GLOBAL ETHICS
AN INTRODUCTION

"This book offers a timely introduction to the emerging subject of global ethics and provides the reader with the theoretical tools and information necessary to understand issues of global importance."

NICK BUTTLE, *University of the West of England*

Global ethics is an exciting and growing field of study. It addresses the most pressing contemporary ethical issues, including torture, scarce resources, poverty, migration, consumption, global trade, medical tourism and humanitarian intervention.

Global ethics is both topical and important. How we resolve (or fail to resolve) the dilemmas of global ethics shapes and limits how we understand human beings, our relationships and social and political frameworks of governance, now and into the future. This is obviously the case with climate change, where our actions now determine the environment our grandchildren will inherit, but it is also the case in other areas, because our decisions about what it is permissible for humans beings to do to each other determines the type of beings we are.

This book introduces the reader to the theory and the practice of global ethics, with particular focus on global governance and citizenship, poverty and development, war and terrorism, bioethics, environmental and climate ethics, and gender justice.

GLOBAL ETHICS
AN INTRODUCTION

HEATHER WIDDOWS

Routledge
Taylor & Francis Group

LONDON AND NEW YORK

For Kit and Gillian

First published in 2011 by Acumen

Published 2014 by Routledge
2 Park Square, Milton Park, Abingdon, Oxon OX14 4RN
711 Third Avenue, New York, NY 10017, USA

Routledge is an imprint of the Taylor & Francis Group,
an informa business

Notices
Practitioners and researchers must always rely on their own
experience and knowledge in evaluating and using any information,
methods, compounds, or experiments described herein. In using
such information or methods they should be mindful of their own
safety and the safety of others, including parties for whom they have
a professional responsibility.

To the fullest extent of the law, neither the Publisher nor the
authors, contributors, or editors, assume any liability for any injury
and/or damage to persons or property as a matter of products
liability, negligence or otherwise, or from any use or operation of
any methods, products, instructions, or ideas contained in the
material herein.

ISBN: 978-1-84465-281-5 (hardcover)
ISBN: 978-1-84465-282-2 (paperback)

British Library Cataloguing-in-Publication Data
A catalogue record for this book is available from the British Library.

Typeset in Minion Pro.
Printed and bound by CPI Group (UK) Ltd, Croydon, CR0 4YY

CONTENTS

ACKNOWLEDGEMENTS

This book has been long in the making. In 2002 the University of Birmingham launched the first Masters in global ethics and in 2005 the *Journal of Global Ethics* followed. Thanks should go to my first colleagues in global ethics: to Donna Dickenson, the first Professor of Global Ethics (who gave me my first academic job), and to Christien van den Anker and Sirkku Hellsten.

Most thanks must go to those who have pioneered the field of global ethics: thinkers who have built on the work of previous thinkers and have carved out distinctive global-ethics approaches. Of these fellow travellers I would first like to thank those I know best: Bob Brecher, Simon Caney, Nigel Dower, Darrel Moellendorf and Leslie Sklair. They have been truly excellent colleagues and working with them on shared projects, publications, workshops and conferences has been a great pleasure. Other global ethicists to whom I am exceptionally indebted – either personally or academically – are Richard Ashcroft, Gillian Brock, Roger Brownsword, Alastair Campbell, Ruth Chadwick, Normal Daniels, Andrew Edgar, Carol Gould, Stan van Hooft, Kim Hutchings, Alison Jaggar, Peter Jones, Graeme Laurie, Fiona MacCallum, Martha Nussbaum, Bhikhu Parekh, Anne Phillips, Thomas Pogge, Sigrid Sterckx, John Tasioulas, Leif Wenar and Gillian Youngs. Particular thanks must go to Bob Brecher for his editing comments, which were well beyond the duties of a reviewer and improved the manuscript no end. I would also like to give thanks to Phil Shiner and his team: an inspirational example of someone working against the odds at the coalface of global ethics.

I would like to thank my current colleagues in the philosophy department of the University of Birmingham, particularly Helen Beebee, Darragh Byrne, Nick Effingham, Alex Miller, Yujin Nagasawa, Jussi Suikkanen and Joss Walker. Special mention should be given to Iain Law and Lisa Bortolotti, co-founders with me of the Birmingham "Health and Happiness" Research Cluster, who provide criticism, humour and support on a daily basis. Helen Harris also deserves special mention for support above and beyond the call of duty. A final, and perhaps most important, thank you to a Birmingham colleague must go to Sean Cordell, who was my research assistant through the final months of this project. His intelligence, patience, humour and reassurance were fundamental in bringing this project to fruition. Others I would like to thank at the University of Birmingham are Leslie Brubaker, Lynne Brydon, Luis Cabrera, Francesca Carnivalli, David Cheetham, John Hick, Heather Marquette, Jean McHale, Stephen Pattision, Nicola Smith, Martin Stringer, Michael Taylor and Simon Yarrow. Thanks must also go to Acumen, particularly to Tristan Palmer, who has been wonderful to work with in all possible ways. The progress of the book has not been easy and a number of delays were experienced. Tristan was understanding and encouraging throughout, and demonstrated a rare trait in current academic publishing: a real interest in the topic.

My final thanks are to my family. The past few years have been eventful – hence the delays: I have given birth to a beautiful daughter, Clara, and lost a magical father. Therefore the book is dedicated to my parents, Kit and Gillian, who in their political activism and community engagement set me on the path to global ethics. I can never thank them enough. Final thanks are to Matthew Hilton, my partner, fellow traveller and inspirational thinker. I thank him for his intellectual rigour, critical analysis, imagination and optimism about what can be achieved.

ABBREVIATIONS

ATTAC	Association pour la Taxation des Transactions financière et l'Aide aux Citoyens
CEDAW	Convention on the Elimination of all Forms of Discrimination Against Women
ECHR	European Court of Human Rights
EIT	economics in transition
FGC	female genital cutting
FGM	female genital mutilation
GHG	greenhouse gases
GNI	gross national income
GRD	Global Resources Dividend
HUGO	Human Genome Organization
IMF	International Monetary Fund
IPCC	Intergovernmental Panel on Climate Change
NGO	non-governmental organization
OECD	Organisation for Economic Co-operation and Development
TRIPS	Agreement on Trade-Related Aspects of Intellectual Property Rights
UDHR	Universal Declaration of Human Rights
UN	United Nations
UNDP	United Nations Development Programme
UNESCO	United Nations Educational, Scientific and Cultural Organization
UNHCR	United Nations High Commissioner for Refugees
UNICEF	United Nations Children's Fund
WHO	World Health Organization
WMD	weapons of mass destruction
WTO	World Trade Organization

1 WHAT IS GLOBAL ETHICS?

INTRODUCTION

Global ethics is a new term that has emerged over the past few decades. In an exceptionally short time it has become established as a recognized area of study: it has a particular approach to ethical dilemmas and some consider it to be becoming a distinct academic discipline rather than a subset of other disciplines. This dramatic growth means that global ethics is an exciting field to be in because those who enter it are committed to discussing, and more importantly to seeking solutions to, the most pressing contemporary ethical issues. Issues addressed in global ethics include the "war on terror", rogue states, child labour, torture, scarce resources, trafficking, migration, climate change, global trade, medical tourism, global pandemics, humanitarian intervention and so on; the list goes on and on. Global ethics is not only topical – these are issues we are all concerned about – but also important. How we resolve (or fail to resolve) the dilemmas of global ethics will determine the framework of future global governance. This will shape and limit the possible relationships and opportunities of all global actors; moreover, decisions made now will affect future generations. This is true not only for problems of climate change, where our actions now determine the environment our children and grandchildren will inherit, but also for decisions about what it is acceptable and permissible to do to human beings. For instance, if we collectively decide that it is acceptable to torture or to buy body parts then we are making judgements about what human beings are, and these decisions will limit and shape what is possible or permissible for future human beings. This is relevant not just for those who are tortured or who buy and sell body parts, but for all of us. If such things are permitted, then human beings will become types of beings who have parts that can be bought and sold, or who can have pain and suffering (to the point of death) inflicted on them in certain circumstances. These things matter in terms of how we understand human beings now and into the future and are at the heart of creating a world where human beings are treated ethically.

Students of global ethics come from many and various backgrounds, including philosophy, politics, public policy, law, theology, international development and sociology. Importantly, students also come from "the field", from policy-making and governance communities and from activist and NGO communities. In the past ten years, numerous monographs, textbooks and edited collections have been published on themes that fall within the broad field of global ethics, such as human rights, global justice, research ethics and environmental ethics. In short, the field is burgeoning and, in terms of ethics, global ethics is a good place to be.

USING THIS BOOK

This book will explore the whole sphere of global ethics. It will consider the most pressing global ethical issues facing the contemporary world, from poverty, through terrorism, to climate change. It will map the ethical responses to such dilemmas. It will consider what sorts of global ethics are currently available and being developed and their appropriateness for addressing global dilemmas. It will present and evaluate theoretical and practical approaches and explore the application of these in the light of key dilemmas.

Very crudely, the first part of the book sets out the theory necessary to understand and analyse the dilemmas of global ethics. These chapters provide the reader with knowledge of the main moral and political theories that are most useful in approaching these issues; together these theories make up the "ethical toolbox" of global ethics. As we shall discover, global ethics is not the kind of area or discipline where theory can be separated from practice. To address the ethical challenges facing the globe, theory, policy and practice must all combine. Unlike other philosophical approaches, global ethics is neither "top-down" nor "bottom-up", but regards theory as necessary for successful practice and practice as essential for informing accurate theory. Accordingly, global ethics is both normative and applied and emerges from and influences policy and practice. The connection of theory and practice is fundamental for global ethics, and something we shall explore further later in this chapter. These early chapters are anything but dry and theoretical, ignoring the realities and limitations of real-world practice. Not only are the policy and practical implications of the theories considered throughout, but Chapters 3, 4 and 5 (the most theoretical chapters) are also meditations on the practical cases studies of Chapter 2.

The case studies detail some of the facts and figures of three controversial contemporary global issues: female genital cutting (FGC), the buying of body parts and torture. These case studies provide an overview of these practices and introduce primary sources, for example quotes from different viewpoints and core documentary evidence. The case studies can be used on their own as useful exercises in exploring these issues, or in conjunction with the early chapters of the book. They are analysed in detail in Chapters 3, 4 and 5, respectively. This is useful in a number of ways. First, it helps in understanding how the theoretical approaches introduced in these chapters play out in practice. Second, it shows how theoretical standpoints colour and shape how the ethical concerns of any issue are seen. Theory is not neutral, but frames what is seen to be ethically important in any given situation; considering how different theories approach such controversial issues shows the importance of understanding theory, not only to make one's own arguments but also to understand where others are coming from and the claims they are making. Third, it shows how global ethics is actually done and the complexity of negotiating these global issues. Exploring case studies helps one to develop one's own position and to test it in light of real dilemmas; for instance, a theoretical approach might seem attractive on paper, but once what this would actually mean in terms of a real-world issue is considered, one might change one's mind. This aspect of case studies is fundamental to global ethics because, unlike much philosophy, global ethics is not an academic endeavour where attempting to win an argument is a kind of philosophical game. Global ethics is concerned with fundamental real-world issues, real injustice, human suffering and global threats, so it cannot be regarded as a mere intellectual exercise; we would worry about the humanity of anyone who treated it as if it were!

The second half of the book looks at specific issues or areas of global ethics: issues of global governance and citizenship, poverty and development, war and terrorism, bioethics, environmental ethics and gender justice. Just as the early theory-focused chapters are full of discussion about policy and practice, so the later chapters on these issues show how theoretical approaches can clarify, critique and influence policy and practice. These chapters focus on some key global-ethics concerns: however, they are representative rather than exhaustive of the core concerns of global ethics. In a book of this size it is unavoidable that more has been left out than has been included, and there are numerous equally pressing global ethical issues that could have been the focus of chapters. For example, there could have been far more discussion about fossil-fuel consumption; scarce resources; international criminal activities such as people-trafficking and drug-trafficking; the role of religion and law and the supposed clash of cultures; business ethics, sweatshops and corporate social responsibility; the role of civil society, anti-capitalist and anti-globalization movements; new social movements and single-issue political campaigns; nuclear war and weapons of war. This list could go on. These issues, and no doubt many others, have claims to being "core" issues of global ethics and no doubt there will be arguments as to why these are more pressing than those that have been included. All that can be said in response is that in selecting these issues the aim is to show the range, complexity and connection of global-ethics issues, not to consider all important issues. To do so would be impossible given their number, breadth and complexity. Even those issues that are included are considered in very partial and limited ways. Whole books could be written on every chapter and the topic would still not be exhausted. Something similar must be said about the omission of many influential theorists of global ethics and global justice. Some key thinkers and arguments are absent for the same reason, and this is not in any way a comment on their import for the topic or usefulness in exploring the dilemmas of global ethics. This book is an introduction, and therefore merely provides a taste of the issues involved and the theories, policies and practices available to address these issues. It is hoped that the ethical toolbox and the illustrations of how global ethics is done will be just as useful when assessing issues not included in the book as for those included.

How you choose to explore these different aspects of the book will depend on your reasons for using the book. If you have a primary interest in one of the global dilemmas, for example contemporary conflict and terrorism, you may wish to focus on Chapter 8 as an introduction to these topics. In addition, you will find the case study on torture useful in thinking about what is acceptable in contemporary conflict. You many also wish to dip in and out of other chapters; something that becomes clear as soon as you begin to examine these global dilemmas in any depth is that it is very difficult to separate one issue in global ethics from others. For instance, other sections that will be useful regarding conflict are found in Chapter 7, where there is a discussion of humanitarian aid and conflict, Chapter 10, where the increasing competition over resources is predicted to become a cause of conflict, and Chapter 11, where rape in war is discussed. You will also wish to explore Chapters 3, 4 and 5 if you are interested in how to understand the rights and wrongs of contemporary conflict, and Chapter 5 will be particularly useful because the case study of torture is analysed using the rights framework set out in that chapter.

WHY GLOBAL ETHICS NOW?

Global ethics is a new and distinctive area of study, so the question is: why now? After all, ethics, understood as an attempt to answer the question "How ought we to live?", goes back to Plato and the earliest philosophy. Likewise, as we shall see, some of the distinctive political approaches of global ethics, such as the cosmopolitan approach, which sees all people in some sense as citizens of the world, also go back to the Greeks. Given this, it would seem that global ethics is continuous with previous moral and political thinking. This is certainly true; but it is also true that there are new ethical dilemmas that arise in the context of globalization. Globalization, and the political, technological and social changes and advances that accompany it, raise new dilemmas, and global ethics is a response to these. For instance, pre-globalization ethical issues could primarily be regarded as local issues. In answering Plato's question "How ought we to live?", we would have been most likely to consider our duties to those known to us: those in our immediate family and community. There would be some duties beyond this and some institutional duties: to rulers (e.g. the king or lord of the manor, which might include taxes, labour and to bear arms); and to religious or cultural bodies (e.g. the Church and her representatives, tribal elders and sacred places). These institutions would also have duties to individuals and to those in the wider network or association, perhaps to a tribe, to a region, to a nation or even to an empire. Yet, before full knowledge of the globe and its people, and the processes of globalization that have made global knowledge and global duties possible, a global ethic would have been nonsensical. This is true, at least, in terms of policy and practice if not in theory. Theoretically there were, of course, candidates for ethics that were believed to be applicable to all, for instance all religious ethics. But recognizing the universal applicability of an ethic is not the same as believing that *all* ethical approaches should take the globe as the proper scope of ethics.

The key claim here is that globalization – the increasing interdependence of global society economically, socially, culturally and politically – has created truly global dilemmas that require global solutions. Global ethics, then, is the response to these new dilemmas. This approach is clearly correct in many ways. No one would deny the phenomenal growth in "global" ethical issues: issues that cannot be addressed within individual nation states or single jurisdictions. Into this "set" of global issues we can place all the topics we shall consider in this book: those of global governance and citizenship, poverty and development, war and terrorism, bioethics, environmental ethics and gender justice.

A GLOBAL ETHIC?

Global ethics is not attempting to promote *a* "global ethic". It is not advocating a particular way of life with a single set of rules, nor is it the promotion of a single principle, set of principles or set of values. Global ethics does not have a solution that people can accept and sign up to; it does not require "moral conversion". Some do wish to establish such a global ethic. For instance, Hans Küng, in his 1993 "Declaration Toward a Global Ethic", presents a list of principles that he believes are shared by all religions (Box 1.1). In these shared values he asserts there is a basis for a global ethic: "a minimal *fundamental consensus* concerning binding *values*, irrevocable *standards*, and *fundamental moral attitudes*" (1993b).

There have been many criticisms of this ethic, not least that it fails to consider those who are non-religious. In addition, it makes controversial and contested

> **Box 1.1 Küng's four "irrevocable directives", which constitute the basis of his global ethic**
>
> - Commitment to a culture of non-violence and respect for life.
> - Commitment to a culture of solidarity and a just economic order.
> - Commitment to a culture of tolerance and life of truthfulness.
> - Commitment to a culture of equal rights and partnership between men and women.

claims, for example that all religions support the equality of men and women. Yet even if it were uncontested that all religions did support such principles, this would not be sufficient on its own to recommend it as a global ethic; that would depend on whether the claims were justified and according to the various criteria of global ethics. There are a number of such solutions – global ethics – some of which we shall consider in the course of the book. Arguably, human rights is such an ethic (to which you sign up or not); as are liberal views that prioritize autonomy over other values. Global ethics explores and utilizes these views to address practice and policy issues, but it does not at the outset support one over another.

This said, although there is not one ethic that global ethics promotes, there is an emerging global-ethics approach. Global ethics does not just consider ethical issues that happen to stretch beyond borders, or any issue with international dimensions; rather, it has a fundamental commitment to including global concerns in *all* ethical reasoning and decision-making. Ethical exploration that addresses international dilemmas or issues that cross borders is not necessarily global ethics. What matters is not just the consideration of global issues, but how these issues are approached and the methodology, ethical framework and assumptions adopted. Increasingly those who work in this field share very broad but identifiable premises and concerns. For instance, one might be concerned about an international issue, such as terrorism or global disease threats, but not have a global-ethics approach. Thus one might prioritize the interests of one group: a ruling party, a nation or a privileged group (e.g. a profession or a demographic cohort, such as an ethnic group or a wealthy group). If one group is prioritized over another and there is a *bias* towards this group and the rights and interests of others are ignored, then a global approach has not been adopted. Thus while there is no global ethic that is being promoted, there are a number of very broad conditions that characterize global ethics. This affects the types of theories global ethicists can adopt. For example, as we shall see in Chapter 3, it is unlikely that a global ethicist can consistently sustain a relativist position, or, as discussed in Chapter 4, a realist position. There are three characteristics or elements that can be traced, and together these broadly define the global-ethics approach: (i) its frame is global; (ii) it is multidisciplinary; (iii) it combines theory and practice

---

Box 1.2 Characteristics of global ethics

- Global in scope
- Multidisciplinary
- Combines theory and practice

(Box 1.2). This said, global ethics is a broad school, and while there are traceable traits, they cover an exceptionally large range of positions and commitments.

GLOBAL SCOPE

The first distinctive feature of specifically global ethics is that the area of ethical concern is always the globe, and the rights and interests of all are significant. Thus when any ethical dilemma is considered, the needs of all must be recognized even if they cannot all be addressed in the response. The global scope of applied ethics is not something new to global ethics and it is at the heart of many of the arguments we shall consider in this book, arguments that were put forward before the phrase "global ethics" was coined. However, while applied ethics *can* be global in scope, there are many examples where in fact it is biased and limited either by specific concerns – for instance, national or professional interests (as for many professional ethics) – or because it prioritizes the needs of one group – a geographical group or a particular group (such as an ethnic group, or simply a wealthy or powerful group) – over those who are vulnerable. There are two ways in which the "global in scope" criterion is evident in global ethics: it necessitates a global frame and it requires that the actions and obligations of individuals, associations and institutions are taken into account.

The global frame

For global ethics the frame within which decision-making occurs must be global: the ethical locus is "the globe". In any ethical analysis it is the globe that constitutes the sphere of concern and thus the needs and perspectives of all global actors are relevant.

This does not mean that all global ethicists are cosmopolitan, a theory we shall discuss in detail in Chapter 4. Many global ethicists are cosmopolitan, but some deny cosmopolitanism, while others are "weak" cosmopolitans. Moreover, even those who aim for full global justice and equality will promote partial solutions despite regarding them as insufficient in the long term. For example, they might endorse supporting nation states that strengthen human rights or promote ethical practice, even though these measures will only partially improve the situation and possibly only for some actors rather than all. However, such solutions, such as nationally enforcing respect for human rights or attaining laws about trafficking or child labour, can be seen as steps towards proper global respect for persons and global justice. In this way the global frame remains in place, in that the aim is that these partial and piecemeal measures will gradually contribute to establishing truly global methods. The global methodology, then, is practical and accepts that impartial and imperfect solutions might be steps on the way to global justice. Yet no matter what theory, policy or practice is ultimately recommended, the global needs of all are factored into the analysis: the frame for ethical analysis is the globe.

In this way global ethics foregrounds the global scope of morality and insists that the rights and interests of those not directly the focus of discussion are not forgotten. This does not mean that it is always possible to meet the needs of all or necessarily to give them equal weight – as discussed above, the best possible solutions may be less than perfect – but it does mean that the needs of all must be visible. The commitment of global ethicists to the global scope of ethics is perhaps most obvious in the growth of discussion of cosmopolitan political theories, which consider the globe the proper unit of ethical concern (discussed in Chapter 4) and in debates about the validity of universalism (discussed in Chapter 3). Key global-ethics thinkers who have been in part responsible for this rethinking include: Charles Beitz, Gillian Brock, Allen Buchanan, Simon Caney, Nigel Dower, Carol Gould, David Held, Stan van Hooft, Alison Jaggar, Charles Jones, David Miller, Darrel Moellendorf, Martha Nussbaum, Susan Moller Okin, Thomas Pogge, Amartya Sen, Henry Shue and Iris Marion Young.

Individuals, associations and institutions

Global ethics is also concerned with all global actors: with the rights, interests and duties of individuals, nations, institutions and associations. Some global ethicists focus on the duties of one group or another, and different duties in different arguments. For example, Pogge and Moellendorf both focus on institutions, but they also have things to say about how individuals relate to institutions and associations and the duties of individuals.

To consider all global actors is to reject the traditional divide in political theory that has classified "ethics" as distinct from "justice", with "ethics" concerned with individual obligations and "justice" with the obligations of institutions. Not only does global ethics not adopt this distinction, but it believes that to address global dilemmas practically action is required at all levels, and that therefore the duties of individuals, associations and institutions are all relevant to global ethics. As Dower puts it:

> Individuals have active responsibilities, responsibilities in practice not merely in theory, towards people in other parts of the world. These include duties of giving aid and opposing practices which undermine well-being, but also, perhaps even more significantly, duties not to be beneficiaries of economic processes which either exploit the poor elsewhere or damage the environment. Likewise states can be seen as having in practice responsibility for human beings everywhere, and responsibility not to continue practices which either damage the environment elsewhere or contribute to negative global impacts on the environment. (2007: 7–8)

How these duties can be constructed and what they are will be discussed in detail in relation to the different dilemmas of global ethics but, in short, just as the rights and interests of all must be considered in analysing any dilemma, so all actors must be considered in the solution. Again this builds on earlier ethicists' work. For example, when discussing ethical responses to famine, which we shall return to in Chapter 7, Onora O'Neill insists that if we are to address famine we need to consider institutional and individual injustices and coercions and the duties of both.

A MULTIDISCIPLINARY APPROACH

The criterion of global scope, which requires that the rights and interests of all are considered and the duties of all actors are necessary to the solution, also leads to the need for a multidisciplinary approach. If global ethicists are going to engage with contemporary dilemmas, then they need to understand the actors with whom they are concerned. This requires more than a moral or political philosophical analysis. It requires expertise from across the spectrum: from economists, lawyers, development experts and sociologists, as well as from the practitioner arenas of activists and policy-makers.

If we take seriously the global frame of ethics then the need for multidisciplinary expertise is obvious. Accordingly, global ethics is fundamentally multidisciplinary. This claim is substantial in that the commitment to multidisciplinarity is not merely contingent on the types of issues global ethics addresses; rather, it is methodological. It is a belief that not only is it pragmatic to approach global ethics taking account of the insights of different disciplines, but also this is the *only* effective way to do global ethics. Global ethics, then, is inherently multidisciplinary, connecting moral and political philosophy with other disciplines such as political science, international relations, law, religious studies, medical ethics and sociology. This methodological distinction again distinguishes global ethics from other forms of applied ethics, which may have come to be multidisciplinary by accident but are not necessarily committed to seeking out relevant information from these other disciplines.

INTERRELATION OF THEORY AND PRACTICE

The third distinctive constituent of global ethics is the insistence that theory and practice are interrelated. Global ethics connects academic debates with the real-world work of policy-makers, practitioners and activists, combining the analysis of practical case studies with rigorous theoretical examination. Theory and practice are regarded as fundamentally interconnected and are both necessary parts of the same pursuit rather than separable endeavours to be conducted in separate spheres and disciplines.

The interrelatedness of theory and practice is seen clearly in leading contemporary global-ethics thinkers, such as Pogge, Moellendorf and Caney. These thinkers not only immerse themselves in political theory and empirical analysis but also actively seek to influence practice and policy. For example, Pogge has long engaged with the injustice caused by the current global intellectual property regime and put forward proposals that are intended to combat some of the injustices of the patent system: something we shall discuss in Chapter 9. The aim of global ethics – as we shall forcefully come to see as we move through the key dilemmas of global ethics in this book – is to affect practice. Its aim is not to come up with consistent and beautiful theories of justice and ethics, but rather to influence policy and practice, to contribute to creating global relations that are more just and reducing and eradicating global injustice and suffering.

In sum, global ethics adopts a comprehensive approach that takes the globe as its ethical locus; it is fundamentally multidisciplinary; and it is based on the premise that theory is necessary for successful practice and practice necessary for accurate theory. Thus global ethics is at once theoretical and applied, and both emerges from and influences policy and practice.

THE GLOBAL-ETHICS COMMITMENT

Taken together these three elements define the emerging discipline of global ethics. Accordingly, global ethics is able to span both micro and macro issues and link questions about individual goodness and justice to political questions about governance.

Furthermore, while global ethics does not endorse a single global ethic, its three identifiable characteristics of being global in scope, multidisciplinary and connecting theory and practice do suggest a broad commitment to justice. Because global ethics is not biased towards any interest group it results in a general bias towards the poor and vulnerable: arguably where the bias of all ethics should be. By considering the needs of all, global ethics brings to the fore the needs of the worst off and highlights the often desperate plight of those who are disadvantaged, economically, socially, politically and culturally. This ethical bias towards the poor, oppressed and underprivileged is a result of taking seriously the needs of all and, as we shall see in Chapter 3, emerges from any moral theory. Arguably, such a bias should be evident in all ethics because it results from any attempt to remove injustice. Global ethics attempts to avoid co-option by interest groups by insisting on a global frame.

Thus global ethicists have a commitment to making a difference in terms of affecting policy and also in terms of their individual actions and commitments. The topics that global ethics addresses cannot be dismissed as just theoretical issues; they require us to act. Again, this is not new. For instance, Peter Singer (whom we shall discuss in Chapters 7 and 10) speaks about the philosopher's duty to act to address famine. Global ethics is a call to action, to action that is effective and informed by robust theory: a call to make the world a more just place. This is summed up by Singer, who was doing global ethics before the term was thought of:

> Discussion, though, is not enough. What is the point of relating philosophy to public (and personal) affairs if we do not take our conclusions seriously? In this instance, taking our conclusions seriously means acting upon them. The philosopher will not find it any easier than anyone else to alter his attitudes and way of life to the extent that, if I am right, is involved in doing everything that we ought to be doing. At the very least, though, we can make a start. The philosopher who does so will have to sacrifice some of the benefits of the consumer society, but he can find compensation in the satisfaction of a way of life in which theory and practice, if not yet in harmony, are at least coming together. (1972: 242–3)

Global ethics requires action from you!

FURTHER READING

- Commers, R., W. Vandekerckhove & A. Verlinden (eds). *Ethics in an Era of Globalisation* (Aldershot: Ashgate, 2008).
- Dower, N. *World Ethics: The New Agenda* (Edinburgh: Edinburgh University Press, 2007).
- Eade, J. & D. O'Byrne (eds). *Global Ethics and Civil Society* (Aldershot: Ashgate, 2005).
- Pogge, T. & K. Horton. *Global Ethics: Seminal Essays* (Saint Paul, MN: Paragon House, 2008).
- Pogge, T. & D. Moellendorf. *Global Justice: Seminal Essays* (Saint Paul, MN: Paragon House, 2008).

2 CASE STUDIES FOR GLOBAL ETHICS

Global ethics is an academic forum for philosophical debate that is not separate from the real world. Rather, it is fundamentally about practice: about how to make the world more just and overcome exploitation and injustice. Global ethics cannot, therefore, be done in a vacuum or an academic ivory tower but must be connected with real-world injustice. Accordingly, global ethicists must think about not just the consistency of their arguments but also the impact of what they say and do to actual people and policy. To this end, and to ensure we think about practice and the implications of our theorizing even in the theoretical section of the book, case studies will be used. There are three case studies – on FGC, the buying of body parts and torture – which will be used to illustrate the theories and arguments that are put forward in Chapters 3, 4 and 5. Introducing case studies in these chapters shows how the theory and practice interconnect and how important theoretical tools are to addressing real-world practices of injustice.

The case studies are intended to be returned to time and time again as you progress through the book and develop your knowledge of global ethics. They can be used in different ways and in conjunction with different chapters. You might find it useful to look at them first – before you have learnt the theories of global ethics – simply to get an initial and untutored reaction. While you will not be able to answer all the questions that follow until you have progressed further, nor understand the moral theories referred to in the questions, you will have a first response that you will find exceptionally useful in working out how you feel about an issue. It may also be useful to return to the case studies when you work through chapters that address related concerns: the torture case study when you look at war in Chapter 8; the body part case study when you look at bioethics in Chapter 9; and the female genital cutting (FGC) case study when you consider gender justice in Chapter 11. Finally, you may also wish to return to the case studies when you have completed the book in order to see how much your views have changed and how you have progressed and developed your thinking and expertise in global ethics.

These three cases were chosen because they are timely and particularly useful for understanding the complexity of global-ethics arguments. Undoubtedly, there could have been many more; we could have considered problems of aid in conflict zones, drug trials in the developing world, wearing of the "veil", ethical shopping and sweatshops, and the patenting of drugs. Developing these as test cases along the lines of the three following case studies could be a useful exercise in seeing the connections between different areas of injustice in global ethics.

These topics are nonetheless developed and discussed in various chapters of this volume. Other topics that are discussed and which could be worked up into global-ethics case studies are: existing and proposed structures of global govern-ance (Chapter 6); aid in conflict zones and fair-trade initiatives (Chapter 7); military intervention in a foreign conflict or crisis on humanitarian grounds (Chapter 8); drug trials in the developing world and the patenting of drugs (Chapter 9); richer nations' industrial pollution and its environmental impact on poorer ones (Chapter 10); and rape in war and forced marriages (Chapter 11).

CASE STUDY FEMALE GENITAL CUTTING

"Female genital mutilation" (FGM), "female circumcision", "female genital cutting" (FGC) and "clitoridectomy" are all phrases that refer to procedures that involve the partial or total removal of the external female genitalia for non-medical reasons. The term we use is not value neutral: the label "FGM" is used by those critical of the procedure ("mutilation" being a wholly negative term); female circumcision is used by those who support or are at least more tolerant of the practice. The term "female genital cutting", or FGC, comes somewhere in the middle of these. Just as the terminology is not value neutral, it is hard to get neutral facts and information on this practice (like many ethically concerning practices that are addressed in global ethics).

The World Health Organization (WHO) distinguishes four types of this procedure:

- partial or total removal of the clitoris and/or the prepuce (clitoridectomy);
- partial or total removal of the clitoris and the labia minora, with or without excision of the labia majora (excision);
- narrowing of the vaginal orifice by creating a covering seal by cutting and appositioning the labia minora and/or the labia majora, with or without excision of the clitoris (infibulation);
- all other harmful procedures to the female genitalia for non-medical purposes, for example pricking, piercing, incising, scraping and cauterization.

FGC is usually carried out on girls under fifteen and the WHO estimates that 100–140 million girls and women have undergone one of the first three forms of this procedure and that around 3 million girls are at risk of such a procedure. Instances of FGC have been reported worldwide: however, it most commonly occurs in western, eastern and north-eastern regions of Africa, parts of Asia and the Middle East and in immigrant communities from these locations elsewhere. In Djibouti, Egypt, Eritrea, Mali, Sierra Leone, Somalia and the Republic of Sudan (formerly northern Sudan) the practice is almost universal and Burkina Faso, Ethiopia, Gambia and Mauritania all have rates of over 70 per cent.

FGC is a traumatic procedure (usually girls are pinned down and it is often carried out in medically unsafe environments and with unsafe equipment, which leads to infection). Long-term documented health risks include pain, lack of sexual feeling, ongoing infections and psychological trauma. In addition, FGC increases risks in childbirth (e.g. post-partum haemorrhaging) and even increases the likelihood of death of newborn babies immediately after birth. For these reasons FGC is opposed by many international organizations including the Joint United Nations Programme on HIV/AIDS (UNAIDS), the United Nations Development Programme (UNDP), the UN Children's Fund (UNICEF), the UN Development Fund for Women (UNIFEM), the UN High Commissioner for Refugees (UNHCR), the UN Educational, Scientific and Cultural Organization (UNESCO), the UN Human Rights Council (UNHR) and the Economic Commission for Africa.

Despite such critiques, FGC continues to be practised and supported by some groups. Many reasons are given for support of the practice, including health, culture and religion, but it is likely that the most significant factor in whether or not a girl undergoes the practice is ethnicity. In places where it is widely practised, it is likely to be supported by both men and women, and those who depart from the practice face social ostracism and condemnation. In such groups, FGC appears to be socially demanded and regarded as socially beneficial and important for a girl coming of age and being prepared for marriage. Thus many girls are proud to undergo the procedure because it signals their transformation to womanhood and without it they may be unable to find a husband; therefore it has implications for economic security. In such groups, FGC is regarded as protecting and preserving a woman's virginity (pre-marriage) and modesty and proper behaviour (post-marriage) as well as being linked to cleanliness and ideals of feminine beauty. Religious reasons are also given by those who practise FGC, although there is no definitive support for this practice from religious texts, and religious leaders differ in their approach. Moreover, the practice

---

Box 2.1 Hannah Koroma, Sierra Leone

"I was genitally mutilated at the age of ten. I was told by my late grandmother that they were taking me down to the river to perform a certain ceremony, and afterwards I would be given a lot of food to eat. As an innocent child, I was led like a sheep to be slaughtered. Once I entered the secret bush, I was taken to a very dark room and undressed. I was blindfolded and stripped naked. I was then carried by two strong women to the site for the operation. I was forced to lie flat on my back by four strong women, two holding tight to each leg. Another woman sat on my chest to prevent my upper body from moving. A piece of cloth was forced in my mouth to stop me screaming. I was then shaved. When the operation began, I put up a big fight. The pain was terrible and unbearable. During this fight, I was badly cut and lost blood. All those who took part in the operation were half-drunk with alcohol. Others were dancing and singing, and worst of all, had stripped naked. I was genitally mutilated with a blunt penknife. After the operation, no one was allowed to aid me to walk. The stuff they put on my wound stank and was painful. These were terrible times for me. Each time I wanted to urinate, I was forced to stand upright. The urine would spread over the wound and would cause fresh pain all over again. Sometimes I had to force myself not to urinate for fear of the terrible pain. I was not given any anaesthetic in the operation to reduce my pain, nor any antibiotics to fight against infection. Afterwards, I haemorrhaged and became anaemic. This was attributed to witchcraft. I suffered for a long time from acute vaginal infections." (Amnesty International 1997)

Box 2.2 Voices in favour of female genital cutting

"The abolition of female genital cutting will 'destroy the tribal system'."

(Kenyatta [President of Kenya] 1938)

"We are circumcised and insist on circumcising our daughters so that there is no mixing between male and female. An uncircumcised woman is put to shame by her husband, who calls her 'you with the clitoris'. People say she is like a man. Her organ would prick the man."

An Egyptian mother (in Assad 1980)

"Circumcision makes women clean, promotes virginity and chastity and guards young girls from sexual frustration by deadening their sexual appetite."

Mrs Njeri, a Kenyan elder (in Katumba 1990)

---

is found among Christians, Jews and Muslims but in no case is it seen as required by all adherents of the religion in question in different cultures (Boxes 2.1, 2.2).

This case study is discussed in Chapter 3. In addition the following questions may be useful in helping to explore this case study.

QUESTIONS

1. What are the key ethical issues raised by FGC? Do these change depending on whether one adopts utilitarian, deontological or virtue theories (as outlined in Chapter 3)?
2. Do you think FGC should ever be permitted? On what grounds and in what circumstances?
3. Are some forms of FGC acceptable and others not? If so, what are the reasons?
4. Whose views are important in working out what is ethical? For instance, is it the girls who will undergo the procedures, the groups they come from, medical experts, human-rights activists or others?
5. How can the norms and values of different cultures be respected and human rights protected?

FURTHER READING

- Amnesty International. "What is Female Genital Mutilation?"(1997). www.amnesty.org/en/library/info/ACT77/006/1997 (accessed May 2011).
- Assaad, M. B. "Female Circumcision in Egypt: Social Implications, Current Research and Prospects for Change". *Studies in Family Planning* 11 (1980): 3–16.
- Bowman, K. "Bridging the Gap in the Hopes of Ending Female Genital Cutting". *Santa Clara Journal of International Law* 3 (2004): 132–63.
- Kenyatta, J. *Facing Mount Kenya: The Tribal Life of the Kikuyu* (London: Secker & Warburg, 1938).
- UN Women. "Eliminating Female Genital Mutilation: An Interagency Statement". www.unifem.org/materials/item_detail.php?ProductID=110 (accessed May 2011).

CASE STUDY BUYING AND SELLING BODY PARTS

Attaining accurate facts and figures regarding the black and grey market in body parts is exceptionally difficult. Nonetheless, it is clear that the market is growing rapidly and that it is global. More people are selling their body parts to people from across the globe; body parts that are bought and sold include kidneys, eggs, sperm, blood and plasma (Boxes 2.3, 2.4, 2.5). This market is sometimes illegal, for example the harvesting of body parts from unsuspecting donors or the sale of parts in countries where such sale is illegal; sometimes it is completely legal, for example the selling of eggs in the US; and sometimes it is "grey", for example practices of infertility clinics in the Mediterranean where "all expenses paid holidays" also provide opportunities for egg-selling. The illegal side of the organ trade and its links with organized crime have put the topic firmly in the public domain and it is a common topic for television, films and discussion as well as an issue for policy-makers. Just as with the case study of FGC, the language is important: terms like "donor" are often used even when what is really being described is a "sale", for instance in the term "paid donation" (a contradiction in terms).

Despite the difficulties, some figures are available. For instance, a 2003 Punjab government inquiry estimated that nearly 3500 people from Sargodha had sold their kidneys through the 1990s to buyers from around the world. In 2006 the BBC conducted an undercover investigation that suggested that China was routinely selling organs of prisoners on death row: under the pretence of seeking a liver for his sick father, the journalist reported that "one hospital said it could provide a liver at a cost of

---

Box 2.3 The effects on donors of legal "paid kidney donation"

Egypt
- 78 per cent reported deterioration in health status.
- 78 per cent spent the money within five months of their donation.

India
- 86 per cent reported deterioration in health status.
- 96 per cent sold their kidneys to pay off debts and 75 per cent were still in debt at the time of the survey.

Iran
- 58 per cent reported negative effects on their health status.
- 65 per cent failed to get out of debt.

(From Shimazono 2007)

£50,000 (US$94,400), with the chief surgeon confirming an executed prisoner could be the donor". Whatever else it may be, the market in body parts is hugely lucrative, particularly for medical merchants and middlemen who broker deals between buyers and sellers. For instance, a 2004 WHO report (Nullis-Kapp 2004) reports medical brokers charging between US$100,000 and US$200,000 to organize a transplant while paying the "donors" as little as US$1000.

Those who support organ sale argue that it is a win–win situation. The buyers win because they are able to access an organ or other body part that they greatly desire and

---

Box 2.4 Voices of kidney vendors and purchasers

"We are worse than prostitutes because we have sold something we can never get back."
                                        A kidney seller (in Scheper-Hughes 2003b)

Mohammed, aged twenty-five, was a casual labourer in Delhi (sending money home to Gujarat). His kidneys were taken by force:

"He said, he was approached by a bearded man as he waited at the early-morning labor market by the Old Delhi train station. The man offered him an unusually generous deal: one and a half months work painting, for 150 rupees a day, with free food and lodging.
    "He was driven four or five hours away, to a secluded bungalow, surrounded by trees, where he was placed in a room with four other young men, under the watch of two armed guards. 'When I asked why I had been locked inside, the guards slapped me and said they would shoot me if I asked any more questions,' Mohammed said, lying in his hospital bed, wrapped in an orange blanket, clenching his teeth and shutting his eyes in pain. He said the men were given food to cook for themselves and periodically nurses would come to take blood samples from them.
    "One by one they were taken away for surgery. 'They told us not to speak to each other or we would pay with our lives,' he said. 'I was the last one to be taken.'"
                                        Mohammed, from Gurgaon, India (in Gentleman 2008)

"Avraham, a retired lawyer in Jerusalem, explained why he went through considerable expense and danger to travel to Eastern Europe to purchase a kidney from a rural worker rather than wait in line for a cadaver organ in Israel: 'Why should I have to wait years for a kidney from someone who was in a car accident, pinned under the car for many hours, then in miserable condition in the intensive care unit for days and only then, after all that trauma, have that same organ put inside me? That organ is not going to be any good! Or, even worse, I could get the organ of an elderly person, or an alcoholic, or a person who died of a stroke. It's far better to get a kidney from a healthy person who can also benefit from the money I can afford to pay.'"
                                        Avraham, an Israeli buyer (in Scheper-Hughes 2003a)

which is either necessary for their survival (e.g. in kidney sale) or essential to meeting an important need (e.g. for sperm or eggs). The vendors win in that they are paid significant amounts of money that otherwise would be unattainable. They can then use this money to make significant differences to their own and their family's situations. But the claim that vendors always win is not borne out by the evidence (see Box 2.4).

In other areas the data are more mixed. For instance, in egg sale it seems that at least some vendors do benefit. The market in eggs and embryos is growing fast because it is increasingly older women who seek to reproduce. As with organ sale, this is a global market, and eggs from younger women are preferred because they are more likely to lead to successful outcomes. To meet this demand for eggs, clinics across the US and Europe buy eggs from "donors"; as with kidneys, "buyers" are more advantaged (socioeconomically, as well as in terms of nationality and ethnicity) and "donors" are from poorer, less privileged demographic groups. For example, clinics in southern Europe (particularly Spain, Greece and Cyprus) purchase eggs from eastern European women to serve the reproductive wishes of western European women from countries where egg-selling is prohibited (Box 2.5). These "donors" go to Spain for a few weeks for a "paid holiday", have their eggs harvested and return to eastern Europe with enough to live on for six months or more. Eggs are also purchased from Spanish students and US clinics routinely advertise in US college newspapers, offering up to US$100,000, depending on how far the donor has the desirable characteristics of education, health, race, physical traits and beauty.

Box 2.5 Svetlana, an egg-seller's story

"Svetlana has a big family secret: she sold her eggs for US dollars. Svetlana did not tell her husband what she was doing because she knew he would be furious. Nor did she tell her mother or her two young children …

"Desperate for money after the birth of her second child, Svetlana had applied for work in the canteen of one of Kiev's growing number of fertility clinics that charge infertile women from Britain thousands of pounds for help in getting them pregnant. Svetlana didn't get the job, but was told that if she needed cash she could sell her eggs. She was told that the process was straightforward and that she would be given US$300 – more if she was a good donor and produced lots of eggs. For Svetlana, like a growing number of Eastern European women, it was too good an opportunity to pass up. Since the birth of her second child she had been surviving on less than US$15 a month. She turned out to be an excellent donor. By the time of her fifth donation, her ovaries, stimulated by the injection of a hormone, produced a batch of 40 healthy eggs. This is four times more eggs than a woman undergoing IVF treatment would produce. The medical staff gave Svetlana an extra US$200 as a reward." (Barnett & Smith 2006)

We have little data on the long-term effects of egg harvesting, particularly on the fertility of the women whose eggs are harvested. However, at least some egg-sellers, especially those who repeatedly sell their eggs, go through unnecessary hormonal stimulation and uncomfortable procedures. Harvesting eggs is not a straightforward matter like collecting sperm. It can be a lengthy, painful and potentially dangerous procedure involving the injection of a powerful drug known as follicle stimulating hormone. Medical experts believe 1 per cent of women undergoing this can suffer serious side effects known as ovarian hyper-stimulation syndrome that in extreme cases can prove fatal. Donna Dickenson reports a number of worrying aspects of this global trade in her book *Body Shopping*:

> [T]he Eastern European and Mediterranean egg-selling clinics routinely extract three or four times the quantity of eggs that would be taken in a well-run clinic. Women are actually given a productivity bonus if they produce high numbers of ova. In one Kiev clinic, for example, women are offered a basic fee of only $300, but given a bonus of $200 if they produce as many as forty eggs. Doses of follicle-stimulating hormone at more than twice the recommended maximum level are routinely used to produce these bumper crops. But the human female is programmed by nature to produce only one or at most two eggs per cycle. (2008: 6)

This said, for most women the process does not seem to be particularly harmful in the short term.

This case study is discussed in Chapter 4. In addition the following questions may be useful in helping to explore this case study.

QUESTIONS

1. What are the key ethical issues raised by the sale of body parts? Do these change depending on whether you adopt utilitarian, deontological or virtue theories (as outlined in Chapter 3)?
2. Do you think that the sale of body parts should ever be permitted? On what grounds?
3. Should all body parts be treated the same? For instance, hair, blood, organs, eggs, whole bodies?
4. Does it matter what the body parts are being used for? For instance, is it different if they will be used for life-saving treatment?

5. If you think the sale of body parts might be permissible in some instances, how would you ensure that exploitation does not occur?

6. Should the laws about which body parts can be sold, if any, apply globally?

FURTHER READING

- Barnett, A. & H. Smith. "Cruel Cost of the Human Egg Trade". *The Observer* (30 April 2006). www.guardian.co.uk/uk/2006/apr/30/health.healthandwellbeing (accessed May 2011).
- BBC. "Organ Sales 'Thriving' in China" (2006). http://news.bbc.co.uk/1/hi/5386720.stm (accessed May 2011).
- Dickenson, D. *Body Shopping: The Economy Fuelled by Flesh and Blood* (Oxford: One World, 2008).
- Gentleman, A. "Poor Donors Duped by Organ-Transplant Racket in India". *New York Times* (29 January 2008). www.iht.com/articles/2008/01/29/asia/kidney.php (accessed May 2011).
- Khan, A. A. "Pakistan's Kidney Donor Crisis" (2004). http://news.bbc.co.uk/1/hi/world/south_asia/4092325.stm (accessed May 2011).
- Nullis-Kapp, C. "Organ Trafficking and Transplantation Pose New Challenges". *Bulletin of the World Health Organization* 82(9) (2004): 639–718. www.who.int/bulletin/volumes/82/9/feature0904/en/index.html (accessed May 2011).
- Scheper-Hughes, N. "Keeping an Eye on the Global Traffic in Human Organs. *Lancet* 361 (2003): 1647.
- Scheper-Hughes, N. "Commentary: A Beastly Trade in 'Parts'. The Organ Market is Dehumanizing the World's Poor". *Los Angeles Times* (29 July 2003). http://pqasb.pqarchiver.com/latimes/access/377365761.html?FMT=ABS&FMTS=ABS:FT&type=current&date=Jul+29%2C+2003&author=Nancy+Scheper-Hughes&pub=Los+Angeles+Times&edition=&startpage=B.15&desc=Commentary%3B+A+Beastly+Trade+in+%27Parts%27%3B+The+organ+market+is+dehumanizing+the+world%27s+poor (accessed May 2011).
- Shimazono, Y. "The State of the International Organ Trade: A Provisional Picture Based on Integration of Available Information". *Bulletin of the World Health Organisation* 85 (2007): 960. www.who.int/bulletin/volumes/85/12/06-039370/en/ (accessed May 2011).

CASE STUDY TORURE

From the mid-eighteenth century, torture has been generally regarded as unaccept-able. The use of torture by the Nazi regime was seen as contravening shared inter-national norms. The global prohibition on torture is stated clearly in Article 5 of the Universal Declaration of Human Rights (UDHR), which states that "No one shall be subjected to torture or to cruel, inhuman or degrading treatment or punishment." The article was supplemented in 1975 by the Declaration on the Protection of All Persons from Being Subjected to Torture and Other Cruel, Inhuman or Degrading Treatment or Punishment (Box 2.6).

Box 2.6 The UDHR's definition of torture

"[A]ny act by which severe pain or suffering, whether physical or mental, is intentionally inflicted by or at the instigation of a public official on a person for such purposes as obtain-ing from him or a third person information or confession, punishing him for an act he has committed or is suspected of having committed, or intimidating him or other persons. It does not include pain or suffering arising only from, inherent in or incidental to, lawful sanctions to the extent consistent with the Standard Minimum Rules for the Treatment of Prisoners."

The 1984 Convention against Torture and Other Cruel, Inhuman or Degrading Treatment or Punishment reiterates this definition. The convention against torture is one of the most successful of the UN's conventions and is ratified by over 130 countries. However, the absoluteness of the prohibition of torture, which seems to be an instance of global agreement, has come into question in the post-9/11 era. In the events following 9/11 it has become clear that not only is torture still routinely prac-tised in "rogue states", such as Saddam Hussein's Iraq, but also by the US and UK who release (rendition) prisoners to countries, including Egypt, Jordon and Morocco, for the purpose of torture. More damaging still, given the power and prominence of the US, instances of systematic torture by US military personnel have come to light.

Table 2.1 details the current systematic practice of torture by both UK and US soldiers in Iraq compiled first-hand by Phil Shiner and his colleagues at Public Interest Lawyers in the course of providing evidence to defend those who have suf-fered such abuse. They have recorded 2193 allegations in total, including 26 cases of detainees being dragged along the ground, 92 allegations of kicking, 77 of punching, 162 of beatings with pistols/rifles/rifle butts/fists/feet/helmets, 20 of being placed in humiliating positions, 36 to forced exposures to porn, 39 of forced nakedness/forced exposure of genitalia and 68 of water deprivation (see Table 2.1).

Table 2.1 Unlawful abuse by agents of the state in SE Iraq

Techniques	UK	US
TECHNIQUES ON SENSORY DEPRIVATION		
Hooding: 1 or 2 sandbags	✓	✓
Hooding: old cement bags	✓	
With plastic blindfold	✓	✓
Silence	✓	✓
Prolonged solitary confinement (with no daylight)	✓	✓
Forced nakedness	✓	✓
"No talking" restrictions	✓	✓
Duct-taping of mouths		✓
TECHNIQUES ON DEBILITY		
Food and water deprivation, including restricted diet	✓	✓
Sleep deprivation	✓	✓
Stress techniques		
Ski position	✓	
Prolonged standing with arms lifted	✓	✓
Prolonged kneeling	✓	✓
Prolonged sitting in required posture	✓	✓
Water bottles on arms	✓	✓
Squatting	✓	✓
Forced exertion		
Running	✓	✓
Water bottles on arms	✓	✓
Prolonged exposure to sun	✓	✓
Temperature manipulation (cold and hot)		
Soaking clothes in water		✓
Dousing with cold water	✓	✓
Detention in unbearably hot locations (containers, buildings with no ventilation, etc.)	✓	✓
Withholding of warmth items	✓	✓
Use of air-conditioning systems (induced hypothermia)		✓
Sensory bombardment		
Loud music		✓
Flashing ("strobe") lights		✓
Loud CD pornography	✓	
Loud radios	✓	
Constant light	✓	✓
Videos of terrorist acts		✓
Prolonged and direct shouting	✓	✓
SEXUAL ACTS		
Forced nakedness (in front of women)	✓	✓
Forced soiling	✓	✓
CD pornography	✓	
Forced watching of pornographic material	✓	✓
Masturbation by soldiers	✓	
Forced masturbation in front of soldiers		✓

Techniques	UK	US
SEXUAL ACTS (CONTINUED)		
Forced simulated masturbation	✓	✓
Women's underwear on heads		✓
Forced oral sex	✓	
Simulated anal sex	✓	✓
Sexual taunts from women	✓	✓
Sexual acts between men and women soldiers		✓
Prolonged attachment to cell bars while naked		✓
Forced humiliating positions	✓	✓
Paraded handcuffed and naked		✓
Urinating on detainees (including hooded heads)	✓	✓
Soldiers' urine offered instead of water	✓	✓
Detainees' own urine offered instead of water	✓	✓
Penetration of anus with objects including broomstick, etc.		✓
Pretended rape/torture/abuse of family members in close proximity		✓
Smearing of (real) menstrual blood		✓
Pubic hair ripped out		✓
Observed on toilet	✓	✓
Simulation of dog on leash		✓
Forced to watch real/feigned sex		✓
Being touched in humiliating ways (in front of women)	✓	✓
Pinching/tweaking of nipples	✓	✓
Touching to genitalia	✓	✓
References to suspected homosexuality of detainee	✓	✓
Taunts regarding bringing mother/daughter for sex	✓	
Ridden like horses		✓
Humiliating medical examinations (sometimes repeated excessively, sometimes invasive)	✓	✓
"Lap dances" from female interrogators		✓
ABUSE		
Soft punching	✓	✓
Forced to sit on hot surfaces	✓	✓
Flexi-cuffing (too tightly)	✓	✓
Flexi-cuffing to rear	✓	✓
Beatings with pistols/rifles/rifle butts	✓	✓
Slapping	✓	✓
Punching	✓	✓
Kicking	✓	✓
Kick boxing	✓	
Kneeing	✓	✓
Pressing face into ground with boots		✓
Death threats	✓	✓
Threats of reprisals (especially to family members)	✓	✓
Threats of rape	✓	✓
Denial of access to open air	✓	✓
No exercise	✓	✓
Minimal/no access to toilets	✓	✓

Techniques	UK	US
ABUSE (CONTINUED)		
Force-fed baseball bat		✓
"Clean beating"	✓	✓
Excessive restraint positions (restricting breathing, etc.)	✓	✓
Mock executions	✓	
Simulated mutilations (knife)	✓	
Threatened multiple burning	✓	
RELIGIOUS/CULTURAL HUMILIATION		
Deprived of prayer	✓	✓
Not being able to be clean to pray (especially during Ramadan)	✓	✓
Throwing Qur'an in toilet in front of detainee		✓
Spitting in food rations		✓
Taunting at prayer		✓
Forced to eat pork		✓
Forced to drink alcohol		✓
Flushing with toilet water	✓	
Role plays ("birthday parties", forced cleaning of cell, etc.)		✓
OTHERS		
Military dogs	✓	✓
Drip feed of comfort items		✓
Verbal violence	✓	✓
Orders screamed	✓	✓
Rifles aimed	✓	✓
Short shackling		✓
Forced howling like dog		✓
Use of pepper spray		✓
Forced injections		✓
Electric shocks		✓
Forced shaving/cutting of hair		✓
Indelible marking of body		✓
Hung from doors, etc.		✓
Forced IV fluids to induce soiling		✓
Forced violence between detainees	✓	

Source: Public Interest Lawyers (www.publicinterestlawyers.co.uk), interviews with torture victims, April 2003–December 2008.

ABU GHRAIB

The most famous abuse of prisoners by US personnel occurred in Abu Ghraib in 2003 under the command of General Janis Karpinski. The story was broken by the *New Yorker* from an army report not meant for public release. The report detailed a list of practices including beatings, waterboarding (repeated near drowning in cold water), sexual intimidation (including sodomizing with a chemical light and perhaps a broomstick, forced masturbation) and terrorizing with dogs. This torture caused public outrage, not least because of the vividness of the photos and video evidence (Box 2.7).

Box 2.7 Torture at Abu Ghraib

"The photographs tell it all. In one, Private England, a cigarette dangling from her mouth, is giving a jaunty thumbs-up sign and pointing at the genitals of a young Iraqi, who is naked except for a sandbag over his head, as he masturbates. Three other hooded and naked Iraqi prisoners are shown, hands reflexively crossed over their genitals. A fifth prisoner has his hands at his sides. In another, England stands arm in arm with Specialist Graner; both are grinning and giving the thumbs-up behind a cluster of perhaps seven naked Iraqis, knees bent, piled clumsily on top of each other in a pyramid. There is another photograph of a cluster of naked prisoners, again piled in a pyramid. Near them stands Graner, smiling, his arms crossed; a woman soldier stands in front of him, bending over, and she, too, is smiling. Then, there is another cluster of hooded bodies, with a female soldier standing in front, taking photographs. Yet another photograph shows a kneeling, naked, unhooded male prisoner, head momentarily turned away from the camera, posed to make it appear that he is performing oral sex on another male prisoner, who is naked and hooded." (Hersh 2004)

Box 2.8 Philo Ikonya's story

In February 2009, Philo Ikonya (author and currently president of the Kenyan chapter of the PEN International Writers Association and a candidate in the 2007 election) was arrested at a small demonstration outside the Kenyan parliament. She was bundled into a car with a male friend, and beaten. In her words:

"'This can't be happening to me', I thought. I told him: 'I've never ever been hit by a man – stop it!' But he hit me again and I yelled: 'Are you going to stop when you break my jaw? What do you want? What have we done?' ... But he kept on hitting us, repeating 'Now the cameras are not here ...'. I thought he was going to finish us between here and the cells – because that's what he was really saying.

"When we got to the police station my lip was swollen and my clothes were torn. He pulled out the young man and slapped him and dragged him upstairs. I was left there. Then some of his colleagues put me in a cell.

"There are horrible things going on in the cells. Every few minutes they were throwing in someone else. The few women that came in were speechless because of previous torture or harassment. One was pregnant. She couldn't talk because women police officers had tortured her upstairs – they had threatened to put pepper in her private parts, even when she told them she was pregnant. And they beat her badly." (Ikonya 2009)

The case study is discussed in Chapter 5. In addition the following questions may be useful in helping to explore this case study.

QUESTIONS

1. What are the key ethical issues raised by torture? Do these change depending on whether you adopt utilitarian, deontological or virtue theories (as outlined in Chapter 3)?
2. Are there circumstances where you think torture might be justified? If so, then on what grounds and in what circumstances?
3. Is it justifiable to violate individual human rights to ensure public security?
4. The table of torture techniques was collated as part of an ongoing legal investigation by Public Interest Lawyers. How much do you think global ethicists should work with lawyers and other professionals? In other words, do you accept the multidisciplinary criteria of global ethics? If so, what does this entail?
5. Can global ethicists be "objective" or "neutral"? More importantly, *should* they be?

FURTHER READING

- Hersh, S. M. "Torture at Abu Ghraib: American Soldiers Brutalized Iraqis. How Far Up does the Responsibility Go?" *New Yorker* (10 May 2004). www.newyorker.com/archive/2004/05/10/040510fa_fact? (accessed May 2011).
- Ikonya, P. "There Are No Cameras Here" (2009). www.irct.org/what-is-torture/voices-of-torture-victims/there-are-no-cameras-here.aspx (accessed May 2011).
- International Rehabilitation Council for Torture Victims. www.irct.org/what-is-torture/voices-of-torture-victims.aspx (accessed May 2011).
- Miller, S. "Is Torture Ever Morally Justified?" *International Journal of Applied Philosophy* **19** (2005): 179–92.
- Office of the United Nations High Commissioner for Human Rights (OHCHR). "Declaration on the Protection of All Persons from Being Subjected to Torture and Other Cruel, Inhuman or Degrading Treatment or Punishment" (1975). www2.ohchr.org/english/law/declarationcat.htm (accessed May 2011).
- Office of the United Nations High Commissioner for Human Rights (OHCHR). "Convention against Torture and Other Cruel, Inhuman or Degrading Treatment or Punishment" (1984). www2.ohchr.org/english/law/cat.htm (accessed May 2011).
- Public Interest Lawyers. www.publicinterestlawyers.co.uk (accessed May 2011).
- United Nations. "The Universal Declaration of Human Rights" (1948). www.un.org/en/documents/udhr (accessed May 2011).

3 MORAL THEORY FOR GLOBAL ETHICS

INTRODUCTION

In order to address the practical issues of global ethics – from climate change, through trafficking and terrorism, to the expansion of the global market to include body parts – we need a methodology. It is not enough to simply say "these are bad practices and something should be done"; we need to say in what ways they are bad and give a reasoned account. As well as analysing the problems, because of the global-ethics commitment to connecting theory and practice and influencing the "real world", we also need to think about ways to improve the situation on the ground. The next three chapters will provide the "toolbox" of global ethics, which will give you the means to approach any dilemma in global ethics. The toolbox will be made up of elements of moral, political and rights-based theories, which will be introduced in turn over the next three chapters. Together these will be sufficient for you to know how to approach any issue. But the toolbox is not "one size fits all". Everyone's approach is different, and what goes into your toolbox and in what order is up to you. You need to choose the moral, political and rights approaches that you believe are most accurate and most effective. You will need to have reasons for your choices and be able to defend your global-ethics position. Then using the tools you have learnt you will be able to *do* global ethics.

This chapter will broadly introduce the basics of some key moral theories. Essentially there are three main approaches – consequentialism, deontology and virtue theory – which prioritize different values and use different methodologies to determine the right and best solutions. Sometimes the conclusions they come to are vastly different but not infrequently, especially when addressing the most pressing problems of global ethics, they come to similar conclusions. You are likely to favour one of these more than others, and this will be the foundation of your global-ethics approach. That said, remember, first, that on many global-ethics issues, all ethical theories will broadly agree; and, second, there are versions of each of these basic theories that overlap with the others. Accordingly, there is no need to assume that favouring one approach means excluding all the aspects of the others (being a rights theorist or a consequentialist does not preclude you from valuing virtues and employing them in your approach, for example). However, you do need to think about your reasons for favouring one particular standpoint over another, or for adopting a more "pluralistic" view that draws on elements of more than one established view; and you must ensure that your argument for doing so is robust and well reasoned.

Before we look at these three theories we need to begin by exploring a key underlying issue in global ethics: the seemingly eternal debate between moral universalists and moral relativists. Universalism takes there to be at least some moral values and standards that hold independently of any particular cultural, political or historical context. The relativist denies this claim, and says that moral norms and practices always arise from, and are understandable only within, certain contexts. This chapter will outline the arguments between universalists and relativists in order to show that all *global* ethics presupposes some form of universalism. To illustrate how important these abstract arguments are in practice, we shall use the case study of FGC from Chapter 2 to explore the different positions.

CAN WE MAKE GLOBAL CLAIMS?

The first questions the global ethicist comes up against are whether or not human beings share moral values, and whether morality differs in different places or times. These really are the *foundational* questions of global ethics: if you do not believe that at least some values are shared globally, or at least that moral frameworks are globally comprehensible and intelligible to those from different backgrounds, then global ethics will be not only difficult to formulate but also meaningless. This is a topic we shall return to time and again. For instance, the appeal to human rights assumes a shared understating of what is valuable about human beings and some kind of common humanity, as we shall see in Chapter 5. Likewise, universalism is assumed in all areas of global governance; for instance, international law relies on some common understandings of justice. Accordingly, in the specific practical issues of global ethics covered in later chapters, from poverty, through war, bioethics and the environment to women's rights, the claim to universal standards is overt. So, for example, codes and guidelines about how to protect medical research subjects are deemed universal, as are rules about protection of prisoners of war and prohibitions on torture.

The universalist claim that there is some shared moral framework does not require that in practice it is universally implemented. As we explore the practical issues of global ethics, we will come to see that one of the problems with global ethics is that practices on the ground do not always reflect the standards set out in global governance rules and codes. But it is important to note that failures in practice do not necessarily show the presence of "different values"; they may merely show a failure or difference in implementation. For example, as the case study of torture shows (Chapter 2, pp. 24–9; returned to in Chapters 5 and 8), the fact that torture happens does not necessarily show that torturers hold radically different moral values or cannot understand the legitimacy of prohibitions on torture; it may show only that they believe torture is justified in certain instances, and to justify these instances they may even appeal to common values. We shall explore all these issues in detail as we address the topical concerns of global ethics. At this stage, the point to bear in mind is that a lack of consistency in practices does not by itself show moral relativism to be true and universalism to be defeated. With that proviso, we shall now look at the universalist and relativist positions more closely.

GLOBAL ETHICS, UNIVERSALISM AND RELATIVISM

As already mentioned in the introduction to this chapter, relativists believe that morality is different in different times and places and applied to different individuals and groups in different contexts, and importantly that morality can be understood only from *within* the group. By contrast, universalists – including all global ethicists – believe that some moral values at least are shared and that moral discourse is meaningful in the global context.

Types of universalism

Accordingly, all the candidates for "a global ethic" adopt universalist approaches. To have any "global" element implies that there is a global understanding of at least some values, even if these are implemented differently. So even a weak "global ethics" that applies in non-uniform ways is not relative, because it assumes that there is a shared vocabulary and understanding of the values (and the practices that protect those values, such as laws and rights). This is obviously true for strong forms of a global ethic – such as divine-command ethics, which deems actions good by virtue of God's willing or permitting them – or any strong set of moral principles or norms according to which global moral judgements should be made (e.g. doctrines of human rights), but it is also true for weaker forms that seek minimum levels of rights or well-being or that argue for gradual convergence in international codes and practices. If any of these global aspects figure positively in an account of moral values and standards, then that account is not relativist, because it assumes, at the very least, the possibility of global communication about values. However, simply not being relative does not mean that a *strong* universalism is being invoked; there are many weak forms of universalism that accept that there is a shared language of values but that do not endorse global duties. Many such theories will be explored in this book, for instance, whether or not there are duties to the distant poor. But first let us explore relativism in more detail, because even though it is in a way irrelevant to the global-ethics debate – simply because if relativism were true, "global" would be incompatible with "ethics" – it is a prominent debate in moral and political theory, and relativist arguments are often used to criticize global-ethics approaches.

Cultural relativism

All forms of non-universalism deny that there are any moral values that are shared by, or apply to, all human beings regardless of context. One way of strongly opposing moral universalism outright is to adopt some form of moral *scepticism*: to question the validity of any of our moral beliefs; or to deny that we can know that a moral judgement is correct or incorrect; or, on some accounts, that it can be rationally justified or unjustified. Most prominent among the opponents of universalism and most relevant for our purposes are cultural relativists, and it is their view that we shall focus on. Cultural relativists are not necessarily committed to this kind of scepticism about moral value and moral thinking *per se*, but they do hold that morality is something that is always and only relative to particular cultures, unlike universalists. Cultural relativism is particularly important for global ethics because it is often presented as undermining global ethics.

Cultural relativists hold that values are culturally dependent: in other words, that values – including moral values – are nothing more than the customs and norms of a particular society. A key argument often given to support the cultural-relativist argument is the argument from difference, developed by J. L. Mackie (1977). The argument from difference claims that moral diversity across times and places shows that there is no shared morality, and thus concludes that there is no one "objective" moral value or set of values in the world independent of those endorsed by particular societies or communities: that the simple fact that there are different moral practices in different places and times is thought to prove that morality is culturally dependent. A frequently used example in textbooks to illustrate how this works is taken from Herodotus' *Histories* (440 BCE; see Box 3.1).

Cultural relativists use examples of difference, here between the Greeks and the Callatians, to argue that there are no universal truths or shared values. Many examples of moral difference can be found in the contemporary context, some of which we shall discuss in the course of this book, for example, regarding the status of women,

---

Box 3.1 The Greeks and the Callatians

"When Darius was King of Persia, he summoned the Greeks who happened to be present at his court, and asked them what it would take to eat the dead bodies of their fathers. They replied that they would not do it for any money in the world. Later, in the presence of the Greeks and through an interpreter (so that they could understand what was said), he asked some of the tribe called Callatiae, who do in fact eat their parents' dead bodies, what it would take to burn them. They uttered a cry of horror and forbade him to mention such a dreadful thing."
(Herodotus, *Histories* 3.38)

---

duties to the poor and the conduct of war. On all these issues people disagree; for instance, some believe that torture is never acceptable and others that it is justified in some circumstances. Cultural relativists argue that the very fact that people disagree about moral issues precludes the possibility of universal moral truth or globally shared values. From this they conclude that morality is nothing more than the practices and views of a particular culture. Essentially, then, moral views are a matter of cultural chance: opinions, norms and customs that vary from one culture to another. Notice that if, as this view holds, values are just cultural norms and practices, then they cannot be compared or judged because there is no universal standard by which to do so. If we buy the cultural-relativist picture, then, morality is simply a matter of following the norms of the culture you happen to be born into. No norms are better or worse, right or wrong; they are simply the attitudes or the evolved preferences of a particular group.

Box 3.2 The argument from difference

1. Culture X holds that action (a) is morally impermissible and culture Y that action (a) is morally permissible.*
2. Therefore, cultures have demonstrably different moral codes.
3. Thus, from 2, judgements about the moral rightness or wrongness of (a) are expressions of conventions and norms that vary between cultures.
4. So, from 3, action (a) cannot be judged either morally right or morally wrong from an objective, universal, non-culturally contextual perspective.
5. Therefore there is no objective or universal moral truth.

*Action (a) could be any action about which cultures disagree. If it helps to understand the argument, substitute examples for action (a), such as abortion, slavery, conspicuous consumption, torture, adultery, pornography, debt, lying, bribery or masturbation.

The cultural-relativist argument has been popular and many consider that it has great advantages, not least its tolerance. It proffers respect for cultural difference and permits (as equally valid) the different moral practices of different cultures. Thus those who adopt cultural-relativist positions do not appear to be open to charges of moral imperialism or moral neocolonialism (charges that are often levelled at universalist positions and will be discussed in Chapter 5 with regard to critiques of human rights and Chapter 7 with regard to development). This wish not to condemn the morals of other groups and people is one that resonates with contemporary Western cultural norms. For instance, consider how often the phrase "You are entitled to your opinion!" is heard in politics and public debate, and the parallel assumption that "You can only speak about something if you have experienced it!"

Now let us look at some of the problems with the relativist position and the argument from difference. First, consider any of the candidate actions given for (a) in the argument from difference (Box 3.2). How is a judgement such as "torture is morally impermissible" consistent with the claim that there is no objective or universal moral truth? Put differently, in making this statement, what would the cultural and moral relativist who thinks torture is morally impermissible actually be *saying* to someone whose culture's moral values permit torture? As a relativist, she could not consistently be trying to persuade them by appeal to some value or thought they both share that torture is wrong, because the key principle of the relativist's argument from difference is that there are at least some values that are *not* cross-culturally shared. So, when faced with such fundamental disagreement, it appears that the consistent relativist must back off and accept that her anti-torture judgement holds for *some* cultures (her own) but not others. Alternatively, then, she could be saying that *her* anti-torture values are superior to those of her opponent's culture. But this is cultural–moral imperialism writ large! It is resonant of the thoroughly relativist-minded empire builders who justified imposing their own values on other "inferior" cultures on the grounds that they were "civilizing" them. As a result, then, relativists who take this approach become, in practice, universalists who promote their own values as universally correct at the expense of all others, which undermines the claims of cultural respect that underpin the position in the first place. These are serious difficulties for relativism as an approach to global ethical issues. On one hand, simply to back off from moral arguments in the face of moral disagreement would not be doing global ethics; on the other hand, moral or cultural imperialism is not what global ethics should be about.

An added problem here seems to be that accepting difference as a *fact* about the way the world is, and tolerating some such differences, does not commit us to believing that there are no objective moral truths. You can, for example, recognize that there are many different cultures and belief systems in the world, *and* tolerate their existence, without having to say that their culture and practices are morally acceptable or immune from your moral criticism. So the statement "Everyone is *entitled* to express their opinions" need not suggest that an opposite opinion is "just as true as our own" or that "all opinions are equally valid". Consider also that, in practice, many countries have laws that prohibit the expression of certain opinions thought to incite racial and religious hatred and violence. Likewise, a number of countries, including Austria, Belgium, France, Germany, Hungary, Israel and Switzerland, have laws prohibiting Holocaust denial. These instances clearly show that as societies we do not practically endorse the talk-show mantra "all opinions are equally valid", but rather the view that some opinions are pernicious and dangerous and should not be propagated. So, once we begin to interrogate the cultural-relativist claims a little it becomes difficult to maintain the simple view that difference shows the absence of objective values or basic shared values. This is not to say that, because we agree that some views or practices are wrong, for example racism or murder, we should automatically jump to a universalist view and ignore difference. But robust cultural relativism does not seem plausible on reflection, especially when we consider the current level of global integration that suggests some form of collective global culture.

With a little thought, then, it seems that the cultural-relativist view – particularly with its alleged attraction of supporting tolerance – is not quite as attractive as it first appears. For a global ethicist to hold a cultural-relativist view is profoundly problematic because it dramatically limits what we can say about the rightness and wrongness of attitudes and practices. And given that ethics is fundamentally about promoting better states of affairs, this is profoundly debilitating. For a cultural relativist, values are not connected to "truth", to what is right or wrong, better or worse: there is thus so much less to debate because there is no question of truth or right at stake. Clearly a global ethicist could not hold this position, because in this framework ethics is never global but is always bound to a particular culture. In essence, what cultural relativism allows is a collection of different cultures with different moral codes that all exist separately. There is no universal standard, or vantage point, from which these moral stances can be judged, argued about or considered. Therefore, important moral differences cannot be discussed and different positions reasoned for because there are no shared moral grounds from which to do this. Rather, this strong construction of moral diversity imposes silence regarding moral matters that does not permit even cross-cultural, never mind global, discussion. If this were accepted there would be little role for ethicists and none for global ethicists. If we think that there are global dilemmas where discussion across cultures is necessary and meaningful, we must reject cultural relativism. Ironically, if cultural relativism were true, then any statement of it appears to be false because it would be a universal claim!

Arguments for universalism

Luckily for the global ethicist, there are many arguments against the cultural-relativist position (Box 3.3) and, as we have already begun to see, the argument from difference can be challenged. Quite simply, the fact that cultures or groups of persons have different opinions does not necessarily mean that therefore there is no objective moral truth or universally shared values.

The first solution would be to say that either the Greeks are right and the Callatians wrong or vice versa. In discussing Herodotus' example, James Rachels (2007) adds a further example – that of "flat-earthers" – to illustrate this. He points out that in some times and places people have believed that the earth is flat, and that there may still be societies that still do. In our society we believe that the earth is round. Therefore there are different possible views about the nature of the earth. However, the fact that there is disagreement about the shape of the earth and some people believe that the earth is flat is not a reason to suggest that there is no true or correct view. Indeed, to suggest such a conclusion is ludicrous. Rather, we think that those who believe that the earth is flat are wrong and misguided. We could add a further very contemporary example of the current argument between creationists and evolutionists. Here again we have an instance of different cultures endorsing different views: the cultures here being ones of religious belief rather than location. Again, the fact that there is a difference in itself is not sufficient to conclude that there is no truth of the matter, or that both are "right" if considered from *inside* the cultures. Again, the response of both groups is to think that the other side is wrong. And, again, many countries in Europe think that it is so important that the "truth" is taught that publicly funded schools are required to teach evolutionary theory as part of the curriculum (e.g. the National Curriculum for England, Wales and Northern Ireland requires that fossil records are taught as evidence of evolution at Key Stage 4). By contrast, in some states of the US both creationism and evolution are taught and presented as rival theories or viewpoints; indeed, some schools in the US require that "intelligent design" is taught. However, again, just because in one part of the world there is no consensus on which of these theories is true it does not mean that there is no truth about the matter; in other words disagreement does not mean that both theories are wrong.

In all these cases – the Greeks and the Callatians, the flat-earthers, and the creationists and evolutionists – it is false to claim that just because there are differences in views, substantive conclusions cannot be drawn about the nature of morality. In fact, in all the cases, most obviously the flat-earth case, it is clear that one side could be correct. Therefore the simple fact of cultural difference does not prove that there is no moral truth or no objective moral values. Of course, to deny that the argument from difference succeeds is not the same as establishing that there *are* universal or shared values, but it is enough to show that the argument from difference is not sufficient to establish that there are no such values. Realizing this is a first step to thinking more seriously about what global ethics and shared values might be.

In addition to this primary argument against cultural relativism – that the argument from difference does not prove that there are no objective values – there are four additional arguments that universalists make, connected to their claims about the failure of the argument from difference.

First, universalists accuse cultural relativists of confusing the underlying values with the manifestation of these practices. As a consequence of this misunderstanding, the cultural relativist exaggerates the difference between cultures. The claim is that when cultural relativists cite the difference between the values of different cultures they are not in fact talking about values, but about the customs and practices that manifest those values. They argue that if we focused on the underlying values there would be far less difference between cultures than the cultural relativists would have us believe. If we return to the example of the Greeks and the Callatians, the universalist might claim that, rather than an argument from difference, this is an argument about practice. In both cultures the aim is to properly respect and honour the dead. Thus the underlying value is that of care and respect for family members in death; the fact that the practices are different says nothing about the underlying values. The apparent gulf between the two cultures disappears on closer enquiry. The disagreements are merely practical ones about *how* the dead are to be honoured (the Greeks burn their dead and the Callatians eat them), not value disagreements about whether or not the dead *should* be honoured. This argument applies well to moral cases – but less well to those of other belief areas, such as the flat-earthers, and the evolutionists and the creationists – but because our primary concern is global ethics, this is not, for us, an insurmountable problem.

Second, universalists argue that the cultural-relativist claim that values are simply cultural norms goes against our moral experience. When people reflect on or act on their moral beliefs they think that something important that matters to them is at stake. People do not think they are expressing cultural norms and opinions; rather, they think that what they are expressing is something that is actually true. The fact that people feel like this is not "proof" that this is the case, but if we are to conclude that values are not "true" in the way that people instinctively believe, then strong arguments need to be made for why we should ignore our moral intuitions. "Projectionist" arguments claim that our feelings about morality are signals about the importance of these matters for social functioning and human flourishing, but they do not mean that values are objectively true.

The third argument that universalists use against cultural relativism is about moral change. If cultural relativism is true then it is difficult to account for moral criticism and moral change. If values are merely non-objective norms and opinions, then how is change possible? For instance, if we think of the abolition of slavery, criticism came from *within* cultures on the grounds that the abolitionists believed that slavery was "wrong". Again, value is tied to beliefs about "right" and "wrong" on grounds that are not simply those of cultural norms but important matters of feeling and commitment.

The commitment to moral beliefs applies to other cultures as well as our own. People do hold certain actions "wrong" and impermissible. Think, for example, of abortion, slavery, prostitution, conspicuous consumption, torture, adultery, pornography, debt, lying, bribery or masturbation, actions that many people have strong moral views on, which they believe are not simply cultural norms. For the most part, people do not believe that torture is impermissible in their own culture but perfectly permissible elsewhere. There are instances where these views can be found, for instance, early colonial views of "uncivilized savages". In such instances, colonials accepted double moral standards on the grounds that the practices of "savages" were less civilized and less moral. Yet, even in this extreme example, the separation of cultures was not absolute and did not continue. It was the appeal to common humanity – recognizing the same values across cultures – that fuelled the abolitionist movement against slavery.

The problem is that there seems no room in cultural relativism for critiquing moral standards if "right" and "permissible" are culturally relative terms. What is right is simply that which is in accord with the norms of the culture in question (and, conversely, what is wrong contravenes cultural codes and norms). If this is true then not only does cultural relativism preclude the criticizing of the codes of other cultures, but it also makes it hard to criticize our own culture. On what grounds would we be able to make such a criticism if values are simply culturally derived? Without some concept of an independent standard, values and practices cannot be judged to be better or worse. Again, the nature of moral critique and change tells against the claims of cultural relativism.

The final argument against cultural relativism is that it presumes cultures are distinct and separable entities. While this understanding of cultures might apply well to the Greeks and the Callatians, it is a problematic view in our increasingly globalized world. While there may be some small groups on the planet who pursue particular ways of life and endorse moral codes oblivious of the wider world, these groups are

---

Box 3.3 Arguments against cultural relativism

- The conclusions of the argument from difference do not follow from the premises.
- It confuses underlying values with application in practice.
- It conflicts with moral experience.
- It ignores that evaluation is fundamental to moral practice.
- It ignores the interrelatedness of cultures in our globalized world.

rare. Cultures may disagree and argue for different values, or different priorities, or different applications of values, but almost all are engaged in the global debate about what *should* be. Thus, in a very real sense, the only culture we can speak of in the moral sense is the global. It might be the case that should we meet species from another planet such arguments would not work but, within human culture, there seems no good reason to think that moral communication is not possible and that there are not at least some shared values.

The number and the strength of the arguments against cultural relativism show that at the very least it is not absurd to argue for moral theories and practices that are not derived from and bounded by cultural norms; in other words, global ethics is possible. If it were not possible meaningfully to discuss moral matters with those who do not share your own culture then the possibility of any global ethics, or meaningful dialogue about values in the global context, would be prohibited. But, the

CASE STUDY 3.1 Female genital cutting

The issue of female genital cutting (FGC) is particularly useful when considering the difficulties involved in arriving at shared views about what practices are acceptable. The case study in Chapter 2 (pp. 15–18) shows that, despite the international criticism of FGC on physical and psychological health grounds, the practice is defended on cultural grounds. For example, Egyptian women who are "circumcised" themselves, and who wish their daughters to be likewise, support it. Cultural relativists must accept not only that FGC is permitted within the culture, but also that the moral status of the practice is determined within the culture. On the relativist view, if a culture deems FGC as important and valuable, then it is; there is no outside or objective standard that can be appealed to in order to critique the practice. A cultural relativist can accept no grounds for criticizing a culturally valuable practice. By contrast, a universalist can argue – using many different moral theories and reasons – that such a practice is morally unacceptable. Extreme practices like FGC, deemed by some to be morally abhorrent, are useful test cases for our ethical thinking. Other useful test cases include torture, slavery, veiling, initiation rights, abortion and arranged marriage: indeed, any practices about which there are strong disagreements, particularly cultural disagreements. Those who oppose such practices argue that these practices are morally unacceptable for a number of reasons (depending on which moral position they endorse): for instance, because they violate human rights (understood to be universally applicable), because they fail to respect persons, or because they do not contribute to human good.

However, before deciding that "of course certain practices are right and wrong or better and worse", we should remember the cultural relativists' caution about adopting our own cultural values and simply attempting to export them (moral colonialism). For instance, Yael Tamir (1996) argues that although FGC is a deplorable practice, we should be suspicious of the mass condemnation of it. In particular, she argues that the way FGC is treated is

cultural-relativist position being far from proved does not mean that the criticisms should be wholly ignored. For example, it is important to remember that even if there are shared dialogue and possibilities of global frameworks and standards, many of the practices in which our values manifest themselves are cultural. Cultural relativism clearly illustrates the danger of believing that our own practices – such as how we treat the dead – are objectively right or wrong. It warns us against cultural superiority and such practices as moral neocolonialism (which we shall return to in Chapters 5, 7 and 11). This said, the recognition that some of our moral practices are culturally constructed does not mean either that there are no right or wrong practices or that all practices are equally good manifestations of some equally respectable value. A universalist position allows us to claim that, because there are universal values, some practices are indeed better and worse than others and either respect or fail to respect certain values. Thus acts and practices can be judged right and wrong, good

markedly different from the way other not dissimilar practices are treated. Practices she lists include "malformations" such as piercing, tattooing and abnormal elongation of lips, earlobes and necks, all of which are done in the name of beauty. She also cites a list of popular Western practices that are damaging to women, including "extreme diets, depilation, face lifts, fat pumping, silicone implants".

It is important to understand that Tamir is not a cultural relativist and she argues that the practices of FGC and the painful practices and procedures that Western women subject themselves to (such as extreme dieting and plastic surgery) should not be endorsed. Indeed, she argues that the same patriarchal values that disempower women underlie all of these practices. What is important about Tamir's argument is that it forces us to think critically about our own values and the grounds on which we can make global claims. In addition, Tamir has a secondary argument that suggests that the problems with our own culture should be addressed first and, worryingly for global ethics, that if there are similar issues in our own culture we should not criticize others. This is worrying because there are no cultures that are without their problems and to endorse Tamir's conclusion would effectively recommend that we silence critiques, activists and reformers. For instance, is it necessary to ensure that all forms of brutality are removed before criticizing torture elsewhere, or that all aspects of racism are removed before racist practices and policies (e.g. apartheid) can be critiqued? To make perfection a condition of critique would effectively be to silence all debate about moral matters. The claim that it is morally wrong to criticize the practices of another culture unless we have rectified all the injustices in our own culture becomes, despite Tamir's own stance, an anti-universalist argument. This argument is addressed directly by Nussbaum (1996). Nussbaum argues that racism in the US was not a reason for not opposing apartheid, just as anti-Semitism in all nations was not a reason not to rescue Jews from the Nazis. She argues that it makes no difference whether the

and bad, better or worse and, importantly, reasons and justifications can be given for this that do not rely simply on asserting the rightness of a particular cultural norm, but on arguing that these practices are better or worse according to the extent to which they are good for human beings.

To help us understand the difference adopting a universalist or a cultural-relativist position makes to how we can do ethics consider the case study of FGC (Case study 3.1).

MORAL REASONS AND ARGUMENTS

So far in this chapter we have explored the cultural-relativist position and established that global dialogue about ethics and values is indeed possible. This done,

injustice occurs on our own doorstep or at the other side of the world. Nussbaum goes on to offer arguments for why FGC should be opposed, and more urgently than the Western beauty practices that Tamir describes.

Nussbaum makes eight arguments:

- FGC is forced whereas Western "beauty practices" are not.
- FGC is not reversible whereas dieting is.
- FGC is performed in unhygienic conditions with disastrous effects.
- FGC is linked to lifelong problems, whereas dieting is not.
- FGC is performed on those too young for consent.
- FGC is performed on those with dramatically lower levels of education, which increases powerlessness and limits opportunities to consent.
- FGC is an irreversible loss of the capability for a certain type of sexual functioning.
- FGC is unambiguously about male domination, whereas Western beauty is more complex.

There are a number of counter-arguments that could be raised against Nussbaum and her claims for the differences between the practices of FGC and Western beauty practices. For example, against both her second and fourth arguments we can object that, while dieting is perhaps reversible, plastic surgery is not and, in at least some cases, extreme dieting and plastic surgery (e.g. if there are complications with implants) do lead to lifelong problems. Moreover, is it really the case that FGC is unambiguously about male domination in a way that breast enlargement is not? In both practices often young girls endorse the procedures (and look forward to the event as a rite of passage). In both, beauty is often thought by both women and men to be enhanced. In both, it is often thought to be in

we must now move on and begin to consider what global ethics might be and how practical issues, such as FGC, might be addressed. The rest of this chapter will begin this process of showing how arguments can be built and reasons given for particular positions. How you build a case for a position and what reasons you consider most important will shape your decision as to the moral theory you adopt. The theory you adopt may well then colour how you see the situation; likewise, situations and experiences may change how correct you believe a moral theory to be. This chapter will outline the three most prominent moral theories – utilitarianism, deontology and virtue theory – and these moral theories will form the basis of your "ethical toolbox". How you understand what is morally right and acceptable fundamentally affects the approach you adopt, as well as shaping the type of arguments you use and the kind of reasons that count most when addressing practical dilemmas. Understanding the moral theories and commitments people have is at the heart of deciphering different moral viewpoints, and an essential first step in

the best interests of the girls for attracting the best husband or otherwise improving their future life chances. Therefore, while Nussbaum's arguments about the importance of critiquing global practices are strong and there are reasons why FGC might be regarded as more heinous than Western beauty practices, there are also questions about whether the failings of the culture with which we are familiar appear less unacceptable than those of other cultures. If we recall the concerns of the cultural relativists, we can see the shadow of critiques about imposing the values of one's own culture on another culture. For instance, the worry about consent and lack of education tends to allot educated Western women more agency than non-Western women. This is an issue we shall return to in the final chapter on gender justice.

What is important for our current discussion is not the rights or wrongs of FGC but that the rights and wrongs of FGC can be meaningfully discussed. Once this discussion is engaged in, a universalist framework has been presumed. To engage in this debate assumes that it is possible to speak across cultures about the rightness and wrongness of the practices of the respective cultures. Accordingly, there is common ground for discussion, debate and understanding from which to make value claims and have ethical arguments. For both Tamir and Nussbaum, there are shared and common understandings about what is at stake, including issues of autonomy, choice, paternalism, power and patriarchy, and thus a universalist framework. Despite Tamir's claims, her comparative argument, which critiques the Western beauty myth and deems it coercive in a not dissimilar way to practices of FGC, is a universalist one. Like Nussbaum, whom she criticizes, she is judging and comparing cross-cultural practices, so a universalist framework is indeed in play. We can draw a key point from the disagreement between Tamir and Nussbaum here. To question the moral legitimacy of actions intervening in other cultures, as Tamir does, does not necessarily imply moral relativism.

making and understanding arguments. People do not need to be moral philosophers – indeed they usually are not – to hold views that fit with one theory or another (or to know that moral theories exist, or their names). However, knowing such theories is invaluable for seeking to challenge an approach or to resolve a conflict. Therefore, understanding moral theory is not merely an academic exercise but indispensable on the ground.

CONSEQUENTIALISM AND UTILITARIANISM

Utilitarianism, along with deontology, which we shall consider next, are the two most prominent types of universalism. Utilitarianism is a form of *consequentialism*. What the consequentialist takes into account when working out whether an action or practice is morally right or wrong is the *consequences*. For the utilitarian and other consequentialists, what matters is the results; all other factors are irrelevant. There are many different types of consequentialism, and indeed many different types of utilitarianism (most importantly utilitarianism divides into act-utilitarian theories and rule-utilitarian theories), but we shall limit our exploration primarily to utilitarianism in general. The fathers of utilitarianism who defined its essential components are Jeremy Bentham and John Stuart Mill, and it is they who set out the main premises of utilitarianism as it is employed in its many and varied versions today.

Utilitarianism asserts that the correct social and moral goal is to make as many people as possible as happy as possible. At its simplest, utilitarianism is the moral theory that promotes the "greatest good of the greatest number". In this theory all human beings are treated impartially and equally, which can be captured by Mill's account of Bentham's dictum, "everybody to count for one, nobody for more than one" (Mill [1863] 1987). As a consequentialist theory, utilitarianism determines the greatest good of the greatest number by considering the outcome or consequences that follow from any act. An act or practice is considered to be morally right if it results in the greatest good for the greatest number of people.

Importantly, then, utilitarianism is *impartial* (sometimes this is referred to as the "principle of impartiality"). No account is taken of relative status and power, whether economic, political, national or ethnic. No partiality or special treatment is morally acceptable on this theory. All human beings are deemed to be of equal moral worth. Importantly for the global ethicist, impartiality extends to distance. It makes no difference if you are near or far; all that matters is how much happiness or goodness will be produced. The impartiality of utilitarianism was radical and revolutionary when it was first articulated. As we shall see in later chapters – when we discuss issues from poverty to reproductive rights – this is still a revolutionary position, and if impartiality were properly applied then the global distribution of wealth as well as key human goods such as health care and education would be distributed very differently.

Maximizing pleasure

For Bentham ([1823] 1907) morality was about increasing or maximizing pleasure and decreasing or minimizing pain. He described pleasure and pain as the "two sovereign masters" of human beings, and he judged all actions according to how much pleasure and pain they produced. Morally right actions and practices promote the most pleasure. He assessed actions using the "principle of utility" (sometimes referred to as the "greatest happiness principle"). The principle of utility "approves" actions that increase happiness, something Bentham believed could be applied to all actions, not only of individuals but also of collective bodies and the government. A right or good action promotes the most happiness, and a wrong or bad action promotes less happiness or even pain. Utilitarianism is therefore a *maximizing* morality. What is morally right or good is the maximization of pleasure or happiness, where "happiness" overall can be increased by adding together the happiness of individual persons as units (sometimes this is called the "aggregative" aspect of utilitarianism). If we take this maximizing element seriously, utilitarianism is very demanding; because you can always create more happiness it is your moral duty always to be continually engaged in doing so. For this reason utilitarianism has been said to be too demanding (something we shall consider in the context of famine relief in Chapter 7).

In Bentham's first version of utilitarianism, "happiness" is equated directly with "pleasure". All that is needed to determine the morally best action is to weigh up the pleasure produced and the pains incurred by alternative courses of action, and choose the one that results in the most pleasure. Bentham set out a number of factors to be considered when making the calculation, namely the action's intensity, duration, certainty, remoteness, fecundity and purity. However, we do not need to be concerned with these in detail, but rather just understand the basic tenet of Bentham's utilitarianism: that what is morally good is measured purely by reference to pleasure and pain.

Utilitarianism is a moral theory with immediate intuitive appeal. Who would not agree that reducing pain and increasing happiness should be at the heart of any moral theory? Yet, even those who directly followed Bentham did not fully agree with his direct equation of happiness with pleasure. They included Mill, Bentham's immediate follower and author of *Utilitarianism* ([1863] 1987). Mill wished to differentiate between different types of pleasure. He argued that some forms of pleasure were (morally) better than others and thus he added an important additional factor to the calculation of happiness: that of "quality" rather than just quantity. Instead of considering only the amount of pleasure and pain, it was now necessary to calculate the value or importance of that pleasure and pain. In Mill's schema, a qualitatively better pleasure might outweigh a greater quantity of a qualitatively poor pleasure: in his words, "better to be a human being dissatisfied than a pig satisfied; better to be Socrates dissatisfied than a fool satisfied" ([1863] 1987).

In introducing the criterion of quality, Mill was attempting to answer the most important question for those who wish to embrace utilitarian theories: what is happiness and how do you measure it? A great advantage of utilitarianism is its simplicity: morality is not complex; all you have to do is measure happiness and do the action that maximizes happiness and minimizes unhappiness. However, this simplicity is deceptive, for what is happiness and how are we to measure it? Once we have to decide between types of happiness and give one type more weight than others – rather than simply measure units of pleasure – measuring happiness is no longer simple because other value judgements are involved.

The extent to which you are convinced that there is a satisfactory way to understand and measure happiness will profoundly influence whether you are convinced by the plausibility and effectiveness of utilitarianism as a moral theory. Three main types of answers can be given to the question of what is happiness: mental-state theories, desire-satisfaction theories and objective-list theories. Each theory has a different understanding of what constitutes happiness and thus of how it can be measured (Box 3.4).

Box 3.4 Happiness for the utilitarian

Happiness is:
- a mental state – "feeling happy";
- desire satisfaction – "getting what you want";
- objective list theories – "having what you need".

There are advantages and disadvantages to each of these theories, and there is space here to give only a brief outline of them. But all have been important and influential, not just in understanding happiness and ethical theory, but also in determining public policy.

Happiness is feeling happy

For many, the idea that happiness is a mental state – that it is about feeling – seems at first to be correct. But if we reflect a little does this still seem plausible? For

Box 3.5 Nozick's experience machine

"Suppose there were an experience machine that would give you any experience you desired. Super-duper neuropsychologists could stimulate your brain so that you would think and feel you were writing a great novel, or making a friend, or reading an interesting book. All the time you would be floating in a tank, with electrodes attached to your brain. Should you plug into this machine for life, programming your life's experiences? If you are worried about missing out on desirable experiences, we can suppose that business enterprises have researched thoroughly the lives of many others. You can pick and choose from their large library or smorgasbord of such experiences, selecting your life's experiences for, say, the next two years. After two years have passed, you will have ten minutes or ten hours out of the tank, to select the experiences of your *next* two years. Of course, while in the tank you will not know that you are there; you will think it is actually happening. Others can also plug in to have the experiences they want, so there is no need to stay unplugged to serve them … Would you plug in? *What else can matter to us, other than how our lives feel from the inside?*"

(Nozick 1974: 42–3)

example, if we are measuring happiness in order to determine which is the morally right action, then should the person who is more exuberant and "feels" happier count more in the calculation? More importantly, does it matter if the feeling of happiness is merited? In other words, does it matter that the happy feeling is a reasonable response to a state of affairs, or is the fact that it is felt all that matters? This has been famously discussed by Robert Nozick (1974), who makes his point using the example of the "experience machine". This is so illustrative it is worth considering in full (Box 3.5).

Whether feeling happy is enough is a theme often explored in science fiction (for instance novels such as *Brave New World* explore whether happiness can be attained by popping a pill, and in the *Matrix* trilogy there is always a character who wants to return to the matrix and "escape reality"). How you respond to the experience machine – would you plug yourself in or is reality important? – gives a good indication of how convincing you will find mental-state theories of happiness. If happiness is a mental state, simply a feeling, then what possible reason could there be for not plugging in to the experience machine? Some people are quite willing to accept this logic and the consequences of the logic and would happily be plugged into the experience machine or take the appropriate drug, whereas others feel morally uncomfortable with such conclusions and seek alternative constructions of "happiness" that include such things as achievements and the completion of projects over the course of a lifetime. The force of Nozick's thought experiment for many people is that is shows that what we see as well-being or happiness is not identical with or reducible to mental states.

Happiness is getting what you want

One alternative is to adopt "desire-satisfaction" theories (a model that has been particularly popular among economists). A desire-satisfaction theory does not focus on mental states when determining happiness, but rather identifies desires and preferences and then claims that happiness is the attainment of those desires or preferences. As with all of these theories there are problems, and in this case one of these is illuminated by considering the way it was originally used in economics. Desire-satisfaction models can be seen as improving on the "feeling" account in so far as they evoke standards with which we can more tangibly measure "utility": the satisfaction of people's desires. Rather than trying to quantify or compare "subjective" feelings that are inside different people's minds in order to calculate whether utility or happiness is being maximized, more explicable measures are appealed to as "utility functions"; a clear example is the amount of money a person has as well as the number and economic value of their possessions. However, a problem here concerns whether the indication of desires and preferences being satisfied amounts to an indication of "happiness", in the sense the utilitarian is looking for, as a measure of well-being and the subject of morality. First, at a given point in time, a person could have all sorts of their desires satisfied at the cost of having many others thwarted at a later time. Second, they could have a present and quite genuine desire to do something that would, perhaps unbeknown to them at the time of desiring, be very bad for them in either the short or longer term. Desire-satisfaction theories get beyond the problems of mere pleasure sensations, but what these two points suggest is that they fail to capture the way in which happiness may be, first, more than subject-dependent (happiness might be more than, or different from, what we happen to desire or wish for); and, second, happiness might make sense only in terms of a complete life (instead of taking account of only present desires and wishes).

Happiness is having what you need

A third option is to adopt an "objective theory", and focus on what is necessary for a happy life. These theories are not concerned only with what people actually desire (as desire-satisfaction theories are), but rather concerned with what we *ought* to desire, or what we would desire if we were fully informed and rational. An example we have already mentioned is in Mill's distinction between "higher" and "lower" pleasures, which goes beyond viewing happiness as merely the satisfaction of actual desires and preferences. That distinction clearly values some of the things a person desires more highly than others, regardless of whether that person feels perfectly content with seeking "lower" pleasures. This theory too has advantages, because clearly we can desire what is not actually good for us (and often as human beings we do just this), but is it really the case that individuals have nothing to say about what actually makes them happy or satisfied? In this theory we might be deemed happy even if we do not have what we actually desire or prefer. Also, such an approach undermines some of the initial appeal of utilitarianism because it is no longer a simple theory, but one that (before it can even begin to be used) must determine what objective goods or values constitute happiness. This complexity comes into view when we ask: what would go on the "objective list" of things that are good in a human life? We shall return in more detail to one influential way of addressing this question when we look at Nussbaum's "capability approach" later in this chapter and again in Chapter 11.

Utilitarianism for global ethics?

Yet, despite the difficulties in determining happiness, utilitarianism remains one of the most compelling and popular moral theories and one that, as we shall see as we move through this book, is influential in much of the real moral decision-making about the practical issues of global ethics, from aid and development to war and humanitarian intervention. The work of Bentham and Mill established the key premises of utilitarianism and their influence can be clearly seen not only in the practical issues of global ethics but also in common moral assumptions: for example, the view that all human beings *must* be morally important, and that making as many people as happy as possible *must* be good (Box 3.6). Also, as many thinkers, like Robert Goodin and Susan Mendus, point out, utilitarianism, in some form, is particularly well suited as a basis on which to make political decisions and policies that affect large numbers of people.

Box 3.6 Utilitarianism

Utilitarianism:
- is the greatest good *of* the greatest number;
- is impartial;
- is consequentialist;
- measures happiness;
- is maximizing.

Because utilitarianism seems to many an obvious and attractive moral theory in the contemporary context, it is easy to forget how radical it was when it was first introduced. Not only did it assert the equality of all individuals (which is still a radical theory if we take it seriously, as we shall see in Chapter 7 when we consider

Singer's utilitarian thinking applied to the issue of famine) but it also runs counter to other moral theories and to much of our usual moral thinking. For example it is important to recognize what it means to say that the *only* thing that morally matters is consequences. If an action is judged morally right or wrong *only* with regard to consequences then no actions or practices whatsoever (whether killing, lying, torture, slavery and so on) are morally impermissible or morally wrong simply in themselves. Likewise, there is nothing that must always be protected, or deemed to be morally good. On such grounds Bentham rejected "rights talk", describing natural rights as a "contradiction in terms", "nonsense" and "fictitious entities", and the French Declaration of the Rights of Man and Citizen (National Constituent Assembly 1789) as "nonsense on stilts". For the utilitarian there are no such things as "rights" that always apply in every circumstance; because every act is only right or wrong in light of the consequences, nothing is "sacred" or intrinsically morally valuable (something we shall discuss in further detail in Chapter 5). In this way utilitarianism overturns conventional moral thinking by denying that certain acts or practices are always wrong. The overturning of conventional morality is shown clearly in Judith Jarvis Thomson's (1985) famous example of the surgeon (see Box 3.7).

CASE STUDY 3.2 Utilitarianism and female genital cutting

For a utilitarian, FGC is not intrinsically right or wrong; its rightness or wrongness is purely determined by the outcome. A utilitarian attempts to establish whether continuing or ceasing the practice has the best outcome. Does continuing or abolishing FGC create the greatest happiness of the greatest number?

To determine whether FGC should continue, the utilitarian begins by considering whose happiness should be taken into account. It might seem simple to say that everyone who is affected should be considered and all should be taken into account impartially and equally and in proportion to utility. However, applying this rule to the real-life case of FGC is not as easy as it might first appear. For example, if in any decision those who are *affected* are those who should be taken into account, whom does this include? Does it include people who disapprove, but who do not themselves go through the practice? Alternatively, should future generations be taken into account (women would arguably benefit if it was stopped now)? If so, how are their potential claims to be balanced? Likewise, how does the utilitarian take account of the claims make by Tamir about patriarchal power relations? Another utilitarian approach would be to think about the greatest happiness overall, which might lead the utilitarian to conclude that this issue was not one that figured greatly in maximizing happiness and therefore is not one the ethicist should focus on.

Having made a decision regarding who should be taken into account, the utilitarian will then need to decide which version of happiness to consider. For example, if happiness is

---

Box 3.7 One life for many?

Imagine yourself to be a surgeon, a truly great surgeon. Among other things you do, you transplant organs, and you are such a great surgeon that the organs you transplant always take. At the moment you have five patients who need organs. Two need one lung each, two need a kidney each, and the fifth needs a heart. If they do not get those organs today, they will all die; if you find organs for them today, you can transplant the organs and they will all live. But where can you find the lungs, the kidneys and the heart? The time is almost up when a report is brought to you that a young man who has just come into your clinic for his yearly check-up has exactly the right blood type, and is in excellent health. Lo, you have a possible donor. All you need do is cut him up and distribute *his* parts among the five who need them. You ask, but he says, "Sorry. I deeply sympathise, but no." Would it be morally permissible for you to operate anyway?

If you adopt utilitarian reasoning – where no acts are ruled out automatically as absolutely wrong – then on what grounds could you criticize the killing of the healthy "patient"? After all, the sum total of happiness brought about by the lives of the five

---

a mental state then all that is at issue in this case is how those who undergo the practice, approve and disapprove, *feel* and how intensely they feel. Such an approach is difficult to implement: how are the feelings of those who wish to undergo the practice – believing it is necessary for them to become women – to be weighed? As long as they feel happy the practice should continue. Or should the net be cast more broadly: should the feelings of the whole community or of all people also be considered? One response would be to argue that the empirical evidence shows the health risks are considerable and therefore continuing the practice would result in unhappiness. But, to conclude this is to adopt an objective view of what constitutes happiness and to ignore both how people feel and their desires. Utilitarians who adopt this "objective" approach can take into account the "health facts", but those who adopt desire- or preference-satisfaction models and more traditional forms of utilitarianism would focus on how people actually feel, not on what is objectively good for them.

There are many conclusions that a utilitarian could make about FGC. And the approach the utilitarian takes to what is happiness and to what counts as a moral fact will colour the resulting moral judgement. To recap, for the utilitarian the right or morally good action is the one that results in the greatest happiness of the greatest number. Before applying the principle of utility and calculating the best action, utilitarians must decide their starting premises:

- Who should be taken into account?
- What counts as happiness and how is it to be quantified?

who are saved is surely more important than the death of the single patient? In utilitarianism the ends really do justify the means; indeed, the means (or the method by which acts are done) have no bearing on the rightness or the wrongness of the act at all. The transplant case shows clearly that our conventional thoughts about morality rebel against conclusions like this one: that it would be morally good, even required, for the surgeon to kill the one healthy person to save five others. This example uses a clearly unrealistic, hypothetical case (a surgeon would not do this and it is unlikely that the healthy "patient's" organs would be compatible with the five patients). But this does nothing to undermine what it shows about the moral theory. Hypothetical examples are useful to our thinking because they clarify what is at issue morally in any particular case or with the application of any particular theory. Thus, hypothetical examples, as long as they are considered with real cases as well, are very useful for clarifying what counts morally.

Utilitarianism (Box 3.8) is not only difficult to fit with common moral intuitions – for example that certain acts are intrinsically right or wrong, irrespective of the consequence (e.g. murder always being morally wrong) – but also with situations that have derived from relationships or special claims. For example, if all that matters is consequences then the historical circumstances that led to an action, such as whether a promise was made, are not relevant when considering what the right action to do is. A promise (or any other commitment, including, for example, relational ones) is morally irrelevant for a utilitarian. Whether and how relationships count is an issue we shall return to throughout the book.

Box 3.8 Summing up utilitarianism

Advantages
- It is intuitively attractive – "Of course it is moral to work for the greatest good of the greatest number!"
- It is unified and simple.
- It embraces the key moral principles of equality and impartiality.
- Almost everyone believes that utilitarian reasoning is correct in at least some circumstances.

Disadvantages
- It conflicts with some ingrained aspects of moral experience.
- It condones actions generally regarded as immoral.
- There are difficulties in measuring happiness.
- It is too demanding.
- It fails to protect individuals.

KANTIANISM

Kantianism is a form of deontology or "duty ethics". Deontological theories present certain acts as intrinsically morally right or wrong irrespective of the consequences of the act. Just as there are many different types of consequentialism there are also many different types of deontology. For instance, many rights theories are deontological (although some are contractual), as are divine-command theories. For our purposes we shall limit our exploration to Kantianism.

Kantianism, named after Immanuel Kant, is like utilitarianism in as much as it is a universal theory intended to apply to all equally in all situations. However, it is vastly different from utilitarianism in both its starting assumptions and in its method of determining the morally right action. Unlike utilitarianism, Kantianism is not concerned with consequences in calculating the morally right action, and it is not a maximizing philosophy: doing what is right is not about maximizing goodness, pleasure, happiness or anything else. In some senses it is impartial, in that it does require that all similar cases are treated similarly and insists on consistency; but, unlike utilitarianism, it can take account of special relationships. Accordingly it can be argued that impartiality is not as thoroughgoing a requirement for Kantian deontology as it is for utilitarianism. This is because a Kantian would think it right and proper to respect duties that arise from relationships, for instance duties to care for family members apply only to these persons and do not apply impartially to everyone.

For deontologists, it is not the outcome of an action that determines its moral rightness, but the status of the action itself and its accordance with moral duty. In colloquial terms, for a deontological theory desirable ends definitely cannot justify bad means: an action is intrinsically right or wrong in and of itself. Therefore if an action is morally right then it is morally required and ought to be done no matter what the consequences and irrespective of any personal reservations, desires, wishes or excuses. Morally right acts are those that quite simply one *ought* to do irrespective of anything else; to use Kant's word they are "categorical".

Kant divided categorical moral "oughts" from hypothetical "oughts". Categorical oughts are those things that must be done by everyone and anyone, while hypothetical oughts are things that we ought to do if we wish for a certain outcome: in other words hypothetical oughts are conditional as in "if I want this then I ought to do that". For example, if you want to be a successful student you ought to read the prescribed books, or if you want to lose weight you ought to diet and exercise. For Kant, moral requirements, categorical oughts, are not conditional in this way but binding on human beings because human beings are rational agents. He argues that morally right actions can be recognized and understood as categorically binding by all rational beings if they reflect on the nature of any action and consider whether or not that action could be "universalizable". By "universalizable" Kant means that if it would be acceptable for the action to become a universally required action then it is an acceptable action. In contrast, if you could not rationally wish that this action was made universally required then it is not an acceptable action.

The categorical imperative

The core principle of Kant's moral theory is the *categorical imperative*. This is used in Kantian theory to determine what is morally right and wrong in a parallel manner to the way that the principle of utility is used in utilitarianism. In the *Groundwork of the Metaphysics of Morals* ([1785] 1997), Kant sets out the categorical imperative as a means by which to judge all actions. The categorical imperative states that you should "act only according to that maxim by which you can at the same time will that it should become a universal law". The categorical imperative is not as complex as it sounds. Quite simply, if you would be (reasonably) happy for everyone to have to perform the same action in the same circumstances then an action is moral; if you would not then it is not.

Kant uses the example of promising to show how his argument works. He presents a case of a person who is forced to borrow money. The person knows that they will not be able to pay it back but they also know that they must promise to pay it back or the money will not be lent. If you turn this act into a "maxim" – a principle of action – then you get the following maxim: "If one needs money one can borrow it by promising to repay it, even if one knows this is impossible." If this maxim (which Kant describes as the principle of self-love) is assessed according to the categorical imperative, it is clear that the action is morally wrong or impermissible. As soon as we consider whether this maxim could be universalized, become a "universal moral law" that applies to everyone in a similar situation, it is clear that it could not. As Kant states, it would contradict itself: promises would cease to be believed because promises to repay money would be worthless; they would be, to use Kant's words, "vain pretences".

In this example of the "lying promise" we can see how the universalizablity criterion in the form of the categorical imperative functions in Kant's framework and the importance of rationality in making sense of Kant's position. For Kant, even if you are in desperate need of money you cannot believe that it is morally right to lie in order to borrow money that you know you cannot repay. For as soon as you consider what it would mean if this action were universalized and everyone acted the same way, the unacceptability of the proposed lying promise becomes clear. The lying promiser cannot respond that they are happy for there to be a rule that everyone in a similar position should act in the same way, because this would not be rational (it would destroy the practices and presumptions of promising and the system would break down). Nor can the lying promiser appeal to consequences – such as that the money is needed to feed his children or for any other "good works" – because these are not relevant, but rather special pleading. The only thing of import in determining whether an action is morally imperative is whether it passes or fails the test of the categorical imperative. In this sense, then, Kantianism can be said to be impartial.

Key to Kant's moral framework is the importance of rationality or, to put it more simply, sound reasoning. Kant does not have much time for excuses for moral failures; nor does he accept that desires or wishes can be so overwhelming that the person could not control themselves and make the reasonable choice. In the *Critique of Practical Reason* ([1788] 1993) he shows how utterly unconvincing he finds such arguments. He uses an example of "irresistible lust" to show that in fact there is no such thing. In his example he asks whether someone who claimed their lust was "irresistible" would still act on it if they knew that immediately after satiating their lust they would be hanged: he suggests that the gallows be erected directly in front of the house. Kant argues that in such an instance the lust would not be acted on, and that as soon as we reflect on such cases we recognize that we are in fact free to choose and to use reason to discover what is morally good. Clearly, for Kant, claims such as "it just happened" and "I couldn't help it" are not real excuses at all, but merely forms of convenient self-deceit. In this instance the "luster" has a self-interested reason that outweighs his desire; despite his lust he restrained himself in order to avoid execution. If you can refrain for self-interested reasons then you can also refrain for moral reasons.

Kantian theory puts acting according to moral duty above human feelings and desires, and places no weight on justification by consequences. Instead it grounds morality in determining conduct by considering what are (or could rationally be) universal rules, from which absolute moral rules are derived. Once you know these moral rules and what acts are right and wrong then they must be followed absolutely and without exception. For Kant, one such absolute rule is that lying is always wrong and morally prohibited. This remains true in all circumstances, and to illustrate Kant's commitment to universalizability we shall consider one final example, Kant's famous "Inquiring Murderer", taken from *On a Supposed Right to Tell Lies from Benevolent Motives* (1797). In this example, Kant argues that a lie always harms another, if not directly in the situation then indirectly in damaging "humanity in general". Just as in the "lying promise" example, the action cannot be universalized because it would damage all promises and all contracts. The absoluteness of the duty to truth, Kant argues, even applies if a would-be murderer asks you to tell the whereabouts of the intended victim. In addition to the general undermining of contracts he also argues that you should not lie because if you do you will be responsible for any unforeseen consequences (including accidentally leading the murderer to his victim).

The more serious worry for Kant is about breaking the universal criteria. Protecting morality and upholding reason means respecting the absoluteness of the moral law. Even in extreme circumstances, such as lying to prevent murder or to prevent starvation, Kant holds to his conviction that lying is wrong because it cannot be reasonably universalized. If we were to make lying a universal law, which we could rationally wish that all persons in similar situations would do, it would be self-defeating. We would undermine the whole system of truth-telling. If lying were universalized then it would very quickly become the case that people did not trust that they were being told the truth. Thus, a successful lie requires that most people tell the truth and therefore relies on lying not being universalized. A purely self-interested action cannot be made into a universal maxim (such that it would be required of all) because it results in contradiction. Put most simply, in cases like these you have an absolute or "perfect" duty to *yourself* to obey – in Kant's memorable phrase – "the moral law within".

To the first formulation of the categorical imperative Kant added a second: that you should "Act so that you treat humanity, whether in your own person or in that of another, always as an end and never only as a means". Some have argued that this is not another formulation of the categorical imperative at all, but rather a second injunction. However, for our purposes of simply understanding a Kantian approach to ethics it does not matter too much if it is a restatement or a second criterion for what is moral. What matters is that it provides a clear set of criteria by which to evaluate moral action. The "ends not only means" criterion is important not only because it provides a high standard for our treatment of others – which is different from utilitarian thinking where it would be acceptable to use individuals as means as long as the consequences were good – but also, importantly, because it insists that this includes not treating oneself as a means. Thus you have duties to yourself as well as to others, which, unlike utilitarianism, makes Kantianism a theory that

CASE STUDY 3.3 Kantianism and female genital cutting

For a Kantian, whether FGC is right or wrong is dependent on whether or not it is universalizable. So for the action to be morally permitted, you would have to be able rationally to will that this action became a universal law. So is it possible to argue that a rational person would wish that practising FGC could be endorsed by, and would not violate, a universal law? Again, as with utilitarianism, it is possible for different proponents of the same theory to argue differently. But, given the negative health outcomes of FGC it is hard to imagine how you could reasonably universalize such a practice. For example, if the argument was about not FGC, but another practice that led to frequent infections and physical suffering, could you argue that this practice should be universalized? A potential counter-argument would be to argue that physical suffering is not intrinsic to the practice and that it could be addressed by ensuring that the practice was carried out in hospital by qualified medical personnel.

Box 3.9 Kantianism

Kantianism:
- is universalizable;
- asserts moral right and wrong, determined by the categorical imperative;
- finds that moral agents are rational;
- treats human beings as ends not only means;
- respects persons.

---

is respectful of the "ends" of individuals and their own projects and concerns. So Kantianism, for all its strictness about moral absolutes, is not over-demanding in the way that utilitarianism is (Box 3.9). That is, a proper part of the moral life is the respecting and giving time to one's own goals rather than simply spending all one's time bringing about the greater good.

Kantianism for global ethics?

The notion that there are actions that are always right or wrong makes Kantianism an important and attractive theory for global ethics.

There are many problems with Kantianism, perhaps most obviously the rigidity of his absoluteness. While many want to say (in conflict with utilitarianism)

The Kantian, having determined, using the categorical imperative, whether FGC was acceptable, would then need to check that it did not contravene the second formulation: that people are always respected as "ends in themselves" and never as means. This criterion allows you to consider issues such as the potentially patriarchal and sexist nature of the practice, as you can ask about whether the autonomy (or "ends") of the women involved is respected. Again, you could come to different conclusions, depending on how you weighted the facts. Yet clearly there are some issues that do appear on this framework and not on the utilitarian framework and vice versa: for example, the Kantian framework does not take account of the "happiness" of those involved but decides on whether the act is right according to whether or not it conforms to the categorical imperative. The Kantian must ask:

- Would it be reasonable for FGC to be a universal law?
- Does FGC respect persons and treat them as ends in themselves?

that lying is generally wrong, and largely irrespective of consequences, they also wish to argue that there are some exceptions where the morally good act is not the one that upholds the general duty to truthfulness. A common case presented as counter-example is that of people hiding Jews lying to the Nazi soldiers who were seeking them. Surely, the counter-example suggests, those people did not have a duty to refrain from lying? Many people would insist that, in fact, they had a positive moral duty to deceive the Nazis if doing so thwarted their evil ends and saved the Jews' lives. There are many more such counter-examples, and it is useful when considering current global dilemmas to ask what normally wrong acts are permissible in extreme circumstances. Such an exercise will help you plot your own moral commitments and convictions. For instance, is it acceptable to steal to prevent starvation? Alternatively, is it acceptable to indulge and have a luxurious Christmas dinner while others are starving? At what point do you draw the line? And most importantly for ethical reasoning, why? On what grounds? What reasons do you think justify your moral solution? Working out where you stand will help you to see both the complexity of moral problems and which type of moral theory is most in accord with your own moral intuitions.

There are further problems with Kantian theories, although we do not need to go into them in detail. For example, what do you do when you have to choose between two wrong acts? Think about the case of the "Inquiring Murderer", where it is both wrong to lie and wrong to assist in murder. Kant would seem to be clear about which act was absolute; but if you simply used the categorical imperative you might conclude that not assisting in murder was equally absolute. A further criticism worth mentioning is that, for some, the absoluteness regarding right and wrong is thought to, wrongly, make morality a system of rules that the moral agent simply has to follow (Box 3.10).

Box 3.10 Summing up Kantianism

Advantages
- It fits with the moral intuition that some things are always wrong.
- It is universal.
- It treats all similar cases similarly.
- It respects persons.

Disadvantages
- There are some conflicts with moral experience (e.g. the "Inquiring Murderer").
- It reduces morality to rules.
- It is legalistic and mechanistic.
- There are conflicts of rules and acts.

VIRTUE ETHICS

Both the universalist theories we have considered have their own problems – most importantly determining happiness and applying the universal criteria – but, they also have some clear advantages. At the very least, understanding these moral theories helps us understand our own and others' moral positions and begin to question the validity of reasons and to judge between better and worse reasons and so better and worse arguments. The third moral theory we are going to consider is virtue ethics. Virtue ethics is very different from the other moral "theories" we have considered, as in some sense it is not a theory as such and has even been called by some an "anti-theory". Many of those who have endorsed virtue ethics began by criticizing other moral approaches (most notably those we have looked at of utilitarianism and Kantianism) for being too reductionist, mechanical and legalistic (see Box 3.11).

Box 3.11 Criticisms

Utilitarianism and Kantianism are:
- *Reductionist* in that they falsely simplify ethics. For example, utilitarianism reduces all morality to happiness, and Kantianism focuses only on the "right" action.
- *Mechanical* in that they suggest that the right or best action can be calculated using a universal formula: either the "principle of utility" or the "categorical imperative".
- *Legalistic* in that these formulas give absolute answers: there is no accounting for circumstance or the various realities of human experience.

In contrast, the virtue-ethics approach does not suggest a formula for determining moral action at all but looks to Plato and Aristotle – the most prominent philosophers in the early Western tradition – and presents a more holistic picture of morality. Aristotle's primary concern in his book on ethics, *Nicomachean Ethics*, is: what is the good person? In virtue ethics, right actions *follow* from good character, from a conception of what a person is like; their character, inner traits, dispositions and motives are important. If we think back to our discussion above, it would matter to a virtue ethicist why and with which motivations a person lied: they would not just be concerned with the act of the lie, its conformity to duty or the moral law, or its consequences. Correspondingly, the characteristic rightness of telling the truth stems from it expressing the virtue of honesty. This focus on character and motive leads virtue ethicists to use words like "good", "admirable" and "kind", as much as they use words like "right", "permissible" and "obligatory". In contrast to utilitarianism and Kantianism, virtue ethics is more strongly "agent-focused": it is concerned with the dispositions, reasons and context of the person acting, which affects the quality of the action, as well as with the "right action".

When discussing virtue ethics it is worth bearing in mind that all moral theories rely on virtues to some extent; or at least the pictures they create of what a moral person is invoke or suggest certain virtues. For example, both utilitarians and Kantians will value rationality, fairness, honesty and justice, because these virtues will aid the carrying out of moral acts on their schemas. Thus some have seen virtue ethics as simply expanding and supplementing the other ethical theories we have looked at. However, it is important to note that by *starting* with virtues of character as the basic explanatory concept in their story of what it means to act rightly, virtue ethics is a distinct approach to moral problems. Furthermore, whichever version is put forward, what all forms of virtue ethics have in common is a conviction that morality and right conduct are too rich and complex to be reduced to rules. Rules can play a part in virtue ethics: for instance, the neo-Aristotelian Rosalind Hursthouse speaks of "V-rules", which prescribe virtuous actions and prohibit those that exhibit the corresponding vice: for example, "do what is generous" and "do not do what is mean". Still, understanding how to "do what is generous" on the virtue ethical account requires developing the appropriate disposition of generosity, so adhering to a "V-rule" has far more to it in terms of character development than just remembering a list of dos and don'ts. So at least when understood in the more familiar sense, rules are not primary features of virtue ethics.

Eudaimonia

Aristotle's theory of the virtues is the starting-point and inspiration for much of virtue ethics. Aristotle's question is: what constitutes the good life? The good life, for Aristotle, is that which is essential to human flourishing, or *eudaimonia*. Eudaimonia is often translated as "happiness": however, it is important to recognize that, for Aristotle, *eudaimonia* is excellence and the goal of life. It is an objective human condition, rather than just a subjective feeling of happiness. *Eudaimonia* is, in this respect, closer to "health" than to "feeling happy". I could *feel* perfectly healthy but not know that I was actually ill. Similarly, one could feel "happy" spending all one's time on hard drugs or plugged into Nozick's experience machine, but not be flourishing – *eudaimon* – in the Aristotelian sense. Note, then, that although the word "happiness" is often used to translate *eudaimonia*, it is better to use phrases such as "flourishing" or "well-being" that connect moral, physical and social goods, and avoid confusing *eudaimonia* simply with pleasure. For Aristotle, *eudaimonia* is the flourishing state of being that is the human goal and to which all other goals are secondary. It is this sense of fulfilment that Aristotle means by *eudaimonia* and which is sometimes translated as "happiness". For him, *eudaimonia* is primary because it is the only thing we do not pursue for the sake of something else. We may strive for a level of material wealth, for example, but we do so *in order* to be happy. We only want money, success, or anything else we desire in the pursuit of *eudaimonia*. By contrast, *eudaimonia* is the one end of all our projects to live well: and the one that has no further end. And, importantly on Aristotle's account, virtues of character are constitutive of a good human life. No human life could be *eudaimon* without the virtues.

The virtue ethicist, then, is concerned not only with right and wrong actions, but more broadly with what constitutes human flourishing. Thus the virtue ethicist is concerned with more than the moral sphere: flourishing and well-being are not only moral but have psychosocial, emotional and physical elements. In practice, a virtue ethicist may endorse similar actions to the deontologist and/or utilitarian as right or wrong, but the accounts that they give of why such actions are right or wrong are different. To expand slightly on the earlier example of honesty, the virtue ethicist is likely to endorse truth-telling as a mark of a virtuous person; yet, this is not because of an objective principle, but because truth-telling is virtuous and something an honest, kind, noble and so on, person would do. A virtuous person will want to act morally because they value morality and consider a flourishing life one that is virtuous. *Eudaimonia*, then, is the goal of the good life, and it is achieved by perfecting the virtues. For Aristotle we will be happiest when we act in accordance with virtue.

The virtues

For Aristotle, there are two types of virtue: the "intellectual virtues" (such as wisdom, both theoretical and practical, scientific knowledge, reason and technical ability for crafts and skills); and the "virtues of character" or the "moral virtues" (such as courage, temperance, beneficence and honesty), which we are most concerned with. Aristotle determines what is a virtue using what he terms the "doctrine of the mean". The doctrine of the mean places the virtue in between the vices, which are the "deficit" or "excess" of those virtues. What lies between too little and too much of something is "the mean". Just as you can have too much to eat or too little – with the optimal amount lying in between – for Aristotle you can have too much or too little of a capability. Both too much and too little are vices, with the optimal amount representing the virtue. Box 3.12 shows some examples. The first column on the left lists what the trait concerns; the second the vice of excess; the third the mean; and the last the opposite vice of deficiency.

In Aristotle's words in the *Nicomachean Ethics*, in finding the mean (mean as in "average") between excess and deficiency, the virtuous person acts "at the right times with reference to the right objects, towards the right people, with the right motive, and in the right way". Some have interpreted this as being simply a doctrine of "everything in moderation", such that the virtuous person would, for example, never get angry. This is a misinterpretation. There may be situations where *that* kind of "moderation" would neither be appropriate nor virtuous, and this is what Aristotle

---

Box 3.12 The doctrine of the mean

Trait concerns	Vice of excess	Virtue, the mean	Vice of deficiency
Danger	Foolhardiness	Courage	Cowardice
Money; resources	Wastefulness	Generosity	Miserliness
Social interaction	Obsequiousness	Friendliness	Standoffishness
Appetite	Over-indulgence	Temperance	Self-sacrifice
Temper	Aggressiveness	Level-headedness	Timidity

---

means when he talks about finding the mean "with reference to the right object". To use one example, temper is a disposition of character, and "level-headedness" is its corresponding virtue between the vices of aggressiveness and timidity. Yet acting from virtue with respect to one's temper does not necessarily mean never being angry

---

CASE STUDY 3.4 Virtue ethics and female genital cutting

As we have seen, it is possible for utilitarians and Kantians to come to different conclusions about whether FGC is wrong (although we have suggested it is less likely that the Kantian will consider it permissible), and this is even more so for virtue ethicists. Nussbaum, whom we discussed earlier, is a thinker in the Aristotelian tradition, and she argues that we can condemn FGC. In this argument she does not directly appeal to the virtues, but her argument does include elements of virtue theory. Most importantly, she begins not with a formula but with experience, and asks what contributes to human flourishing. Nussbaum's approach is to derive a list of basic human capabilities or functions that are necessary to the flourishing of all human beings (this returns us to the "objective list" idea we encountered in the discussion of utilitarianism, although its formulation here by Nussbaum has a strong Aristotelian flavour in its *eudaimonic* basis). Together with Sen she developed the "capability approach", which we shall return to in Chapter 7, when we consider Sen's approach, and again in Chapter 11, when we consider Nussbaum's formulation with respect to gender issues.

Nussbaum's list of capacities functions as an account of what is required for human flourishing. She is attempting to map out the good life, which does not simply mean survival, but a life that has opportunity and some scope for choice and creativity. Nussbaum's capabilities (1999) are:

- life (not dying prematurely);
- bodily health (health, food and shelter);
- bodily integrity (freedom of movement without fear of assault);

---

at anything or anyone whatever the situation, because the "mean" is not meant to be merely a constant and perfectly balanced emotional psychological condition. Being virtuous does not require emotional sterility, but quite the opposite. The appropriate expression of the mean in the face of a gross injustice might well be to feel aggrieved and display appropriate anger – righteous anger – and not to be calm or detached. To be calm and unaffected in such a situation may in fact be a vice.

Perhaps the most difficult problem for the virtue ethicist is determining the virtues and working out how they fit together. We can see the difference if we compare Aristotle's virtues with some of those of Jane Austen. As well as drawing on the classical tradition of which Aristotle is a key part, Austen is clearly influenced by Christianity in citing faith, hope and charity as key virtues of characters in her novels. Alasdair MacIntyre (1982) discusses Austen's virtues and the overarching role she gives to the virtue of "constancy", which, according to MacIntyre, concerns the "unity of a human life" and is a prerequisite for exercising the other virtues. Just

---

- senses, imagination, thought (education and freedom of expression);
- emotions (freedom to love and form attachments);
- practical reason (living in accord with one's conception of the good life);
- affiliation (living with others with respect and dignity, including the capacity for justice and friendship);
- other species (proper relations with animals, plants and nature);
- play (recreation and laughter);
- control over one's environment (including political participation and material work and ownership).

Nussbaum's approach offers one way for a virtue ethicist to address the issues. For instance, if Nussbaum were to apply her capability approach directly she would need to ask:
- What constitutes human flourishing?
- Does FGC contribute to such flourishing and to a good life?

Other virtue ethicists, for instance those who focus on the virtues rather than human flourishing, might ask:
- What virtues are manifested in FGC?
- Would a virtuous person engage in FGC?

Yet other virtue ethicists, for instance care ethicists (whom we shall return to in Chapter 11), would simply ask:
- How is FGC expressive of, or conducive to, caring?

as a Kantian has an apparent problem when duties conflict, so a virtue ethicist might have problems when virtues conflict. Which virtues should have priority and when? It is a little easier for virtue ethicists because, unlike Kantians, they can argue for circumstance-sensitive accounts, in which a necessary part of being a good, virtuous person is knowing how to act in a particular situation without having to appeal to codified moral rules or duties. Yet this only takes virtue ethicists so far if they do not wish to fall into relativism and all the problems we have seen that that entails.

Virtue ethicists do not wish to suggest that virtues are relative, but they do admit differences in application. The moral virtues are learned virtues, virtues that are attained by habit and practice. They are "character building". Thus we are not born virtuous (although we are born with the ability to be virtuous). To become virtuous we need to practise virtue and be taught virtue as children, and it is by practising acting on virtues – by repeatedly acting courageously or telling the truth – that we become courageous or truthful. Likewise, if you get into the habit of lying or behaving either cowardly or in an over-aggressive manner you will gradually become a person who lies – a habitual liar – or someone who is overly passive or overly aggressive in their dealings with others.

Virtue theory and global ethics?

The key problem of virtue ethics for global ethics is often seen as an advantage of the theory. Virtue ethics is context sensitive (see Box 3.13) and in this lies the danger of relativism. For many this is an attractive aspect of virtue ethics because it offers an explanation for failures of moral motivation and explains why injustice breeds injustice. If you are not taught morality – or worse, suffer injustice – then virtue may not be attractive and vice may seem more profitable. For others the learned nature of morality is a reason for rejecting virtue ethics for two reasons: (i) it suggests that morality is not a simple calculation able to be performed by any rational person; (ii) it requires relationships of teaching, encouragement and training that in turn require a community. If morality is not taught, does it mean that people cannot be virtuous? If so, this is a problem for the global ethicist.

Box 3.13 Key characteristics of virtue ethics

- What we should "be" is the basis of what we should "do" (good persons are prior to right actions).
- Emphasizes human flourishing.
- Emphasizes good character and development of "practical wisdom".
- Emphasizes inner traits, dispositions and motives of persons.

The trouble with making virtue something learned is that it ties virtue to community, which returns us to the debate at the beginning of the chapter between universalists and relativists. As we discussed, both Kantian ethics and utilitarianism stress the importance of universality. In these theories, what is moral in one place at one time is also moral at all relevantly similar places and times and, what is more, anyone can work out whether an act is morally required or forbidden using the mechanism of the theory (the action that produces the greatest happiness for the greatest number, or the action that is in accord with the categorical imperative). This universalism seems to be in stark contrast to the agent-relative picture of virtue ethics, which is about good character. How can virtue ethicists respond? First they can assert that some virtues are universal and valued by all societies, such as, for example, honesty, care for the young and concern for justice (although they may be expressed in different ways). Thus, although there may be different practices, the underlying virtues are the same. As we saw at the beginning of the chapter, this is a standard universalist response. Likewise, virtue ethicists can counter the related criticism that if virtue is taught by the community then those within are forced to accept the values of that community and there will be no possibility of revolutionary or dissenting voices. The virtue ethicist argues that this is not the case, because the virtues lead to human flourishing, of which at least some aspects are universal: so critique of immoral practices arises from loving the virtues and attempting to be virtuous. In these ways virtue ethics remains a universal theory with all the benefits of universalism, as discussed in the first section of the chapter (see Box 3.14). This said, making virtue theory globally applicable remains an ongoing task for global ethicists committed to virtue and one we shall explore in this book.

Box 3.14 Summing up virtue theory

Advantages
- It considers the whole person.
- It is agent-focused.
- It respects actual persons and their commitments and relationships.
- It permits appropriate partiality.

Disadvantages
- It is complex.
- It has difficulty defining virtues.
- Conflicts of virtues are difficult to negotiate.
- It is difficult to apply globally.

CONCLUSION

This chapter has given you the first and most important parts of the toolbox necessary to do global ethics. Knowing about these moral theories will help you understand and criticize the arguments of others and help you to develop and use your own arguments. We began this chapter by considering the cultural-relativist argument and the problems this poses for global ethics. We then explored the three key moral theories that form the main theoretical tools to criticize and build arguments. As you critically use these theories and what you have learnt in this chapter to assess real dilemmas of global ethics, remember that these are intended to serve you not only when you write essays, but, more importantly, when you argue about what matters and what should be.

While all of the moral theories we have considered in this chapter are universal, they are very different. And thus even when they come to the same conclusion regarding how you should act in any given situation, the reasons for the differences are important. Which moral theory you endorse colours moral action and signals that there are differences of moral opinion that are crucial to understanding the moral pictures of the world that are in play. The discussion of FGC has shown the importance of moral theory, because which moral theory you choose changes the way you see the "facts" and which "facts" you think are important. As we saw above, a "lie" is not a fact in a simple sense. For example, in the case of the "Inquiring Murderer" for the Kantian, the lie is the morally relevant fact; for the consequentialist the lie is not relevant in itself, but only in so far as it is or is not an effective means to producing a good outcome; and, for the virtue ethicist, it depends partly on the motives of the lie and the wider context – for instance, was the liar dishonest for self-gain or did she lie regretfully and out of compassion (for the victim)? If the latter, then perhaps the demand of compassion outweighs the virtue of honesty in this situation. However, this said, the differences between moral theories and those who endorse these theories can be exaggerated. Often, in fact, moral theorists will largely agree, and the disagreement will be between those who do not care about morality at all and those who do, not between different types of ethicist. Sometimes the strongest arguments can be built using arguments that reach the same conclusions from all theories in order to make the strongest possible case that will result in actual change. When doing global ethics we should always remember that the end goal is not the best moral theory, but the best world.

FURTHER READING

- Darwall, S. (ed.). *Consequentialism* (Oxford: Blackwell, 2003).
- Hursthouse, R. *On Virtue Ethics* (Oxford: Oxford University Press, 1999).
- Kant, I. *Groundwork of the Metaphysics of Morals*, M. Gregor (ed.) (Cambridge: Cambridge University Press, [1785] 1997).
- Kant, I. *On a Supposed Right to Tell Lies from Benevolent Motives*, T. K. Abbott (trans.) (1797). http://oll.libertyfund.org/?option=com_staticxt&staticfile=show.php%3Ftitle=360&chapter=61937&layout=html&Itemid=27 (accessed May 2011).
- Mackie, J. L. *Ethics: Inventing Right and Wrong* (Oxford: Oxford University Press, 1977).
- Mill, J. S. *Utilitarianism* (Harmondsworth: Penguin, [1863] 1987). www.efm.bris.ac.uk/het/mill/utilitarianism.pdf (accessed May 2011).
- Nussbaum, M. "Double Moral Standards? A Response to Yael Tamir's 'Hands off Clitoridectomy'". *Boston Review* (October/November 1996). http://bostonreview.net/BR21.5/nussbaum.html (accessed May 2011).
- Nussbaum, M. *Sex and Social Justice* (Oxford: Oxford University Press, 1999).
- Rachels, J. *The Elements of Moral Philosophy*, 5th edn (London: McGraw-Hill, 2007).
- Sen, A. & B. Williams (eds) *Utilitarianism and Beyond* (Cambridge: Cambridge University Press, 1982).
- Tamir, Y. "Hands off Clitoridectomy". *Boston Review* (Summer 1996). http://bostonreview.net/BR21.3/Tamir.html (accessed May 2011).

4 POLITICAL THEORY FOR GLOBAL ETHICS

INTRODUCTION

Many, but not all, global ethicists and proponents of global understandings of ethics and justice are "cosmopolitans". Essentially this means that they reject positions in international relations or moral theory that limit the scope of duty and obligations to a particular community or geographical location and that they regard all individuals as equal members of the global moral community. There are global ethicists who do not regard all individuals as equal members of the global community: for instance they might make distinctions in terms of nationality, culture or gender, or they might regard the global community as less important than national communities. Thinkers like this may still be global ethicists in terms of being able to "do" global ethics, if they still consider all global actors in their moral decision-making (even if they do not accord all persons the same weight in their reasoning). In other words, if thinkers apply the "global in scope" criterion outlined in Chapter 1 then they can contribute to the global-ethics debate.

In Chapter 3 we considered universalism and the moral theories we can use to address the issues of global ethics. The moral theories we considered – ultilitarianism, Kantianism and virtue ethics – originate from the disciplines of ethics and moral philosophy. These provide the background you need to do global ethics; they are the first tools of your "ethical toolbox". This chapter adds to that toolbox theories of justice and draws not only on moral philosophy, but also on political philosophy and theories of international relations.

We discovered in Chapter 3 that which moral theory you use changes the way you see the facts, both in terms of what facts you can see and with regard to the priority you give them, and this is no less true of which political approach you adopt. Just as your moral theory has an impact on what you believe to be morally important and what you deem good or right moral conduct, so the political theory you adopt provides the framework within which you conceive of what is just and the limits of justice. In other words, the political framework influences the scope within which you apply your moral theory, and together the moral and political theories you adopt will determine whether you are a global ethicist or not and what type of global ethicist you are.

The main question when considering global ethics from this political perspective is: what are the bounds of justice and morality? For example, do political borders, such as state, regional or national borders, have bearings on our moral duties? Do we have more duties to those whom we have more in common with, for instance, fellow nationals? If moral duties are influenced by political structures and boundaries, then are current systems fit for purpose? In short, what, if any, is the ethical significance of borders? This chapter will explore the different ways political theorists answer these questions and whether or not such answers are compatible with global ethics. We shall not only consider cosmopolitanism (the view most closely associated with global ethics), but also a range of competitor views. It is also important to remember that while the cosmopolitan voice may be very strong in global ethics (and it is likely that all cosmopolitans would be happy to call themselves "global ethicists"), you do not have to be a cosmopolitan to claim to be a global ethicist and certainly not to add to the global-ethics debate. For instance, some global ethicists hold society of states perspectives and nationalist perspectives, and yet still endorse some global duties. Some of these views might be considered "mixed" views or "weak cosmopolitanism", because they subscribe to cosmopolitan views in some areas (say perhaps, in terms of meeting basic needs or a duty to respond to disasters or emergency situations) but not in others. The only view that is completely incompatible with any global-ethics approach, however weak that view might be, is the realist view. The realist denies any conception of a global moral community and any global duties of justice and it is hard to imagine how a global ethicist could take this position without being self-contradictory.

The theories presented here and in Chapter 3 provide the key theoretical tools the ethicist employs to address the pressing concerns of contemporary global ethics (Box 4.1). This is not to say that once you understand these moral and political theories you have all you need to "do" global ethics. On the contrary, you will need to keep adding to your toolbox – you will need more theoretical tools: for instance, those provided in the next chapter on human rights; more empirical knowledge about the world (e.g. that provided in Chapter 6 on the actual functioning of the systems of global governance); and most importantly, as you progress in global ethics, you will add to your toolbox your real experience about how these theories work in practice and how practical cases of global ethics influence how you interpret your theories. This said, when you combine the theories of Chapter 3 and those of this chapter you will have the basic tools you need to begin to do global ethics. These theories are your starting-point. What the rest of the book does, particularly the later chapters,

---

Box 4.1 The global-ethics toolbox

- Moral, political and rights theories.
- Understandings of global governance and global institutions.
- Practical experience.

---

is to consider in more detail the core topics of global ethics, and in these chapters you will begin to see how these global-ethics tools are used in practice in relation to poverty, hunger, health and war. More importantly, as you study such issues and find your own examples of global injustice, you will come to see, not only how others have used these theories, but how you could use them to put together your own arguments and actually do global ethics (rather than merely read, write or talk about other writers doing global ethics).

This chapter introduces cosmopolitanism and analyses current cosmopolitan approaches. It considers criticisms of the cosmopolitan position, including realism, nationalism and internationalism, and the difficulties in applying cosmopolitan approaches to current global institutions. It also considers the nature of justice and, in particular, how broad the "scope of justice" is. As discussed in Chapter 1, to do global ethics at all, one must believe that the scope of justice is global, in that all global actors must be considered in moral decision-making. There are various ways in which this criterion can be met: for instance, strong cosmopolitans believe that all individuals (irrespective of race, nationality, gender and class) should be taken into account in exactly the same way; weak cosmopolitans consider all actors, but believe that there are differences in how individuals should be taken into account. For example, they might think that although there are some duties of global justice, states are still important.

COSMOPOLITANISM

We shall begin by considering cosmopolitanism, which, as its name suggests, holds that there is a "moral sphere" that transcends national or cultural boundaries, and hence that moral obligations are global in scope. We shall look at versions of cosmopolitanism and some views opposed to it, and place these views in the context of the debate about global justice.

Just as there are many different types of utilitarianism, Kantianism and virtue theory, so there are many types of cosmopolitanism (many of which we shall come across as we explore the application these theories in later chapters). The term "cosmopolitan" has been used in general terms both positively and negatively: to denote a well-travelled, multiculturally aware, worldly and experienced person – a good thing;

and to insult foreigners and dangerous outsiders (as it was used of Jews and Bolsheviks by the Nazis) – a bad thing. The term "cosmopolitan" originates with the Stoics and is derived from "*cosmos*" meaning "world" and "*polis*" meaning "state" or "city". The Stoics, from whom the term "stoical" is derived, were a school of ancient Athenian philosophers founded in the third century BCE, who argued for the universal reason of nature (*logos*). In keeping with this view of nature and humans' part in it, the Stoics claimed that they were citizens of the world, and identified themselves with, and owed allegiance to, all humanity, not just their local geographical, religious, ethnic or cultural group. The Stoics' conviction that they were "citizens of the world" still captures the essence of contemporary cosmopolitanism. While there are many different versions of cosmopolitanism, they all consider the moral sphere to be the global sphere in that their community is in some sense the global community and that there are at least some duties of justice that extend beyond national or state boundaries.

The first defining feature of cosmopolitanism is that the moral sphere is global for at least some obligations: that there are some duties that go beyond national borders (and for some strong cosmopolitans all duties of justice are global). The second is the emphasis on the individual: the conviction that it is the individual that has moral worth, rather than entities such as family, ethnic, cultural, religious or national groups (or at least that these are only morally significant in that they are made up of individuals who have individual moral worth). The third feature of cosmopolitanism is equality: all individuals have equal moral worth. These three elements are standard in different definitions of cosmopolitanism. A commonly cited definition is that of Pogge, one of the foremost contemporary global ethicists (Box 4.2).

Not surprisingly there are similarities between the universalism we looked at in Chapter 3 and cosmopolitan theories, because all are concerned with the global scope of morality and affirm the moral worth of all individuals. Indeed, Kant's thinking was highly influential for contemporary cosmopolitans, who are often considered to be putting Kant's notions of universalizability and rationality into the theory and practice of the political arena. Consider also Kant's imperative that we should never

---

Box 4.2 Cosmopolitanism according to Thomas Pogge

According to Pogge, cosmopolitanism comprises:

"First, *individualism*: the ultimate units of concern are *human beings*, or *persons* … Second, *universality*: the status of ultimate unit of concern attaches to *every* living human being *equally* – not merely to some sub-set, such as men, aristocrats, Aryans, whites, or Muslims. Third, *generality*: this special status has global force. Persons are ultimate units of concern for everyone – not only for their compatriots, fellow religionists, or such like."

(Pogge 1994a: 89–90)

treat persons only as means, but always as "ends in themselves", which clearly affirms the moral status of each individual. Likewise, the impartiality of utilitarianism fits well with the second criterion of cosmopolitanism. When we come to Chapter 7 we shall see how utilitarianism and strong cosmopolitanism combine in the work of Singer, and his arguments that we all have global duties to act to alleviate poverty.

Despite these similarities, it is important to note that the moral theories of Chapter 3 and these political theories are not directly parallel. For example, cosmopolitans do not focus on issues of impartiality and its requirements in quite the same way that

CASE STUDY 4.1 Cosmopolitanism and the sale of body parts

In order to explore how cosmopolitanism and its competitors function we shall now use the example of selling body parts (see Chapter 2, pp. 19–23).

Moral and political reasoning in relation to the sale of body parts
In order to consider cosmopolitan responses to the sale of body parts, a brief comment on the relation between moral and political approaches and between the theories of this chapter and Chapter 3 is useful. It is important to remember that the "cosmopolitan" aspect of the response is only part of the response. How global ethicists will address the sale of body parts will depend on their moral, as well as political theoretical, convictions. For instance, if we think back to Chapter 3, whether a cosmopolitan thinker is utilitarian, deontological or a virtue ethicist will affect his or her final position. Kantians will either accept or oppose the sale of body parts according to whether they believe that the action is intrinsically right, asking questions such as "Is this treating human beings as ends in themselves?" or "Is this universalizable?" A utilitarian will consider whether selling body parts leads to more or less overall happiness. Either of these moral philosophical approaches could be relevant to the global debate and – as discussed in Chapter 3 – if one takes the universalizablity criterion of Kantianism or the impartiality criterion of utilitarianism seriously then both *should* be making global claims. However, these moral theories begin with the actions of individual moral agents: is it right for individuals to sell their kidneys? While such reasoning should always take account of all persons, the starting-point is focused on the individual. By contrast, because of the third and fourth criteria of cosmopolitanism – that it is global in scope and considers political structures and institutions – the cosmopolitan approach is different, in that it is overtly concerned to address the relationships of groups and institutions as well as individuals, and in addition it focuses on structural networks and frameworks of governance as well as individual duties. Therefore, as well as focusing on the rightness and wrongness of individual actions, cosmopolitanism considers the political and practical aspects of carrying out such actions. For example, cosmopolitans (and political philosophers in general) will often consider how rights are best attained and how duties can be fulfilled and needs met as well as what those rights and duties might

moral theorists (of whatever variety, whether utilitarian, Kantian or virtue theorists) do. For instance, the debate about partiality and impartiality in moral philosophy focuses on whether or not you can have special obligations by virtue of the nature of your particular and often personal relationships. Prominent in these discussions are family relations, for instance duties to your children or parents, and professional relationships, for instance duties of teachers to their students and doctors to their patients. When cosmopolitans argue that all individuals should be treated as morally equal they are not denying such special relationships (as someone defending

be. Accordingly, it is no surprise that cosmopolitans concern themselves primarily with the institutions that are responsible for ensuring moral practices and the political and legal mechanisms by which justice can be attained. This difference in language and focus (not content) will become clearer when we consider the institutional focus of some particular cosmopolitan thinkers, including Pogge and Moellendorf, both here and in later chapters.

The concerns of moral and political philosophers are not distinct, but overlap. Good moral philosophers will consider the impact their reasoning has on groups and should consider how judgements about individuals influence issues of structure, governance, policy and practice. And, as we saw in Chapter 1, the need to connect theory to practice and for practice to be influenced by theory is the third component of global ethics. Likewise, then, good political philosophers will connect their work on international relations and the duties of institutions with the individual agents who make up those states and nations. For most who are trained in either moral or political philosophy (rather than in global ethics directly) the starting-point will be a little different: one beginning with the individual agent, the other with political structures. As we have discussed, to do global ethics we must do both and connect individual and group action. It is worth noting that in some theories it is impossible to separate the two. For instance, virtue ethics focuses on the virtuous person, but considers that for people to be virtuous the institutions and governance mechanisms must also be virtuous.

Given this, the cosmopolitan (and indeed all political thinkers) will focus not only on whether it is right, permissible or good for a certain person to sell their organs in this particular instance, but they will immediately consider the political and governance implications. Thus with regard to organ trade they are likely to discuss not only what is morally permissible, but how such trade is to be effectively regulated and monitored (if permitted) and, if not permitted, how vulnerable persons are to be protected from black and grey markets in trade and pressures of exploitation.

A cosmopolitan approach to the selling of body parts
From our initial discussion of cosmopolitanism we can begin to sketch what would be the elements of a cosmopolitan response to a market in human body parts. In order to show the difference between cosmopolitan and other views most clearly we shall consider a strong

impartiality in moral theory would). But the focus of cosmopolitans is political, rather than personal, and therefore personal relationships are not their primary concern. Cosmopolitan theorists focus on the content and weight of obligations across state boundaries. Thus, while parallel in some ways, these debates are not the same. In moral discourse the focus is on duties of individual agents to other individual agents (as we shall see in detail when we look at Singer's utilitarian approach to addressing global poverty), whereas in political discourse obligations are seen primarily in terms of political structures.

---

form of cosmopolitanism: the view that *all* duties of justice are global duties. Borders are regarded as morally insignificant, so national or regional approaches are unjust. This goes against the view expressed by Charles Erin and John Harris (2003), who propose a strictly regulated system of offering financial incentives for organ "donation" that "would be confined to a self governing geopolitical area such as a nation state or indeed the European Union". We shall return to this discussion in Chapter 9.

A first point to consider is which ethical approach should be adopted. For instance, a deontological cosmopolitan will believe that selling organs is right or wrong depending on questions such as whether or not kidney sale respects persons. This will not be considered in terms of one particular case, but will ask whether or not persons can be respected in the requisite institutions. Here the global criterion and the political criterion are clearly active. For instance, let us consider the case of egg sale. A non-cosmopolitan ethicist who is considering egg sale in the US may decide that, overall, egg sale is justified once a number of conditions are met, for instance that a "fair price" is set and that it is clear that egg vendors have given their fully informed consent and that they are guaranteed appropriate medical care both during and following the procedure. Obviously there are many problems with such a view, for instance regarding the possibility of a fair price. But, these problems are profoundly exacerbated when one takes a strong cosmopolitan view.

A strong cosmopolitan must consider the global and political implications of this, which changes the issues dramatically. For instance the issue of a fair price is compounded when one considers the poverty of many who are selling their body parts and the current black and grey market. Brazil, Egypt, India, Moldova, Pakistan, the Philippines and Romania are among the world's leading providers of trafficked organs. In these countries eggs and organs are purchased from live donors. Given the wealth inequalities between these countries and the countries organ purchasers come from, the impossibility of developing a global fair price increases the ethical dangers of such a market. Globally, dangers such as exploitation and inducement become far greater than if, for instance, the US market is considered in isolation. Likewise, the difficulty in ensuring standards of health care and appropriate accountability if vendors and purchasers are travelling between countries is far more problematic globally.

The final feature of cosmopolitanism, which is little discussed in political theory (perhaps because it is assumed), is that it focuses on the political realm. This is of importance in global ethics where, as discussed in Chapter 1, we are concerned not only with the political realm, but also with individual and personal demands of global ethics, and also duties of other non-political actors, such as NGOs and civil society. Hence the need to combine moral theories with political theories. The differences between universalism and cosmopolitanism are ones of focus rather than of content. In some instances the arguments are the same: for example, often

Such considerations show us that the cosmopolitan commitment does not mean just that duties and rights (for instance, perhaps, property rights in one's own body or reproductive rights) must be extended to be globally applicable, but the global-in-scope criterion might, in fact, affect what is deemed morally acceptable. Therefore a cosmopolitan and a non-cosmopolitan who endorse the same moral theory might come to different conclusions about whether or not the sale of body parts is permitted. For instance in the case of kidney-selling, the cosmopolitan might be convinced that the extreme nature of global inequalities makes the dangers of legalized organ sale too great for it be considered (even if, on a national level, the dangers might be manageable).

Consider the fourth criterion, that of political structures. Suppose the strong cosmopolitan concluded that the dangers are extreme but, even so, the crisis of scarce organs and the long waiting lists for life-saving transplant treatment are so severe that sale should be permitted. They might decide (on consequential grounds because it would increase happiness, or on Kantian grounds because it was respecting persons by saving lives) that kidney sale was justified; then, however, they would proceed to address the political issues. Questions would include: how can a market in organs be constructed so as to avoid as many of the dangers as possible? Here considerations about institutions and structures would be crucial.

Remember, adopting cosmopolitanism does not lead to only one outcome; a strong cosmopolitan could endorse or reject the sale of body parts. What it does require is that certain issues are *considered*, issues that all ethicists do not take into account sufficiently: for instance the global nature of the moral community and the political structures required. We shall return to the sale of body parts later in the chapter and explore how particular types of non-cosmopolitans approach the issue. When doing global ethics it is easy to assume that cosmopolitan and global approaches dominate. However, this is not the case. In fact, many thinkers endorse explicitly anti-cosmopolitan positions and even more endorse weak versions of cosmopolitanism. In the case of body parts the current reality is extremely non-cosmopolitan. There is no global legislation about whether or not body parts can be bought and sold and as a result there is an increasing phenomenon of "medical tourism", where people travel from one jurisdiction to another to buy what is illegal in their own country.

Box 4.3 Cosmopolitan views

For a view to be cosmopolitan:
- the individual must be the key unit of ethical concern;
- all individuals/every individual must be equivalent units of ethical concern;
- it must apply globally;
- the primary focus is the political.

---

cosmopolitans defend universal value claims using similar arguments to those of Chapter 3 against cultural relativism. Yet, while these theories overlap and share both origins and primary tenets, and indeed often theorists, the difference of focus is at times important for understanding the arguments people are using and the claims they are making in a given circumstance. These differences will become clearer as we explore different versions of cosmopolitanism; for now, cosmopolitanism can be summed up by four criteria (see Box 4.3).

These four claims commit you not to a position where all obligations of justice are global, but rather to a more minimal view that there are at least *some* global obligations that go beyond national borders. The view that there are some, however minimal, global obligations of justice has been termed "weak cosmopolitanism". By contrast, "strong cosmopolitanism" holds that the global sphere is the *only* moral sphere: that to consider any lesser sphere is unjust and immoral. On this view, all duties of justice are global duties, because national or regional borders are morally insignificant and ethically irrelevant. For the strong cosmopolitan principles of justice that apply within a society or nation should apply *globally*, because when it comes to deciding who gets what in terms of goods, resources and rights, there are no moral grounds for preferring one group, race, nation or society over another. Perhaps most simply put, nationality (and many other forms of group membership) is a mere accident of birth and of no moral significance whatsoever. Accordingly, cosmopolitans endorse a number of different views depending on how strong or weak their cosmopolitan commitments are and on the number and type of duties that they believe are global. Therefore, to understand what adopting any particular type of cosmopolitan theory entails in practice, we need to explore different types of cosmopolitanism in a little more detail (Box 4.4).

Simply because you endorse moral cosmopolitanism of one sort or another, this does not entail any particular commitment to how this should be put into practice, for example, in terms of global governance or institutions. Some argue for institutional and legal cosmopolitanism and claim that the moral claims of cosmopolitanism require the establishment of global institutions to enforce and administer the duties and responsibilities that moral cosmopolitanism entails. But it is important

---

Box 4.4 Different versions of cosmopolitanism

- Weak: *Some* moral obligations go beyond borders and apply to all persons.
- Strong: *All* moral obligations go beyond borders and apply to all persons.
- Moral: *All* individuals have equal *moral* status.
- Institutional: Global institutions, structures and associations (not just individuals) are required to fulfil the obligations of global justice.

---

to remember that embracing cosmopolitan claims with regard to ethics does not necessarily commit you to any global institutional political commitments (although those who endorse strong theories of cosmopolitanism often argue that the logic of cosmopolitan theory must lead to such practical endorsements if it is to be effective). We shall return to this issue in Chapter 6.

We shall return to Case Study 4.1 and explore these issues in more detail both later in this chapter, when we look at non-cosmopolitan reasoning about body parts, and in Chapter 9, when we explore bioethical dilemmas. Before we do this, though, we shall consider in a little more detail theories of justice and how cosmopolitans extend the "bounds" of justice from states and to the global community. We shall begin by outlining Rawls's account of justice and its important place in the development of global ethics.

RAWLS'S THEORY OF JUSTICE

To understand the emergence of global ethics in the past few decades we need to understand contemporary approaches to justice as a key focal point of political theory and theorizing. To do this one must consider the work of John Rawls on justice. It is Rawls, particularly in his 1971 book *A Theory of Justice*, who has informed the most prominent contemporary theories of global justice and been especially influential on the work of current cosmopolitan theorists and proponents of global ethics, including Brock, Caney, Moellendorf and Pogge. So although Rawls himself did not consider his theory of justice to apply globally, it is his theory and his proposed principles of justice that have inspired much current cosmopolitan thinking.

Rawls's *A Theory of Justice* sets out principles of justice that are intended to be adopted by all. Rawls argues that fair principles of justice are those that would be agreed in the *original position* (Box 4.5). The original position is a hypothetical agreement that Rawls proposed as a means to work out what the principles of justice should be and to ensure that once determined they would be binding. Rawls claimed

---

Box 4.5 Rawls's "original position"

"This original position is not, of course, thought of as an actual historical state of affairs, much less as a primitive condition of culture. It is understood as a purely hypothetical situation characterised so as to lead to a certain conception of justice. Among the essential features of this situation is that no one knows his place in society, his class position or social status, nor does any one know his fortune in the distribution of natural assets and abilities, his intelligence, strength, and the like. I will even assume that the parties do not know their conceptions of good or their special psychological propensities. The principles of justice are chosen behind a veil of ignorance. This ensures that no one is advantaged or disadvantaged in the choice of principles by the outcome of natural chance or the contingency of social circumstances. Since all are similarly situated and no one is able to design principles to favour his particular condition, the principles of justice are the result of fair agreement or bargain."   (Rawls 1999a: 11)

---

that principles derived from the original position were those that all free and rational persons concerned with their own self-interest would agree to. Once the principles had been decided in this way, then, they would be applied to all further situations to determine the just or fair solution. These principles could then be used to constitute the foundation of a just and rational society.

The original position is essentially a thought experiment that Rawls believed resulted in fair principles of justice that would be accepted by all. In the thought experiment, those who are considering what is just are blinded to their own situation in order that they come up with fair principles for all, rather than biased principles that benefit people and groups in one situation and circumstance rather than another. Key to the original position's claim to fairness in the design of the principles of justice is the *veil of ignorance*. Crucially, those behind the veil of ignorance do not know if they are rich or poor, strong or weak, black or white, male or female and so on. Essentially the aim is to remove any concern that arises as a result of a person's actual situation or social circumstances in order to ensure that the final principles are unprejudiced.

The veil of ignorance strips individuals of their particular characteristics, biases and concerns and assures that, rather than cater to their own particular needs and attempt to skew the system to benefit themselves or their own group, principles of justice that are fair to all will be devised. The claim is that the veil of ignorance makes the principles of justice free from economic, social, cultural, religious, gender and class biases. In Rawls's (1999a) words, "the veil of ignorance ensures that all are equal in the original position".

In Rawls's theory the first principles of justice are determined behind the veil of ignorance. These principles are then used to resolve all future issues of justice and to reform institutions. Once the foundational and original principles are agreed, they are to be applied in further hypothetical situations in order to develop more detailed rules and social structures. According to this picture, then, just institutions and social structures are those that conform to these principles of justice and which would have been agreed by rational persons behind the veil of ignorance. Moreover, and very importantly, he argues that because the principles agreed on are rational, chosen by rational individuals, they can be explained and justified.

Rawls's principles of justice

Rawls argues that there are two principles of justice (Box 4.6) that those in the original position would choose: equality regarding basic freedoms and the difference principle.

Principles of justice, then, are first about equality and, second, prohibit actions, practices and institutions that further disadvantage the already most disadvantaged. In effect the "difference principle" is a kind of minimum baseline that is intended to prevent a person becoming more disadvantaged than they already are. According to this principle, an action that makes the already poorest and most disadvantaged more disadvantaged is unjust. The difference principle does not rule out advantaging the already advantaged, but it allows this *only* if it also improves the position of the disadvantaged. If this is not the case then the action is not acceptable.

Rawls intends that the first principle of justice will secure the equality of citizens and their liberties and the second will secure fair distribution of wealth and positions of power. Therefore each principle covers a range of issues: the first principle of equality includes issues ranging from political liberty to the freedom to hold property

---

Box 4.6 Rawls's principles of justice

The first principle of justice

"Each person is to have an equal right to the most extensive scheme of equal basic liberties compatible with a similar scheme of liberties for others." (1999a)

The second principle of justice

"Social and economic inequalities are to be arranged so that they are both a) to be of the greatest benefit to the least-advantaged members of society (the difference principle) b) offices and positions must be open to everyone under conditions of fair equality of opportunity." (1999a)

Box 4.7 Features of Rawls's principles

The first principle: Equality of "basic liberties of citizens"
- Political liberty (the right to vote and be eligible for public office).
- Freedom of speech and assembly.
- Liberty of conscience and freedom of thought.
- Freedom of the person and the right to hold property.
- Freedom from arbitrary arrest.

The second principle: Fair distribution
- Fair distribution of income and wealth.
- Fair organization of authority, responsibility and chains of command and distribution of positions therein.

---

and the second is concerned with distributive justice and the structural and governance mechanisms by which such justice can be assured (Box 4.7).

The scope of Rawls's principles of justice and the fact they include commitments to civil liberties as well as to distributive justice require that issues of practice are addressed as well as theory. Accordingly, a pressing question is how the principles of justice are to be implemented. For Rawls, the principles apply fundamentally to what he calls the "basic structure" of society: that is, the key institutions that *define* rights and shape the way we can and cannot live our lives in a society; in other words, to the structure of society and the governance mechanisms, for instance, legal frameworks and political institutions. Examples Rawls uses are: the legal institutions of the protection of free thought and liberty of conscience; the economic institutions of competitive markets and private property; and the social institution of the family. Put simply, such institutions to a great extent determine who gets what, and so should be the primary subject of the principles of justice. This approach means that concerns of justice are focused on the institutions, procedures and policies that affect the practical realities of who gets what and how free real individuals actually are. As we shall see, these elements of Rawls have been taken up by contemporary global ethicists.

Rawls's methodology, and the position he seeks to establish by using it, is expressly *liberal*. The focus of the original position thought experiment is on formulating principles that then ensure a fair arrangement for all persons and liberty for each of them. This approach has been widely critically discussed, and one problem worth mentioning is that it appears to overlook the social relationships in which the hypothetical parties will inevitably end up in actual society. Rawls says that although the parties are divested of knowledge of their particular social role or status, the parties must know that there are all sorts of different roles and statuses, one of which each will come to occupy. But could a party in the original position not rightly worry not just about which particular position she is going to occupy but also about the relationship of her position to *other* positions, in other words about what society and her relationships within it will be like? The question then is whether the parties would choose quite the principles Rawls thinks they would, and we consider this question later in the chapter when discussing a global application of Rawls's idea by Brock. But the worry about social relationships also underpins a more general concern about the conception of the individual person in Rawls's and other liberal positions; namely, whether it conceives of moral persons in an unrealistic and undesirably isolated and individualistic way. We come to this kind of criticism in Chapter 11 in the discussion of feminism and the ethics of care.

Rawls and global justice

Despite the importance of Rawls's work as an inspiration and basis for many contemporary accounts of justice, Rawls himself does not offer an account of global justice. Interestingly, Rawls considers that the principles of justice apply only in the domestic realm and *within* borders. For Rawls, international justice, which he addresses in his later work *The Law of Peoples*, consists not in the application of his two principles of justice directly to individuals and the basic structures of societies in the global realm, but in respect for a minimal set of human rights. Rawls sees the global ethical realm as a "society of peoples". Essentially, then, Rawls limits the global application of his account of justice to the respecting of *peoples* rather than individuals globally. On this view "peoples", not individuals, are the moral loci in the international realm. Such an account wholly conflicts with the founding premises of cosmopolitan thinking – that all individuals count equally – and particularly with strong cosmopolitan thinking for which borders are morally irrelevant. In fact, Rawls offers essentially two accounts of justice: one contained in the principles of justice and one concerned with global justice. His account of global justice, unlike his theory of justice, is state-centred: no longer do all individuals count equally behind the veil of ignorance. Rather, he offers a separate set of eight principles for the governance of the international order (see Box 4.8).

This approach is state-centred: states themselves are, on this view, bound by a common set of moral rules. This is similar to a "society of states", an approach we shall discuss in a later section of this chapter, but what is important to note now is that this approach is markedly different from the one he espouses for determining principles of justice within states.

The issue of the importance of justice in other states is one that Moellendorf raises in his book *Cosmopolitan Justice* (2002). Moellendorf wonders whether a society-of-states-type approach is really compatible with Rawls's view. He draws attention

---

Box 4.8 Rawls's principles of international morality

- Peoples are free and independent, and their freedom and independence are to be respected by other peoples.
- Peoples are to observe treaties and undertakings.
- Peoples are equal and are parties to the agreements that bind them.
- Peoples are to observe the duty of non-intervention (except to address grave violations of human rights).
- Peoples have a right of self-defence, but no right to instigate war for reasons other than self-defence.
- Peoples are to honour human rights.
- Peoples are to observe certain specified restrictions in the conduct of war.
- Peoples have a duty to assist other peoples living under unfavourable conditions that prevent their having a just or decent political and social regime.

---

to Rawls's sixth principle of international morality: that states must honour human rights. Honouring human rights is, of course, more limited than the principles of justice that Rawls proposes for governing domestic justice; but even this goes beyond upholding the morality of the international realm according to a society-of-states model. To ask about whether human rights are honoured is to express concerns for individuals within other states and to fail to fully respect state values of independence and non-interference. While the concern for human rights might be limited, and perhaps not equivalent to concerns for the rights of co-nationals, it is an instance of individuals being units of ethical concern rather than states. So if some concern about individuals is permitted on the international model, why does this not extend to full concern? Moellendorf's (2002) question is: "why not *global* 'justice as fairness': i.e. why not global justice according to Rawls's two original, 'domestic', principles of justice?"

Rawls's conception of justice, despite the limited nature of his own theory of international justice, has inspired many cosmopolitans to expand his ideas to the global sphere. Cosmopolitan thinkers have attempted to answer Moellendorf's question, and have attempted to apply Rawls's two principles of justice globally. In such theories the "original position" is thought of as being a global position rather than one within a state. Beitz adopts this kind of approach to ethics in his book *Political Theory and International Relations* (1999). This approach begins with the cosmopolitan rejection of the moral significance of national boundaries or borders. For cosmopolitans these are simply empirical accidents and do not have any moral significance. Accordingly, they should not have any weight in moral reasoning and certainly they present no limit to our moral and social duties. Therefore if we apply Rawls's argument for the "original position" globally we should take no account of borders. Thus the parties in the original position behind the veil of ignorance should not only not know where they will stand in a particular society (in terms of wealth, position, gender, etc.) but in addition should not know *which* society they will be part of. The argument is that the veil of ignorance can be used to remove bias *between* societies just as easily as it can be used to remove bias *within* societies.

Using this line of argument, Beitz claims that the principles of justice (especially the difference principle, which addresses socioeconomic inequalities) would and should be chosen from a hypothetical "global original position". His claim is that shifting the scope from the national to the global does not affect the content of the principles, which are in fact appropriate global principles. Moreover, he argues that the argument works with global individuals and not with states. To apply the difference principle to states is to fail to take into account economic diversity within states. He claims that this supports a cosmopolitan view rather than a society-of-states view, because "it seems obvious that an international difference principle applies to persons in the sense that it is the globally least advantaged representative person (or group of persons) whose position is to be maximised" (1999).

Moellendorf and global associations

Moellendorf takes a not dissimilar approach to Beitz. In his book *Cosmopolitan Justice*, Moellendorf uses Rawls's theory to defend – against Rawls's law-of-peoples view – the global application of his two principles of justice.

The form of cosmopolitanism that Moellendorf adopts is *institutional cosmopolitanism*. Institutional cosmopolitanism is based on a distinction between moral duties in general and duties of justice. Thus Moellendorf is a theorist who distinguishes between "justice" and "ethics". As we discussed in Chapter 1, global ethics embraces duties of both individuals and institutions. However, Moellendorf, from a political philosophy background, finds the distinction helpful because it allows him to separate out those dilemmas that can be addressed structurally from other moral dilemmas. He argues that a failure to distinguish between duties of justice and other moral duties has resulted in confusion for some forms of cosmopolitanism, particularly as regards the moral duties someone owes to those close to them (e.g. duties to family or compatriots), rather than duties of justice. Hence, by separating the justice and other moral duties in this way, he is making sure that the cosmopolitan commitment to respecting all individuals irrespective of place of birth and status is not confused with the moral debate about impartiality and special duties (as discussed in Chapter 3). Duties of justice do arise in general from moral duties in the sense that if persons in general did not have moral duties then there could be no duties of justice. Yet, duties of justice are different from such moral duties in that they are socially acquired and regulated: they require association as a necessary prerequisite.

Moellendorf focuses not on the duties of individuals, but on the duties of institutions and on public and policy structures and on mechanisms of governance. Public institutions should not prefer one group or class of persons above others, because this would suggest unfair discrimination. Moellendorf's distinction between moral duties of individuals and duties of social justice establishes the importance of associations and institutions in his picture. He argues that if there is no association between different persons and groups then there would be no duties of justice. Institutions are required to implement justice; hence his second claim that duties of justice are often carried out indirectly. For Moellendorf, then, justice is concerned with negotiating and regulating the associations of public life with the appropriate principles, rules and practices.

Global associations

Given Moellendorf's claims about the nature of duties of justice there must be an appropriate global association that meets the institutional requirements. Moellendorf argues that the appropriate association already exists: the global economic order. He argues that this association has evolved along with capitalism and the globalization of markets, and that it is an association that necessarily connects all individuals throughout the globe. For Moellendorf, the rise of the "global economy" and the fact that the international network of commerce is no longer structured around the insular economies of particular nations creates a much wider, global, association that influences everyone affected by it. He argues that because economic impact is not confined to nations or particular societies, nor are duties of justice. Consider, for example, the number of consumer goods that Western societies import, thus creating and sustaining a demand for them. Often the relatively low (for Western consumers) price of these items depends directly on their being produced by sweatshop labour in other countries. For Moellendorf, if there is an injustice in this situation then it is clearly a matter of *global* injustice: one that implicates persons or institutions across the world and not just those within one society, nation, political state or people.

The effectiveness of his argument for institutional cosmopolitanism depends on whether this non-voluntary global association exists. Moellendorf argues that it does and moreover that it is unavoidable. The global economic order is something individuals and states cannot realistically choose not to partake in; therefore participation is involuntary. We have to be part of this association whether we like it or not. Moreover, this association directly affects the moral interests of almost everyone on the planet. He argues that owing to our involuntary membership of this association, duties of justice exist not only between compatriots but between persons globally. In Moellendorf's picture it is membership of this economic

---

Box 4.9 Moellendorf's claims

About justice
- Duties of justice are different from general moral duties.
- Duties of justice are primarily *institutional* rather than between individuals.
- Because duties of justice are institutional they are often fulfilled indirectly.
- Duties of justice occur within *associations*.

About global justice
- For there to be global duties of justice there must be an appropriate *global association*.
- The *global economic order* is such an association.
- Accordingly there are *global duties of justice*.

---

association, rather than citizenship of a state or membership of any other association, that makes us part of the global association and allots us global duties of justice.

Moellendorf recognizes that the global association is not the only association within which we have duties of justice; we also have such duties to associations such as cities, provinces and states, and in fact are members of multiple sociopolitical associations. Moreover, these associations may not be prioritized in a simple manner; for example, if you live near a border you might have more in common with those who live near to you but on the other side of the border than to fellow nationals who live far away; similarly a farmer in Oklahoma may have more in common with a farmer in Italy than with a Wall Street financier. Given this, Moellendorf does not think duties of justice can be prioritized in a simple formula: for example, that you owe duties to compatriots before global duties. Priorities of duties of justice will change depending on circumstance. Sometimes commitment to justice will require that non-compatriots will come first, and sometimes duties to compatriots will take precedence. For Moellendorf there is no *general* priority of one over the other. Rather, because we have various associations (one is global, another may be provincial, and so on), we also have various duties to justice, some of which may conflict. In cases of conflict – say, between the duties of justice we have to compatriots and duties to non-compatriots – the conflicting duties have to be weighed against each other. The important point here is that we do not begin to resolve such a conflict, nor see that justice is served, by simply declaring, in advance, that one association is the winner.

Brock's non-egalitarian cosmopolitanism

We have seen some ways in which cosmopolitans develop Rawls's theory of justice and argue that his two principles should apply directly at the global level. Another explicitly cosmopolitan view holds that all people have equal moral worth and makes use of Rawls's methodology – the original position – while denying that this leads to the application of economic equality found in Rawls's difference principle.

Brock (2009) takes Rawls's model and applies it to the global setting, where the parties in the global original position are seeking "a fair framework for interactions and relations among the world's inhabitants". Mirroring Rawls's veil of ignorance, Brock's parties know about the inequalities of poverty and affluence, health and security and so on, but are shielded from knowing their particular nationality or citizenship, and hence from predicting the situation of poverty or affluence, security, war or peace, health or illness they are likely to end up in.

Brock claims that the parties here would *not* arrive at Rawls's egalitarian principle, which, as we saw, states that any inequality is justified only if it is to the advantage of the least well off: the difference principle. They would, says Brock, select a less demanding principle that secures a *minimum* standard for a decent life and for the prospects of such a life, as well as certain basic freedoms. In other words, for Brock, taken globally, rational persons would choose a minimum standard of a decent life, without the clause that allows inequalities of opportunity only if they drag that minimum upwards. Brock cites empirical evidence for this conclusion from controlled experiments undertaken by Norman Frolich and Joe Oppenheimer, in which the overwhelming majority of subjects, under conditions modelled on the original position, chose her preferred principle over a difference principle.

Brock defends her theoretical view that global justice is primarily about *all* people being afforded the chance of a decent life, where this means, basically, the opportunity to meet basic needs and to enjoy basic freedoms: for example, the basic needs of shelter, food, sanitation and protection from illness, basic education, and the freedom from violence and economic slavery. Brock states that enabling people to meet such needs and enjoy such freedoms, even minimally, requires "fair terms of cooperation", and the social and political arrangements to underwrite these goods. Hence her starting-point is a set of universal entitlements that global political institutions should uphold, and in this sense her account is a thoroughgoing form of cosmopolitanism.

Yet, in terms of its focus and structure – on basic human needs and freedoms and the political conditions that can enable these – it is important to see that this view, while committed to a standard of living below which no person should fall and holding to the cosmopolitan conception of the equal *moral* worth of people globally, is not primarily committed to making socioeconomic conditions *equal*. Hence, to a large extent, Brock's account of global justice can be seen as *non*-egalitarian, even though she is expressly concerned with improving the plight of the world's poor and implementing global justice. Where an egalitarian view holds that, as far as possible, the gap between rich and poor is closed, Brock is more concerned with raising the lower standard to a certain minimal "decent" level and less concerned with what happens above that level. So, if we were to imagine representatives of the world's population positioned on a ladder, with the least well off at the bottom and the better off further up, Brock's view is that many are now too low down and should be raised to a rung that represents at least a minimally decent life. Whether doing so, in fact, increases equality for all on the ladder is not, for her, the primary question of global justice.

Pogge's version of institutional cosmopolitanism

As we have seen, cosmopolitans agree on the equal moral status of individuals globally, but they may disagree about what this entails regarding global socioeconomic equality: for instance, as Moellendorf suggested in his version of institutional cosmopolitanism, whether or not the "global association" is sufficient to require global duties. Pogge (2002), as Moellendorf suggested in his version of *institutional cosmopolitanism*, which he compares with *interactional cosmopolitanism*. An "interactional" view is concerned with individual duties; for instance, fulfilling human rights is a duty that individuals have to others directly. The scope of cosmopolitanism is "interactional" because it sees rights and duties – and their violations – in terms of interactions between persons. On the institutional view, the duty to uphold human rights is ascribed directly to institutional schemes rather than to individuals; again, like Moellendorf, for Pogge there is a distinction between the duties of individuals and institutions.

In Pogge's institutional form of cosmopolitanism, individuals do have obligations not to participate in unjust institutional schemes; therefore individual duties are entailed by this institutional approach. A good way to distinguish between the views is to consider Pogge's example of how each would address the question of slavery. Taking the human right not to be enslaved, an interactional view would hold that by virtue of this right, all persons have a duty not to enslave each other, while the institutional view would oblige all legal and economic institutions not to recognize or allow practices in which persons are owned and used as slaves. In turn, individuals are obliged not to take part in or support institutions that facilitate slavery. For Pogge, an important difference between the interactional and the institutional view is what each says about people who are themselves neither slaves nor slaveholders. Someone taking the interactional view can hold that a "third party", someone who as an individual does not enslave anyone, has no responsibility towards people who are enslaved: they are not in the relevant "interaction" with slaves to incur a duty.

But on the institutional view, the right not to be enslaved obliges these persons not to uphold the institution of slavery or the institutional order that keeps it in place. Therefore, and importantly for global ethics, Pogge explicitly formulates the connection between individual and institutional duties.

Generalizing from this example, Pogge (2002) is able to reject the arguments of rich and powerful people who, taking an interactional line, claim they have no obligation to the very poor in other countries because they are not directly involved in any violation of their rights. Pogge's focus on the direct, "first-order" duties of global institutions of which rich people are part, rather than on the direct duties of interactions between persons, implies a "second-order" duty on anyone involved with such institutions. "Our negative duty [a duty *not* to do something; more on this in Chapter 5] not to cooperate in the imposition of unjust coercive institutions triggers obligations to protect their victims and promote feasible reforms that would enhance the fulfilment of their human rights." We shall return to this in Chapter 7, and see how this view bears on the way we think about our obligations to the world's poor. But, for now what is important to note is the way that thinkers such as Pogge and Moellendorf are developing cosmopolitanism, and that their focus on institutions makes it far less easy for individuals to claim that if they do not have direct relations with distant individuals then they have no duties to them.

In the remainder of the chapter, we look at some alternative political theories to cosmopolitanism. Some of these can be regarded in some forms as weak versions of cosmopolitanism, or at least friendly to cosmopolitanism; other forms can be seen as being in opposition to cosmopolitanism. We shall also consider realism: an approach that directly opposes cosmopolitanism and denies its basic principles.

CASE STUDY 4.2 The society-of-states approach and the sale of body parts

If we return to the selling of body parts, we can see clearly the difference between a society-of-states approach and a cosmopolitan approach. In the domestic realm the reasoning of the two theorists might not be too different. Both would be concerned in the domestic sphere with the rights and wrongs of individuals' actions and characters; so, depending on their ethical theory of choice, they would be considering best consequences, respect for persons and human flourishing. Obviously there would be some difference in their reasoning; most importantly, the cosmopolitan will be factoring in concern for all global persons whereas the society-of-states theorist will be concerned only for those within the state. However, both will be concerned for individuals as the units of moral concern. For the cosmopolitan thinker this is still true in the international setting. The cosmopolitan theorist continues to employ the same moral framework globally as domestically; for them there is only one moral framework. Understanding the theoretical philosophical and political com-

THE SOCIETY-OF-STATES APPROACH

Rawls's approach to global justice, which we looked at earlier in this chapter, can be thought of as an example of what others have developed as the "society-of-states" view. However, it is worth mentioning that Rawls himself does not use that term and we should resist casting Rawls as a simply society-of-states theorist, for reasons that should become apparent as we look more closely at this position as developed by more recent proponents, such as Terry Nardin (1983). The society-of-states approach argues that the international moral order is one that is made up of states and that states are the units of ethical consideration. Accordingly, states have moral duties to other states, not to individuals within those states. Moral duties that states are required to respect are those of non-intervention, sovereignty and independence. Thus the society-of-states approach regards the international sphere as a moral sphere with its own rules of good conduct. What counts as morally good or right in the international sphere is different from what is good or right in the domestic sphere. Therefore, although both the international and the domestic realm are governed by moral rules, they are governed by *different* moral rules. In the domestic realm the unit of concern is the individual, and moral issues concern what is right or wrong for individuals; in the global realm the unit of concern is the state and what is right or wrong for states. These are completely separate moral realms that respect quite different moral values.

A key criticism of the society-of-states view – clearly illustrated by the case study – is that it simply ignores moral concerns in the global sphere. By switching frameworks from the domestic to the global it effectively sidesteps issues of duties to

mitments of different factions helps one to understand how and why different policies and practices are endorsed by different groups and why.

For the society-of-states theorist, as soon as one moves from the domestic realm to the international realm, the framework changes. The concern is no longer for individuals, but only for states. What is respected in this framework are things that are valuable to states, such as independence, sovereignty and non-interference. The moral concerns of the domestic realm are quite simply regarded as irrelevant to the international realm when it comes to relations between states. Therefore a society-of-states proponent will be concerned only about these state-centred issues and it is hard to imagine an instance in which principles of sovereignty or independence might be undermined by the sale of organs. If the trade in organs was so great that the health of the nation was undermined and thus its capability for independence and defence might be threatened, the society-of-states proponent might object to the sale of body parts. But, for the most part such ethical issues simply do not figure in the society-of-states schema.

individuals. Is it really the case that states have nothing to say about how other states treat individuals within those states? While this may have historically been the reality of how states interacted, increasingly it seems unacceptable to consider it to be morally correct to have no concern for how those in other states are treated. This is seen increasingly in laws that stretch beyond borders; one example is laws about sex tourism. US citizens, for instance, can be prosecuted for sexual activity with prostitutes under the age of eighteen in other countries, even if that activity is legally permissible under the laws of that particular country. In addition, this approach conflicts with international conventions, such as the Geneva Conventions or the UDHR. In practice, the society-of-states approach still accounts for most dealings between states. For the most part, states do not intervene with how other states treat their citizens; however, this is not always the case, as we shall see in Chapter 6, where humanitarian intervention will be discussed.

The international community is vocal in its criticism of perceived mistreatment of citizens of other states and perceived human-rights violations. For example, in Zimbabwe, leading members of the main opposition party – the Movement for Democratic Change – were intimidated, beaten and imprisoned prior to supposedly "free" elections, adding to Zimbabwe's profile as a "pariah state" on the international scene. Likewise Burma, a military dictatorship, regularly suppresses free speech and, according to Human Rights Watch, human trafficking and forced labour – including child labour – are commonplace. This is not simply ignored by the international community and Burma is currently subject to nineteen UN resolutions calling for democratization and human rights.

As well as states taking stands on how other states treat their citizens, citizens also take stands across borders. Think, for instance, of consumer campaigns and boycotts of certain goods. Famous and successful boycotts of South African produce as well as sporting events were carried out against apartheid (in the 1970s and 1980s) and against specific companies who were implicated. In 2005, the food giant Nestlé was sued by the Washington-based International Labor Rights Fund for using forced child

---

CASE STUDY 4.3 Nationalism and the sale of body parts

For a nationalist, the political and the moral sphere are not completely separate, as they are for the society-of-states proponent, and thus moral considerations do count in international politics. But the moral obligations one has, or approaches one takes, to fellow nationals are different from those that one has to those beyond borders. Thus the nationalist may well have a different attitude regarding the treatment and remuneration of women who donate and sell their eggs to fellow nationals as compared to eggs being received from or donated to recipients in foreign jurisdictions. Some nationalists, such as Miller, whose argument we

labour, and the sports-clothing company Nike has come in for widespread public criticism for using cheap sweatshop labour in developing countries, for example in Naomi Klein's book *No Logo* and Michael Moore's documentary film *The Big One*.

The globalization of our world suggests that a system that considers states as isolated and unconnected is increasingly unrealistic. Individuals travel between states, permanently or temporarily; also, many communities are global – for instance business communities, academic communities and activist communities – and, as discussed in Chapter 1, many of the most pressing ethical challenges are global in nature. Taken together these changes render the society-of-states picture increasingly out of date. This said, it is important to remember that in the political realm the state-centred view is still dominant. It is still governments of states, for the most part, who negotiate and implement international policy. These issues of governance structures will be returned to in Chapter 6.

NATIONALISM

A second alternative approach is nationalism. Nationalism does not refer in this context to nationalist political parties or extreme, usually right-wing, political sentiments, but rather to a moral and political claim that nations are ethically significant. Nationalists in this sense argue that what rights and duties we have to others is affected in part by nationality and that we have special obligations to fellow nationals (or compatriots) that we do not have to non-nationals.

Those who defend the nationalist view argue that the claim that we have duties to our compatriots that we do not have to others is not strange, but in fact is assumed by most political actors and policy-makers, as well as by the voting public in democracies. For example, health or education policy is determined in any country with regard to the needs and wishes of nationals, and it is nationals who will suffer or

consider on page 92, claim that a special commitment to co-nationals is compatible with a commitment to universal human rights. Thus the question for a nationalist like Miller, who also endorses human rights, is twofold: (i) is the market in organs morally acceptable domestically; and (ii) if so does the international market in body parts breach human rights (or any other moral obligations beyond borders)? If it is both domestically morally acceptable and desired *and* it does not breach the less stringent global obligations, then the selling of body parts will be deemed ethical. What is crucial to note is that what is required to protect those beyond borders, in this instance compliance with human rights, is not equivalent to the duties and obligations owed within borders to fellow nationals.

benefit from any change in policy. Indeed, if the voting public suddenly discovered that their taxes, which they believed were being used for national and local services, were found to have been used to benefit members of other countries, and at the expense of the home country, there would be an outcry. Thus such national parochialism is thought to be in line with common-sense morality and experience. But, nationalism denies a key assumption in the universalism that underpins the standard cosmopolitan view. That is, it explicitly denies that individuals are necessarily *equal* units of concern regardless of nationality. On the nationalist view, your compatriots take moral priority over non-compatriots, although this does not mean that a nationalist does not consider non-compatriots morally *at all*. The nationalist claim does not deny that there are some duties beyond national boundaries, but claims that there are special duties within national boundaries.

For some, all such boundaries are states. However, this has been rejected on a number of grounds, and others argue that this is not the case because a state may cover more than one nation and those with a shared identity may be found in more than one state. In his book *On Nationality* (1995), Miller favours a cultural interpretation of national identity, such that recognizing nationality need not override other ways in which we define ourselves, such as ethnicity. Miller sees conceptions of nationality as significant for personal and communal self-understanding. He argues that cultural–national identities are legitimate sources of personal identity: the way we define ourselves as persons. Therefore he argues that nationality is something that distinguishes people and grounds their loyalties and interests. For Miller, this supports the view that prioritizing your nation is sometimes justifiable. Accordingly, we are justified in citing obligations to our co-nationals that have special, non-global status. He adds that nations are *justified* in seeking political self-determination: hence he is not merely describing the way in which nationality is significant, but saying also that this is a good thing.

Proponents of nationalism argue that, based on a common history and a national character that feeds into cultural identity, there are special duties to fellow nationals that do not apply to non-nationals. The argument that persons have special duties to some people that they do not have to all is not a controversial one. For example, nearly all ethicists would accept that there are particular duties to family members, or to those with whom one has a personal relationship due to one's roles (e.g. doctor to patient). However, those who distinguish between duties of justice and other duties would argue that these are not duties of justice, as discussed above. There are exceptions, for instance Singer (1972), who has argued that it makes no difference morally whether someone you are in a position to help is in front of you or on the other side of the world. We shall explore his view further in Chapter 7. But most ethicists do allow special relationships. Nationalists argue that just as there are special duties, for example, to family members, there are also special duties to your nation. Just as you can argue for cosmopolitanism using different moral theories, so too can you argue

---

Box 4.10 Arguments from nationalists

- There are certain *special* obligations to compatriots/co-nationals that do not necessarily extend to non-compatriots.
- These special obligations do not preclude there also being some global obligations.
- These special obligations, like other special obligations, are not strange but are morally justified.

---

for nationalism using different moral theories; for example, on contractual grounds that nations are mutually beneficial societies, or according to utilitarian reasoning that such boundaries are useful ways of allocating more general duties (see Box 4.10).

POLITICAL REALISM

The final position we shall consider is that of the political realist who takes a very anti-cosmopolitan stance and could perhaps be regarded as the "arch-enemy" of the cosmopolitan. The kind of political "realism" we shall be referring to is to be understood in something like the everyday sense of "being realistic" about the way things are and about what needs to be done. The term "realism" in philosophy can be used to describe the view that things, such as moral or aesthetic qualities, exist – are "real" – independently of our thoughts and perceptions of them. In what follows, when we mention "realism" we shall mean specifically political realism, and will not be talking about this sort of philosophical realism. The realist view of the ethics of international relations is perhaps the traditional view of international interaction. Philosophically it draws on Thomas Hobbes and his particular picture of the "state of nature".

Box 4.11 The Hobbesian state of nature

In Hobbes's words, in the states of nature there is:

"no place for industry, because the fruit thereof is uncertain: and consequently no culture of the earth; no navigation, nor use of the commodities that may be imported by sea; no commodious building; no instruments of moving, and removing, such things as require much force; no knowledge of the face of the earth; no account of time; no arts; no letters; no society; and which is worst of all, continual fear, and danger of violent death; and the life of man, solitary, poor, nasty, brutish, and short."

(1994: 76)

The British philosopher Hobbes argued that morality derives from the rules that are necessary when human beings live together in social groups. This is a "contract" theory of morality, sometimes called "social-contract theory" or "contractarianism": social rules and the mechanisms for enforcing them are agreed (contracted) by human beings as they move into social arrangements. For Hobbes, people "before" or "outside" the "social contract" are in a "state of nature". This is summed up in his now famous description of life in the state of nature as "solitary, poor, nasty, brutish, and short". The state of nature, on Hobbes's view, is essentially a "constant state of war", without any association between individuals, and therefore without the cooperative endeavours that are necessary for improving life. The Hobbesian state of nature is a very unattractive and undesirable picture of human life.

In Hobbes's model, in order to escape the state of nature, human beings begin to cooperate with each other, realizing that together it is easier to meet basic human needs and to improve chances of survival. In order for such cooperation to take place, agreement is necessary to ensure that people will not be harmed and to ensure that agreements will be kept. This agreement Hobbes terms "the social contract" and it is from this that moral codes are derived. Morality, then, is not an essential or intrinsic part of human being or relationships (indeed, in the state of nature even relationships are not essential to human beings – something that contradicts the universal need for some nurturing, parenting relationship for survival). Rather, morality is a cooperative scheme: a set of social practices and conventions that works if the majority of persons whom it affects participate in it. Individuals choose to cooperate from self-interested motives. Such a scheme is set in place by rules agreed on by people who, as rational beings, seek the mutual benefits of such a scheme.

Realists argue that this state of nature is the condition of the international order and therefore no rules of morality apply (or should apply) in this arena. They argue, following Hobbes, that the social contract requires the assurance that everyone will comply with the rules if rational people are to agree to abide by it. Hobbes argues that this requires that there is a government or power that is able to ensure that people comply

---

CASE STUDY 4.4 Realism and the sale of body parts

If we consider how realists would approach our case study about the selling of eggs and kidneys, the simple answer is that they would not. Realists might well deem the market in body parts simply not their concern, but a moral matter to be addressed in the moral sphere, not a political matter to be addressed in the political sphere. It is possible that realists might deem the matter their concern if they deemed some aspects of the case political, although again they would address these purely as political matters, matters of power, rather than as moral matters. For example, it is possible to imagine that a relatively

and, if there is not, then it is not in individuals' self-interest to comply with the social contract. In the arena of international relations there is no such powerful governing body or authority and thus no contract and no moral obligations. So war would seem to be an unavoidable state. Certainly this is what Hobbes thought. In the international context the state of nature describes the situation between states. Accordingly, every state (just like every individual in the original state of nature) is entitled to seek its own self-interest. Not only are there no moral rules in the international realm but because there are no moral rules what a state *should* do is to seek its own interest. Thus for the realist a state should always do what is in the national interest.

Box 4.12 The realist's arguments

- Morality is a set of rules that rational people agree to for their mutual benefit.
- Others must also comply for it to be in an individual's self-interest to comply.
- Some authority or government is necessary to ensure compliance.
- In the international arena there is no such authority.
- Therefore it is not rational for states to comply with moral rules because they have no guarantee that others do.
- Therefore there is no morality (moral rules) in the international arena.

For the realist, morality simply does not exist in the international sphere. Hans Morgenthau, a predominant proponent of this position in the twentieth century, asserts the non-moral nature of political realism in his book *Politics Among Nations* (1948; Morgenthau & Thompson 1985). He emphasizes the independence of the political realm, stating that the political sphere is "autonomous", and not one to which the standards or methods of interpersonal morality apply. He argues that morality may itself be highly relevant in many areas of life, but it has no place in thinking about the political affairs of states or in international politics. In his words,

---

poor country might regard the purchasing of organs from its citizens as a practice that weakened the country politically – against the national interest – and thus move to stop the practice. Likewise one could imagine a country worrying about an influx of "donors" on "paid holidays" as a gateway to illegal immigration, or conversely a country might wish to encourage the practice in order to address the scarcity of organs. However, such actions, and the many other possible reasons one could imagine, would always be for political reasons – actions taken because they were believed to be in the national interest – with no regard for any other issue, and certainly not moral issues. For realists, moral concerns about the sale of body parts are, like all other moral concerns, quite simply not their concern.

"while the individual has a moral right to sacrifice himself in defence of such a moral principle, the state has no right to let its moral disapprobation of the infringement of (that moral principle) get in the way of successful political action, itself inspired by the moral principle of national survival". International politics and relations are concerned with the interests of states understood in terms of their powers. To impose another framework is to import inappropriate standards to the realm of the political.

International relations is a sphere in which morality is simply not relevant. For a realist, then, the only concern when it comes to addressing ethical dilemmas is what is in the national interest; and national interest is interpreted in political terms of power. The realist sees nations much as Hobbes saw individuals in his pre-societal "state of nature". Here it is important to consider that to be a political realist is not necessarily to be anti-moral or an amoralist. On the realist view, the global order just is not a subject to which a moral order is relevant, because the arrangements of nations in the world (at least as things stand) preclude there *being* a moral community.

CONCLUSION

This chapter has introduced the key theories of political philosophy and understandings of global justice. When these political theories are added to the moral theories of the last chapter the basic ethical toolbox for global ethics is in place. To this will be added rights theories (in Chapter 5) and a more detailed understanding of the nature of global governance and global institutions (in Chapter 6). Indeed, we have already begun to raise some of the issues that will be explored in later chapters. The introduction of institutional cosmopolitanism in this chapter shows that considering the global structure and institutions is not just a matter of empirical knowledge, but also has moral implications. For instance, is the global economic order sufficient to constitute an association? If so, what is its mechanism? Do institutions such as the World Trade Organization (WTO) and the International Monetary Fund (IMF) constitute governance of this association? Alternatively, do we need to move to other forms of institution and even to a world government if duties of justice are to be adequately fulfilled?

When you approach pressing contemporary ethical dilemmas you should apply the tools you have learnt to use. As we have seen, the political theory you endorse does not automatically provide you with the answer to prescribing what ethically *should* happen. However, if you combine political and moral commitments then you begin to get some answers. Which moral and political theories do you endorse? What conclusions do you actually come to?

Although this chapter has not given simple answers to what a global ethicist should endorse, it has shown us the scope of global ethics. For instance, a global ethicist clearly cannot be realist: a realist denies the global scope of morality. Conversely, it makes a lot of sense for a global ethicist to endorse a cosmopolitan position of one form or another. Yet, to say this does not end the debate. Which form should be adopted? Institutional cosmopolitanism? Do you agree with Moellendorf that global justice depends on associations rather than individuals? Do you wish to adopt a strong or weak form? Are duties to all individuals the same, or is it acceptable to have some duties to compatriots only? If so, how are these balanced?

How you answer these questions will determine how you do global ethics and what kind of global ethicist you are, indeed, whether you think that there are in fact global-ethics issues at all. For instance, if you are a realist this debate is completely irrelevant. This said, those who adopt society-of-states approaches and nationalist approaches still have much to offer the global-ethics debate. How much depends on how much weight they give to global duties. For instance, the society-of-states advocates might still wish to endorse human rights (or another global set of obligations): how is this to be done? Likewise, the nationalists might in fact endorse substantial global obligations, even if these are not as high as the duties owed to compatriots. Thus there is much still to be determined, and it mostly depends on which arguments you are convinced by. Chapter 5 will help in making such judgements. It considers human rights as a possible "global ethic", as well as suggestions of basic rights and minimal standards. This debate will add to the ethical toolbox and help you decide what you think is actually right or wrong; it will give you the tools to make arguments in support of your position.

FURTHER READING

- Beitz, C. *Political Theory and International Relations* (Princeton, NJ: Princeton University Press, 1999).
- Brock, G. *Global Justice: A Cosmopolitan Account* (Oxford: Oxford University Press, 2009).
- Brock, G. & H. Brighouse. *The Political Philosophy of Cosmopolitanism* (Cambridge: Cambridge University Press, 2005).
- Caney, S. *Justice Beyond Borders: A Global Political Theory* (Oxford: Oxford University Press, 2005).
- Mandle, J. *Global Justice: An Introduction* (Oxford: Blackwell, 2006).
- Moellendorf, D. *Cosmopolitan Justice* (Cambridge, MA: Westview Press, 2002).
- Pogge, T. "Cosmopolitanism and Sovereignty". *Ethics* **103** (1992): 48–75.
- Rawls, J. *A Theory of Justice* (rev. edn) (Cambridge, MA: Harvard University Press, 1999).
- Van Hooft, S. *Cosmopolitanism: A Philosophy for Global Ethics* (Stocksfield: Acumen, 2009).

5 RIGHTS THEORY FOR GLOBAL ETHICS

INTRODUCTION

Chapters 3 and 4 introduced the main moral and political theories that form the basis of the global-ethics toolbox. To these can be added additional theories and perspectives, for instance, legal theory, social theory, cultural critiques and, perhaps most importantly, empirical evidence from policy and practice and hands-on experience. Your ethical toolbox grows as you learn and experience more and continue to add theories and knowledge of how such theories play out in practice. In this chapter we shall add one final theory to it: rights theory. Over the past half-century, talk about human rights has gradually grown until it is familiar in all forums of debate: academic, policy and practice. In addition, rights are very familiar in popular discourse about ethics and politics: as O'Neill (2008) comments, the "rhetoric of human rights is all around us – perhaps never more so than at present in the English-speaking world". Other examples can be found easily in newspapers and popular media, for instance when people talk about their rights being violated, even when there appears to be no specific human right being directly violated; an example of this we consider in this chapter is whether being subject to excessive noise could constitute a violation of human rights.

The wide application and acceptance of rights makes them of crucial importance in developing global ethics, because human rights are the most obvious candidate to be considered a global ethic in the current system of global governance. As we saw in Chapter 3, global ethics requires some kind of universalist approach and human rights offer a means to assert universal respect for all human beings simply on the grounds that they are human (without the need for any additional supporting reasoning). Thus, human rights as a global ethic has the advantage of already being established in both global and local governance systems. Accordingly rights-based approaches are practical and realistic ways to address global injustice, although, as we shall come to see in this chapter, rights, both in theory and practice, are not without their problems.

Rights theories can be supported using different moral and political theories. For instance, as we saw in Chapter 4, cosmopolitan thinkers use rights theories: weak cosmopolitans to present some global minimum standard and strong cosmopolitans to argue for some kind of global governance and enforcement of standards. Moral theories also include rights: for example, a Kantian uses rights in order to ensure that the respect for persons is maintained, and a virtue ethicist may endorse rights as being important in establishing a community that will lead to human flourishing. Likewise, utilitarians will support rights if they believe that this will lead to the best consequences; rule utilitarians often defend rights. A rule utilitarian is someone who defines the right action as the one that complies with a rule that, if generally followed, would maximize overall happiness. So, as John C. Harsanyi (1980) has noted, rule utilitarianism can "fully recognize the moral validity of … rights and obligations precisely because of its *commitment* to an overall moral strategy". This is in contrast to the view of the act utilitarian, who would look at individual *acts* and assess whether the benefit would outweigh the harm in each particular case.

While all sorts of theorists can endorse rights, there are some theories that fit more easily with rights than others. Kantianism is regarded as being the most natural home for rights-based theory. Utilitarians will support human rights only as far as they believe they lead to the best consequences, not because they believe there is any intrinsic value in rights themselves. And virtue ethicists, while wishing to promote human flourishing, may worry about the individualism of rights and their lack of context awareness. All these tendencies to support and critique rights will be explored in this chapter, and by the end you should have a better understanding of the nature of rights and how useful they are in moving towards a more just world.

In order to explore the nature of rights and how they function in global-ethics theory and in the practical campaigns to create a more just world, this chapter will consider definitions of rights, the establishment of rights and the theoretical constructions that underpin them. We shall consider what human rights are supposed to be and their function, and how they are implemented and enforced (or not), in particular with regard to the prohibition on torture; and we shall examine some important criticisms of both the theory of human rights and the practical efficacy of their universal application. The case study of torture will be used to illustrate and clarify the arguments and theories discussed in this chapter. The case study can be found in Chapter 2 (pp. 24–9).

GLOBAL HUMAN RIGHTS

Defining rights

A first problem with rights theory is determining what counts as a human right. Many supposed rights are asserted in popular discourse even though no corresponding human right is actually established in human-rights documents. For example, in 2003 a group of campaigners and residents near London's Heathrow Airport took the airport to the European Court of Human Rights on the grounds that aircraft noise was contravening their human rights (see Verkaik 2003). Now, there is no specific right concerned directly with noise pollution, but the group cited article 8 of the European Convention of Human Rights (Council of Europe 2010), parts 1 and 2, which runs as follows:

1. Everyone has the right to respect for his private and family life, his home and his correspondence.
2. There will be no interference by a public authority with the exercise of this right except such as is in accordance with the law and is necessary in a democratic society in the interests of national security, public safety or the economic well-being of the country, for the prevention of disorder or crime, for the protection of health or morals, or for the protection of the rights and freedoms of others.

The group's case, then, was clearly based on their claim that their private and family lives were not being respected. In assessing and balancing the interests of the community as a whole, the court ultimately disagreed, and the group lost its case. This is an example of how differing interpretations of human rights can be offered. It also shows that simply *stating* that you have a right does not mean that it actually exists.

Similar discussions happen in academic circles too. For instance, there is much discussion about reproductive rights (which we shall return to in Chapter 9) but, in terms of the UDHR, reproductive rights are not explicitly mentioned. What is asserted is the right to found a family (United Nations 1948: article 16), and the importance of bodily integrity (article 5), which forbids torture and cruel or inhuman treatment and punishment. Taken together, these rights can be used to claim that no one should be physically prevented from conceiving and bearing children; or conversely that no one should be forced to carry a child. Yet while having children clearly does contribute to human flourishing, and some aspects of having and raising children are accordingly protected in the declaration, there are no "reproductive rights" as such.

Thinking about reproductive rights helps us understand some of the complexities surrounding rights claims. For instance, if reproductive rights were explicitly named in the UDHR what might these be? Would a reproductive right be a negative right not to be interfered with? How would this be interpreted? Would it be the right to be left alone to practise contraception and abortion? If so, would this right require that contraception and abortion be publicly funded? Such a policy would be controversial. For example, although abortion has been legal in the US since 1973, legislation was passed in 1976 to prohibit funding from the Federal Government's Health and Human Services Department. What of those who are unable to conceive: what do reproductive rights mean for them? Do reproductive rights extend to rights to have access to reproductive treatment and technology? This would have huge global resource implications and would be successful only for some.

These examples show that, although very prominent, rights theory is by no means unproblematic. Rights need clear definition, and consensuses about how to interpret them: what do they entail and, importantly, who has a duty to give to the rights-holder that which is owed? Rights in a vacuum do not entitle the rights-holder to anything unless the corresponding duty and the person or institution charged with fulfilling that duty can be identified. This in itself can be a problem for rights, for while rights always imply that someone has a duty, identifying exactly who has this duty and ensuring they act on it is not always easy; indeed, this is the reason that some theorists prefer to avoid the language of rights and focus on duties instead (as we shall see when we consider O'Neill's arguments to address poverty in Chapter 7).

Establishing universal human rights

Although there are problems with defining and implementing rights, *claiming* that human rights are universal seems at least plausible, even if *implementation* is still some way off. For instance, as we shall see, the UDHR, which was originally ratified by forty-eight nations of the UN, has essentially been endorsed by all countries, and in different forms integrated into national laws and statutes. Thus, the European Convention on Human Rights establishes human rights as legal entities, and rulings from "lower" national courts can be overturned if they conflict. Accordingly, the European Court of Human Rights has become a last court of appeal for those living within its jurisdiction. For example, in 2009 the European Court of Human Rights (ECHR) ruled against the mandatory display of crucifixes in all classrooms in Italy. The ECHR ruled that it violated the rights of parents to choose which, if any, religion their children were to be educated within, and furthermore that it undermined "pluralism in education, which is essential to preserve a democratic society". ("Pluralism" here means equal respect and toleration of a number of faiths or beliefs.) And in 2008, the ECHR overruled French court rulings that prevented a lesbian woman from adopting a child, also awarding damages to the woman and charging the legal costs to the French state. Accordingly, human rights are powerful legal instruments that give force to the universal moral values that underpin them. It is for this reason that many cosmopolitans (strong and weak) engage with human-rights theory and key global ethicists use rights theory in support of their claims. For instance, Pogge uses human-rights theory to argue that freedom from poverty is a human right (an argument we shall return to in Chapter 7); and Caney uses human-rights theory to argue for environmental justice, on the grounds that the effects of fossil fuel consumption, namely global warming, infringe human rights by undermining fundamental interests, an argument we shall return to in Chapter 10.

However, while it may be the case that human rights are the best established candidate as a basis for a global ethics they are by no means globally secure. For instance, although the declaration of human rights theoretically binds all nations, they are not "legally binding" in the way domestic laws are: that is, they are not "binding" in the sense that countries or individual representatives of those countries are actually brought to account for breaches of these human rights. In fact, human rights are often more evident in their breach than their observance, and the full protection of all persons globally from human-rights violations remains an ideal. But, even though human rights are not, as yet, universally established and protected as envisaged in the UDHR, the fact that there is some universal agreement about what human rights are, or should be, is significant in itself. To return to the argument of Chapter 3 regarding universalism and relativism, the fact that the UDHR is ratified by countries from Europe, Asia and Africa belies claims of relativism. The original declaration in 1948 was voted for by, among others, Afghanistan, Argentina, Australia, Bolivia, Brazil, Burma, Canada, Chile, China, Cuba, Denmark, Ecuador, Egypt, Ethiopia, France, Guatemala, Haiti, Iceland, India, Iran, Iraq, Luxembourg, Mexico, New Zealand, Nicaragua, Pakistan, Panama, Paraguay, Peru, Syria, Thailand, Turkey, United States, Uruguay and Venezuela. As we have seen in the case of the European Convention on Human Rights, more localized interpretations and applications of the principles of the UDHR have emerged. Other examples are the American Convention on Human Rights (also known as the Pact of San José), adopted in 1969 (see Inter-American Commission on Human Rights 1979), and the African Charter on Human and Peoples' Rights (also known as the Banjul Charter) adopted in 1979 by African heads of state under the Organization of African Unity (see African Commission on Human and People's Rights 1981).

Moreover, as well as there being some universal consensus about respect for persons in the form of respecting human rights, there are emerging governance mechanisms and sanctions that are intended to encourage, and in certain instances even enforce, some respect for human rights. Thus the International Criminal Court can actually prosecute individuals for genocide and other crimes against humanity, and this can be seen as the international legal imposition of the most basic human rights even though these rights do not themselves have the same status as laws. Much of the international campaigning against apartheid in South Africa during the 1970s and 1980s was mounted as a defence of human rights, as is the current campaign against Burma's military junta's brutal suppression of free speech and dissent, and use of child and forced labour. Human-rights violations are recognized as global injustices, not just by activist and campaigning groups, such as Human Rights Watch and Amnesty International, but also by the international political community: as when in November 2009 the General Assembly of the UN adopted a resolution "strongly condemning the ongoing systematic violations of human rights and fundamental freedoms" in Burma.

Yet, just as enforcement by nation states is less than complete, so too are international responses intended to protect and enforce rights. For instance, although there is much NGO reporting of human-rights violations in China (such as Amnesty International's recent campaign against the death penalty), there is little international action taken to attempt to force China to comply with human-rights norms. Amnesty International reported on 23 August 2010 that while China has proposed to reduce by thirteen its sixty-five crimes punishable by death, this measure is in fact unlikely to reduce the number of executions, a number about which China remains less than transparent. Another recent example of the failure to universalize human rights is the actions of coalition forces in the recent wars in Iraq and Afghanistan. In these conflicts the US and UK in particular have been criticized for undermining human rights by permitting violations against civilians and by using torture. We shall explore this issue both as a case study for this chapter and in Chapter 8. This is worrying because it could be argued that at times when respect for persons is under threat, such as times of emergency or conflict, respecting human rights is particularly important; it is in these situations that violations are most likely.

Such failures of the international community to prioritize human rights are an issue for the global ethicist. It suggests that states act to promote human rights only when it is in their best interest, or at least not directly against their interest, to do so. This would suggest, if we think back to the theories of Chapter 4, a realist or perhaps a society-of-states approach, rather than a cosmopolitan approach. So again, although human rights may have some features of a functioning global ethic, they are limited both theoretically and in application. But, what human rights do is universalize the notion that all individuals possess rights simply by virtue of being human. This claim might be regarded as substantial in itself and its general acceptance, however inadequate the practice, is significant. In addition, although declarations of human rights such as the UDHR do not have the same legal status as laws that can be enforced, they nonetheless provide a basis on which international pressure, and popular campaigns, can be mounted. So even if we acknowledge that the UDHR lacks full legal power, this need not stop theorists and activists alike from appealing to the principles of human rights as a powerful tool in the cause of global justice.

The development of rights

When considering human rights it is important to recognize that human rights as established in the current global system are not always directly equivalent to rights as understood in philosophical theories. While philosophical views do, of course, feed into how human rights are regarded, particularly with regard to how they are established and justified, how they work in practice is largely a matter of law and governance mechanisms. As we saw in Chapter 3, a philosophical right is generated from a particular moral theory. For instance, a Kantian might develop rights by using the categorical imperative to establish universal rights and duties. However, this theoretical underpinning is not necessary for using and understanding human rights. The current concept of human rights is a recent phenomenon, as is the network of international law that developed in the second half of the twentieth century to support them. The first document to enshrine human rights is the UDHR of 1948, which was constructed in the aftermath of the Second World War with the intention of ensuring that there were certain minimum standards regarding the protection of individuals (Box 5.1).

Human rights are often talked of as having evolved through three generations of rights:

- First generation rights are civil and political rights.
- Second generation rights are economic, social and cultural rights.
- Third generation rights are rights of peoples.

The 1948 UDHR embodies first and second generation rights but is silent about the third. This has become a prominent issue in recent years and is key to concerns about indigenous persons and group rights. This is an issue we shall explore using examples later in the book, in Chapters 9, 10 and 11. In Chapter 9 in particular we shall consider whether there are group rights to protect indigenous groups from having their genetic make-up taken without the permission of the group as a whole; or to protect groups in the developing world from having their "traditional knowledge" taken for Western developments without adequate compensation for the community. Key questions here are whether groups themselves can have rights that are something separate from collecting all individual members' rights together. Can we, for example, identify a *community's* right to live on and use a piece of land by virtue of its history and ancestry, where such a right is not just reducible to the rights of, say, *individual* farmers, business owners or residents? In such instances, it is questionable whether respecting only individuals' rights is sufficient to protect the interests of these groups.

The kinds of civil and political right protected in the UDHR are those concerned, for example, with freedom from interference by the state: free association; free speech; safety; and freedom from discrimination. Key political rights are participation in

Box 5.1 The Universal Declaration of Human Rights

The UDHR recognizes that:

"[T]he inherent dignity and ... the equal and inalienable rights of all members of the human family [are] the foundation of freedom, justice and peace in the world."

(United Nations 1948: Preamble)

The UDHR states that:

"All human beings are born free and equal in dignity and rights."   (Article 1)

"Everyone is entitled to all the rights and freedoms set forth in this Declaration, without distinction of any kind, such as race, colour, sex, language, religion, political or other opinion, national or social origin, property, birth or other status."   (Article 2)

"Everyone has the right to life, liberty and security of person."   (Article 3)

"No one shall be held in slavery or servitude."   (Article 4)

"No one shall be subjected to torture or to cruel, inhuman or degrading treatment or punishment."   (Article 5)

"Everyone has the right to recognition everywhere as a person before the law."

(Article 6)

"All are equal before the law."   (Article 7)

"Everyone has the right to an effective remedy by the competent national tribunals for acts violating the fundamental rights granted him by the constitution or by law."

(Article 8)

"No one shall be subjected to arbitrary arrest, detention or exile."   (Article 9)

"Everyone is entitled in full equality to a fair and public hearing by an independent and impartial tribunal, in the determination of his rights and obligations and of any criminal charge against him."   (Article 10)

"Everyone ... has the right to be presumed innocent until proved guilty according to law in a public trial."   (Article 11)

"No one shall be subjected to arbitrary interference with his privacy, family, home or correspondence, nor to attacks upon his honour and reputation."   (Article 12)

"Everyone has the right to freedom of movement and residence within the borders of each state."   (Article 13.1)

"Everyone has the right to leave any country, including his own, and to return to his country."   (Article 13.2)

"Everyone has the right to seek … asylum from persecution." (Article 14)

"Everyone has the right to a nationality." (Article 15)

"Men and women of full age, without any limitation due to race, nationality or religion, have the right to marry and to found a family … [and to] equal rights as to marriage, during marriage and at its dissolution." (Article 16.1)

"Marriage shall be entered into only with the free and full consent of the intending spouses." (Article 16.2)

"Everyone has the right to own property." (Article 17.1)

"No one shall be arbitrarily deprived of his property." (Article 17.2)

"Everyone has the right to freedom of thought, conscience and religion." (Article 18)

"Everyone has the right to freedom of opinion and expression." (Article 19)

"Everyone has the right to freedom of peaceful assembly and association." (Article 20)

"Everyone has the right to take part in the government of his country, directly or through freely chosen representatives." (Article 21.1)

"Everyone has the right of equal access to public services." (Article 21.2)

"The will of the people shall be the basis of the authority of government." (Article 21.3)

"Everyone … has the right to social security and is entitled to realization, through national effort and international co-operation and in accordance with the organization and resources of each State, of the economic, social and cultural rights indispensable for his dignity and the free development of his personality." (Article 22)

"Everyone has the right to work, to free choice of employment, to just and favourable conditions of work and to protection against unemployment." (Article 23.1)

"Everyone … has the right to equal pay for equal work." (Article 23.2)

"Everyone … has the right to just and favourable remuneration." (Article 23.3)

"Everyone has the right to form and to join trade unions." (Article 23.4)

"Everyone has the right to rest and leisure, including reasonable limitation of working hours and periodic holidays with pay." (Article 24)

"Everyone has the right to a standard of living adequate for the health and well-being of himself and of his family, including food, clothing, housing and medical care and necessary social services, and the right to security in the event of unemployment, sickness, disability, widowhood, old age or other lack of livelihood in circumstances beyond his control." (Article 25.1)

"Motherhood and childhood are entitled to special care and assistance." (Article 25.2)

"Everyone has the right to education." (Article 26)

"Everyone has the right freely to participate in the cultural life of the community." (Article 27.1)

"Everyone has the right to the protection of the moral and material interests resulting from any scientific, literary or artistic production of which he is the author." (Article 27.2)

"Everyone is entitled to a social and international order in which the rights and freedoms set forth in this Declaration can be fully realized." (Article 28)

"Everyone has duties to the community in which alone the free and full development of his personality is possible." (Article 29.1)

"In the exercise of his rights and freedoms, everyone shall be subject only to such limitations as are determined by law solely for the purpose of securing due recognition and respect for the rights and freedoms of others and of meeting the just requirements of morality, public order and the general welfare in a democratic society." (Article 29.2)

"These rights and freedoms may in no case be exercised contrary to the purposes and principles of the United Nations." (Article 29.3)

"Nothing in this Declaration may be interpreted as implying for any State, group or person any right to engage in any activity or to perform any act aimed at the destruction of any of the rights and freedoms set forth herein." (Article 30)

(See United Nations 1948 for the full declaration.)

government and the right to legal justice and a fair hearing. Social, cultural and economic rights include those to education, employment, formation of families, health and social welfare. The current UDHR emphasizes the first class of civil and political rights over the second group of social, cultural and economic rights. Thus it prioritizes civil and political rights. One reason for this is that political and civil rights are thought to *generate* cultural and economic rights. In other words, cultural and economic rights can come about only if basic political and civil rights are first in place. To illustrate this thought, a defender of this prioritization could ask, rhetorically, how the cultural right to education, or the "right to rest and leisure, including reasonable limitation of working hours and periodic holidays with pay" (Article 24), could be upheld without first having the political and civil rights "to life, liberty and security of person" (Article 3) and those prohibiting slavery or servitude (Article 4). This said, as we shall see in later chapters, others argue the opposite: that civil and political rights are meaningful only if one has sufficient economic subsistence rights to exercise first generation rights.

Box 5.2 Human-rights declarations, conventions and covenants

- Convention on the Prevention and Punishment of the Crime of Genocide (1948)
- European Convention for the Protection of Human Rights and Fundamental Freedoms (1950)
- International Convention on the Elimination of all Forms of Racial Discrimination (1965)
- International Covenant on Civil and Political Rights (1966)
- International Covenant on Economic, Social and Cultural Rights (1966)
- American Convention on Human Rights (1969)
- International Convention on Elimination of Discrimination Against Women (1979)
- African Charter on Human and People's Rights (1981)
- Convention against Torture and Other Cruel, Inhuman or Degrading Treatment or Punishment (1984)
- Convention on the Rights of the Child (1984)
- Declaration of Principles of Indigenous Rights (1989)
- Vienna Declaration and Action Programme (1993)

Since the UDHR there have been numerous further declarations, such as those found in the International Covenant on Economic, Social and Cultural Rights, as well as declarations that are concerned with particular groups (such as women and children) and declarations to prevent specific breaches (such as genocide or discrimination). The main declarations of this sort are listed in Box 5.2.

CASE STUDY 5.1 Torture in theory and practice

Analysing the case study of torture is different from the case studies we have looked at in the previous two chapters: FGC and the buying of body parts. In both these cases there are potential advantages for the individual involved. For instance, there are arguably cultural and identity benefits for girls who undergo FGC, and those in favour of the sale of body parts argue that to permit sale is to respect the autonomy of individuals and allow them to decide what will produce the best outcome in their situations. In the case of torture there is no conceivable and realistic benefit for the tortured. The justification is solely on the grounds that it will benefit others.

If rights protect human beings then the prohibition on torture, from a human-rights perspective, at least at first glance, is incontrovertible. Torture contravenes human dignity and human rights and is always impermissible. The UDHR and the widely ratified UN Convention against Torture and Other Cruel, Inhuman or Degrading Treatment or Punishment that followed suggest that torture is a practice that international human-rights law completely outlaws.

We have so far mentioned that some of these conventions and declarations do not have full legal status, but that they have been "ratified" by nations. In this context, "ratification" means the nation itself actually implements the declaration or convention. Thus the country must use its own laws and governance mechanisms to establish the rights. So a country can "sign up" to a covenant without ratifying it in its own laws and procedures. For example, 174 nations have signed the International Covenant on Civil and Political Rights, but eight of them, including China, Laos and Pakistan, have not ratified it. Governments also attach conditions to ratification, which in some cases attracts criticism on the grounds that they compromise or undermine the agreement in practice. For example, the US Senate ratified the covenant but with several reservations, an important effect of which is that, in the words of a Senate Executive Report, "the Covenant will not create a private cause of action in US Courts". Thus the Senate agreed to the covenant and then ratified it, but, importantly, in a way that prevents legal process being brought against the government if it transgress the rights it specifies. Critics claim that this makes the ratification no more than lip service, and renders the covenant all but useless as a potential legal instrument for those who might need it most.

THE HISTORY OF RIGHTS

The contemporary conception of human rights is one that emerged in the aftermath of the Second World War and it is from this point that the current predominance of

However, as the case study so clearly shows, torture continues to be practised and not just by "rogue states" or those outside the law (such as terrorists, bandits and warlords) but by legitimate states, such as the US and UK, who claim to be defenders of human rights. How can we understand this mismatch between the recognition that torture continues to happen and is at least tolerated with the absolute prohibition of the convention? If outlawed practices continue even when there are international human-rights laws in place, then what use are such laws? As Oona Hathaway (2004) claims, there does not seem to be a correlation between ratifying the convention and a reduction of torture.

Explanations for the mismatch between theory and practice are various and we shall explore them as we go through the chapter. Possible explanations include: the fact that rights do not actually exist so are only upheld when it is in a country's best interests; that rights are only one set of values among others and do not always take priority; or that there are disagreements about how rights are defined and what is prohibited by the convention against torture.

human rights can be traced. The current dominant version of human rights emerged from previous understandings of rights. The idea can be traced to the beginnings of Western philosophy, with rights drawn from Aristotle's conception of natural law and the rights of citizens, and from the commitment of the Stoic philosophers to a universal moral or natural law (in Chapter 4 we saw that it was the Stoics who first used the term "cosmopolitan", meaning "citizen of the world"). This idea of natural law continued through the transition to Christianity and features strongly in medieval Christianity, particularly in the tradition of natural law found in the work of Thomas Aquinas (c.1225–74), who built on Aristotle, a tradition subsequently developed by many thinkers including Hugo Grotius and, especially, John Locke. The basic idea behind natural law is that laws do not depend on any particular historical situation or sociopolitical arrangements: in other words, they do not depend in any way on how people happen to be at a given time. Rather, natural laws stand above any particular culture and are independent of such considerations. They are therefore always binding. They are set either by God (in Aquinas's version) or by the nature of human beings: human beings are just "like this" (as in Aristotle's version which, as we saw in Chapter 3, starts ethical enquiry with the question "What is the good life?", this view has also been developed by some contemporary virtue theorists, such as Philippa Foot and Rosalind Hursthouse). If we think back to the distinction we made in Chapter 3 between universalism and relativism, natural-law theory can thus be seen as a kind of universalism writ large: it applies to all human beings regardless of whatever worldly situation they find themselves in. Gradually in the Enlightenment, rights thinking began to gain prominence in ethical and political thinking over natural-law thinking. A key Enlightenment thinker who promoted rights was Kant (whose theory we discussed in Chapter 3).

John Locke and natural rights

John Locke declared that there are certain "natural rights". In his influential work *Second Treatise of Government* (1689) he famously argued that we are bound by moral rights to preserve "the life, liberty, health, limb and goods" of others. In other words, there are rights to life, to freedom and to own property. It is unjust to fail to respect these rights in others and, for Locke, it is also unjust to fail to respect these rights in ourselves (e.g. by committing suicide). For Locke these are "natural" rights in that they are rights that arise simply from human nature, because human beings are the sort of beings they are.

Locke was explicitly building on the natural-law tradition of Christian thinking (originally from the Stoic philosophers). Accordingly, he not only asserted the existence of these rights but also considered the role of government in supporting and establishing such rights: as we have already noted, asserting rights without a theory that ascribes a corresponding duty to another person or institution is ineffectual. Locke argued that the role of government was to protect and enforce the rights we possess in the "state of nature" by establishing and enforcing the rule of law. It is worth noting that Locke's understanding of the state of nature is completely different from that of Hobbes, discussed in the previous chapter. For Locke, human beings are bound by nature to respect certain rights – natural rights – and therefore morality is a natural feature of human beings. For Hobbes, nothing is binding in the state of nature, human beings have no intrinsic value and morality is simply convention.

For Locke, then, natural rights always exist: they are integral to human being. However, he suggests that in the state of nature, before formal institutions and government, these rights are vulnerable to those who do not observe the rules of justice and respect rights. Property is particularly unsafe and insecure in the state of nature. In order to secure rights, people are willing to leave the state of nature and to join with others in society in order to mutually protect the natural rights of life, liberty and property. Here the argument is similar to Hobbes's argument: it is mutually beneficial for individuals to come together in social structures and communities.

Rights to life and liberty

In many ways this Lockean conception of rights forms the background for the contemporary conception of human rights and we can trace the emphasis on life and liberty in the UDHR and subsequent conventions. In political terms, the ideas of natural rights became most obviously influential in the US and in France. In the US the American Declaration of Independence speaks of "unalienable rights", first to "life", and then to "liberty and the pursuit of happiness" (National Archives n.d.; see Box 5.3).

The unalienable rights and self-evident truths of the American Declaration of Independence (Box 5.3) sound very similar to Locke's version of natural rights. Likewise, very similar ideas were found in the French Revolution and the founding document of the Republic, the Declaration of the Rights of Man and of the Citizen (National Constituent Assembly 1789; see Box 5.4).

Box 5.3 Extract from the American Declaration of Independence

"We hold these truths to be self-evident, that all men are created equal, that they are endowed by their Creator with certain unalienable Rights, that among these are Life, Liberty and the pursuit of Happiness. That to secure these rights, Governments are instituted among Men, deriving their just powers from the consent of the governed." (National Archives n.d.)

> **Box 5.4 Extracts from the Declaration of the Rights of Man and of the Citizen**
>
> "Men are born and remain free and equal in rights." (Article I)
>
> "All the citizens, being equal in the eyes of the law, are equally admissible to all public dignities, places, and employments, according to their capacity and without distinction other than that of their virtues and of their talents." (Article VI)

Both the American Declaration of Independence and the Declaration of the Rights of Man and of the Citizen stress the importance of freedom and of equality: not surprisingly, as both are replacing monarchies and overtly rejecting previous feudal hierarchies in favour of egalitarian ideals of social relationships. Yet, the limits of equality presented in these documents can be questioned: for example, neither considered that women were entitled to be bearers of such rights. Furthermore, both focus on the rights of the citizen and the role of the state: thus the American Declaration of Independence insists that governments are established to secure these rights for citizens (and if they fail to do this the government can be replaced). So while declaring that "all men are created equal", the declaration is really only concerned with male citizens and the protection of rights is fundamentally tied to the protections of the state. This tension between the universal claims of rights and the reliance on states to enforce the protections of rights remains a key tension in the contemporary debate about human rights (something we shall explore further in Chapter 6).

In addition to rights declarations of specific countries, such as those of America and France, there were also a number of particular conventions aimed at international cohesion on particular issues, including, for example, conventions on slavery (Brussels Conference Act 1890; Slavery Convention [1926]) and on the conduct of war (Hague Conventions [1899, 1907]; Geneva Conventions [1949]). Such conventions aimed to create an international standard in these areas and can be seen as the beginnings of the establishment of global norms and governance mechanisms. Yet, like the American and French declarations, and the eventual UDHR, it is states that must uphold and enforce such rights and good practices.

TYPES OF RIGHT

We have already mentioned "generations" of human rights, which describe three kinds of human institutions and interactions (civil and political; economic and social; and those of whole "peoples") that "generate" rights. The history of rights shows also that there are different kinds of right: rights that function in different ways in different circumstances and which address different moral concerns. What follows is a survey of some of these key distinctions.

Positive and negative rights

A basic distinction that is often made when discussing rights is between "negative" and "positive" rights. A negative right is one that requires only that other people do nothing to violate that right. To caricature the situation, they are rights to be left alone and to exercise your rights in peace. So if I have a negative right not to be physically attacked, this requires only that everyone else refrain from attacking me. By contrast, positive rights are those that require other people to act: actually to do something. If I have a positive right to physical *protection* from attack, this requires that someone else – for example the police force – is thereby required to do what is necessary to provide that protection. Thus positive rights make positive demands on others whereas negative rights do not make demands that anyone *do* anything.

Intrinsic and instrumental rights

Where the negative–positive distinction is between what rights do, a further distinction is found in the justification of rights: in other words, the way in which we value them and the reasons we have for doing so. One view, adopted by Thomas Nagel, is that rights are "intrinsic". On this view, the value of rights is simply that they recognize and protect the *intrinsic* value of people: a value that people *just have* and that we must respect, period. Recall Kant's deontology, discussed in Chapter 3, which enjoins us always to treat people as "ends in themselves". Nagel follows Kant here by denying that rights are to be respected because of some benefit or good they bring about for persons or communities. Rather, they are rights in the first place *because* they respect the intrinsic value of individual persons.

An alternative view, defended by Allen Buchanan among others, is that rights are "instrumental". On the instrumental view, rights are valuable because of the conditions brought about as a consequence of these rights being upheld. Thus this view adopts a form of consequentialism, and has also been characterized as "teleological" ("goal-led"; from the Greek *telos*, meaning purpose or end). In contrast to the intrinsic view, what matters about rights on this account is that they provide and allow a good or minimal standard of life for people they affect. So on Buchanan's view, rights are things that are put in place to protect people's interests and enable them to flourish. Thus they are like instruments that bring about something we are *aiming* at; namely, a good, decent and flourishing life.

Within these basic categories, rights are also commonly subdivided into claim-rights, liberty-rights, powers and immunities. This "classic" fourfold analysis of rights was first proposed by Wesley Hohfeld (1919), but is now a fairly standard account. Peter Jones (1994) sets them out in the following way:

1. Claim rights: Claim rights are simply that: a claim that one person has on another. For one person to have a claim-right someone else must have a duty. So, "suppose A and B enter into a contract in which B undertakes to pay A a sum of money. A then has a right to that money and B has a reciprocal duty to pay A that sum."
2. Liberty rights: Liberty rights are rights to freedom, to dress, to speech, religion and so on. They are really the "right" not to be hindered in doing something that one should be able "freely" to do. Therefore the duties of others are non-interference.
3. Powers: Powers are rights to actions that one is "empowered" to do. For example, "I have the right to vote in that I am legally 'empowered' to cast a vote in an election; someone who is not enfranchised is not so empowered."
4. Immunities: Immunities are rights not to be subject to the "powers" of others. Simply put, they make you "immune".

Basic rights

These distinctions give some understanding of rights and how they function, but who or what gets which rights and why? One answer to how rights should be implemented and given priority is to distinguish between "basic rights" and other rights. This line of argument suggests that there is a certain minimum level of basic rights that must be enforced and which is necessary for all other rights to be exercised. This approach was championed by Henry Shue, in *Basic Rights* (1980). He argues that there are some rights – basic rights – that should take priority over other rights.

Rights are defined by Shue (1980) as "the rational basis for a justified demand". In other words, a right is essentially a demand that you can make of others and expect to be met. For a person to have a right it needs to be socially guaranteed and therefore there must be good reasons to justify such rights and to account for why the demands of the rights-holder should be met. Rights, then, are claims that allow one to make demands that are "socially guaranteed". The arrangements that socially guarantee a right may be legal, but they may also be customs and other social practices.

Minimal basic rights provide a minimal protection for the most vulnerable in order to ensure survival. Essentially, they are about meeting basis needs, such as to food and shelter, to ensure that all human beings are accorded a minimal standard

> **Box 5.5 Shue's basic rights**
>
> Shue's basic rights:
>
> - provide minimal protection against "utter helplessness";
> - protect the defenceless against devastating threats;
> - function as a restraint against otherwise overwhelming economic and political forces;
> - guarantee to meet some basic needs;
> - provide a minimal standard no one should be permitted to fall below.

of respect. Minimal basic rights set a level below which no one should be permitted to fall. Shue outlines a number of conditions of basic rights, outlined in Box 5.5.

Essentially these are "rights of desperation" and fit particularly well into discourse about what should be provided in emergency situations and to those living in exceptionally poor countries. A life that does not have these basic rights is unacceptable for Shue; moreover, he argues that all other rights are dependent on the enjoyment of these basic rights. So basic rights are a prerequisite for exercising all other rights. Given this, Shue argues that basic rights should take priority over all other rights. The basic rights that should take highest priority, for Shue, are security rights, subsistence rights and liberty rights.

For Shue, these rights are the minimum necessary for an acceptable level of existence. Without basic rights in these areas it is impossible to imagine an acceptable life. You need to be protected from the threat of assault, torture, rape and murder if you are going to be able to function at all. For Shue, it is impossible to function, even minimally, if you are not free from violence. In addition, minimum rights to security are necessary to exercise other rights. For example, a right to freedom of religion or to found a family is not much use if you will be beaten or murdered if you attempt to exercise those rights. Thus security is a basic right not simply because it is valuable in itself, but because no other right can be enjoyed if physical security is not protected. Without physical security all other rights are meaningless.

Similar reasoning is applied to minimal subsistence rights: rights to unpolluted air and water as well as adequate food, clothing, shelter and some basic health care. Shue argues that, like security rights, subsistence rights are basic rights because they too are necessary for the exercise of all other rights. Subsistence rights ensure that people have the essentials to reach a minimum level of health and activity. He argues that if you lack basic-level subsistence then you are vulnerable and suffer just as profoundly as if your security rights are violated. Indeed, you may be even more vulnerable, because the person lacking subsistence will be too weak to fight back if their security rights are threatened. Therefore subsistence rights, for Shue, are also basic rights.

The third basic right, for Shue, is the more standard right to liberty. Essentially this is a right to be able to pursue reasonable projects that do not harm others. Again this is a basic right because, if you do not have basic liberty, you cannot enjoy other rights.

For Shue, all these basic rights – security, subsistence and liberty – are minimal, and a life that falls below the minimal level indicated by these rights will be morally unacceptable. Although, for Shue, these rights are minimal, many critics would argue that in fact these rights are very demanding. In particular, they do not respect the standard forms of reasoning we have discussed above: that civil and political rights take priority over social and economic rights and that negative rights take priority over positive rights. Shue explicitly includes in his list of basic rights not only the civil and political rights of liberty and security, but also the social and economic right of subsistence.

The usual liberal argument is that security rights and liberty rights are negative rights, requiring only that people refrain from attacking or murdering others: thus these are usually seen as relatively easy to grant. In contrast, a right to subsistence is usually regarded as a positive right that requires others to act to meet subsistence needs: something seen as more demanding on the liberal model.

Shue rejects this neat divide between positive and negative rights. He denies the liberal claim that the negative rights of liberty and security are easy to grant and should take priority. He argues that a right to physical security requires far more than the description of negative rights suggests. In fact, he claims that ensuring that security and liberty rights can be exercised requires resources and entails positive duties whereas the negative-rights model suggests that all that is required is that one refrain from violating another's security rights. For Shue, this is not sufficient to maintain a minimum security right, because such rights also need protecting. He argues that substantive positive action is required to do this, for instance, putting in place a law-enforcement system and all that this entails. Likewise liberty rights also

---

CASE STUDY 5.2 Basic rights and torture

Shue's discussion of basic rights shows that there is much debate within the rights framework about how rights are to be understood and who has a duty to protect rights and to re-establish rights that have been violated. It is these differences between rights theorists that are central not just to the theoretical debate, but to what happens in practice. For instance, if you adopt Shue's understanding of a security right you are accepting far greater responsibilities than if you adopt the usual liberal understanding of security as a purely negative right to be left alone.

require positive action actively to protect liberty; again, infrastructure and governance mechanisms are required.

Conversely Shue argues that subsistence rights are not neatly classified as positive rights. Sometimes, for example, as in a famine, subsistence rights do require positive actions from others, such as the delivery of food aid. However, at other times subsistence rights will take the apparently negative form of having the right to the opportunity to support oneself. Therefore, he argues, subsistence rights might not in fact require more onerous actions than those required by security and liberty rights. All rights require structural and institutional support and therefore all make positive as well as negative demands. Shue argues that subsistence, security and basic liberty rights all have the same structure and place similar demands and entail similar correlative duties. He suggests that basic rights have three duties that correlate to them; duties to avoid, protect and aid (Box 5.6). This is true just as much for rights to security as it is for rights of subsistence.

Box 5.6 Shue's duties

- Duties to *avoid* depriving.
- Duties to *protect* from deprivation.
- Duties to *aid* the deprived.

All three duties – to avoid depriving, to protect from deprivation and to aid the deprived – apply to all basic rights. The duty to avoid depriving is the duty not to eliminate a person's security or their only available means of subsistence; the duty to protect is a positive duty to protect against the deprivation of security and subsistence; and the duty to aid is a positive duty to those who are unable to provide their own security or their own subsistence.

We can see this definitional difference working in practice if we return to the case study of torture. What is understood by the right to be protected from torture is fundamental to what is deemed to be permitted. If one adopts Shue's reasoning, torture in any of the forms listed in the case study would be prohibited because it would certainly violate basic rights and prevent the exercise of other rights. By contrast, the US approaches the right very differently. Notably, while the US has outlawed torture, anything that is nearly torture is deemed permissible. For example, George W. Bush infamously stated that he did not believe that waterboarding – which simulates the experience of drowning – was a form of torture. Accordingly, the US has ratified the convention but it has not used the UN's definition; rather, it has adopted a "state-protective" definition of torture instead (see Box 5.7).

Rights as trumps

In considering the question of what kinds of right are being evoked in human-rights talk, one thing that becomes clear is the kind of priority we assign to rights. Priority is important both with regard to the status of rights compared with other kinds of values and when considering how different rights are prioritized against each other. For instance, as we saw above, a standard way of prioritizing rights is to regard negative rights as taking priority over positive rights. Another common view we have already mentioned in this chapter – although criticized, as we shall see later, as a Western view – is to assert the priority of civil and political rights over social and economic rights. Shue offers an alternative hierarchy of rights, prioritizes basic rights over other rights and argues that these basic rights should always be protected.

Whichever *theory* of rights you endorse, it seems true to say that you will ascribe a special status to some rights. For instance, even when rights are discussed informally, in statements such as "You have no right to speak to me like that", you are asserting not merely that a wrongdoing has been committed, but that it is a wrongdoing that cannot be justified by appeal to some other considerations. This seems true when we consider universal human rights. When people cite an action as violating a human right, they mean to ascribe some special force to the claim; namely, that there has been a violation of something valuable to all humans, and that this is a fundamental violation of a right that we think inviolable – full stop, no balancing or trading off with other benefits or reasons.

Ronald Dworkin has described this quality of rights as their ability to "trump" other considerations, such as the wider social or economic benefits of a society. The ascription of a right, then, in Dworkin's terms, "trumps" other reasons there may be for other courses of action. In relation, and additionally to the supposedly *universal* quality of human rights discussed so far in this chapter, this illustrates further the supposed "inalienability" of human rights: the idea that these rights cannot simply be ignored in the face of other concerns or sacrificed to other ends or purposes, whatever the benefits or consequences of them might be.

CASE STUDY 5.3 Rights as trumps and torture

Dworkin's suggestion that rights are trumps is one that activists frequently adopt in order to draw attention to human-rights abuses and also to attempt to get legal and civic protections against human-rights violations. However, the status of rights as trumps assumes that rights can never be violated no matter what the consequences might be. If we return to our case study of torture we can see that it is at least questionable that rights are, or should be, always regarded in this way. For instance, there are many instances where it

---

Box 5.7 US definition of torture

In order to constitute torture, an act must be *specifically intended* to inflict *severe* physical or mental pain or suffering; and that mental pain or suffering refers to *prolonged* mental harm caused by or resulting from:

- the intentional infliction or threatened infliction of *severe* physical pain or suffering;
- the administration or application, or threatened administration or application, of mind-altering substances or other procedures calculated to disrupt *profoundly* the senses of the personality;
- the threat of *imminent* death; or
- the threat that another person will *imminently* be subjected to death, *severe* physical pain or suffering, or the administration or application of mind-altering substances or other procedures calculated to *disrupt profoundly* the senses of personality (USCIS 2010).

Key here are the words *severe*, *profound* and *imminent* and how these are interpreted. Presumably the torture techniques documented in the case study are not severe enough to be considered torture using this definition, although clearly they do fit under the usual definition of "cruel, inhuman or degrading". Therefore, key to enforcing human rights is not just achieving a global agreement to the right in general but getting a global agreement to the details. The US interpretation of what constitutes torture goes against not only the view of theorists such as Shue, but also more usual definitions in international law and practice. For example, usual definitions given substance by international tribunals and judgments would regard as torture beatings that might not be severe enough to break bones or be likely to result in imminent death but do cause intense pain. Other techniques such as the use of stress positions, threats of rape and other mutilations would also normally be considered torture.

---

can be argued that individuals' human rights are justifiably violated in order to serve some greater good. This has become a particularly powerful argument in the post-9/11 era and often the debate has been presented as one of protecting security versus protecting civil liberties and human rights. This reasoning has been used to justify torture in at least some circumstances, or at least to deem it as the "lesser evil" – the least bad option. The classic case in which torture has been said to be justified or permitted is the "ticking bomb", as set out by Michael Walzer (1973) (see Box 5.8).

In *Taking Rights Seriously* (1977), Dworkin sets out his defence of rights in opposition to what he sees as the prevailing theory of law in Anglo-American political and moral theory. On Dworkin's view the prevailing theory has two elements, the first of which is legal positivism. This, roughly, is the idea that what any laws or rules say is only ever legitimate by virtue of being laid down by an institution. So, for example, any statement of law that says "it is forbidden to torture" makes sense only when understood as "it has been ruled by [a court, a legislature, the monarchy, or whatever] that torture is forbidden", and thus any talk of its being prohibited by something like a "natural law" is meaningless. According to Dworkin, the second element of the prevailing or "ruling theory" is that institutions should make laws that maximize social welfare. Thus Dworkin claims that the dominant view favours a utilitarian perspective regarding the aims and function of the legal system. Unsurprisingly, Dworkin sees this view as owing much to Bentham's philosophy.

Dworkin's main argument against this "ruling theory" is one that is based on the view that rights are trumps. For Dworkin, rights are understood as things to which individuals have recourse to prevent the goals of a community or society as a whole imposing on, or taking something from, an individual. To use the torture example, suppose it could somehow be shown that torturing an individual really would serve society well as a whole (perhaps by not only extracting vital life-saving information from a potential mass killer but also calming the public and averting widespread civil unrest, say). On a Dworkin-type view of individual rights (where the right of the individual can, and must, trump public and common interests), that individual must be protected by rights.

In terms of implementing human rights, Dworkin's legal theory, opposing legal positivism, argues that legislators and judges can and should sometimes adjudicate "hard cases" – ones where either the nature of the case or the legal procedure is not clear cut – according to principles based on the rights of those involved, rights that are not necessarily specified by laws but are fundamental rights: trumps. Thus one could take Dworkin's view and apply it to the international arena. Human rights might be neither "natural" nor decreed by convention, but still we might need them to protect individuals. And a proponent of this view might add that only a theory of *individual* rights can do this.

In the case of the ticking bomb (Box 5.8), how do you respond? Is it acceptable to use torture? If the suspect does not speak, many innocent people will be killed; but if torture is used, a gross violation of human rights will have occurred. In this case many are willing to say that, although undesirable, torture is acceptable here: the "least worst" option. Notoriously, Alan Dershowitz (2002) has argued that a method for sanctioning torture in just these circumstances should be devised, and he has suggested "torture warrants" as a means of regulating instances of torture. Dershowitz claims that the current situation is hypocritical, because torture is currently practised but not legal. He argues that he is normatively opposed to torture but

---

Box 5.8 The ticking bomb

A suspected terrorist is held by the security forces. The terrorist has information about a planted bomb or imminent biological, chemical or other serious threat. Hundreds of innocent civilians will die if the suspected terrorist does not "break" and give the interrogators the information they need to halt the attack. The terrorist has refused to give any information despite the best efforts of the interrogators using normal tactics.

---

it happens currently, and "it would certainly be employed if we ever experienced an imminent threat of mass casualty biological, chemical, or nuclear terrorism". Given this, he argues, it is better to recognize and legalize the practice in certain extreme instances, and legally sanction torture with a warrant, rather than allow it to continue, known about but ignored. Indeed, he suggests that such legislation would actually reduce the practice of torture, because only in these instances would it be permitted, in contrast to the current situation, in which, while legally disallowed in practice, the use of torture is increasing.

Others continue to deny that torture is ever acceptable, some on the grounds that it simply does not work and others on the grounds that it is an unacceptable violation of rights. In *Torture and the Ticking Bomb* (2007), Bob Brecher denies the acceptability of torture on both counts, arguing that the utilitarian defence of its effectiveness fails, and that the practice is anyway impermissible on human rights grounds. He thus rejects the permissibility of torture in all cases. Where Dershowitz can be seen as proposing the containment and monitoring of torture as a regrettable practice that will inevitably continue (a bit like arguments for "decriminalization" of some illegal drugs), Brecher sees torture as something that should not be permitted and, moreover, does not work, thus failing even on the utilitarian grounds that Dershowitz himself proposes.

Even if you reject the use of torture it does not necessarily mean that you must do so by endorsing Dworkin's line that rights are "trumps" in all cases. For instance, even if you think human rights are such that torture is never permitted you might think that there are other scenarios where it would be justified for individual rights to be sacrificed in order to attain other public goods, for example in a public health scare. Is it acceptable to weight public health over individual rights in instances of pandemic illnesses, and to put people in isolation, even if this means effective imprisonment of those who carry the disease? This would be a severe violation of their liberty rights, but perhaps one that you think justified.

CRITIQUES OF THE RIGHTS FRAMEWORK

Our discussion so far has shown that human rights have made some advances in terms of becoming an effective form of global ethics. In particular they have some global acceptance and recognition and they are embedded in international local and regional laws, making them more practicable than many other possible global ethics. However, our discussion has also shown that there are many problems in establishing and implementing human rights. Some of these difficulties are theoretical; what should count as a human right; how can rights be prioritized; and are there different orders of human rights that merit different levels of respect? Other difficulties are practical: if a human right is established then who is responsible for meeting that right; what are the duties of states; and how can the non-implementation and enforcement of rights be addressed? Difficult though these problems are, all of these concerns come from within the rights framework. They are internal criticisms regarding the scope and implementation of rights rather than primary criticisms that question the validity of the rights framework in general. In the rest of this chapter we shall look at some more basic criticisms of the rights framework as a whole, beginning with an objection from classical utilitarianism.

Bentham's rejection of rights

The most basic criticism of human rights concerns whether there are such things as "natural" rights that exist prior to and independently of social and political constructs: societies and states. These criticisms are as long-standing as the arguments for rights themselves. Perhaps most famously, Jeremy Bentham (whom we met in Chapter 3 as the father of utilitarianism) denounced the rights enshrined in the French Declaration of the Rights of Man and of the Citizen as "nonsense on stilts". Bentham claimed that while we might reasonably want the conditions that rights supposedly prescribe – protection from harm and the provision of goods, for example – it is "nonsense" then to move to the claim that there *are* such rights: that such rights actually exist. In his words, "a reason for wishing that a certain right were established, is not that right; want is not supply; hunger is not bread" (2011b: Preliminary Observations, Article II). For him, rights are only and always created and implemented by people and the idea of "natural rights" is "rhetorical nonsense – nonsense upon stilts".

Certainly in a utilitarian theory of ethics such as Bentham's, some kinds of "prescriptible" rights *may* be useful, but they hold no special, privileged place in moral theory or practice; certain rights should be formulated and respected and upheld if they produce the greater happiness for the greatest number, but not if they do not. Many contemporary utilitarians argue in favour of always upholding human rights on these grounds; indeed, this is why Dershowitz's argument fails even on utilitarian grounds. But, establishing just what rights do and do not produce is a matter of social experimentation – working out what produces the best consequences and more human well-being – and not simply a matter of stating that there are rights and expecting them suddenly to be met.

Marx's rejection of rights

A second important critic of the emergence of rights was Karl Marx. Like Bentham, he regarded the supposedly natural basis of rights as nonsense, and saw them as constructions that served the ideology of the bourgeoisie. Marx denied that rights protected equality and thought that, in fact, they promoted inequality, because they protected the rights of the bourgeoisie over those of the working class. Marx was particularly critical of rights that he thought promoted individual egoism and competition in capitalist societies, such as property rights. As we saw in the earlier discussion, rights to property and ownership – key capitalist rights – are primary in early rights theories, such as Locke's.

Many Marxists have argued that Marx was not anti-rights in general, but was against these types of rights and the ways they were constructed, exercised and protected. Marx is not necessarily critical of the idea of people *having* certain rights and entitlements *per se*, but of a particular liberal conception of rights that he sees as the dominant one. That is, Marx was criticizing the concept of rights that emerged from the conditions of liberal bourgeois society. He does think that people are entitled to certain things and should be free from certain constraints. For instance, especially in his earlier writings such as *The German Ideology* (with Friedrich Engels; 1845–46), Marx was greatly concerned with the way in which workers under capitalism were prevented from realizing their nature as "species beings", hence prevented from flourishing as humans should in a way that arguably has close parallels with Aristotle's idea of *eudaimonia* (see Chapter 3).

In Marx's key critique of liberal rights, "On the Jewish Question" (1844), he argued that the furtherance of political rights – rights to practise religion or to own property – protect only certain *political* freedoms. Moreover, these rights that are universally

---

Box 5.9 Rights according to Bentham and Marx

According to these critics rights are:

- nonsense!
- absolute rubbish!
- fictitious!
- bourgeois!

ascribed to everybody ("the rights of man") are actually political constructs of a certain sort; rights of the bourgeois ideology that have become mythically imbued with the status of "natural" and pre-societal truths about human beings *per se*. For Marx, such *political* rights are obstacles to achieving human freedom, by marking off the political sphere from that of "civil society". So, for example, the right to religious worship legally ensures that no particular religion is favoured or discriminated against, and property rights protect people's use and ownership of possessions. But this leaves intact precisely the religious practices and the institutions of property themselves within civil society, which Marx saw as impediments to full *human* emancipation. For Marx, then, the ascription of supposedly universal and individual liberal rights moves institutions such as private property and religion into a personal and supposedly non-political sphere.

Perhaps we can illustrate Marx's thinking here with an actual recent example used earlier in this chapter: the 2009 judgment by the ECHR prohibiting the previously mandatory display of the crucifix in Italian classrooms. On a view like Marx's, such a measure could be construed as implementing a political right that, through political legislation, removes religiosity from schools. In doing so, however, it does not remove religion or any of its institutionalized practices (including the oppressive and inequitable ones) from human lives at all. Rather, it helps confine religion and its practices to the sphere of civil society, where oppression continues just as strongly as, or perhaps more strongly than, if it were endorsed by the political state.

Feminist critique of human rights

Feminist theorists, including Gould, Jaggar and Sarah Ruddick, have launched substantial criticisms of the liberal construction of rights and the model of the person that underlies that framework. In particular, and like the Marxist critique in some ways, feminists are critical of the lack of awareness of social context in the rights model and the dangers of imposing a particular liberal Western (and feminists would add "male") construction of rights. The rights model is concerned primarily with individual rights and it does not easily take account of context and relationships. Feminists critique this as a male model that fails to give due attention to the embedded, historical and relational aspects of human beings. Accordingly, feminist thinkers have sought to amend this model of person and rights in order to supplement the liberal model. Such thinkers believe that rights should be reframed, revised or supplemented to protect communal and relational goods as well as individual goods. This is an issue we shall return to in Chapter 11. For now, it is important to note the influence of the feminist critique and its similarities to socialist critiques as well as the non-Western critique we shall consider next.

The non-Western critique of human rights

Like the Marxist and feminist critiques, the non-Western critique does not necessarily deny the theory of human rights itself (or reject rights in all forms). Rather, it claims that what have *actually* become known as "universal" human rights have developed not from a universal human standpoint but from a particular Western one. This is a similar concern to that of Marx: a concern about the types of rights that are assumed; a liberal and arguably Western set of rights. However, some non-Western critics do argue that any rights are inappropriate for non-Western cultures and that other value frameworks (such as those of virtues or duties) make more sense.

The criticism that human rights are not global but are Western impositions or forms of "moral neocolonialism" is one that the global ethicist needs to address if human rights are to play a part in any framework of global ethics. The claim is one that originated in the Asian values movement – associated originally with Malaysia and Singapore – and that has spread across Asia and Africa. Elements of this critique have been taken up everywhere outside the West. The roots of this critique are generally traced to Lee Kuan Yew, former Prime Minister of Singapore, who, along with Mahathir Mohamad, former Prime Minister of Malaysia, are regarded as the founders of the Asian values movement. Yew attributed Singapore's speedy economic achievements to Asian values, which he presents as standing in contrast to Western individual rights. The Asian values movement denies the primary "Western rights" of liberty and instead promotes more communal values, such as hard work, thriftiness and discipline, and aims to benefit the family and the community rather than the individual. Proponents reject "Western" individual rights not only on the grounds that Asian values are different, but also that they are superior. For instance, Mahathir has denounced individual Western values as being responsible for community breakdown and the erosion of respect for marriage, family values, elders and important customs, conventions and traditions.

Those who critique rights from a non-Western perspective argue that the West endorses broadly individual moral values – autonomy, freedom and choice – and that Asian (and other non-Western) cultures endorse broadly communal values – respect for community, relationships and family and the "good life" rooted in community. To

---

Box 5.10 Western versus non-Western

	Western – individual	Eastern – communal
Values	Autonomy, freedom, choice	Community, relationships, family
Persons	An autonomous, isolated, free, choosing individual	A connected, community-defined, relational-being

---

give a caricature of this debate, the moral agents who exhibit these values are diametrically opposed. The "Western" moral agent is an autonomous, isolated, free, choosing individual and the Asian moral agent is a connected, community-defined, relational-being. So different are these persons that they could almost be different species.

This characterization of Western values and personhood has been widely criticized, using the anti-relativism arguments we discussed in Chapter 3. Western individuals are not these isolated beings making choices in a vacuum. To present human beings as making judgements outside their culture and background is to ignore the historically and socially constructed nature of human beings. The non-Western picture is no better: an amalgamated creature, conjoined to relations and family with no distinguishable personhood or identity. Such a person would be entirely passive and lack any sense of self, personal preference and decision-making ability, and would even lack the ability to form relationships: again, not a realistic picture of a human being. Therefore at most there is a spectrum, with some ethical systems having a tendency to prioritize some values and others different values. This said, all ethical systems must – if they wish to represent real human beings and their decisions – take into account both the communal and individual aspects of human agency. As we have seen in Chapters 3 and 4, a core claim of global ethics is that there are shared global values and therefore shared pictures of human beings. For instance, the virtue-ethics tradition, which we discussed in Chapter 3, is not a rights-based tradition, although it is a Western tradition. As we saw, much of virtue ethics focuses on human flourishing understood in relational, historical and communal contexts. Likewise, as we have just discussed, feminist ethicists also launch critiques of over-individualist understandings of persons and rights. Therefore, to suggest a strong divide between Western and non-Western approaches seems too extreme to be justified.

Other criticisms of the Asian values movement have been levelled at their intentions. For instance, the motivations of the proponents of Asian values have been criticized, and the movement presented as little more than a means to deflect accusations of human rights abuses and to support unjust authoritarian political systems. A little less critically, the promotion of Asian values has been described as merely a convenient way to promote economic and political progress. In his 1997 lecture "Human Rights and Asian Values", the economist and political theorist Amartya Sen denies that authoritarian anti-human-rights governments do in fact further such political and economic projects. He also questions the notion that there is a distinct set of Asian values that are in tension with human-rights thinking. By contrast, he argues that respect for human rights is not historically an exclusively Western concept.

This said, even if some of the claims of the Asian values movement are flawed, global ethicists should not dismiss concerns about the imperialism of Western ethics. In particular, the claim that human rights do not express universal values, but promote a particular Western view – an over-individualistic, liberal view – is worthy of consideration, not least because it echoes Marxist and feminist concerns.

The prioritizing of civil and political rights over economic rights – for instance, the focus first on liberties rather than provision of basic goods – could be seen as a view particularly well suited to more affluent Western nations whose concern is the maintenance of capitalism. By contrast, poorer and developing nations might believe that economic rights to a basic subsistence should be prior to civil and political rights. Therefore, at the very least, we should be critical of which rights are being claimed and who is likely to benefit.

CONCLUSION

This chapter has introduced rights theories and the problems with such theories. Human rights clearly are an important part of contemporary global ethics and are used by policy-makers and activists to attempt to create more just global structures. However, although human rights can be seen as crucial in the development of global ethics – most importantly they are global and they have some legal force – they are by no means uncontentious in theory (what are they and how are they established?), in policy (which should be given priority?) or in practice (how can they be enforced?). Yet despite the difficulties, human rights carry moral force and are perhaps the best means we currently have for recognizing and calling attention to global injustices. Therefore, whatever one ultimately decides about their scope and status, they undoubtedly have a place in the global-ethics toolbox.

As we have seen, rights theories combine with the moral and political theories of Chapters 3 and 4, and together add to the moral framework. How you regard the status of human rights will depend on which moral and political theories you endorse. For instance, you are more likely to believe that human rights are some kind of natural right if you endorse deontological theories. Or perhaps if you are a virtue ethicist you might think that human rights are useful to protect core values and virtues that enable human flourishing. Therefore, even if rights do not fit perfectly with your theory, you might still regard them as useful for protecting core human values and enshrining in law appropriate duties that contribute to the good life. If you are a utilitarian you might, like Bentham, think that natural rights are nonsense, but this does not mean that you will not find them useful if they produce the best consequences.

Similarly, your attitude to rights will be influenced by the political theory you adopt. For instance, some regard human rights as conflicting with cosmopolitanism, because rights are essentially state-limited: granted by states to citizens. It is states that sign up to the UDHR, rather than citizens. Others believe that human rights are important first steps towards global duties and ethics. They argue that international pressure can be used to force states to protect human rights. For such thinkers the mechanism might be state-based but the result is a global respect for rights. Others suggest – as we shall see in Chapter 6 – moving away from state concepts of citizenship towards global understandings of citizenship. This move might remove some state power in the conferring of rights and ensure a more global framework.

Whatever you think of the nature and scope of rights theoretically, you might think that they are politically useful. For instance, activist and pressure groups use the language of rights to ensure that their cause is stated in the most powerful language, something we explored in this chapter, when we considered the notion of rights as trumps. Certainly in terms of sound bites and activist goals, a "right to basic needs" that demands respect might be more effective than general pleas for food, shelter and health care. In later chapters we shall consider practical issues of global ethics – from poverty to the environment – and you will get a chance to explore both the status you believe rights have and how useful they are in any given context. For instance, do you think Shue's concept of basic rights would be effective in solving problems of global poverty (Chapter 7)? Or are rights too individualistic for encouraging development? Following from this, who can have rights? Only individuals? If so, how are group goods, for instance those of the environment, to be protected (something we shall return to in Chapter 10)?

How you answer these questions about rights will feed into your own moral framework and, in combination with the moral and political stand you take, determine the ethics you will promote. By now you should have a fairly clear idea of your theoretical position and be ready to address the practical issues that follow. Next we shall consider the structures of global governance and debates about global citizenship.

FURTHER READING

- Buchanan, A. *Justice, Legitimacy, and Self-Determination: Moral Foundations for International Law* (Oxford: Oxford University Press, 2007).
- Dershowitz, A. *Why Terrorism Works: Understanding the Threat, Responding to the Challenge* (New Haven, CT: Yale University Press, 2002).
- Dworkin, R. *Taking Rights Seriously* (London: Duckworth, 1977).
- Jones, P. *Rights* (New York: St Martin's Press, 1994).
- Locke, J. *Second Treatise of Government*, C. B. MacPherson (ed.) (Indianapolis, IN: Hackett, [1689] 1980).
- Marx, K. "On the Jewish Question". In *Selected Writings*, D. McLellan (ed.), 49–62 (Oxford: Oxford University Press, [1844] 1977).
- Nagel, T. *Equality and Partiality* (Oxford: Oxford University Press, 1991).
- Sen, A. "Human Rights and Asian Values". Sixteenth Morgenthau Memorial Lecture on Ethics & Foreign Policy (New York: Carnegie Council on Ethics and International Affairs, 1997). http://www.cceia.org/resources/publications/morgenthau/254.html/_res/id=sa_File1/254_sen.pdf (accessed May 2011).

- Shue, H. *Basic Rights: Subsistence, Affluence, and US Foreign Policy* (Princeton, NJ: Princeton University Press, 1980).
- United Nations. "The Universal Declaration of Human Rights" (1948). www.un.org/en/documents/udhr (accessed May 2011).
- Walzer, M. "Political Action and the Problem of Dirty Hands", *Philosophy and Public Affairs* 2 (1973): 160–80.

6 GLOBAL GOVERNANCE AND CITIZENSHIP

INTRODUCTION

As well as working out what is ethical and what we should do, global ethicists also need to think about *how* we can move towards a more just world. As discussed at the beginning of the book, global ethics combines theory with policy and practice. So as ethicists we need to be concerned with the mechanisms of global governance and with institutions and associations that can be used to deliver justice. In Chapter 5 we looked at rights theory, and human rights are perhaps the most obvious instance of the establishment of global ethics in international systems of global governance. In addition, there are many other institutions and associations that are part of the global-governance framework, some of which are connected and overseen by the United Nations, such as the WTO and IMF. In addition to our discussion in this chapter, we shall revisit concerns about the global system of governance throughout the rest of the book: the globally agreed Millennium Development Goals (Chapter 7); the International Criminal Court and the Geneva Conventions (Chapter 8); the Agreement on Trade-Related Aspects of Intellectual Property Rights (TRIPS) (Chapter 9); the Kyoto Protocol (Chapter 10); and the Convention on the Elimination of all Forms of Discrimination Against Women (CEDAW) (Chapter 11).

Accordingly, much of your understanding of global governance and the impact of the various global institutions and associations of global justice will be developed when you consider the dilemmas of global justice in greater detail in the remaining chapters. However, it is important to have a broad understanding of the institutions and the connections between them in the current global framework and to think about what kind of political and social global infrastructure would be most suited to delivering global justice. To this end, we shall consider: the possibility of global government and citizenship; the institutions and associations of global governance; and the global economic order and some of the ethical issues that arise from it, such as economic migration. In the final section we shall consider proposals about how the global economic system might address global injustice: the Tobin tax, the Global Resources Dividend and the Clean Hands Trust.

GLOBAL GOVERNMENT AND CITIZENSHIP

In Chapter 4 we discussed the rise of the political theory of cosmopolitanism. As we saw, the notion of being a "citizen of the world" is not a new one, but goes back to the beginning of Western thought. Yet, in the context of globalization, the notion of global citizenry takes on new meaning. What might global citizenship mean in a globalized context? What duties fall on global citizens and how are such duties enforced? The notion of global citizenship is explored by Dower and Williams (2002).

There is a spectrum of views about the institutions and duties that global citizenship requires. Some argue that for global citizenship to be meaningful there must be a global government or other form of global authority that forms an association. "Citizen" is a technical term that denotes a particular form of political relationship: that between citizen and the state. "Citizenship", then, is not in itself a moral concept or one describing personal identity, but rather a term that describes a particular political and institutional relationship. For those who take this line, a realistic and robust understanding of global citizenship requires a global government; therefore, global ethicists should be working towards establishing such an institution. Luis Cabrera (2004), for instance, discusses the possibility of a world state.

But there are problems with seeking to establish a global government. Not least, to change systems of government, from our current state-based system to one of global government, would be no simple change. It would require a sea change in global structures and institutions, requiring global consensus, determined political will and huge political and practical reformation. Such a change – even if there were public and political support – would be long and difficult. The practicalities of removing the state as the locus of control and organization, and nations as focuses of identity, would be colossal. Indeed, it is hard to imagine the enormity of such change. However, before even considering the practicalities that would be involved in such a global overhaul of institutions, there would need to be almost complete global consensus about its desirability. As we shall see clearly in the next few chapters when we look at the most pressing contemporary challenges – from conflict to climate change – it is difficult to get global agreement even on single issues where cooperation is clearly in everyone's best interest: think of the failures to get global consensus in climate change, for instance the US's refusal to sign the Kyoto Protocol and the relative ineffectiveness of the Copenhagen Accord. If it is impossible to get what many think of as relatively minor agreements on such pressing issues, then it would seem incredibly unlikely that we could reach global agreement on something far less necessary. In short, what is in it for states? Very little. They would lose power and no longer be able to protect and give preference to the rights and interests of their citizens. Even the poorest states could find reasons not to move to a global government, even though the population of such countries would be likely to benefit most from the eradication of states. Moving towards a global state would destroy the power (and wealth) of those in power in such countries, whether governments, juntas or warlords.

So given all that, and remembering the global-ethics commitment to theory and practice together, it might seem better to promote more realistic steps towards global justice, rather than advocating a proposal that is likely to be dismissed out of hand as impractical and unrealistic. The proposals we shall consider in the later sections of this chapter – which suggest ways of using the global economic system to promote global justice – support a step-by-step approach. Rather than advocate dramatic changes, they seek to gain support from across the political spectrum (from left to right) and from all global actors (global institutions, states and businesses), and they use the existing framework to address injustice. A final concern regarding the prospect of a global government is about centralizing power in one place. If there is only one source of power, then there is always a danger of what would happen if control fell into the hands of a dictator or some other form of oppressive government. Advocates of global government argue that appropriate checks and balances could be built into the system. However, for some the idea of one centralized power is disturbing.

Accordingly, some people wish to promote a moral idea of citizenship, similar to that of the Stoics' original view. Global citizenship is then an ethical stance and a statement of community and identity. Dower presents a version of this view, arguing that we are all global citizens simply by virtue of being human beings who live in a global community. However, he distinguishes between this type of global citizenship, which applies to everyone, and "active" global citizenship. Dower says:

> only some human beings are "active" global citizens because they accept responsibility to pursue global concerns. Being a global citizen is not merely a matter of accepting a global ethical framework; it is belonging to and partici-pating in a wider community which finds expression in a variety of institu-tions within global civil society which already exist but which a global citizen is committed to develop and strengthen. (2002: 40)

Dower thus sees citizenship as a moral attitude and position, and one that goes beyond simply thinking of yourself as part of a global community. It also requires action that helps move towards stronger global institutions and frameworks of global governance, rather than recommend an immediate jump to global government.

Again, this is a practical commitment to using and developing current governance systems.

In light of some of the views we discussed in Chapter 4, we can see that just as not all theorists of global ethics endorse cosmopolitanism, nor do they all recognize this model of global citizenship as part of global ethics. While Miller's nationalist view, for example, claims to accommodate many duties beyond borders, he argues for the special status for national and cultural identity. This denies global citizenship as a moral concept at least in the strong sense that Dower has in mind, while still affirming some global duties.

GLOBAL INSTITUTIONS AND GOVERNANCE

United Nations

The architecture for the current system of global governance developed in the aftermath of the Second World War. The current international order is institutionalized in the UN and the institutions and associations that derive from it, including the human-rights declarations, conventions and covenants we discussed in Chapter 5. The UN is an organization created to engender cooperation between states, a mechanism by which their relationships can be managed and a forum for international discussion. Nation states remain primary in the UN system and, as we saw with human rights, power ultimately remains with states, not with any international body. The UN relies on cooperation from states and the power it has is essentially that of individual states: it has no power of its own. This said, the establishment of international norms – such as the UDHR – provides standards that states are expected to uphold and sustain. The UN funds and supports a number of organizations dedicated to addressing particular global concerns (see Box 6.1).

Box 6.1 United Nations organizations

UNCTAD	UN Conference on Trade and Development
UNDP	UN Development Programme
UNEP	UN Environmental Programme
UNFPA	UN Population Fund
UNHCR	UN High Commissioner for Refugees
UNICEF	UN Children's Fund
WFP	World Food Programme

Box 6.2 Specialized agencies

- International Labour Organization (ILF)
- International Monetary Fund (IMF)
- UN Educational, Scientific and Cultural Organization (UNESCO)
- World Bank
- World Health Organization (WHO)
- World Trade Organization (WTO)

This is not an exhaustive list, but gives only those most obviously useful for global ethics.

In addition to these organizations there are a number of separate agencies, some of which existed before the establishment of the UN. These are independent of the UN, with their own membership, budgets and programmes. However, although separate from the UN they nominally come under the UN umbrella and are loosely coordinated by the UN Economic and Social Council (see Box 6.2).

The establishment of such organizations and associations has resulted in some shift towards global norms and has placed concomitant expectations on states. For instance, the regional measures to enforce human rights – discussed in Chapter 5 – have led to a recognition that there are values that must be respected and which trump national sovereignty. Likewise there has been a gradual emergence of the view that legitimate states must respect human rights, and those that fail to do so are deemed to be "failing" or "rogue" states. Such states are subjected to criticism from the international community and sometimes the international community will act against such states, either employing economic sanctions or even using force in the case of humanitarian intervention (a topic we shall return to in Chapter 8).

International law

Another sphere of global governance is international law, which regulates relations between states. Human rights can be thought of as such a law, in that states agree that rights have special status that places them above national laws. Other examples are the rules of war and conflict, the most well known being the Geneva Conventions (although arguably these go back generations with notions of honourable conduct in battle and codes of chivalry). These rules aim to limit the most inhumane practices of war and, increasingly, the most barbaric weapons. Those who ignore these rules can be tried in international courts for "war crimes" or "crimes against humanity". In Europe, individuals responsible for war crimes, including genocide, in Bosnia during the 1990s have been tried in the Hague, Netherlands, and prosecuted under the International Criminal Tribunal for the Former Yugoslavia. Similarly, the International Criminal Tribunal for Rwanda, established by the UN Security Council, has the specific aim of bringing to justice those responsible for "genocide, crimes against humanity and serious violations of international humanitarian law committed in Rwanda during 1994".

Such international norms and the fact that those who transgress them can be brought to account in some form are concrete examples of global structures of governance. While limited, such structures do show that national sovereignty no longer rules supreme in terms of the behaviour of states, either towards each other or towards their own citizens.

THE GLOBAL MARKETPLACE

Global economic structures and global trade constitute a powerful global association, so much so that Moellendorf (2002, 2009a) argues that it is enough of an association to establish global duties of justice, as discussed in Chapter 4. Participating in the global market is unavoidable for most people and states. Trade provides links between individuals (producers and consumers) and between states in terms of trade and national income; and many companies are international in terms of the goods and services they produce and their delivery. In addition, international financial markets are increasingly interconnected to the point where it makes little sense to see the financial market as anything but a global one. As a result, a financial crisis in one country has significant impact on other countries. In the early 2000s, for example, more and more people in the US were given access to mortgages they could not realistically afford, owing to the demand from banks and Wall Street investors, who "bought" the mortgages believing them to be steady sources of income (mortgage-holders make large deposits and subsequent regular payments). For a time this was how it worked, and debtors paid their mortgages by obtaining other forms of easily available credit: paying off debts by getting into more debt. In 2006 the "bubble" finally burst, with massive levels of mortgage defaulting (failing to pay) which in effect reversed the supply and demand relation of the "boom" (so now there were too many houses and too few buyers) and house prices plummeted. The "subprime" crisis in the US was global because the trade in "subprime" mortgages was worldwide. Hence the collapse of the US housing market in 2006 has led to global recession, the effects of which are still being felt and will be for some time to come.

The primary actor in managing the international economic order is the WTO, which developed out of an earlier regime, the General Agreement on Tariffs and Trade, which was essentially a trade agreement. The WTO (established in 1995), however, has significant power and aims to reduce tariffs and barriers to trade. As barriers have been reduced there has been increased pressure for states to comply to global norms and move towards freer trade. For instance, as well as regulating tariffs and quota systems, national laws and their impact on international trade are increasingly being considered in the international system. The IMF was established in 1945 to manage the international economic order. It monitors states' economic health and provides funds to those in need in return for internal restructuring as deemed necessary by the IMF. The IMF aims to promote efficiency and stability in global financial markets.

ETHICAL CRITICISMS OF THE GLOBAL ECONOMIC SYSTEM

Despite the fact that global ethicists broadly welcome the move towards global institutions and frameworks that at least include all nations and people within their scope, there are many criticisms of global institutions. For instance, as we shall see in Chapter 7, there are criticisms of the simplistic economic development measures that have been favoured by the IMF and WTO, which fail to take into account actual standards of living and quality of life and focus rather on economic measures such as income of individuals or communities. As a result, these measures miss the fact that people who live in largely agricultural and subsistence economies with robust family and community networks might have almost no income, but yet be able to meet many of their basic needs, as well as have some quality of life. Such people appear exceptionally poor on such economic measures, but in fact are better off than those with some income, but who are unable to meet all their basic needs. Moreover, in these circumstances the person may have left their families and social networks in order to attempt to earn money in an urban environment. By focusing on economic measures alone it can appear that a country is poorer than it in fact is, or, more worryingly, that it is "developing" and economic standards are improving, while in fact people's quality of life is deteriorating. This sort of criticism was levelled at the Structural Adjustment Programmes implemented by the World Bank and the IMF in the 1980s and 1990s, which placed conditions on loans given to developing countries. Key conditions of these programmes were greater privatization and the removal of trade barriers, thus encouraging foreign investment. The stated rationale for this is that the country receiving the loan is forced to become more efficiently market-focused, thus encouraging its economic growth. However, the programmes often destroyed local infrastructure, failed to improve living standards and arguably increased corruption.

Moellendorf (2005) launches somewhat similar criticisms of the WTO from his egalitarian perspective. He argues that although the theory behind the WTO is that all will benefit as trade is liberalized, in reality it does not work out quite like that.

The model of economic growth on which the WTO is founded assumes that "trade liberalisation should increase global economic efficiency and lead to increases in aggregate production and consumption". In other words, free trade should benefit all: poor and rich, consumers and producers. Moellendorf counters this claim on a number of grounds. First, he asks whether the WTO does in fact promote free trade, and whether it does this equally. Moellendorf suggests that it does not. For instance, the removal of protections and tariffs to ensure unhindered world trade means that developing countries are unable to protect young and developing industries, and this is not comparable to the position of the developed countries that did in fact protect their own industries in the early years. Given that developed countries did this and that it seems to have contributed to successful development, not to permit and encourage it in other countries is a form of injustice. Moreover, the injustice arising from the refusal to allow developing countries to protect young industries – debilitating in itself – is further compounded by the fact that the WTO is not so insistent with regard to developed countries. Simply put "the WTO's policy of tolerating developed-world protectionism against underdeveloped countries is seriously unjust".

Second, Moellendorf argues that even if free trade did produce efficiency and development as the theory claims, this alone would not be sufficient for ethical justification. Egalitarian considerations about distributive justice also need to be taken into account. For instance, issues of unjust differentials in wealth (the fact that arbitrarily some are born in circumstances of plenty and others in abject poverty) need to be remedied in a satisfactory ethical economic system. So, if liberalization requires the removal of protections and tariffs, on the grounds that they disrupt the free market and create inefficiencies, one result is that it will be impermissible for developing countries to protect subsistence agriculture and emerging industries. Moellendorf (2005) suggests that for such policies to be acceptable, compensation must be offered to farmers because "pursuit of agricultural trade liberalization would require the WTO to provide income support for displaced subsistence farmers, and this would require institutions of taxation and transfer".

Moellendorf argues that these injustices are a direct result of the way the WTO is managed and organized. First, he shows that underdeveloped countries are marginalized from WTO decision-making processes, because they are unable to fund participation and attendance. He suggests this could easily be addressed by putting mechanisms in place to subsidize the voices of the poor in order to allow them access to the debate. Second, following Singer, he argues that the WTO (like other institutions) prioritizes economic efficiency over other goods. Singer himself argues that in addition to failing to respect quality of life, economic measures also ignore other values, such as environmental ones. As we shall see in Chapter 10, the extent of the environmental challenge means that a framework that fails to take into account other ethical concerns will be lacking when it comes to addressing global dilemmas.

Moellendorf's final point is the effect that WTO agreements (e.g. TRIPS) have on other areas of development: as we shall see in Chapter 9, this agreement has reduced the access of the poor to essential drugs. Simply put, although the agreement applies to all it does not affect all in the same way. It benefits and protects rich countries – the exporters of intellectual property – and impoverishes poor countries – the importers of intellectual property.

Economic migration

A key feature of the globalization of the economic order is the increase in migration as people attempt to improve their own economic situations (by emigrating) and those of their families (by sending remittances to their home countries). There are many contemporary forms of movement between jurisdictions, states and regions. It can be voluntary, but there is also a global phenomenon of forced movement and labour, as in instances of "human trafficking" for prostitution or domestic or agricultural work. The US Department of State (2005) estimates that "600,000 to 800,000 men, women, and children [are] trafficked across international borders each year". In anticipation of Chapter 11, where we shall look at some global gender inequality issues, it is also worth pointing out that "approximately 80 percent are women and girls and up to 50 percent are minors".

Economic migration in itself is nothing new; think for instance of the various tides of economic migration into the US from Europe. According to the US Office of Immigration Statistics, in the first decade of the twentieth century more than a million people from Italy and another million from Russia arrived and obtained legal permanent resident status, while more recently, in 2009, 17,000 from the UK and 54,000 from India did the same. The post-war period has seen a huge increase in migration of people. Primarily, economic migrants move to the developed world, and in the era of globalization, awareness of the possibilities of other ways of life is far greater. In particular, the information age means that you are likely to be aware of your relative situation. If you are poor you are likely to know it and this might provide impetus for you to choose dangerous and exploitative options in order to improve your situation. For instance, some women "choose" to be "trafficked" for prostitution in order to improve their families' situation despite sometimes knowing the risks; or young men attempt to cross the sea from Africa to Europe despite the numbers who die in the crossing. In 2009 an estimated seventy-five people attempting this journey died at sea; they had, like many, made their way to Libya and set off in rubber dinghies to reach the Italian island of Lampedusa. The website Fortress Europe carries a collection of press reports from 1988 to 2008, which together report more than 14,000 deaths of migrants attempting to reach Europe either by sea or across the Sahara Desert.

Remittances

One area that is currently receiving interest is the impact of short-term economic migration, usually by one person in order to send back money – "remittances" – to parents, children, family and the wider community at home. Perhaps the most familiar picture is of the male migrant worker who leaves to work elsewhere and sends money home to his family, such as the South African miners who live in dormitories and rarely return home, earning on average about 3000 rand (275 euros; US$350) per month; or the eastern European seasonal agriculture worker, who comes to the UK to pick fruit every year in harvest time, works long hours for a minimal wage and again lives in dormitories; or the female domestic labourer, such as Filipina maids in Hong Kong and the Gulf states. In a number of these instances without such migrant labour some industries would fail; for instance, when employment has been relatively high in the UK, and thus much less of the population needs to take lower-paid jobs, agriculture has relied on migrant agricultural labourers. Likewise, much care work, including childcare and care of the elderly, is done in the US by legal and illegal immigrants, often from Mexico.

Clearly there are many global ethics issues concerning economic migration: not least whether or not economic migration turns migrants into second-class citizens. For example, is it acceptable for migrants to do jobs that domestic workers reject as being "beneath them" or are considered too poorly paid? Similarly, is it unacceptable exploitation for women to care for the children and elderly parents of the rich when often this means they are unable to care for their own children and family? In other words, is economic need sufficient to justify such interactions and working practices? And what is the role of legislation in this? For instance, is a global minimum wage necessary to protect people from at least the most extreme forms of exploitation? Perhaps other forms of labour regulation are required, such as ensuring holidays or rights to paid family visits? Labour regulation might help the situation for some economic migrants but it does nothing to protect those who are illegal migrants. They are, in effect, "stateless" and therefore in many ways the most vulnerable of all groups we are concerned with in global ethics, because, as we discussed in Chapter 5, rights are granted by states to their citizens, so those who lack states lack rights. So those who migrate illegally are effectively right-less, an issue that global ethicists seek to redress.

Despite the ethical concerns that arise from migration – and the significant injustices that migrants suffer – there are those who do improve their situations in this way. And remittances from migrant workers have contributed to economic growth in migrants' countries of origin. In 2010, *The Economist* reported that "Remittances [in the Philippines] are now equivalent to 11% of the economy." Thus, in at least some instances, economic migration has resulted in some of the benefits that the migrants hoped for. That said, we should recognize that many find themselves in situations that amount to little more than contemporary forms of slavery.

In addition to the use of migrant labourers to perform jobs that are low paid and which domestic labourers do not want to do, migrants are also drawn from skilled populations. Indeed, those most able to attain legal migration are not the relatively unskilled discussed above, but those who are most skilled. Those most in demand by the developed world are professional and skilled workers, and immigration policies are designed accordingly. Thus the most highly trained in the developing world have the best chance of migrating to the developed world. Such migration leads to a loss of skilled work in the developing world, where such skills are already scarce; hence this movement has been termed the "brain drain". In a 1994 report, for instance, the UNDP estimated that India, China, South Korea and the Philippines together lost 145,000 skilled scientifically trained workers to the US between 1972 and 1985. Another example is the active recruitment by the UK's National Health Service of medical professionals from the developing world. According to Riccardo Faini's (2006) statistics, Africa has lost 30 per cent of its best educated manpower, primarily to the UK and the European Union.

While remittances from low-paid labour do contribute to development of the migrant's country of origin, the migration of the most skilled seems to contribute less. In theory, skilled migration should contribute more, because such workers earn more and therefore have more to send back. Moreover, these are educated persons who migrate legally and who are much less likely to suffer exploitation than low-skilled migrant labourers. But, in practice, and as people settle in new countries, this does not happen; families join them and less is returned to the country of origin. Thus the claim that the negative effects of the brain drain – losing key skilled workers who have been trained at the cost of the country – are negated by the benefits from remittances seems false.

USING GLOBAL ECONOMIC STRUCTURES TO ADDRESS INJUSTICE

Economic sanctions

There are many ways in which the global economic system is used to attempt to address injustices. For instance, the IMF and the WTO, despite criticisms, aim to increase development, and the IMF provides resources for those in need. Another prominent way that the economic system can be used is by implementing economic sanctions, often as a way of addressing non-economic injustices. For instance, economic sanctions were introduced by some countries against apartheid South Africa in the 1960s, although a call from the UN General Assembly to implement international economic pressure was resisted by many. As domestic resistance grew, so did international awareness of apartheid, and corporations and businesses decided to disinvest in South Africa, while many individual Western consumers heeded a call from the anti-apartheid African National Congress to boycott the purchase of South African products. In addition, a sporting boycott was widely endorsed by individuals and sporting institutions, as when in 1970 the International Association of Athletics Federations agreed to suspend South Africa from its membership. This movement reached critical mass during the 1980s and it had a significant effect on the South African economy and contributed to a dramatic rise in "capital flight": the flow of capital and investment out of the country. While some critics argued that sanctions adversely affected poor South Africans – the black people on whose behalf the sanctions' supporters were supposed to be campaigning – they undoubtedly wielded pressure on the regime, arguably figuring as an essential catalyst in its eventual downfall. In addition, the consumer boycott is an important example of how individuals can act even when their governments do not.

Sanctions were also employed internationally – and more controversially – against Iraq by the UN Security Council from 1990, following the first Gulf War, to 2003, the beginning of the second. Intended initially to put pressure on Saddam Hussein's regime to withdraw from Kuwait and pay reparations, and then to disclose details of alleged weapons of mass destruction (WMD), sanctions banned all trade and financial dealing with Iraq, with the exception of some medicines and foodstuffs if provided in "humanitarian" circumstances. As a country whose economy relied heavily on exporting its oil, these sanctions hit Iraq, and its people, hard. There was significant controversy surrounding the toughness of these sanctions and whether and to what extent they led to an upsurge in infant illness and mortality and illiteracy rates (indices that had been falling during the1980s, prior to sanctions). The UN recognized that "even if not all suffering in Iraq can be imputed to external factors, especially sanctions, the Iraqi people would not be undergoing such deprivations in the absence of the prolonged measures imposed by the Security Council and the effects of war" (UN Security Council 1999).

In addition to such standard measures, other ways of using the economic system to address injustice are being developed by political, policy and activist communities. These are measures that could be adopted relatively easily and without any radical overhaul of current systems of global economic governance. Thus they aim to be practical and realistic and are designed to have as wide appeal as possible across the political spectrum. These proposals – especially Pogge's and Leif Wenar's – are excellent examples of the way global ethicists address policy and practice directly and are willing to build partial solutions that will be adopted relatively easily as steps on the way to creating a just social order.

Tobin tax

Perhaps the most well known suggestion for moderating the current system is the Tobin tax. The original proposal came from James Tobin, a prizewinning economist, but it has been developed and supported by a variety of economists, political and development theorists as well as by policy-makers and activists. Tobin taxes are sales taxes on currency trades that cross borders, the idea being to restrict short-term large investments that capitalize on temporary fluctuating exchange rates. Recent Tobin-tax proposals have received considerable political interest. For instance the then UK Prime Minister Gordon Brown raised it at the 2009 G20 summit of finance ministers and continued to support the proposal in early 2010, emboldened by US President Barack Obama announcing his own plans to curb the risky financial ventures of Wall Street banks. A few months later, the European Parliament voted for an EU Tobin tax, although at the time of writing this has yet to be implemented. It has also inspired huge amounts of civil society activism: attempts to bring it to the attention of policy-makers are spearheaded by the Association pour la Taxation des Transactions financière et l'Aide aux Citoyens (ATTAC) network, which was set up to campaign for the adoption of the tax. ATTAC is now a huge and important activist network with branches in over forty countries and around 1000 local groups.

Exactly how Tobin taxes would be administered and enforced depends on the version adopted, but the intention is that they could be implemented relatively easily and without introducing new and potentially expensive layers of bureaucracy and administration. Thus it is likely that they would be managed and enforced by nation states, as indeed many forms of global governance are, including human rights, as discussed in Chapter 5.

The level of the tax would be relatively low (between 0.1 and 0.25 per cent), yet even this negligible cost for the taxpayer would create significant revenue: estimates range between US$100 billion and US$3000 billion annually. This revenue would then be used to meet recognized global needs; for instance, for aid in emergency situations, to address chronic poverty by improving opportunities and infrastructure, and to fund adaptations and mitigations in response to climate change. In addition to the usefulness in meeting global needs, other advantages of the Tobin tax are that it would encourage a greater level of stability in financial markets. Currently, an enormous proportion – up to 90 per cent according to some estimates – of currency trade is short-term speculative trade. It is this short-term trade that is most likely to lead to financial crashes. The claim is that longer-term investments connected to production and infrastructure would be affected relatively little, whereas short-term damaging trades would reduce. If advocates of the Tobin tax are correct, there are few downsides to this tax: it costs little, produces much and makes global financial markets more stable (Box 6.3).

Box 6.3 Benefits of the Tobin tax

- It is easily implemented;
- costs little to the wealthy and powerful;
- reduces volatility in the market by discouraging short-term currency trade;
- provides revenue to meet global crises (from poverty, to emergency situations, to climate change);
- introduces beneficial global governance and encourages international cooperation.

Global Resources Dividend

Another proposal comes from Pogge, one of the foremost global ethicists. In Chapter 7 we shall consider Pogge's argument that we have a negative duty to assist the poor because we are not only ignoring, but causing, poverty. For now we shall consider his proposal for a Global Resources Dividend (GRD).

The GRD is a mechanism for compensating the poor for their low use of natural resources. Pogge (2001) bases his proposal on the premise that "those who make more extensive use of our planet's resources should compensate those who, involuntarily, use very little". The GRD suggests that while nations control their resources, they are "required to share a small part of the value of any resources that they use or sell". This payment is a "dividend", because the poor "own an inalienable stake in all limited natural resources". The dividend should be managed in simple and transparent ways, so it is clear that everyone is paying their fair share and the costs are kept low.

As with the Tobin tax, Pogge intends his proposal to be practical, realistic and easily implementable. He calls his proposal "modest" because it does not require any restructuring of systems of global governance and relies on current national structures for implementation. Pogge argues that modesty is important if it is to gain support among governments and institutions, and thus to have any chance of being introduced.

Box 6.4 Advantages of the Global Resources Dividend

- It is easily implemented;
- costs little to the wealthy and powerful;
- brings benefits through participation (through incentives to comply);
- provides revenue to relieve extremes of global poverty;
- benefits the environment.

Pogge also insists that extreme poverty and radical inequality could be addressed with a surprisingly small GRD. He argues that a dividend of 1 per cent on global products would reduce severe poverty and result in an "acceptable distributional profile" in a short period of time. He estimates that a GRD of 1 per cent would raise around US$300 billion annually, which would be US$250 for every person below the international poverty line. At a relatively small cost for the wealthy and in a very short time, extreme poverty could be eradicated. The final aim of the GRD is that the poor will "be able to meet their own basic needs with dignity".

Pogge believes that, given the relatively small cost and the great benefits (see Box 6.4), the GRD would not be difficult for most countries to adopt. Moreover, additional incentives could be built in to the operation of the scheme. For instance, he suggests that progress should be rewarded and, in cases of non-compliance, other means of using the funding to address poverty should be sought. In situations of extreme non-compliance, sanctions could be implemented using the current decentralized sanction mechanisms. Duties could be imposed on imports from non-compliant countries until an equivalent amount of money to the GRD is reached. However, he argues that it would not be in any country's interests to avoid paying the GRD given the relatively small cost, especially when compared with the potential loss in foreign trade that would result from non-compliance.

In addition, Pogge suggests that the GRD should be focused on those goods whose reduction in use contributes to conservation. The GRD could be used to help address environmental degradation and climate change as well as global hunger.

Clean Hands Trust

A final proposal for reforming the current system is proposed by Wenar (2008). Wenar's proposal to establish a "Clean Hands Trust" is another illustration of the global-ethics commitment to combining theory and practice. Like the Tobin tax and Pogge's GRD, the Clean Hands Trust is intended to be both modest and based on already existing laws and mechanisms. Again the aim is that it is easily implementable and a step on the way to addressing the "resource curse". Wenar argues that his proposal introduces no new rules or principles but simply requires that the normal rules of the market are properly enforced.

His starting-point is that the first issue that needs to be addressed in the global market is not inequalities but the violation of property rights and the toleration of theft. He argues that currently "the international commercial system breaks the first rule of capitalism in transporting stolen goods", and that it "does so on an enormous scale".

To establish the claim of mass trafficking in stolen goods he maps the "resource curse". The "resource curse" describes the fact that in many resource-rich countries there are many extremely poor people. Thus it seems that being rich in resources is not, as one might imagine, correlated to development. This is explained by various factors that beset countries that rely on the export of natural mineral resources for a large part of their national wealth. Wenar lists three conditions: (i) countries of this type typically have authoritarian regimes that control and exploit these natural resources; (ii) there are often civil conflict and coup attempts, which are in part attempts to gain control over natural resources; (iii) these countries exhibit lower rates of growth, so that even though the "country" is wealthy, this does not result in improved living standards for the majority. To illustrate his claims he uses examples from Nigeria, Sierra Leone, the Democratic Republic of the Congo and, particularly, Equatorial Guinea.

Like Pogge, Wenar argues that we are all implicated in causing and sustaining the resource curse. He states that the "resources" are only part of the picture; the other part is who purchases the resources. In short, the international community purchases the resources and thus is culpable. Wenar suggests that the problem lies in a failure of institutions to enforce established rules of the market and, in particular, to enforce already globally recognized property rights. He bases his claim on Article 1 of the International Covenant on Civil and Political Rights or the identical Article 1 of the International Covenant on Economic, Social and Cultural Rights (covenants that are signed up to by over three-quarters of member states). Most importantly Article 1 (in both covenants) states that "all peoples may, for their own ends, freely dispose of their natural wealth or resources" (see OHCHR 1976). He argues that this principle of national ownership is widely established and recognized and its requirements can be met in a variety of ways in national, collective and private ownership. However, there are some small circumstances where ownership of natural resources cannot be established, and in these cases there is no right of ownership of natural resources and thus no right to sell. Selling national resources by those who lack a legitimate right, Wenar claims, is tantamount to selling stolen goods. The current international regime buys resources from those who control them, essentially those who have the power within the country: typically authoritarian regimes, warlords and juntas. Effectively, the current global regime respects the "might makes right" rule (by which power supposedly amounts simply to legitimate authority). This is clearly unacceptable to Wenar and a violation of the most basic principles of the market: that one must have ownership of what one sells. Moreover, the purchaser cannot be regarded as "innocent" if they could reasonably be expected to know that the goods are stolen: a not unreasonable assumption if you are purchasing raw materials from a junta, brutal dictator or warlord.

Wenar sets out the conditions for rightful ownership of national resources. He sets the bar deliberately low in order to win over as many as possible to his proposal. Wenar lists three minimal conditions that must be met if the government or power are to be deemed to have sufficient legitimacy to sell the country's natural resources: (i) citizens must be able to find out about the sales; (ii) they must be able to stop the sales without incurring severe costs; (iii) they must not be subject to extreme manipulation. None of these conditions are met if citizens do not have minimal civil liberties, such as some free press and mechanisms to comment and protest with no fear of arrest or retaliation. Wenar suggests that we identify countries where citizens lack these basic civil liberties using the ratings of Freedom House, an independent NGO that is widely recognized and respected. Wenar suggests that any countries that receive Freedom House's worst rating (states with "virtually no freedom", and where "political rights are absent or virtually non-existent") should be regarded as failing to have legitimate rights to sell the country's natural resources.

Wenar's solution is that once these countries are identified, the international community should refrain from purchasing from them. However, he recognizes that not all states in the international community will comply – for instance China – and it is to address this that he suggests a Clean Hands Trust. This trust would be set up in the name of the people of the country where the resources originated. If China, say, bought oil to the value of US$3 billion from a country (Wenar's example is Sudan), then America (and presumably other members of the international community) would put a tariff on Chinese imports until an equivalent US$3 billion had been collected. This money would then be handed over to Sudan once minimal conditions of governance had been met: in practical terms, once the country is no longer in the lowest Freedom House category. Wenar argues that this will ensure that consumers in the developed world are no longer implicated. It will also ensure that the people of countries under the resource curse are no longer robbed, because the value of their stolen property will be returned. It will reduce incentives to countries such as China to purchase from these countries because it will increase the price of their exports. And, finally, it gives an incentive to people and rulers in the resource-cursed countries to improve the governance structures so that they can receive the money from the Clean Hands Trust (see Box 6.5).

Box 6.5 Advantages of the Clean Hands Trust

- It is easily implemented;
- costs little to the wealthy and powerful;
- provides revenue to relieve extremes of global poverty;
- reduces revenue to warlords, dictators and juntas;
- reduces conflict in the most conflict-ridden countries;
- Gives impetus for establishing legitimate government;
- strengthens the global order by enforcing property rights;
- improves on traditional sanctions because it focuses on the guilty and ultimately benefits innocent citizens.

CONCLUSION

All these proposals for change rely on a belief that civil society can influence policy-making; indeed, without such convictions, networks such as ATTAC would not exist. Pogge argues that there are many historical examples of the effect of moral convictions on international justice, most obviously the ending of the slave trade. He suggests that similar "moral mobilization" is necessary to end global poverty. There are many ways to do this: lobbying for political change; participating in the usual parliamentary processes; changing our basic consumption choices – recall the consumer boycott of South Africa – or purchasing "fair-trade products" (see Chapter 7); and participating in other forms of consumer activism. Whatever else, we can conclude that while the global economic system is blamed for many of the current global injustices, it can also be used to redress those injustices. This recognition is important, because the global economic system is too often treated as if it were outside human influence and agency. Clearly this is not the case. The rise of global institutions such as the IMF and the WTO shows how the global economic system can change in response to the wishes of the international community in order to manage and institute globally approved policies. For instance, TRIPS, which we shall return to in Chapter 9, and which has caused such controversy, is relatively new (coming into effect on 1 January 1995). Just as TRIPS can be introduced, so can other policies, such as the Global Resources Dividend or the Clean Hands Trust. Therefore, even if you do not conclude that it is worth proposing a form of global government at the current juncture, nor should you conclude that there is nothing that can be done to change global institutions of governance.

This chapter has again brought home just how interconnected are the issues of global ethics. Economic measures are used directly to address economic injustice, for instance to encourage development, but also for non-economic reasons, for example when sanctions are used to attain political ends. In addition, what is practically possible is constrained by the frameworks and institutions in place, and while states remain the primary political structures of societies, there are those who will fall between the cracks, such as those made stateless and so effectively rights-less as a result of illegal migration. If there were a global system of government, or even some way of globally ensuring the rights of all (irrespective of states), then this would not happen. Likewise, how we prioritize different values affects how we measure injustice and this influences how we are able to address other issues and injustices. To take one such case, which we shall discuss in the next chapter, if we only consider economic development we miss other important indicators of development.

FURTHER READING

- ATTAC website. www.attac.org (accessed June 2011).
- Brock, G. *Global Justice: A Cosmopolitan Account* (Oxford: Oxford University Press, 2009).
- Cabrera, L. *Political Theory of Global Justice: A Cosmopolitan Case for the World State* (London: Routledge, 2004).
- Dower, N. & J. Williams (eds). *Global Citizenship: A Critical Reader* (Edinburgh: Edinburgh University Press, 2002).
- Faini, R. "Remittances and the Brain Drain". IZA Discussion Paper No. 2155 (Bonn: Forschungsinstitut zur Zukunft der Arbeit (IZA), 2006). ftp://repec.iza.org/RePEc/Discussionpaper/dp2155.pdf (accessed May 2011).
- Fortress Europe website. http://fortresseurope.blogspot.com/2006/01/press-review.html (accessed June 2011).
- Moellendorf, D. "The World Trade Organization and Egalitarian Justice". *Metaphilosophy* **36** (2005): 145–62.
- Pogge, T. "Eradicating Systemic Poverty: Brief for a Global Resources Dividend". *Journal of Human Development* **2** (2001): 59–77.
- Tobin Tax Initiative website. www.ceedweb.org/iirp/ (accessed June 2011).
- Wenar, L. "Property Rights and the Resource Curse". *Philosophy and Public Affairs* **36** (2008): 2–32.

7 GLOBAL POVERTY

INTRODUCTION

In moving from local to global frameworks the unjust distribution of wealth is perhaps the most pressing issue of global injustice. What ethical reasons and justifications are there for 10 per cent of the world's population holding 90 per cent of the world's wealth and resources? This chapter will address this unjust distribution of wealth, with a particular focus on the north–south divide (as always, such terms as "north", "south", "Western", "non-Western", "developing" and "developed" can be problematic and should be regarded as mapping general trends rather than as definitive definitions).

The problem of poverty is to some a perennial problem, and some argue that it is one that is irresolvable. This said, in the context of globalization the issues of global poverty cannot be dismissed so easily. This is true both politically, where there are international and national programmes for debt relief and aid, and also individually, as individuals respond to appeals for aid in huge numbers. The Organisation for Economic Co-operation and Development (OECD; 2010) reports the level of Official Development Assistance (a term that refers to international aid provided by government institutions) as (in US dollars or equivalent):

- US$28 billion from the US (0.2 per cent of its gross national income [GNI]);
- US$11.5 billion from the UK (0.52 per cent GNI);
- US$6.4 billion from the Netherlands (0.8 per cent GNI); and
- US$2.7 billion from Australia (0.29 per cent GNI).

As for charitable donations from the public: according to a 2010 report by Global Humanitarian Assistance, in 2008 the US donated on average per citizen $14; the UK $14; Saudi Arabia $29; and, most generously, Luxembourg $114. As images of poverty – from natural and man-made disasters – are beamed on to television screens, claims of ignorance can no longer excuse inaction. It is impossible for a member of the rich world (the developed world) not to know of their relative privilege or of the fact that most of the world's population is not so privileged. Yet, despite this knowledge and the number of horrific images of famine that have been watched in homes in the West, the problems of poverty are no less than they were three or four decades ago. The report *Rethinking Poverty* by the UN Department of Economic and Social Affairs (2009) opens with the depressing statistic that in 1981, some 820 million people in the world were undernourished, and that by 2008 the figure had risen to over 950 million.

One standard and "absolute" financial indicator (a flat rate that is not proportional or relative to other material or social factors) of extreme poverty is the World Bank's poverty line of an income of US$1.25 per day per person. The same report shows an overall decrease in the number of people below this line from 1981 to 2005, from 18,000 million to 13,000 million. There are two points to note about this trend. First, while much of this progress has been made in the East Asia and Pacific region of the developing world, the figure for Sub-Saharan Africa has steadily increased from 212 million to 388 million. Second, the report notes that the global financial crisis after 2005 "will in all likelihood erase progress made over the last decade in reducing extreme poverty". In addition, remember the point made in Chapter 6 about the problems with income-only measures, which are unable to take into account other factors that contribute to actual living standards.

This chapter will consider why, despite the obvious needs of the global poor, it is still the case that the problem of poverty is largely unaddressed and that disparities in wealth are greater in 2010 than they were a quarter of a century ago. In 2006, commenting in the *Sunday Times* on the World Institute for Development Economics Research report he helped compile for the UN, economist Professor James Davies said: "Income inequality has been rising for the past 20 to 25 years and we think that is true for inequality in the distribution of wealth" (Brown 2006). This chapter will explore the global-ethics response to these injustices of poverty and of global inequalities in wealth, using the ethical toolbox created in Chapters 3, 4 and 5 to apply a global-ethics framework that incorporates universalist ethical theories, cosmopolitan frameworks and principles of distributive justice.

GLOBAL POVERTY

Given our discussions in the earlier chapters, at first glance it is difficult to understand why the problem of extreme poverty has not yet been adequately addressed. If we think about our ethical toolbox, it seems unlikely that the existence of poverty could ever be justified. What possible argument could be advanced in defence of global poverty and such stark inequality? None of the moral theories of Chapter 3 could support such injustices and suffering; in terms of the political theories of Chapter 4, only a thoroughgoing realism could accept such global injustice, while nationalist and society-of-states theories would support meeting basic needs beyond their own borders at least to the point where survival was no longer threatened; and Chapter 5 would suggest that at least some basic rights should be met. If you consider the rights specified in the UDHR it would seem that even the most basic rights to survival – simply to stay alive – are routinely violated (or at least fail to be upheld). Article 25 the UDHR states that "everyone has the right to a standard of living adequate to the health and well-being of himself and his family, including food, clothing, housing and medical care". Those in extreme poverty clearly do not have these basic rights and, as discussed in detail in Chapter 5, those who lack basic rights to survival and subsistence are unable to exercise other human rights. Moreover, the UDHR not only outlines rights, but also stresses that they should be realized (as Pogge points out). Thus Article 28 continues that "everyone is entitled to a social and international order in which the rights and freedoms set forth in this Declaration can be fully realized". Those in poverty do not have these rights and it would seem that little is being done to uphold the promises about realizing and securing such rights.

Of course, you might not adopt a rights-based approach and therefore not see poverty as a violation of rights: however, it is likely that in one way or another you consider massive global inequality and poverty as bad things. Likewise, you do not have to accept rights to recognize that in the world today, most people do *not* have access to the goods listed in Article 25; they do not have an adequate standard of living. This is recognizable on any theory of ethics or justice, and although it is theoretically possible to deny any and all duties to others, this is unusual, inhuman and perhaps even sociopathic. It is reasonable to think that extreme poverty is morally unacceptable and therefore that there are moral and political questions about how extensive duties to the poor are and how these can be fulfilled.

It is hard to understate the extent of the problem of poverty and for some it is the very size of the problem that makes it so difficult to address. Quite simply, it is overwhelming. A great number of people in the world live in abject poverty, while a smaller number enjoy luxuries. The facts about this situation are startling. Pogge (2005) observes that in today's world the problems of severe poverty – starvation and malnutrition, illness and poor health, low life expectancy, dependency, social exclusion and effective slavery – affect billions of people. In his words, "the annual death toll from poverty-related causes is around 18 million, or one-third of all human deaths, which adds up to approximately 270 million deaths since the end of the Cold War". "Poverty-related causes" can include not only starvation or malnutrition but also diseases preventable by basic health care and sanitation. The 1999 World Health Report by WHO gives a detailed breakdown of these causes and numbers of deaths in different parts of the world. Most striking are the summary estimates of mortality by "Communicable diseases, maternal and perinatal conditions and nutritional deficiencies": these accounted for 34 per cent of deaths in areas defined by WHO as "low income", but only 6 per cent in high-income areas. These figures are in spite of the growth of average income worldwide and advances in technology.

But the ethical problem is perhaps even more drastic than the facts and figures suggest. For as Pogge notes, this inequality *could* be largely addressed. Pogge (2005) states that the 44 per cent of the global population that falls below the World Bank's "more generous" poverty line of US$2 per day consumes only 1.3 per cent of global production, and could rise above this line by consuming just 1 per cent more. In contrast, 955 million people in better-off countries use 81 per cent of global production.

We shall look at three ethical responses to the problems in addressing poverty as set out by Singer, O'Neill and Pogge. These responses show the ethical imperative to address the issue of poverty from any ethical standpoint. They also highlight the extent to which the issue is not addressed in practice and the fact that this is partly owing to the dominance of realism and the reliance on states in the global system, as we discussed in Chapters 4 and 6. So, for example, the lack of a global ethical outlook may be a result of realist assumptions about the absence of a genuinely global moral order of nations, or nationalist assumptions about the priority of our own political community and its needs over those that are beyond its borders. (Nationalist systems, however, do recognize duties of aid in emergencies and basic rights, so those who adopt this approach might accept global disparities, but are still likely to find extreme poverty unacceptable.)

Singer's utilitarian approach

We shall look first at Peter Singer, a contemporary utilitarian working in this field, and his argument that there is a duty to provide famine relief, and then at O'Neill's Kantian approach about duties to feed the poor. Both of these thinkers, using supposedly conflicting moral theories, conclude that there is a strong moral duty to give to the poor, and that this is a mandatory "duty of justice" and not an optional "duty of charity". While not all ethicists would agree with Singer and O'Neill, if you take seriously the principles of impartiality and universalism that we discussed in Chapter 3 then it is hard to deny these conclusions. It might be possible to limit the duty in some way; however, good reasons would have to be given for not taking the implications of these principles to their logical conclusions. Thus, although perhaps uncomfortable for the privileged if you adopt either a utilitarian or Kantian approach, these conclusions are difficult to refute on moral grounds. It is very difficult to come up with *moral* arguments in defence of global poverty or, conversely, for the holding of vast wealth.

At the time of famine in East Bengal, Singer wrote a now famous article, "Famine, Affluence, and Morality" (1972), in which he criticized the response of both affluent individuals and affluent countries. Although his argument takes as its starting-point the emergency of this particular famine, it applies equally to all circumstances of poverty. Indeed, he states clearly that the argument is equally applicable to poverty whether or not it is brought about by an emergency situation (such as a famine). Singer argues that the traditional assumptions of moral thinking – which regard meeting the needs of those in distant countries as issues of charity rather than obligations of justice – are wrong.

He begins with what he considers to be two relatively uncontroversial premises:

(i) "Suffering and death from lack of food, shelter and medical care are bad."
(ii) "If it is in our power to prevent something bad from happening, without thereby sacrificing anything of comparable moral importance, we ought, morally, to do it."

To illustrate the logic of this second principle Singer uses the following example: "If I am walking past a shallow pond and see a child drowning in it, I ought to wade in and pull the child out. This will mean getting my clothes muddy, but this is insignificant, while the death of the child would presumably be a very bad thing." Taken together, Singer suggests, these relatively uncontroversial premises lead to a startling conclusion: just as there is a duty to rescue the child from the pond there is a duty to relieve famine, poverty and inequality. If this is true then two generally held moral assumptions, which we shall now examine, have been overturned.

The first assumption Singer denies is that geographical closeness is morally significant. That is, he denies that there is any moral difference if the child is a neighbour's drowning child or an Indian child dying of starvation. In arguing against this assumption, Singer claims that while being near to someone in need of help might make it more likely that we *can* and *will* assist, this does not show that we *ought* to prioritize the needs of someone nearer over someone further away. At one time in history, argues Singer, it may have been that people were in a position to help the needy in their own village or town, whereas trying to help those further afield would have been futile or impossible. In this case, locality might have been a justification for helping some and not others owing to the limits of travel and communication. However, this is simply not the case today. The reality of, for example, famine and its effects are visible across the world through news and other media, and the ability to assist is evident: physically in the work of international aid agencies and financially in the form of giving to famine-relief charities. Given these facts (and Singer wrote several decades ago, since which time mobility and global communication has increased), there is, according to Singer, no justification for discriminating on geographical grounds. There is no moral difference between the near and the far away.

This argument makes a direct appeal to the universal moral principles of utilitarianism: those of impartially and equality. This is in keeping with Mill's summary of Bentham's principle "everybody to count for one, nobody for more than one". Singer regards this first argument as morally uncontroversial (although non-universalists, such as the cultural relativists we discussed in Chapter 3, would disagree).

The second assumption that Singer strongly resists is that a person's duty to help another person is lessened if there are millions of other people who also could help. So, in the case of global famine, the fact that many other people are in a position to help starving people on the other side of the world – for example in the country itself or in bordering countries – would not lessen your moral duty to help. In this case he claims that the only significant difference is a psychological one: people are likely to *feel* less guilty if many others in a similar situation have also failed to save the child. But there is, for Singer (1972), no difference in moral responsibility. He also argues that the duty to attempt to save the drowning child from the pond is clear even if there are other people in a position to save that child. Thus he suggests that the obligation to help the world's poor is equally shared, and not lessened for any one person by virtue of its being shared. He argues that "most of the major evils – poverty, overpopulation, pollution – are problems in which everyone is almost equally involved".

So Singer's two conclusions are that:

- Proximity or distance are morally insignificant.
- The number of people who could perform the saving action is morally insignificant.

Singer derives from this his final conclusion that there is a moral duty to give to famine relief at least to the point at which nothing morally significant has been sacrificed, or, in other words, to the point where giving more would cause suffering to oneself or one's dependants. To give to this level is not being "good", "charitable" or "generous", but simply doing your moral duty.

Singer's argument appears radical. It upsets traditional moral assumptions: that to give in this way is not worthy of praise, but is just your required moral duty. Conversely, not to give is to be failing morally and worthy of censure and condemnation. He argues that not to give to famine relief while you spend money on anything beyond necessity is morally unjustifiable. Singer claims that, for example, when we buy clothes in order to "look good" and update our unfashionable wardrobe rather than give to the poor, we are doing something wrong. To carry on wearing unfashionable – although still warm and serviceable – clothing and give the money saved to famine relief would not be any great sacrifice. For Singer, making such insignificant sacrifices in order to prevent another person from starving is, simply, what we ought morally to do.

Box 7.1 Utilitarian elements of Singer's argument

- It is universal.
- It follows principles of impartiality and equity.
- Morality is determined in terms of maximizing social utility.
- Moral goodness is understood as the maximal reduction of suffering (if not quite the maximization of the good).

In Singer's argument we can see the utilitarian theory at work in this practical topic of famine relief (Box 7.1). His moral commitment is universal: not to family, community or nation first, but to all people globally. In utilitarian fashion he calculates what is morally good or right by weighing up the relative pains and pleasures of persons equally. On the "pain" side of the equation would be the suffering of the poor (in this case the famine victims) and on the "pleasure" side would be the pleasure of the rich in purchasing lifestyle goods that go beyond what is needed to avoid pain. As a result he is able to conclude that it is a moral duty for all affluent people to give to causes such as famine relief (and equally to all those who are suffering). This would reduce significant pain at a cost of very little reduction of pleasure (for the pain reduced by preventing starvation is not comparable to the lack of pleasure for the rich in buying unnecessary additional goods).

In fact Singer (1972) does not go as far as he might in this utilitarian argument, since he does not argue for pleasure to be fully maximized and explicitly states that the second principle "requires us only to prevent what is bad, and not to promote what is good, and it requires this of us only when we can do it without sacrificing anything that is, from the moral point of view, comparably important". If he were to take a fully utilitarian line he would not stop with preventing bad but move to promoting good. It would seem that he decided that his conclusions were radical enough without fully following the utilitarian line regarding the maximization of the good. However, although he does stop at the prevention of what is bad, he clearly is still committed to utilitarian conclusions (even if he does not press them in this argument) because he wonders whether this goes far enough and whether one is in fact required to give beyond the point where oneself and one's dependants might suffer, which he calls the point of "marginal utility".

O'Neill's Kantian approach

Onora O'Neill is an important contemporary Kantian who has written on moral theory and on many issues of policy and practice, from bioethics to famine. In a now famous article, "Rights, Obligations and World Hunger" ([1987] 2008), she argues for why a Kantian approach is the most effective ethical approach for addressing world hunger. O'Neill addresses this topic from a very different angle to Singer and Pogge, although she comes to very similar conclusions. Her theory is a theory of obligation, of duty, which is very similar to rights thinking. However, O'Neill prefers an obligations theory, believing, for reasons we shall explore, that it is more effective than a rights-based theory.

O'Neill, like Singer (1972), begins by outlining some of the horrendous facts and figures about world hunger and the disparities between the rich north and the poor south and points out that simply knowing the facts is not enough. She emphasizes what we have learnt in putting together our ethical toolbox: that knowing the facts of a situation does not tell you what you should do and what matters in an ethical situation. In other words, what matters is what we *do* in response to those facts. As we saw in Chapter 5, there are many constructions and interpretations of rights, and O'Neill's point is that which interpretation is adopted matters. Many prevalent interpretations, for example those that emphasize political and civil rights over economic and social rights, are not adequate to address world hunger. For O'Neill, too, many constructions of rights do not address human needs and relegate the addressing of poverty to charity, which for her (like Singer) is an unconvincing answer. She argues that while it is possible for poverty to be eradicated by charity, it is unsatisfactory to see it in these terms. This is because, for O'Neill, making poverty eradication the concern of charity gives it the status of an optional act that is "supererogatory": that is, beyond what is obligatory. On this understanding, says O'Neill, the "haves" of this world are in a position to see helping the poor as an especially admirable moral action: a praiseworthy option rather than an absolute requirement. Correspondingly, the "have-nots" are in no position to claim any entitlement to help. They cannot make *demands*, but only beg for assistance. Relying on such requests is simply not enough to address the problem; in O'Neill's words it is "witheringly inadequate". Thus on the charity view, people dying of starvation can appeal to richer people's sense of benevolence and hope for the best, but they cannot make a claim in terms of their right or entitlement that demands aid from the rich.

Given this, O'Neill prefers an overtly Kantian approach where ethics and justice is focused on obligations rather than on rights. She argues that this is a less passive model of persons than either the utilitarian or the rights-based model. In an obligations model, rather than being units in the calculation or claimants of rights, people are agents with the power to require changes directly, not wait for others to deign to grant their rights. In other words, O'Neill sees obligations as prior to rights, because a right is effectively meaningless unless there is someone who has the duty to honour that right.

In keeping with what we have said about the nature of rights in Chapter 5, O'Neill says that we cannot make sense of a right until we establish "who has what obligation to do what for whom under which circumstances". Broadly speaking, what this means is that to talk about a right that one person has is always to talk about an obligation that someone else has to honour it by providing something or refraining from doing something. For example, a right to education obliges someone or some institution to provide it; a person's right not to be attacked obliges everyone not to attack them (think back to the discussion of Shue's understanding of basic rights to security). Now, in the context of global poverty, O'Neill thinks that talking predominantly about the "rights" of the poor – rights to food, shelter, clothing or education, for instance – focuses too heavily on one side of this equation at the expense of the obligations side. Thus to ascribe rights to impoverished people who have no power to enforce these rights is, by itself, virtually meaningless and, perhaps more importantly, practically ineffective. What is needed instead is a primary focus on the obligations that the better-off nations and institutions have to the worse off. In short it puts the onus not on the poor to demand their rights, but on the rich, who have an absolute duty to address poverty. Clearly O'Neill's emphasis on obligations has similar aims to at least some of the conceptions of rights we discussed in Chapter 5 with regard to what she wishes to protect and claim. Thus it is not a disagreement about what an ethical outcome or just distribution is, but rather a disagreement about how best such issues should be constructed and understood to result in the poor being made better off.

As we have discussed, Kant uses the categorical imperative to work out what is morally right and tell us what should be done. Key to Kant's method was the requirement that actions are "universalizable": that practices and actions must be something one could rationally wish that all people can do. Applying this to the issue of hunger, O'Neill argues that while we cannot, for example, make it the case that everyone in the world could eat exactly what I eat or share exactly the same shelter, we can nevertheless make the *principles* of living and the structure of social and political institutions consistent, such that they and their benefits are "shareable by all", and then see how such a principle would apply to particular situations.

Using this methodology, O'Neill considers coercion and deception and argues that they cannot be universalized. In other words, they do not pass the test of the categorical imperative because they cannot be shared by all: it is impossible for everyone to be coercers, because they need people to coerce; and not everyone can reasonably be deceivers, as we saw with the case of lying, because they need people to deceive. Therefore, O'Neill claims, one principle of justice is non-coercion. The obligation not to coerce others rules out various immoral acts, such as murder and torture, but, importantly, O'Neill argues it is particularly pertinent when considering obligations to the poor; for the poor are, by definition, in a position to be coerced. As O'Neill puts it, we the rich can easily make the poor "offers they cannot refuse". In other words, the rules of economic fairness might be enough to protect justice in the case of transactions between roughly equal partners: for example, two rich nations

---

Box 7.2 Kantian elements of O'Neill's argument

- It is universal.
- It uses the categorical imperative (the criterion of "universalizablity") to determine obligations.
- It prioritizes duty.
- It respects individual persons and their needs as "ends in themselves" and never as means to something else.

---

conducting commerce. But when one party is poorer and a great deal less powerful than the other, the powerful nation has the upper hand, such that they can set up dangerous industries in urban areas, or charge crippling investment conditions or set conditions on giving aid.

What is needed to prevent this is not only a focus on the rights of poor individuals and the duties of rich individuals, but a view that also includes the obligations of institutions, corporations and governments not to coerce in these ways. O'Neill's claim, then, is that injustices such as coercion can be made visible and addressed on a Kantian model of obligation in a more effective way than they can on a rights or utilitarian model (see Box 7.2). An obligations approach explicitly includes obligations of institutions as well as individuals; something that we saw in Chapter 5 can be problematic for rights-based approaches. Moreover, an obligation model lays the burden of action not on the vulnerable party to demand rights, but on the stronger, wealthier party, who must discharge their obligation to act.

Pogge's cosmopolitan and negative-rights approach

So far in this chapter we have looked at Singer's utilitarian argument that we have a moral responsibility to help the world's poor if we are in a position to do so; then at O'Neill's Kantian claims that what matters most in the theory and practice of addressing global poverty are obligations and that there are obligations to assist the poor. Both these views take there to be certain obligations that richer people, institutions or nations have to help poorer ones. But what kind of obligations are these? Both these thinkers argue that the duty to aid the poor is one that requires action if we are in a position to help. Thus, these duties to the poor are "positive duties" to do something, not "negative duties" not to harm. Think back to Chapter 5 and the distinction between positive and negative rights: positive rights are those that require others to act if they are to be met and negative rights are those of non-interference – the right to be "left alone".

The duty Singer is talking about is a positive duty *to* help – to alleviate poverty – irrespective of the causes of poverty. Similarly, O'Neill's formulation of our obligations to the world's poor is not based only on negative duties *not* to bring about poverty (although she does evoke at least one negative duty not to coerce the poor), but also on a *positive* obligation to assist them. By contrast, a wholly negative characterization of our duty to the poor would be limited to requiring us to avoid causing or exacerbating poverty: to avoid causing harm to others by our actions. This would allow us to overlook poverty that we did nothing to bring about or make worse. By formulating our obligations in Kantian terms of universalizability, O'Neill expressly rejects a wholly negative view. For by accounting for these obligations in terms of principles we could all rationally make universal and thereby live under, she is claiming that we are positively obliged to see to it that everyone has enough to eat, and not just that we are morally obliged to avoid harming them or making them hungry.

So both Singer and O'Neill's approaches require that positive obligations to the world's poor be recognized. As we saw in Chapter 5, many people regard negative rights as stronger than positive rights, and therefore believe the duty "not to harm" is primary (although some thinkers, like Shue, rejected this distinction). Those who think that the claim of negative rights and duties is prior to that of positive rights and duties will find Singer and O'Neill's arguments weak. They will argue that positive obligations are not strong enough to make the duties of assistance required in the ways that Singer and O'Neill claim. For example, Western governments might argue that they owe less to far-away famine victims than to the less well off within their own borders, even though this poverty is less extreme. This claim is not based on distance alone nor on national partiality, but on the claim that because the government has a direct impact on its own poor people, it has a strong negative duty *not* to pursue policies that make them worse off or keep them in poverty, which alleviating poverty beyond its own borders would inevitably entail. So there is a negative duty on the government not to harm that is stronger than any positive duty to aid people whose poverty it has no direct part in.

To counter such claims Thomas Pogge, in his famous book *World Poverty and Human Rights* (2002, 2008), denies that duties to the poor are positive duties, and reframes them as negative duties. He claims that to fail to help the global poor is to violate negative moral duty: a duty not to harm.

Pogge begins by denying the popular assumption that we are *responsible* for global poverty simply because we have done nothing to prevent it. In Pogge's scheme we are not culpable because we are bystanders who have simply stood by and done nothing as an unjust state of affairs has developed. Rather, in failing to help the poor, Pogge argues, we are culpable in failing our negative duty to stop *bringing about* the injustice. Thus we have responsibilities because of our *actions* rather than our *inaction*. The crux of Pogge's position is that world poverty is the direct responsibility of the richer world: that we have caused the poverty and directly harmed the poor.

Accordingly, we have strong negative moral obligations to alleviate poverty – to do no harm – and not weaker positive obligations to help.

Pogge's argument depends on the premise that world poverty is largely brought about and sustained by richer Western economies and institutions. For the duty to alleviate poverty to be negative, Pogge must establish that such poverty is *caused* by the rich; they must be fully implicated to avoid being simply bystanders. In defence of this crucial premise, Pogge argues that world poverty comes about from an international order largely imposed and upheld by richer Western nations: from shared social institutions (such as the World Bank and the IMF discussed in Chapter 6); from poorer nations being excluded from the use of their natural resources (such as when Western magnates and, more recently, corporations have established themselves in foreign countries to utilize crops and minerals, not to mention cheap labour); and, relatedly, from the historical effects of colonialism and war.

Reframing the argument as one of negative rather than positive duties allows Pogge to avoid some of the objections that can be made against a positive duty to aid the poor: objections it is harder for Singer and O'Neill to avoid. One such objection, which takes our obligations to alleviate world poverty as positive but which rejects Singer's impartiality claim, says that it is understandable, and may be defensible, for citizens and governments to be concerned with those nearer to them. Pogge states that this may indeed be a defensible claim when it comes to positive obligations, but that it is not for negative ones. To use an analogy, we might intuitively put our positive duties to care for members of our family as overriding those we have to others, without doing anything immoral. But if we were to privilege the negative duty *not* to harm our family above the same duty to refrain from harming anyone, including strangers, this would be harder to defend. As we saw in Chapter 5, we have a universal, basic duty not to harm people or violate their rights. By framing duties in this way, Pogge does not need to address the nationalist's claim that it is legitimate to prioritize certain positive obligations to compatriots over duties to those beyond borders. Again, this works only with positive duties. The duty not to harm – a negative duty to refrain from action rather than a positive duty to act – is incumbent on us all. In the case of global poverty, our duty is to *refrain from action*, not to *make* people suffer and to stop *causing* suffering – wherever and to whomever it occurs: not a positive duty of action.

A second objection levelled at Pogge (and other advocates of duty to the poor) is the claim that poverty is not primarily caused by the international order, but rather by the unstable, and often brutal and corrupt, regimes of poorer and developing countries. Pogge rejects this claim and argues that even if such regimes may be directly responsible for exacerbating poverty, developed nations, in supporting and literally "buying in" to such regimes, thereby sustain and perpetuate not only those regimes but also the unstable conditions under which, for example, military coups are commonplace. Using the case of Nigeria in the 1990s as one example,

---

Box 7.3 Duties to the poor are not duties of generosity

"The common assumption, however, is that reducing severe poverty abroad at the expense of our own affluence would be generous on our part, not something we owe, and that our failure to do this is thus at most a lack of generosity that does not make us morally responsible for the continued deprivation of the poor. I deny this popular assumption."

(Pogge 2005)

Pogge (2008) puts the point powerfully in terms of there being no moral difference between trading with, and thereby sustaining, a tyrannical regime that "dispossesses" its people of natural resources and stealing from them directly. He claims that to pay General Sani Abacha imposes "a second undue harm on the poverty-stricken Nigerian population: not only is the oil taken away for our consumption (and much environmental damage done) without their consent, but their tyrant is also propped up with funds he can spend on arms and soldiers to cement his rule". Furthermore, for Pogge all that is needed to make international governments complicit in this way is that they *recognize* these regimes: in other words that they allow them to act on behalf of the people whom they rule; to borrow and to dispose of their countries' resources in that capacity. Thus the presence of a corrupt or wicked

---

Box 7.4 Key objections to global duties overcome by a negative duty argument

- "Where poverty is the responsibility of a regime which exacerbates it in their country, there is no duty for other nations to alleviate it" (Pogge 2008).
  By contrast, we do have a duty if we recognize, trade with or interact with such regimes.

- "Alleviating poverty in other countries may be a generous act, but doing so is not our moral *duty*" (Pogge 2008).
  By contrast we have a negative duty to address the poverty we have caused. This is not an optional duty of charity.

- "Helping those in poverty may be a *positive* duty, but we have stronger positive duties to help those nearer to us than those further away, so we are entitled to deny impartiality – and thus give preference to our own country" (Pogge 2008).
  By contrast alleviating poverty is a negative duty not to harm. Negative duties are universal and take precedence over positive duties.

---

government does not itself absolve the international order of its responsibility for the conditions that such a regime may perpetuate. In Pogge's view we in richer, developed nations can claim neither that "it is not our responsibility" nor that we are unable to help nor that helping would be going beyond a negative moral duty *not* to sustain poverty.

Like Singer and O'Neill, then, but using a very different approach, Pogge also concludes that the duties to the poor are not those of charity or generosity (Box 7.3).

The difference between Pogge and Singer and O'Neill is that, for Pogge, the duties to the poor derive from the fact that the rich cause and therefore are responsible for poverty. These are negative duties not to harm, and thus duties it is harder to deny (Box 7.4).

A duty to aid

The arguments of Singer, O'Neill and Pogge show that there is a strong case for a duty to aid the poor. These theorists use different methodologies and arguments but they all assert that the ethical approach is to alleviate poverty. Moreover, they all believe that the duty is not one of charity or generosity, to be undertaken after duties to those nearer to us. For all three the continued fact of global poverty shows that we have failed in our moral duties: that we are morally culpable.

From all ethical perspectives, then, the current distribution of global resources is unjust, and our collective failure to address such indefensible inequalities shows just how difficult we find it to be ethical when it will cost us something, even when we know that we should be. After all, the ethical imperative to meet the needs of those who are starving is not an issue of ethical dilemma or controversy, as is so often the case in ethics, for example, when it comes to balancing rights. Rather, all ethical theories tell us that poverty, particularly extreme poverty, is wrong: it does not increase happiness, it does not respect persons and it does not allow people to engage in the good life. Given this, the explanation for our reluctance to address these issues cannot be defended.

So the task of the global ethicist is to attempt to engage not only in theoretical debate about whether or not there is a duty to the poor, but also to engage in debates about what are the appropriate policies and practices that are needed to address poverty. So far in this chapter we have established that there is a moral duty to address global poverty and that not to act on this duty or to come up with reasons why it is not necessary to do so is immoral. In the rest of the chapter we shall consider how such duties can be implemented. In order to meet the challenges of global poverty we need to know what kind of development and poverty-alleviation programmes are most successful; for instance, what type of aid is effective and also what kinds of measurement of development work best.

ADDRESSING POVERTY

In order to address global poverty we need first to work out what addressing poverty would mean. Is it sufficient to meet basic needs – for instance, to provide adequate shelter and food – or is more required? One way in which such goals have been formulated is in the UN Millennium Development Goals.

Millennium Development Goals

The "Millenium Declaration" was adopted by the UN General Assembly at a summit meeting in 2000. It was agreed to by all 192 member states and comprised a series of goals concerned with eradicating extreme poverty and disease and promoting education and access to other social resources. There are eight development goals (Box 7.5), which are broken down into targets and indicators.

The eight goals subdivide into targets and specific indicators that are intended to map progress. The targets for the first goal – to eradicate extreme poverty and hunger – are found in Box 7.6.

Box 7.5 Millennium Development Goals

Goal 1: Eradicate extreme poverty and hunger.
Goal 2: Achieve universal primary education.
Goal 3: Promote gender equality and empower women.
Goal 4: Reduce the child mortality rate.
Goal 5: Improve maternal health.
Goal 6: Combat HIV/AIDS, malaria and other diseases.
Goal 7: Ensure environmental sustainability.
Goal 8: Develop a global partnership for development.

Box 7.6 Targets of the first Millennium Development Goal

- Halve, between 1990 and 2015, the proportion of people whose income is less than US$1 per day.
- Achieve full and productive employment and decent work for all, including women and young people.
- Halve, between 1990 and 2015, the proportion of people who suffer from hunger.

AID

As we noted in the introduction to this chapter, "Official Development Assistance" is aid that is given by governments, individually or in collaboration with other states such as with UN programmes. Some aid measures can be specifically humanitarian, as in the case of sending food or other resources in direct response to crises such as floods or earthquakes. Another kind of aid is development aid, which, as its name suggests, is supposed to improve and sustain economic development over the longer term. Next, we look at some problems raised by critics of aid. These criticisms are usually directed at development aid, although they may also relate to aspects of humanitarian aid. Furthermore, as we shall see in the case of aid in conflict situations, the distinction between humanitarian and development aid is not always clear-cut.

Problems with aid

There are many criticisms of aid, and we can only touch on them in this chapter (see Box 7.7). The first is that aid, while it addresses the worst suffering in an emergency, does little to address long-term poverty, as evidenced by the figures at the start of the chapter. Second, aid, especially in the form of emergency and food aid, is a short-term fix that has damaging effects on economic and social infrastructures. For instance, food aid undermines the sale of what food there is, which in turn undermines the livelihoods of those who supply and trade in the market. A third criticism is that aid is "top-down" rather than "bottom-up". What is meant by this is that rather than work out what the most effective forms of aid would be in particular instances, development agencies and policies import their own standards and priorities. Often these are about meeting particular global goals, which are determined by donor goals. As a result, programmes too often fail to see the needs on the ground so that, despite the intention, the aid is ineffective. For example, an outside aid agency, driven by a strong and commendable egalitarian rationale and concern for universal

---

Box 7.7 Criticisms of aid

- Responsive and emergency focused.
- Reduces rather than builds capacity and infrastructure.
- Top-down rather than bottom-up.
- Relies on an economic view of development.
- Encourages corruption.
- Used to meet other political and economic agendas.

---

human rights, might attempt to distribute aid equitably among a number of different groups, when in fact the requirements of these groups might differ greatly. Hence, laudable as the aid agency's values may be, they may not in practice produce the most effective distribution of aid if they overlook local states of affairs. A fourth and connected criticism is that development is often measured by inappropriate standards. Often economic metrics are primary when considering development, and income per capita has been a standard measure of development. However, the problem with such measures is that they do not necessarily map onto actual standards of living. For example, those with low or no wages in a subsistence economy with strong family and social networks who are able to access basic goods may actually be better off than those who earn some wage but who lack necessary goods. A fifth criticism is that the infrastructure of aid is a big industry in itself and often one that represents the largest source of wealth in a poor context. As a result, aid can encourage corruption and abuses of power in conflict situations (an issue we shall return to) but also in any situation where resources and opportunities to gain wealth and goods are rare. A final criticism is that aid does not often come without conditions. Aid can be given in return for other goods, such as access to land, political allegiance, trade agreements, conversion to a particular religious belief and numerous other goods. This is particularly well documented in the case of the Cold War, where aid was given or refused according to which "side" a country was on and the strategic benefits of sustaining its allies. So, for example, during the later part of the Cold War, Fidel Castro's socialist Cuba received significant subsidies from the Soviet Union, while the right-wing dictator in Chile, Augusto Pinochet, benefited similarly from the US. Many argue that aid, and development work in general, always comes with such conditions, for instance, current aid to Afghanistan and Pakistan as part of the "battle for hearts and minds".

Aid in conflict zones

In addition to these general problems with aid there are particular problems with giving aid in conflict zones. However, given that conflict breeds refugees and emergency situations, and that emergencies breed conflicts, emergency aid is often desperately needed there. Of the criticisms above, the claim that aid encourages corruption is particularly important. In such instances there is often no legitimate authority that can authorize access and give permission to aid agencies or that can provide some infrastructure by which aid can be delivered. In such circumstances aid agencies are forced to negotiate with warlords in order to deliver emergency aid. Not surprisingly, those who control aid in a conflict zone have a powerful advantage over those who do not; so much so that it has been suggested that aid prolongs conflict rather than relieves suffering in such conflict zones.

Linda Polman (2010) addresses this issue in her recent book documenting the role of aid in recent conflicts. She suggests that aid has now become "a strategic aspect of warfare" and that, since the end of the Cold War, development and humanitarian agencies are often the biggest players in conflict zones. Polman reports that the International Committee of the Red Cross estimates that every major disaster now attracts 1000 national and international aid agencies. Aid is big business, and certainly the biggest and best financed business in conflict zones when normal economic and social structures have collapsed. As a result, Polman argues, much of the conflict in war zones revolves around warring parties attempting to control as much aid as they possibly can. Aid thus becomes a target for conflict and a sustainer of conflict as well as a reliever of mass suffering.

Polman documents the details of how this happens with examples from a number of conflicts, including Rwanda, Sierra Leone, Afghanistan and Biafra. She describes the 1994 genocide in Rwanda, in which extremist Hutus systematically murdered an estimated half a million Tutsis and moderate Hutus. As a result of the following conflict, two million Hutus left Rwanda (including those who had committed the genocide). This resulted in a humanitarian crisis of huge proportions and approximately three-quarters of a million Hutu refugees found themselves in a refugee camp near Goma. Polman describes how the camp became a media circus, with each NGO claiming higher death rates in order to be back on the news in the north, in part to attempt to increase giving and donations, which would be used to alleviate suffering with aid. What was not mentioned in these news broadcasts was that many of those in the camps were responsible for the genocide. Her conclusion is striking: "abundant humanitarian aid was all that enabled the Hutu extremists to carry on their extermination campaign against the Tutsis in Rwanda from UNHCR camps in Goma". She goes on to describe how humanitarian aid was pretty much the only source of income the Hutu leadership had access to; without it it is likely that their military infrastructure and aims would have collapsed relatively quickly.

SUSTAINABLE APPROACHES

These problems with aid are well documented. But, if aid is not effective then what is the alternative? To do nothing – as we have seen from Singer, O'Neill and Pogge – is unethical. However, to be ethical aid must also be effective. Other longer-term approaches have been tried that attempt to engender long-term development rather than meet short-term needs. The attempt to build capacity and infrastructure has become an increasingly important aspect of the work of development NGOs. This is true not just in the amount of aid they give to long-term projects, but also in the increasing attention NGOs give to attempting to influence policy and to lobbying rather than just to emergency relief. Oxfam, for example, is engaged not only in emergency and humanitarian relief and development programmes in more than a hundred countries, but also in public campaigns designed to put pressure on government institutions. Examples of these are those that were run by coalitions of NGOs, such as Health and Education for All and Jubilee 2000, among many others.

One approach has been not to "aid" as such, but to enable poor people to engage in the marketplace and to attain the skills or capital to support themselves. Increasingly, NGOs and other aid agencies have seen the shortcomings of a top-down approach to international aid and the need for more localized systems of delivering aid. For instance, in *Ethics of Global Development* (2008), David Crocker writes about Sabina Alkire's involvement in Oxfam's community development projects in Pakistan. Here, Alkire and Oxfam used "local facilitators" to assess the effectiveness of its projects with a view to continuing with or modifying them. In other words Oxfam did its quality control at the particular and grassroots level, rather than by looking from above at broad indicators that supposedly apply generally across different cultures and situations. There are a number of other approaches that attempt to do this, for instance anti-corruption schemes such as that of the OECD, and micro-finance schemes such as the Co-operative Bank's initiative that gives financial support to small businesses in poor countries.

Fairtrade

Perhaps the most well known of these alternative approaches to aid is the Fairtrade movement. The phrase "Trade not Aid" began as a mantra of the Right, who objected to giving foreign aid on the grounds that it is damaging to economic growth. Peter Bauer is illustrative of this popular approach. He has long argued that aid is an inappropriate intervention into an economy, and results in a catalogue of undesirable effects. First, it encourages the growth of bureaucracy and big government (always bad from a right-wing perspective). Second, aid is often given by and to governments and thus increases the power and wealth of those in public office. This leads to ill effects in that it makes government positions more attractive and therefore lures talent from entrepreneurial roles to public administration.

In short, according to this model, aid results in the growth of bureaucracy and administration rather than in the development of wealth-creating infrastructure. Thus although aid might meet short-term needs, in the long term it stultifies economic growth and arguably creates cultures of dependency. You do not have to accept this claim to recognize that the creation of long-term resources and sustainable development that gives people the means to support themselves is preferable to the short-term fixes of emergency aid. Moreover, the benefits of such strategies are not only beneficial in terms of economic development but also address psychological and emotional cycles of dependency. This type of approach is summed up in Christian Aid's strapline: "Give a man a fish and you feed him for a day. Teach a man to fish and you feed him for life." The Fairtrade movement embeds this commitment.

The Fairtrade movement has been successful in part because it is heavily promoted by development NGOs, such as Oxfam, Christian Aid, CAFOD, Traidcraft and Tearfund. The movement towards fair trade is part of the move towards policy and sustainable approaches that NGOs have increasingly adopted over the past few decades. Fairtrade and similar initiatives are attempts to begin to address poverty in ways that extend beyond aid. These have had some real successes; for instance, the successful mainstreaming of the Fairtrade logo has been acclaimed as one of the most significant retail trends of the past few decades and sales are in the hundreds of millions. Ethical shopping has become big business and, importantly, buying Fairtrade products, like other forms of consumer activism (such as the boycott of Nike), gives individuals some power, however limited, to address issues that usually seem beyond their reach.

There are, of course, criticisms of this movement: there are right-wing objections that Fairtrade undermines normal market forces, and a more standard criticism that the Fairtrade movement is so small that it does little to address injustice but rather serves to salve the consciences of the Western consumers who purchase the products. In addition, there are left-wing criticisms: that it endorses a capitalist market model. Despite its failings, Fairtrade is an important development in terms of global ethics. It addresses the issue at all levels: it engages in the institutions of global trade, and allows individuals to act in small ways, which in turn serves to establish global relations and connections across borders. In addition, the purchasing of Fairtrade products has become normal, which increases knowledge of poverty and also establishes global responsibilities.

THE CAPABILITY APPROACH

We shall finish this chapter by considering the capability approach to development, which attempts to avoid some of the problems with simple understandings of development. The capability approach is primarily associated with the work of Amartya Sen (1979, 1999; Nussbaum & Sen 1993) and Martha Nussbaum (1988, 2000), although it has been broadly adopted in both theoretical work regarding issues of quality of life and theories of human flourishing, and has influenced the development and implementation of policy and practice; consider its obvious presence in the thinking behind the United Nations Development Reports. The beginnings of the capability approach were first outlined by Sen in his 1979 Tanner Lecture,

"Equality of What?", where he criticized contemporary understandings of equality and presented an "alternative formulation of equality".

The capability approach arose out of dissatisfaction with the available tools for evaluating and monitoring development, in particular those that derived from utilitarian agendas and aggregate measures, and those based on asserting a list of "primary goods". Sen is critical of utilitarian models and economic models because they do not take account of the differences between individuals and their different needs. Because utilitarian methods measure the total of well-being, or utility or happiness (as we discussed in Chapter 3), it is difficult for utilitarian accounts to accommodate distributional inequalities rather than focus on one measure. Often these measures are economic, such as income per capita. For example, a utilitarian model would conclude that poverty had been reduced if income per capita had increased. Likewise, Sen rejects desire and preference satisfaction models because they focus only on personal preference and mental reactions. Thus, he rejects typical utilitarian calculators of well-being, such as psychic utility or preference-fulfilment, as not being effective forms of social evolution.

Sen (1979) also criticizes "primary goods" models of development on the grounds that they do not "adequately take account of the diversity of human beings". In other words, they assume that all people are basically the same, with the same needs. Sen argues that if this were the case, a list of primary goods that all people needed would be a reasonable way to assess people's well-being. This is not the case, however, and Sen argues that "in fact, people seem to have very different needs varying with health, longevity, climatic conditions, location, work conditions, temperament, and even body size (affecting food and clothing requirements)". The different needs of different people suggests that simply to list the "goods" that people need, and then measure the extent to which they are lacking them, is not sufficient to ensure development.

Sen argues that we should not be looking for any single measure. Nor, he says, should we be ticking goods off a list to determine the development needs of a certain person. As Alkire (2002) says, when commenting on Sen's approach, we should look at real individuals, at "what persons are actually able to do or be ... not ... the pounds of rice they consume".

Sen's approach is to be concerned with the reality of people's experiences rather than with external measures. Therefore he focuses on capabilities; on the actual capability of agents to "be" and to "do": a person's "beings and doings". Capability is about what a person is able to be and do determined by the background social context, the endowments of the individual and opportunities and choices afforded to the individual.

"Capability" refers to a set of beings and doings, or "functionings", as they are often termed. The particular combination of functionings (the functionings set) is variable by individual and context, as in turn is the resulting construction of capability. Capability is thus worked out by seeing what "functionings" a person has and can exercise. These functionings are not the same for everyone, and what is a valuable functioning for one person is less valuable for others. Capability is about having sufficient appropriate functionings to lead a fulfilled life (and the *freedom* to choose what type of life to lead). Thus the valuable functionings (beings and doings) that make up capability are open to negotiation and change from one context and individual to another. Flexibility is important for Sen, as it allows us to recognize different needs and contexts: if this were not the case "we might be as worried about the rich person fasting as about the starving poor" (Alkire 2002). There is flexibility between individuals and between different social contexts and regions. This allows us to consider a very broad range of functionings: some are elementary or basic and valued by all, for example "being adequately nourished and being in good health" (Nussbaum & Sen 1993), and others are more complex and valued differently.

Furthermore the selection of capabilities takes place at a number of levels – some collective, some individual. Thus choices about capability, about the actual set of functionings, need to be made in different contexts and by different individuals and groups according to the values and priorities of that context. The resulting definition of capability is not predetermined (at least in Sen's work) by the mere adoption of the approach, and accordingly key functionings need to be selected to assess capability in any given circumstance. Judgements still need to be made, and arguably the downside of flexibility is that it is too indeterminate. This is Nussbaum's view, and why in her version she has a normative list of functionings (something we discussed in Chapter 3 and shall return to again in Chapter 11).

There is a freedom to move between sets of functionings and to value different functionings combined in different ways. Freedom construed in this way is not just about "choice" but includes social and political policies that engender greater or lesser freedoms. Freedom, for Sen, is a substantial concept that is connected with the actual capabilities that you have, not just with individual control and choice. Sen does not adopt the liberal-choice model of freedom, but broadens the scope of freedom to include social and political policies that engender greater or lesser freedoms. For instance, when he speaks about freedom from malaria, he argues that given a choice we would choose a malaria-free environment. Therefore, public programmes to drain malaria ponds enhance our freedom, even if these were not choices individuals explicitly made, because only if such communal measures are taken is there the "freedom" to live in a malaria-free environment. So, for Sen, "being free from malaria" or "freedom from hunger" are not just "rhetoric". He argued that "there is a very real sense in which the freedom to live the way one would like is enhanced by public policy that transforms epidemiological and social environments" (Nussbaum & Sen 1993). Freedom in the capability approach indicates more than simply autonomous, individual choice as championed by the liberal model. Freedom in this approach is conceptualized as positive as well as negative – in terms of the discussion in Chapter 5, it is a positive right to experience certain freedoms as well as the negative right to be "left alone".

> **Box 7.8 Advantages of the capability approach**
>
> - It has a global framework;
> - is local and context-sensitive;
> - includes individual and group values.

The capability approach has three advantages over other models of development, especially if one is looking for globally suitable models. First, the mix of functionings – some elementary and some more complex – allows a global framework that is still sensitive to local and individual differences (in this it is similar to Shue's basic-rights approach). Second, its flexibility makes it less open to accusations of moral imperialism or moral neocolonialism. And third, because it includes both individual and communal concerns and sees freedom not only as individual choice but as collective responsibility, the divide between individual rights and communal goods is reduced.

The capability approach has been influential in practice and in particular has fed into UN thinking about how to measure development. Drawing directly on the capability approach, the UNDP (1998) defines "human development" as a "process of enlarging people's choices. Enlarging people's choices is achieved by expanding human capabilities and functionings." In these measures economic development alone is not regarded as a sufficient model of development.

The values endorsed by the UNDP, and which inform the Human Development Reports, state that development should not only increase economic status but also should:

- be equitable;
- enhance human well-being;
- encourage democratic participation;
- be environmentally sustainable;
- support cultural flourishing; and
- promote human rights.

CONCLUSION

This chapter has explored some of the issues of poverty and development that are central to global ethics. It has shown that there are no ethically good reasons to justify global inequalities and therefore shown clearly that global ethics is not just about theoretical debates about the nature of duties or the nature of justice. The three arguments presented from Singer, O'Neill and Pogge show that there is an unquestionable duty to address global poverty. Given the strength of the duty, it is difficult to account for the fact of the continuing and extreme poverty of most of the globe's population. In the second half of the chapter we considered various approaches to addressing that problem and the need for effective approaches and alternative possibilities for measuring and ensuring development.

Given the scope of the topic, it is not surprising that there are many more issues and policies that could have been addressed. However, I have demonstrated both the extremity of the problem and how it connects with other issues in global ethics. For instance, as Pogge so strongly pointed out, the mechanisms of global governance implicate all global actors in causing and sustaining poverty. In addition, conditions of poverty exacerbate other global-ethics concerns, such as human-rights violations and sustaining and causing war and conflict (as we touched on in the discussion of aid). Thus this chapter has shown us the connectedness of global-ethics issues and how the ethical toolbox can be applied, and has forcibly brought home the need for action at every level: individuals need to act in lobbying and personal giving to NGOs; states need to act through foreign policy as well as development policy; and global institutions and the global community need to act so as not to cause poverty as well as to give aid in emergency situations.

FURTHER READING

- Crocker, D. A. *Ethics of Global Development* (Cambridge: Cambridge University Press, 2008).
- O'Neill, O. "Rights, Obligations and World Hunger". In *Global Ethics: Seminal Essays*, T. Pogge & K. Horton (eds), 139–55 (Saint Paul, MN: Paragon House, 2008).
- Organisation for Economic Co-operation and Development (OECD). *Fighting Corruption: What Role for Civil Society? The Experience of the OECD* (Paris: OECD, 2003). www.oecd.org/dataoecd/8/2/19567549.pdf (accessed May 2011).
- Pogge, T. *World Poverty and Human Rights: Cosmopolitan Responsibilities and Reforms* (Cambridge: Polity Press, 2002).
- Pogge, T. "World Poverty and Human Rights". *Ethics and International Affairs* **19** (2005): 1–7.
- Polman, L. *War Games: The Story of Aid and War in Modern Times* (London: Viking Press, 2010).
- Sen, A. "Equality of What?" The Tanner Lecture on Human Values (1979). www.tannerlectures.utah.edu/lectures/documents/sen80.pdf (accessed May 2011).
- Sen, A. *Development As Freedom* (New York: Knopf, 1999).
- Singer, P. "Famine, Affluence, and Morality". *Philosophy and Public Affairs* **1** (1972): 229–43.
- United Nations Development Programme (UNDP). "Glossary of Terms" (1998). http://hdr.undp.org/en/humandev/glossary/ (accessed May 2011).
- United Nations Millennium Development Goals website. www.un.org/millenniumgoals/bkgd.shtml (accessed June 2011).

8 GLOBAL CONFLICT: WAR, TERRORISM AND HUMANITARIAN INTERVENTION

INTRODUCTION

In Chapter 7 we explored perhaps the most pressing issue of global ethics: the huge injustice of global poverty and global disparities in wealth. This chapter will address an equally challenging issue for global ethics: that of war, conflict, terrorism and all forms of military intervention. A key difference between war and conflict and issues of global poverty is that the suffering and violations of human rights that arise in war and conflict are *always* caused by human agency. War and conflict is *always* someone's responsibility, so if the "harm principle" (a negative duty not to harm) we discussed in Chapter 3 holds, it should be at least possible to map duties of compensation and redress, even if it is difficult to enforce these in practice. In Chapter 6 we considered arguments about who had duties to meet the needs of the poor and, in this chapter, similar arguments will be considered about duties to those who are suffering from conflict, particularly in the final section on humanitarian intervention. In addition, issues that we have discussed in all the previous chapters about the scope of global duties and whether or not there are duties to distant others come to the fore when we consider the ethics of war and conflict.

Questions about whether political violence is ever justified are at the heart of global ethics. Violence and killing are unethical acts. The question is not whether these are "good" acts. They are not. The question is whether they can ever be justified. For example, is violence permissible if it prevents worse violence? Answering this question remains one of the most difficult ethical conundrums. For while there is general agreement that violence is wrong, there is also a general acceptance that in some instances it is permissible: for example, in self-defence, to prevent atrocity, to protect the vulnerable or as an action of last resort. But, even if one does wish to argue that violence is permissible in certain circumstances, characterizing exactly what these circumstances are is no easy matter. Moreover, as difficult as it is to characterize such situations for individuals, it is even more difficult to do it for larger groups and for states where violence becomes institutionalized and politically sanctioned, as it does when wars are waged.

For those who think that violence is sometimes permissible – pacifists believe that violence, whether individual or state, is never justified – much ethical time and effort is given to attempting to characterize those circumstances where violence is justified. It is the attempt to clarify this issue that explains the posing of familiar ethical questions: would it have been ethically acceptable to kill Hitler or Stalin (or any other "evil" leader whose actions resulted in the death of millions) as a child? In other words, is preventative violence acceptable and justifiable in instances where the "perpetrator" is still innocent? If we expand this to state violence, is it acceptable and justifiable to engage in war "pre-emptively" to prevent a bloodier later conflict? This has become a key issue in contemporary debates about wars, for example, to prevent "rogue states" from acquiring nuclear weapons or other WMD, or to prevent mass starvation or ethnic conflict; we shall return to this later issue in the last section, on humanitarian intervention.

This chapter will address key issues of global conflict, particularly whether or not the use of force can ever be justified. It will consider traditional "just-war" approaches that claim that force can be justified for humanitarian reasons. It will consider contemporary forms of warfare, such as terrorism, and the extent to which traditional frameworks for assessing the ethical validity of war are appropriate, and will build on the discussion of torture in Chapter 5 to continue the debate about individual and communal rights. In these ways the distinctive elements of war and conflict as ethical issues in the contemporary global context will be assessed.

JUST-WAR THEORY

The traditional way ethicists have judged whether state violence is permissible is by the application of "just-war" theory. Just-war theory is a mechanism to determine the circumstances in which war is justified. Moreover, it aims to control, limit and often even forbid war and, importantly, it attempts to respect the humanity of the enemy and to uphold morality even in times of conflict. It is intended to be used before a conflict to help leaders decide whether it is permissible to engage in war, but is also used after the event to determine whether or not the war was justified. At the time of writing in 2010, for example, the debate continues over whether the US-led invasion of Iraq in 2003 (which we shall use as an example throughout this chapter) was, all things considered, justified or whether it was nothing of the sort and even constitutes a war crime. Both defenders and critics of the Iraq War commonly evoke arguments and concepts employed in just-war theory. For example, some critics say that it was a purely aggressive act of war that had nothing to do with defence (even though it was disingenuously publicized as necessary for international security) and therefore cannot be considered just. Some supporters claim that it was reasonable to suppose at the time that Saddam Hussein was developing WMD and that therefore this risk provided a good enough reason – a just cause – for invading, even though that supposition later turned out to be largely false. Others argue that the regime was so unjust that the aim of changing that regime was sufficient to justify this conflict.

Just-war thinking is influential and it is this thinking that has shaped much of the international law and codes of practice on conflict that are accepted by the member states of the UN. Just-war theory addresses two aspects of warfare:

- *Jus ad bellum*: the justice of going to war.
- *Jus in bello*: the justice of the conduct of war.

Distinguishing between these two aspects of war is important, since a war might be justified in that a violent response was necessary, for example to prevent greater violence or numbers of casualties. However, if the conduct of war is not all that it should be, for example, innocents are killed or unethical weapons or tactics are used, then going to war might be justified but the practice of war render it unethical. Conversely, one could have a conflict that was deemed unjust in that it should never have been begun, but the combatants could have nonetheless behaved justly, or honourably, in perpetrating the (unjust) conflict. Depending on the questions you are trying to answer, you will focus on either *jus ad bellum* or *jus in bello*. If we consider the recent conflict between the Western coalition and Iraq, both issues arise. For example, *ad bellum* questions can be asked over whether going to war was justified. Were there good enough reasons to go to war? Here relevant matters might include whether or not those who declared war believed (and had sufficient reason to believe) that there were WMDs and therefore a global threat. There are also *in bello* questions: for example, accusations of torture at Abu Ghraib (mentioned in the case study for Chapter 5) would fall into this category.

JUS AD BELLUM

Just-war thinking has a long philosophical history and the modern framework for this thought owes much to Christian scholars, particularly Augustine, whose work on war in *On the City of God* (written in the fifth century CE) influenced Aquinas. Aquinas's work on war can be found in his famous work *Summa Theologica*, written around 1270. There he sets out three moral criteria or principles that have become the basis of all subsequent just-war theory. Aquinas is primarily concerned with *jus ad bellum*, or what justifies or legitimizes the resort to war and violence, rather than with how war should be conducted. For Aquinas it is possible for a war to be justified if it meets three criteria. First, it must be waged on the authority of a legitimate prince. Aquinas was concerned that war was not waged for private interests, but in the best interests of the "common weal of the city". In more contemporary language, a legitimate war should not serve the interests of the few but those of the majority and therefore serve the common good or public interest. Second, a "just cause" is required; in other words war should be waged only in order to right some wrong or other. Examples Aquinas uses include avenging wrongs and making amends for wrongs inflicted on subjects, or restoring that which has been unjustly seized. This raises issues not just of whether a war can be just, if its cause is just, but also whether there is a duty to wage war on behalf of others to redress wrongs, for example in a case where the subjects of a state are suffering and being wronged. This is an issue we shall consider in a later section on humanitarian intervention. Third, a "right intention" is required: the intention must be to bring about better circumstances, not to inflict harm or to attain power.

Since Aquinas, these three have been expanded and now include: legitimate authority, just cause, right intention, probability of success, last resort and proportionality (Box 8.1). These appear in different orders in different lists. Yet, priority is not significant in determining just war because all the principles must be met for a war to be just. Sometimes a seventh principle is also included: comparative justice. This principle requires that in order for the resort to the use of force to be permissible, the injustice suffered by the party using the force must be significantly greater than that suffered by the party being forced. In other words, in a situation of conflict, while someone may not be fully or perfectly justified in attacking, they may be more

---

Box 8.1 The six criteria for a just war

1. A just war must be waged by a *legitimate authority*. It cannot be waged by a private body and usually this "legitimate authority" is interpreted as meaning a state.
2. A just war must have a *just cause*. It must be waged for a good reason; possible reasons might include self-defence or to prevent a greater injustice.
3. A just war must have a *right intention*. It can only be for good purposes, not for attaining goods or power.
4. A just war must have a strong *probability of success*. A war in a futile cause is not just.
5. A just war must be a *last resort*. All reasonable peaceful alternatives must have been seriously explored and exhausted.
6. A just war must be *proportional*. The principle of proportionality requires that a just war must have benefits that are proportionate to the anticipated harms.

---

justified than the side they attack, in which case they may be permitted to do so by this principle.

Applying just-war theory

Despite the fact that just-war thinking has been hugely influential in shaping international law and global norms regarding when war is justifiable, employing the theory in actual cases is no easy matter. Each criterion is open to different interpretations and in practice this leads to huge disagreements about which wars are in fact just and which forms of conduct are possible. Interpreting just-war theory has always been a difficult task and, arguably, this has increased in the contemporary global context, when wars are typically not between states (and certainly not between the rival princely states that Augustine and Aquinas envisaged). For instance, recent "global" wars are characterized by forms of guerrilla warfare, insurgency and so-called humanitarian interventions. None of these fit the model of two states at war with each other, and this makes a number of just-war criteria problematic. For instance, can non-state actors (such as guerrilla groups) ever have legitimate authority? Does legitimate authority require a UN sanction in current systems of global governance? Moreover, no longer is a typical war one where two armies fight each other at a battleground, and the war is tracked through a number of discernible battles. When wars were fought like this it was relatively simple (especially when soldiers wore uniforms of primary colours) to recognize who was a combatant and who was not. In many current global conflicts it is often exceptionally difficult to distinguish between non-combatants and combatants. Problematic as this is in many situations, it becomes even more complex in even less traditional "wars", as we shall discuss later, concerning the "war on terror". However, although such questions make the just-war criteria more difficult to apply, the complexity of current warfare arguably makes applying them even more necessary. The more difficult it is to determine the moral rightness or wrongness of a war, the more mechanisms to do this are needed. Thus, the complexities in application and interpretation do make just-war theory less simple than it might first appear and it is often possible for those on both sides of a given conflict to argue, using just-war principles, that it is their side that is justified. Because the complexities are in the interpretation, it is important to think about the kind of issues that arise when applying just-war theory to conflicts.

1. Legitimate authority

The criterion of legitimate authority was originally intended to stop wars between rival families and factions and to ensure that something as important as going to war was in the relatively safe hands of a lawful authority (whether a sovereign or a recognized ruling body). The criterion is intended to ensure that war is not waged for private ends. For Augustine and Aquinas, what constituted legitimate authority was relatively unproblematic: Christian princes were those with legitimate authority to wage war, an authority that not only came from the recognition of the people but was ordained by God. The location of legitimate authority continued as relatively unproblematic – a power that belonged to established and recognized rulers – until relatively recently. In the postcolonial era, establishing legitimate authority by this means became problematic, because often the struggles against the colonial powers were viewed as legitimate (at least in hindsight). Moreover, some struggles that have involved violent elements have been supported by the international community to some extent. The African National Congress in South Africa during the apartheid era, for example, was seen by many across the world as the primary and most coherent group of legitimate resistance. And whereas the Provisional IRA in Northern Ireland never received official support from any state during the 1970s and 1980s, it was nevertheless not always officially denounced; in 1981, Prime Minister Margaret Thatcher refused to engage with any of the demands of the IRA-led prison hunger strikers and her uncompromising stance drew international condemnation.

In addition, the legitimate authority of states to wage war has been tempered by the introduction of the United Nations Charter in 1945. The charter continues to grant states the right to take up arms in self-defence, but action that goes beyond this needs the authorization of the Security Council. The effectiveness of the Security

---

Box 8.2 The UN, legitimacy and the Iraq War

The lack of a UN Resolution has been a point of much debate regarding the 2003 invasion of Iraq. In 2002, the UN passed Resolution 1441, which demanded that the regime comply with its "disarmament obligations". Iraq agreed to the Resolution and weapons inspectors were allowed into the country. No WMD were found, although the report by the inspectors did "not contend that weapons of mass destruction remain in Iraq, but nor do they exclude that possibility". The UK, the US and Spain then proposed a second Resolution that declared that Iraq had failed to fulfil the obligations to disarm set out in Resolution 1441, thereby making a case for the use of force. However, the second Resolution received support from only four of the Security Council (the three who proposed it plus Bulgaria), and nine affirmative votes are required for a Resolution to be passed. In addition, France opposed the Resolution and, as one of the five permanent members, could have exercised its power of veto. The Resolution was withdrawn, and the legitimacy of the subsequent invasion is thus often questioned in terms of UN procedures, with defenders of the war claiming in response that the UN's inaction over Iraq only underlined the need for the "coalition of the willing" to use force regardless of UN approval.

Council is a matter of debate, however; in particular the power of veto of the five permanent members (China, France, Russian Federation, UK and USA) means that the council often fails to approve actions because of national agendas rather than for global reasons. For instance, the NATO invasion of Kosovo in 1999 was carried out without a UN Resolution. It is a matter for debate why a Resolution was not sought for what was explicitly a war that fitted at least most of the criteria of just war in that it was done to right wrongs and to stop a threat to international peace and security. However, given the relationship between Serbia and Russia (one of ethnic and historical closeness and loyalty) getting a resolution would have been almost impossible. Although this war was generally deemed legitimate on humanitarian grounds, it did not have the necessary legitimate authority if this is now constituted by a UN Resolution.

2. Just cause

Some causes are more obviously just than others. For instance, most people would regard self-defence as an uncontroversial justification for war. This is recognized in the UN Charter, which grants states a right to defend themselves against aggression and to assist allies who are attacked. Self-defence is perhaps the only wholly non-problematic "just cause", at least for those who accept that it is possible for war to be justified. Other possible just causes include the righting of wrongs and intervention to stop suffering. Whether or not the prevention of suffering constitutes a just cause is an issue we shall address later when we consider humanitarian intervention. Yet, although this justification for war is controversial, there are conflicts where it has been widely accepted as sufficient to constitute "just cause". For example, the 1998 NATO action in Kosovo fits this category and was widely supported. Righting of wrongs is also controversial; but *how* controversial usually depends on how grave the "wrong" is seen to be. For instance, the 1990 invasion of Kuwait by Iraq was deemed to be so grave a wrong that the UN sanctioned the coalition response.

Difficult as it is to determine just cause in instances of righting wrongs and humanitarian intervention, it is perhaps even more difficult in instances of "pre-emption". An understandable first response to pre-emptive strikes or war would be to say that they can never be morally justified or establish just cause, as in these instances aggression, however threatened, has not yet occurred and therefore might never occur. Cases where pre-emptive actions have been deemed just are instances where it has been deemed that there was enough evidence convincingly to claim that attack was inevitable and therefore a pre-emptive action did qualify as self-defence. It is this claim, that it was necessary to pre-emptively attack the Taleban in order to prevent further al-Qaeda attacks, that was used by the US to justify the 2001 action against Afghanistan and which was accepted by the UN Security Council.

But, because of the uncertainty about actual rather than threatened aggression, pre-emptive "just cause" is difficult to establish.

3. Right intention

It is not hard to see why right intention is problematic when it comes to establishing whether or not a conflict is just. It is notoriously difficult to establish an individual's intention in any ethical act, let alone the intention of a state: there are questions about whether it is even intelligible to speak about a state's intentions. In situations of conflict there will inevitably be numerous intentions that could be attributed to a state that chose to wage war.

Right intention clearly precludes certain reasons, such as revenge or the attainment of goods or territory, as permissible reasons for going to war. However, rarely are reasons for going to war unitary: more often they are complex. According to the theory, having additional reasons for going to war that do not constitute "right intention" does not invalidate the claim that the war is just. What matters is that the central purpose of the war is a good one and therefore that right intention can be claimed.

It is here that the problems arise: determining what is the primary motive is fraught with difficulty. If it is accepted that other reasons may be in play, and what matters is simply how they are prioritized, it can be a difficult juggling act to ascertain whether the good reason really is the primary reason. For instance, if we again consider the 1990 Gulf War and the 2003 invasion of Iraq, there was much discussion about whether the "real" motive of the US and its partners in the coalition was to establish control of Iraq's oil or for strategic advantage. Clearly these reasons do not qualify as a "right intention" for war. Yet, as long as they are not the primary intention, according to just-war theory, it does not undermine the claim that the war was just. In the first Gulf conflict the UN deemed the intention was correct: to right the wrong of the seizure of one UN member by another. The 2003 war is more controversial.

In addition, right intention requires that the aim should be a more just outcome for all, not just for your own side. Again, this is a more complex and more important criterion in current warfare and unsurprisingly the recent 2003 invasion of Iraq is a conflict where right intention is contested. We have seen already in this chapter that, in the 2003 case, whether there was in fact a just cause for going to war is controversial, and it is even more controversial whether there was right intention. Many people claim that the WMD pretext was dubious: that perhaps there was at best only a suspicion, which was presented with more certainty than was warranted by evidence. They thus doubt that finding and removing WMD really was the intention. Another reason often given for intervention has been that it liberated Iraq from a tyrant: critics see this as a justification "after the event" that was underemphasized in the run up to the war and then stressed when the original purported intention – disarming Iraq of WMD – began to look increasingly implausible.

4. Probability of success

If a war is to be just then there must be a real chance that it will be successful. While it might be considered noble for individuals to "martyr" themselves for a cause they believe in, the just-war criteria do not permit this for a nation. According to just-war theory, if a war is not likely to result in a better outcome for the population than other options then it should not be entered into. Success does not necessarily mean outright victory; it may also mean that certain objectives are met (perhaps defending core resources, cities or people might count as "just"). Or perhaps a "defeat" that leads to better terms for the population in a negotiated peace might be "better" and therefore more successful than if occupation had occurred unopposed. What is important in judging this is that what counts as success must be considered reasonable and in the best interest of the people of the nation. Probability of success is a contentious point in the debate over the war in Afghanistan (2001 onwards), for example. Sceptics point to the fact that the war is unlikely to be "won" against a thinly spread enemy comprising pockets of ruthless guerrilla fighters sheltering among rural communities in a vast mountainous landscape. They cite the fact that no less a war machine than the Soviet Union's army ultimately failed to defeat just such opposition, then in the form of Afghan "mujahideen", when it invaded in 1980, and to the length, bloodiness and eventual defeat of the US military campaign in Vietnam.

5. Last resort

Last resort does not mean that any and all possible measures must have been exhausted for a war to be just. If this were the case war would never be justified, because it would be almost impossible to claim that there were absolutely no other options. Even perhaps the worst-case scenario of occupation and even slavery constitutes another option. Therefore "last resort" means a last reasonably acceptable option. Importantly, diplomatic methods and other non-violent possibilities must be explored before a war can be justified. However, the balance of argument is difficult because there may be circumstances where waiting too long to resort to force is to do greater damage in the long run. For example, as we shall see in the final section of this chapter, arguably the damage done by the reluctance of the international community to use force in situations like the Rwandan genocide in 1994 or the more recent and ongoing crisis in Darfur have resulted in much greater injustice than a swift resort to force would have done.

6. Proportionality

A final and important criterion of just war is that it must be proportional, and proportionality serves as a useful balance to all the other criteria. For instance, when considering "probability of success", while it may be the case that a ruler or nation wished to count "success" as, say, preserving a holy site or some other national space, even if this could be justified as a "success" it is doubtful that it could be deemed "proportional", because as a justifying condition, proportionality demands that the beneficial consequences of waging war outweigh the harm it causes. Thus, even if those planning war had every chance of preserving their holy site or space (thus meeting the "probability of success" requirement), the proportionality requirement would deem it impermissible, for example, to bomb schools or commit genocide in order to do so.

In current global conflicts that involve superpowers (the US being perhaps the current global example), the likelihood of the superpower being defeated is low; accordingly the duty of proportionality – the beneficial consequences outweighing the harms of war – becomes higher. In other words, the stronger and more powerful a state is, the greater its chance of success, so the more responsibilities it will incur for the consequences of that success. This has led some to argue that a third group of just-war principles should be instituted that recognize post-conflict obligations. These are referred to as *jus post bellum* principles and they propose a duty of care to the population to ensure rebuilding and restructuring after conflict as well as to protect the populations' basic rights.

JUS IN BELLO

Whereas *jus ad bellum* concerns the justification for going to war, *jus in bello* principles govern the conduct of combatants. These attempt to preserve some standards of moral conduct in war, and are essentially a recognition that even though normally immoral actions are sanctioned in war, this does not mean that morality itself is suspended. Some actions remain prohibited, for instance killing the innocent, executing prisoners of war and disproportionate damage (such as polluting land or water, or burning farms and villages in order to make tactical advances). It is principles like these that have informed codes, norms and expectations of the proper conduct of war. Thus the Geneva Convention is an attempt to establish an internationally binding account of *jus in bello*. There are three principles of *jus in bello*: discrimination, proportionality and military necessity (Box 8.3). Together these attempt to limit the extent of the violence of war and to ensure that there is as little harm as possible; and that where harm does occur it is unavoidable if the aims of the just

---

Box 8.3 Three principles for conducting war justly

1. *Discrimination*. To be just combatants must distinguish between enemy combatants and non-combatants.
2. *Proportionality*. To be just the harms of any action must be proportional to the gains.
3. *Military necessity*. To be just any action must be militarily necessary to achieve the end with the minimum harm.

---

war (as determined using the *jus ad bellum* criteria listed above) are to be met. For a war to be just, *both* the *jus ad bellum* and the *jus in bello* criteria must be met. A just war is ethical in its aims and intentions and in how it is conducted in practice on the ground.

1. Discrimination

Although the *jus ad bellum* principles tend to be the focus of much academic and political debate when attempting to justify conflict, in many ways the conduct of war is primary when considering the ethics of conflict. Moreover, how the war is actually conducted can influence views about the original justification of the war. If a war is carried out in an unjust manner, the justice of going to war will be obscured and compromised. The first principle of just war, that of discrimination (sometimes called distinction), is a long-standing and important principle of warfare. Historically it can be found in codes of honour that have ruled the behaviour of warriors from the ancient world, from Roman legionnaires and Samurai warriors to medieval knights' codes of chivalry, and contemporary formulations are found in the Geneva Conventions. Obviously such codes have changed over time but all distinguish in one form or another those who are "legitimate targets" and they give guidance regarding the proper conduct of battle.

In just-war theory the vocabulary used is that of "innocence" and "legitimate targets". Essentially, legitimate targets are those who are involved. Determining "innocent" parties is no easy task. One traditional route has been to draw a distinction between non-combatants and combatants; and it is this reasoning that lies behind respect for prisoners of war in the Geneva Conventions. However, this would exclude those who incite violence or who order violence, as well as those who contribute to it materially (e.g. workers producing weapons), and it has been argued that this is too narrow a definition in contemporary warfare. We shall return to this issue later in the chapter when we discuss terrorism and contemporary forms of warfare. Here it is sufficient to recognize that the principle of distinction is complex, and far more so in the contemporary context than in previous generations.

Irrespective of how "innocence" is determined, it is important to note that the principle of discrimination does not prohibit the death of innocents; it is recognized that in war innocent people must die. What it does require is that these deaths are limited and proportional, that they are unintended and that they are justified by the third principle of military necessity. Accordingly, the death of innocents must not be the purpose of the operation; it must be unintended and unavoidable.

2. Proportionality

The principle of proportionality is very similar to the parallel *jus ad bellum* principle. Acts must be appropriate and not excessive. The vagueness of this principle and the difficulty of determining whether an act is proportional is one of the main points on which just-war theory is critiqued. For instance, your cause and intention profoundly influence what level of violence (e.g. civilian causalities) is permissible. Thus, as in *Jus ad bellum*, proportionality should provide a check that limits excessive violence.

3. Military necessity

The principle of military necessity requires that an act is militarily justified. In other words, it must be required to bring about the military goal; it must be effective. Again, there are difficulties of discrimination and proportionality here; for instance, a target might be regarded as a "military necessity" but reaching it might involve some civilian casualties (some collateral damage). An additional part of just-war theory that can be used to address this is the "doctrine of double effect", which is intended to help to make distinctions between what is permissible in such contexts.

The doctrine of double effect

The doctrine or principle of double effect (meaning "side effect") again has roots in Aquinas's work (*Summa Theologica* II-II, qu. 64, art.7), and is sometimes employed in just-war theory to argue that an action that is (genuinely) militarily necessary is permitted even if there are significant civilian casualties. For instance, in evoking this doctrine, it may be permissible to bomb an enemy weapons factory if this will end the war quickly and if it is the only means of doing so, even if it is in a vulnerable area where there will undoubtedly be many casualties as a "side effect" of this action. According to the doctrine, such an action is permissible if it meets the five conditions of the doctrine (Box 8.4).

> **Box 8.4 The doctrine of double effect**
>
> 1. The action must be either morally good or indifferent in itself (e.g. ending the war quickly by bombing the munitions factory).
> 2. The bad effect must not be the means by which one achieves the good effect (e.g. killing people is *not* justifiable as a means to destroying the factory).
> 3. The intention must be to achieve the good effect. The bad effect must be an unintended side effect, although it may be foreseen (e.g. casualties are not *intended* in the raid on the factory, although it is known that they will occur).
> 4. The good effect must make up for or outweigh the bad effect (e.g. the benefit of ending the horrors of the war must compensate for, or be greater than, the evil of killing in the action).
> 5. The action must be the *only* way of achieving the (justified) end.

The doctrine of double effect invokes the standard principles of just-war theory, particularly proportionality. However, the means and ends condition (condition 2) and condition 3 do provide new concerns and conditions. One cannot use a bad effect to create a good one; therefore policies such as blanket bombings of cities are problematic within the doctrine if the intention is to kill civilians in order to end the war, rather than to attack a military target. Applying this doctrine is notoriously difficult, particularly when we consider the third criterion of intention. How is it possible to prove that the "intention" is to achieve the good effect?

PACIFISM

For some, just war is impossible and therefore theories about justifiable war are inadequate; the only ethical approach is to eschew violence altogether and to adopt pacifism. Just-war theory denies that the prohibition on killing is absolute: killing, violence and war are not always the worst option. Dower outlines different variations of non-violent theories, pacifism and pacificism, in *The Ethics of War and Peace* (2009). Essentially, pacifist and non-violent approaches to war and peace are extensions of the ethical commitment not to kill (and perhaps to non-violence in general).

Those who adopt non-violence have an ethical commitment to non-violent responses to others (whether individuals or institutions). This is either based on a belief that violent acts are not an ethically justifiable response to oppression and violence or it is a tactic that, for one reason or another, is deemed to be successful in engendering social change. It is possible that those who use it as a "tactic" may not share a deeper commitment to non-violence; however, given the violence with which non-violent protest is often met it is likely that those who regard it as a mere tactic will be provoked into violence. Famous examples of the use of non-violence to engender political, social and cultural change are the Indian independence move-ment in the mid-twentieth century and the 1960s civil rights movement in the US. Non-violence is a general position against violence; in contrast, pacifism centres on war and the view that waging war is morally wrong. Some pacifists might not be opposed to all violence, but only to war. There are different types of pacifists and Dower (2009) distinguishes between "absolute/deontological/principled pacifism and contingent/consequentialist pacifism". The discussion in Chapter 3 should enable you to work out the difference in these two theories. In short, the absolute pacifist believes that war is always wrong irrespective of the consequences, whereas the consequentialist pacifist rejects war just because of its consequences: it brings about more bad things than good things. If it were shown to be otherwise then, on this view, war would no longer be deemed wrong.

In addition to general arguments against violence, there are further reasons paci-fists give for opposing war: in particular, that war dehumanizes both soldiers and those whom they kill in a way that undermines their own humanity and denies respect for the humanity of others. Such dehumanizing happens in a number of ways: first soliders, in a real sense, have to be dehumanized in order to be able to carry out their duties; and second, they must dehumanize others. Soldiers must deny their respect for others and their rights and, as Dower says, "forget or suppress their knowledge of the essential humanity of the enemy soldiers. Soldiers have to be turned into efficient 'killing machines'." The trauma involved in such inhumane attitudes is clear and "it is often recognised that such training actually hardens and maybe sometimes brutalises soldiers and certainly those actually involved in combat are often left with various forms of trauma and psychological problems". A second reason is that war is necessarily indiscriminate and "innocents" are unavoidably killed, especially in modern warfare. For the pacifist, the doctrine of double effect does nothing to negate the horror of civilian death. In war civilians are killed (often in disproportionately large numbers when compared to combatants) and this is anticipated and planned for.

For some, non-violence and pacifism are not regarded as the ethical options, but on the contrary as unethical and even cowardly responses. Attempting to "shame" individuals or groups is thus a fairly standard response to pacifism; think of the white feather used to shame conscientious objectors and their families in the First World War in the UK. Those who reject pacifism consider that there are occasions when war is justified and even necessary, for example, because the evil that will be done if violence is not used is greater than the evil of the war itself. For example, they might think that some things are just so evil that all means, including war, must be used to stop them: that some wrongs are so great that it is better to die trying to prevent them than to stand by. For many this is a justification for war and for other kinds of violence, both personal (e.g. self-defence in response to domestic violence) and political (e.g. "freedom-fighting"). The "evil" of the Nazis was certainly offered as a justification for the Second World War. If you conclude that violence is sometimes ethically required then you need to find a mechanism for judging when violence is justified and when it is not.

CONTEMPORARY FORMS OF CONFLICT

The just-war theory – despite all the difficulties in application – is historically the method that has been adopted to do this and perhaps its longevity is itself an indication of its effectiveness. However, there are questions about whether, even if effective in the past, just-war theory continues to be the most appropriate theory in the contemporary global context. Armies are increasingly deployed on missions that do not neatly fit the assumptions of just-war theory. Increasingly, states do not go to war with other states (or coalitions of states with other coalitions) but with non-state actors, and for reasons that are not neatly accommodated in the just-war framework. Two types of conflict that are particularly difficult to accommodate in the just-war framework are those of terrorism and humanitarian intervention, and we shall consider these in the remaining sections of the chapter.

Terrorism

To say that one person's terrorist is another person's freedom-fighter is a cliché, and like many clichés it is also true. If a terrorist can "fight for freedom", then at least some forms of terrorism (or political violence) must have some case for moral justifiability. If this is so, then, just as a framework is necessary to judge whether war is justified, so too a framework is necessary to assess other types of political violence, including terrorism. Some people believe that the only form of violence that is ever justified is that carried out by armies of a legitimate force; in terms of just-war theory they believe that the only "legitimate authority" is a state. For those who think this, acts of "terrorism" can never be justified, irrespective of the cause, but others argue that some acts of political violence that are not committed by state actors are indeed justified and can even be heroic. To take an example, were members of the French Resistance in the Second World War justified in committing acts of violence? They were not part of any legitimate army and they certainly did not identify themselves as combatants, yet many would argue that their violent acts were justified and morally acceptable. What about other cases, such as the acts of violence committed against the apartheid regime in South Africa? Considered in terms of just-war theory, these instances of terrorism were not sanctioned by a state and thus arguably lack the "legitimate authority" necessary for political violence to be justified. Conversely, some argue that these acts of political violence were justified, and in terms of just-war theory were supported by "right cause" and "just intention". In standard just-war theory, failing even one criterion would be sufficient to render the war unjust; however, some argue that either legitimate authority is a criterion that does not always need to be met, or alternatively that it does not necessarily have to be derived from the authority of the state. Some thinkers have developed such arguments in order to attempt to extend just-war theory to acts of political violence that extend beyond traditional models of war in order to incorporate contemporary warfare.

Terrorism as a just war?

To justify terrorism using just-war theory seems at first glance to be a difficult task. Before one can even consider whether any terrorist action can meet the principles of just-war theory, one must first make some judgements about the conflict itself. Is a sequence of violent acts, such as a number of killings or bombs, or even an insurgent activity, enough to be considered a "war"? Some would argue that it is. Sometimes terrorists themselves wish to be regarded as combatants in a war. To return to an earlier example, the Provisional IRA always maintained that it was engaged in a war to free the six "occupied" counties of Northern Ireland from the British state. So strongly did these terrorists wish to be regarded as "soldiers" and, when captured, as political prisoners rather than as criminals that, in order to get the British government to accept this, a number of them went on hunger strike, Bobby Sands being the first and most famous of ten prisoners who died in the cause. At other times states fighting terrorists use the rhetoric of war: thus the US and UK governments spoke of a "war on terror" as a response to the 9/11 terrorist attack on the twin towers in New York and the Pentagon. Moreover, not only was the rhetoric of war used, but explicit references were made to "just-war" arguments by coalition leaders to justify the recent conflicts in Iraq and Afghanistan. For example, speaking at the 2010 inquiry into the invasion, the then UK Prime Minister Gordon Brown said of Iraq: "I believe we made the right decision for the right reasons", arguably appealing to the right-intention condition; and adding that his "feeling was and still is that we cannot have an international community that works if we have either terrorists who are breaking these rules or … aggressor states that refuse to obey the laws of the international community" (Dower 2009), apparently proposing that the cause was just and that it was just for reasons of self-defence and security.

Yet, even if these prior issues can be addressed, and the conflict can be deemed a "war" and an appropriate enemy identified, there are still problems in applying just-war theory to terrorism. For instance, the legitimate-authority criterion needs to be rejected or substantially revised, as too would the *jus ad bellum* criterion. However, given that both war and terrorism are forms of political violence that have similar goals and aims – for example, liberating or protecting a particular people or group – then it is at least worth trying to find a way in which they can be ethically judged in comparison with each other.

Jus ad bellum and terrorism

If terrorism – or some forms of terrorism – are to be assessed according to the just-war criteria, there has to be potential for the six just-war criteria outlined above to be met: legitimate authority, just cause, right intention, probability of success, last resort and proportionality. Of these, the one it is impossible for terrorists to meet is legitimate authority if, as noted above, legitimate authority implies that only states may engage in political violence. For some, such as the US Department of State (2006), which defines terrorism as "premeditated, politically motivated violence per-petrated against noncombatant targets" and its perpetrators as "subnational groups or clandestine agents", terrorists can never have legitimate authority and so can never engage in justified acts of political violence.

To suggest that all violence by non-state actors is a form of terrorism and can therefore never be justified seems inconsistent with other standard practices and attitudes. For example, the justness and appropriateness of political violence by non-state actors is recognized on occasions where there is a failure of sovereignty or legitimate rule: people have a right to overthrow unjust and illegitimate rulers. This is an argument that has been successfully used to justify much military intervention (e.g. NATO in Kosovo 1999) as well as resistance to oppressive occupiers (e.g. the French Resistance or resisting colonial occupiers). If this is the case then perhaps the legitimate-authority criterion of just war should be revised. It could be dropped as "essential"; but the danger of this would be that individuals or extreme groups could engage in acts of political violence that were not in any way representative of a significant group of persons. Another alternative is to suggest that to claim legitimate authority depends on establishing representation (e.g. of a significant and identifi-able group) and perhaps even requiring evidence of some kind of participation to ensure representation.

Jus in bello and terrorism

Even if one could revise the legitimate-authority criterion so that the *jus ad bellum* criteria could potentially be met by an act of terrorist political violence, there are still a number of problems with the typical conduct of terrorism. Key aspects of the just conduct of war, like the wearing of uniforms and the need to discriminate between combatants and non-combatants, do not seem to fit the nature of terrorist campaigns.

The typical form of violence employed by terrorists is that of guerrilla warfare, involving small mobile groups of armed fighters who are not under the auspices of a national or state army, and who characteristically employ tactics such as raids and sabotage. For this type of warfare to be effective, it relies precisely on the fact that it is difficult to distinguish combatants from civilians, and therefore it seems to be in direct conflict with, and so contravene, the first (and arguably most important) principle of *jus in bello*: the principle of distinction. Moreover, not only do those engaged in political violence typically fail to distinguish combatants from non-combatants, but in fact targeting civilians is a key tactic of many terrorist campaigns, and indeed part of how terrorism is sometimes defined. While the Comprehensive Convention on International Terrorism – an ongoing proposal being discussed in the UN at the time of writing – has so far not agreed on a conclusive definition, it seems fair to say that "terrorism" always involves specifically bringing about, through violence, fear and terror in certain non-military populations or communities as a means of achieving a political objective.

Therefore, just as with the criterion of legitimate authority, the principle of distinction needs to be reformed in some way if terrorist acts are ever going to be deemed justifiable on just-war criteria. Of course, you may think that discrimination is so important that it could never in any circumstances be justified to target non-military personnel and therefore that any act of political violence that did this should immediately be condemned as unjust. But some argue that it is not quite this simple. For instance Held (2004) suggests that it is far more difficult than standard just-war theory allows to distinguish between civilians and legitimate targets. In the context of the 9/11 attack she asks whether flying planes into the World Trade Center was significantly different from the attempt on the same day to fly a plane into the Pentagon. If the principle of distinction is interpreted as clearly distinguishing between military and non-combatant targets, then it would seem that the attack on the Pentagon might not be terrorist, because it was a military target, whereas the attack on the World Trade Center would be. It is easy to find more examples of acts that are difficult to define, or seem to be wrongly defined, if we endorse a strict distinction between combatants and non-combatants. For instance, there are examples of acts that are standardly not called terrorism but on this definition become such, such as the Second World War bombings of Hiroshima, Nagasaki, Dresden and Coventry.

Held also argues that not only is it difficult to separate military and civilian targets easily, but also that innocence and culpability do not neatly fit with such distinctions. She uses the examples of the leaders of populations and voting populations and wonders whether those who contribute to and endorse public policy and those who determine it are really less legitimate targets than those who are soldiers in the army; particularly if the army is a conscripted army (Held uses the example of the Israeli army). If you agree with Held then the principle of distinction needs to be rethought and cannot be used to rule out all so-called terrorist acts as unjustifiable.

She argues that both states and terrorist groups should be judged on other aspects of the war, for instance its purpose (cause and intention) and the way it is carried out (how proportional it is). Thus she suggests that some acts, such as torture, are unjust whoever carries them out, and she speaks of the unjustifiability of "state sanctioned torture", which she calls "state terrorism". She argues that both war and terrorism that kills indiscriminately are more unjust than political violence, which does not.

In these ways it may be possible to extend just-war theory to include terrorism. But it would require some major revisions to both *jus ad bellum* and *jus in bello* principles. Accordingly, some have rejected this project and argued that it is simply inappropriate to try to consider this type of violence using the just-war framework. Others argue that it is important to use the framework: (i) for the pragmatic reason that we need to be able to judge different types of violence on the same scale; (ii) for more ideological reasons – that if just-war theory can be used by one side to attempt to justify violence, then it should at least in principle be possible for the other side to employ the same framework.

Security and civil liberties

A key issue of all aspects of the global-ethics debate is how we balance the rights and interests of individuals and groups. This is an issue we considered in Chapter 5 when we asked about the status of the values of human rights; for instance, are rights "trumps", and in what circumstances can individual human rights be violated? One possible example is the "ticking-bomb" case, discussed in Chapter 5, and whether it is justified to violate individual rights for the greater good. A parallel example is the violation of individual human rights in instances of pandemics or public-health crises, where rights of liberty are infringed in order to stop infection spreading and for the public good. This is an issue we shall revisit throughout the book: in Chapter 9 we consider the rights of groups; in Chapter 10 we consider whether individuals' rights can be limited to address climate change; and in Chapter 11 we consider whether protecting the cultural rights of groups undermine individuals' rights. Balancing the rights of different parties is a constant challenge for the ethicist and one to which there is no obviously right or easy answer.

In terms of this debate about war and terror, there are questions not just of whether it is acceptable for the human rights of all citizens to be curtailed for the public good, but, more controversially, about the legitimacy of targeting certain groups, particularly the counter-terrorism method of targeting certain ethnic and religious groups, usually young Muslim men. There are consequentialist arguments about the *effectiveness* of such counter-terrorism; although potentially useful in the short term, such tactics are arguably counter-productive in the long term because they alienate whole communities and result in radicalizing youth to produce more terrorists. There are also rights-based reasons for refusing to support such discrimination and the systematic violation of the human rights of certain groups. The Amnesty International (2004) report on racial profiling calls for the end of ethnic profiling, and argues that it directly affects "Native Americans, Asian Americans, Hispanic Americans, African Americans, Arab Americans, Persian Americans, American Muslims, many immigrants and visitors, and, under certain circumstances, white Americans". Amnesty International takes the permission to violate the human rights of some as a standard counter-terrorist practice, and finds it to be dangerous not only for those whom it targets, but for all of us: "When law enforcement officials focus on what people look like, what religion they follow, or what they wear, it puts us all at risk."

HUMANITARIAN INTERVENTION

Humanitarian intervention is a relatively new phenomenon and one that is particularly interesting in global ethics. Humanitarian intervention is a military intervention undertaken for humanitarian reasons; for example, in order to prevent mass violation of human rights, as in a genocide situation; or in circumstances where states have collapsed into civil war and continual conflict. Humanitarian intervention clashes with the principle of non-interference in the internal affairs of sovereign states, which we discussed in Chapter 4, and the very existence of humanitarian intervention as a possibility – one that has been evoked in a number of situations – suggests movement away from a realist framework and towards some framework of global cooperation.

International law can allow force to be used for purposes of self-defence and in collective actions overseen by the UN Security Council and, as expressed in the UN Charter, this can be on the grounds of maintaining "international peace and security", itself a move away from the principle of non-intervention. As we have seen in Chapters 5 and 6, while there are global standards of human rights, the protection and maintaining of such rights is the task of states. There is no global form of government and, as discussed in Chapter 6, those who are essentially stateless are often deprived of rights. What happens then to states who do not protect the human rights of their citizens, or worse, actively violate such rights? If human rights are "inviolable" and "universal" as the language of the UDHR (discussed in detail in Chapter 5) asserts, should there not be a mechanism to ensure that rights are protected even in situations where the government who should be doing so fails in its duty of protection?

When one considers some of the horrors of humanitarian crises, such as the genocide in Rwanda (where an estimated half a million Tutsis and others were killed by Hutu militia groups), it is hard not to think that humanitarian intervention is justified. Indeed, how can it not be if one wishes to take human rights or global duties with any degree of seriousness?

Yet, although humanitarian intervention clearly respects many of the aims of global ethics (see Box 8.5), there are also reasons why some global ethicists would not wish to endorse it, or at least treat it sceptically.

A primary question for an ethicist is whether it is ever justified to use force, especially in the form of contemporary military force, to prevent or address humanitarian concerns. For instance, if you are a pacifist then it would not be acceptable to use force to stop a possible injustice, because this would simply be to add yet more evil. Likewise, many of the problems of applying just-war theory emerge also in considering the possibility of justifying humanitarian intervention. Can you be relatively certain of the outcome, and of proportionate casualties? Indeed, what are proportionate casualties in such circumstances? Some would argue that states cannot justify losing, or injuring, any soldiers to defend non-compatriots from suffering. Thus no military casualties are justified. This claim might be criticized from a cosmopolitan perspective; yet it resonates strongly with public opinion, for in general the public is not very tolerant of soldiers dying in far-off places, especially if they cannot see it as necessary to defend the domestic population. Arguably, it is for this reason that the NATO humanitarian intervention in Kosovo (1999) relied on air power rather than on ground forces: the coalition knew that there would be little public tolerance for the war if soldiers started returning in body bags. However, this also meant that there were probably more civilian and non-combatant casualties in Kosovo than if ground forces had been used. In short, the difficult calculations necessary in just war are even more complicated when it comes to humanitarian intervention.

As well as it being hard to apply just-war reasoning to humanitarian intervention – particularly with regard to proportionality and justifying conflict when there is no threat to the state – there are further concerns. Perhaps the two most important concerns are abuse of the system and difficulties in consistent responses.

Box 8.5 Humanitarian intervention

- Respects the "inviolate" and "universal" nature of human rights.
- Takes duties of global justice seriously.
- Respects all human beings, not just citizens.

Misuse

The possibility of abuse is not hard to imagine: wars being waged in the name of humanitarian intervention, but actually in order to advance the interests of certain groups or states. Arguably, one example is Hitler's claim that the invasion of Czechoslovakia was to protect the German public, where the justification offered can be seen as, in a sense, humanitarian: waging war to "save" the German people. A more recent and explicit example is the recent Iraq War, where one of the reasons expressly given for the invasion in President George W. Bush's White House address (22 March 2003) was to "free the Iraqi people" (White House 2003). This is not a simple case because other, non-humanitarian reasons were given, as we have seen. In addition, and importantly, this war did not attain a UN Resolution and therefore cannot strictly be regarded as an official humanitarian intervention. The debate about the "real" reasons for waging war will continue to be controversial. This example might make you wonder whether it is ethical for humanitarian reasons to be used in this discussion at all, given that they can sometimes be used to justify acts that would be otherwise regarded as ethically insupportable.

Consistency

A further problem is consistency. If humanitarian intervention is used in one situation then should it also be used in other similar situations? In practice it is not. For instance, humanitarian intervention was used in Kosovo, but not in the more devastating situations of Rwanda and Darfur. If ever humanitarian intervention is justified, it was justified in Darfur. According to Save the Children (2007) over seventy children under the age of five were dying daily; over two-thirds of the population (around four million people) were dependent on humanitarian aid; and two million people were in refugee camps in order to escape the conflict. Yet no international response was launched, except for a limited and inadequate deployment of African Union troops, who have neither the numbers nor resources to protect civilians. As the then UN Secretary General Kofi Annan (1999) said, we need to know "why states are willing to act in some areas of conflict, but not in others where the daily toll of death and suffering is as bad or worse". Many conclude that – sadly – humanitarian intervention is never a primary reason for action. Thus there may be instances where the international community will engage in humanitarian intervention, and for humanitarian reasons, but only if there are also other reasons for action: if the country is strategically important or there are other gains to be made. States seem unwilling to engage in instances where there are *only* humanitarian reasons. In Rwanda and Darfur, the humanitarian crisis was such that if any duty to protect against human rights violations and injustice exists, action should have been taken.

> **Box 8.6 Problems with humanitarian intervention**
>
> - The "humanitarian claim" might be abused.
> - It is difficult to justify force as a preventative measure.
> - It is difficult to publicly justify military casualties to defend non-compatriots.
> - There are practical problems about who decides when it is justified and on what criteria.
> - There are practical problems about insisting that states go to war when it might not be in their interest.

But it was not. It seems that the international community does not wish to risk its troops and spend money to protect African civilians from the violence of their own leaders or would-be leaders. Thus humanitarian intervention might be one reason among others, but it seems that it is never the only reason. This is problematic not just in terms of consistency – some humanitarian crises are not addressed when they should be – but it also increases the force of the "abuse" argument. If humanitarian crises only ever provide a partial reason for intervention, the previous claim that it simply provides a rhetorical justification to cover other, less ethically acceptable, motives for going to war is strengthened.

The future of humanitarian intervention

From an ethical perspective there are important reasons why – despite the difficulties – we should not dismiss humanitarian intervention. Humanitarian intervention is important for global ethics not just because it provides a globally accepted means to address some of the worst injustices and human rights violations, but also because it recognizes that there are positive global duties.

The failure of the international community to intervene in Rwanda and Darfur of course represents a significant failure for those who do believe in some responsibility to protect. In these instances we might wish that humanitarian intervention had been robustly pursued. As Annan (1999) said, Rwanda "showed us how terrible the consequences of inaction can be in the face of mass murder" and "the international community stands accused of doing too little, too late". Those who agree with Annan wish to find ways to ensure that humanitarian intervention to address extreme humanitarian catastrophes is undertaken in the future. In other words, ways need to be found to initiate intervention on humanitarian grounds *alone* and, furthermore, not to rely on states to find additional reasons to provide the necessary motivation to go to war. Other mechanisms could be put in place to ensure that there is legitimate authority to reduce the possibility that humanitarian intervention is abused. There is still an issue of how states can be motivated – or required – to commit their forces to such conflicts where their own states are not directly involved. Some have suggested that a possible solution could be a standing UN force, to which states contribute but that they do not direct: something along the lines of NATO, but global. Given our discussion in Chapter 7 about global government and the need for solutions to be practical, realistic and achievable, perhaps (at least in the short term) we should seek solutions that use existing mechanisms and are therefore more likely to be implemented.

Responsibility to protect

The responsibility to protect is receiving increasing attention. It was first discussed in a 2001 report by the International Commission on Intervention and State Sovereignty, and followed up by discussion at the 2005 UN World Summit (Box 8.7).

The importance of the responsibility to protect is discussed in detail by James Pattison (2010) and Nicholas Wheeler (2000). They report the increasing interest in the topic, and the large numbers of research and advocacy centres that have been set up to think about it. Humanitarian intervention is only part of the responsibility to protect; other duties are also important. Force therefore becomes only one aspect of the responsibility to protect, which takes the focus away from a single-conflict framework. Moreover, humanitarian intervention is justified by the responsibility to protect *only if* it has Security Council authorization. So the 2003 Iraq War would not count as humanitarian intervention. This condition reduces some of the concerns about the misuse of humanitarian intervention to provide an ethical justification for an action that is really undertaken for other less admirable reasons. Moreover, such intervention must be in response to a state's failing to address key human-rights abuses, such as ethnic cleansing, crimes against humanity, war crimes and genocide.

Because responsibility to protect is broader than military or humanitarian intervention and introduces additional elements – the "responsibility to prevent" and the "responsibility to rebuild" – it might at first glance seem to be more demanding and therefore less likely to receive support from states. Yet, Pattison (2010) argues, because the military aspect is less prominent in the responsibility-to-protect agenda, it may receive greater support than strong humanitarian-intervention doctrines alone. He suggests that those in the global south can be resistant to humanitarian-intervention agreements on the grounds that they fear that such interventions will be directed at them, either because they are involved in human rights abuses, or because humanitarian intervention might be used as an excuse for invasion. Others are resistant because they fear that humanitarian intervention reduces state power and sovereignty in general. However, while the military element may be downplayed

Box 8.7 The 2005 UN World Summit

Main outcome

"Clear and unambiguous acceptance by all governments of the collective international responsibility to protect populations from genocide, war crimes, ethnic cleansing and crimes against humanity. Willingness to take timely and decisive collective action for this purpose, through the Security Council, when peaceful means prove inadequate and national authorities are manifestly failing to do it." (United Nations 2005)

Resolutions 138–140 under the heading "responsibility to protect populations from genocide, war crimes, ethnic cleansing and crimes against humanity"

138. Each individual State has the responsibility to protect its populations from genocide, war crimes, ethnic cleansing and crimes against humanity. This responsibility entails the prevention of such crimes, including their incitement, through appropriate and necessary means. We accept that responsibility and will act in accordance with it. The international community should, as appropriate, encourage and help States to exercise this responsibility and support the United Nations in establishing an early warning capability.
139. The international community, through the United Nations, also has the responsibility to use appropriate diplomatic, humanitarian and other peaceful means, in accordance with Chapters VI and VIII of the Charter, to help to protect populations from genocide, war crimes, ethnic cleansing and crimes against humanity. In this context, we are prepared to take collective action, in a timely and decisive manner, through the Security Council, in accordance with the Charter, including Chapter VII, on a case-by-case basis and in cooperation with relevant regional organizations as appropriate, should peaceful means be inadequate and national authorities are manifestly failing to protect their populations from genocide, war crimes, ethnic cleansing and crimes against humanity. We stress the need for the General Assembly to continue consideration of the responsibility to protect populations from genocide, war crimes, ethnic cleansing and crimes against humanity and its implications, bearing in mind the principles of the Charter and international law. We also intend to commit ourselves, as necessary and appropriate, to helping States build capacity to protect their populations from genocide, war crimes, ethnic cleansing and crimes against humanity and to assisting those which are under stress before crises and conflicts break out.
140. We fully support the mission of the Special Adviser of the Secretary-General on the Prevention of Genocide. (United Nations 2005)

Box 8.8 The responsibility to protect

It includes:
- the responsibility to prevent;
- military/humanitarian intervention;
- the responsibility to rebuild.

---

in the responsibility to protect, some think that we should make sure that it does not get removed altogether. For instance, Pattison (2010) states that "if we ignore, overlook, or exclude forcible military intervention from the responsibility to protect, we will be adopting a head-in-the-sand approach about the hard choices that will sometimes need to be made about military intervention".

CONCLUSION

In this chapter we have explored the ethics of contemporary wars and conflicts. In particular, we have looked at whether force can be justified and by what criteria; we have asked whether in the global context traditional justifications of war, deriving from the just-war theory, are appropriate, and especially whether the equation of legitimate authority with states holds in terrorist conflicts or in situations of humanitarian intervention. In considering how the global ethicist addresses conflict and war we have also considered whether force can be used as a means to address injustice (e.g. in humanitarian intervention) and if so whether we need to reform the governance structures we considered in Chapter 6.

There are arguably no "right" answers to the dilemmas that global war and conflict raise, but there are types of approach that the global ethicist is more likely to adopt. For instance, the global-in-scope criterion is likely to prohibit a response that considers that it is only states that have legitimate authority; it is also going to require recognition that there are duties to those in distant lands if their human rights are violated. However, recognizing that there are such duties will not tell you what these duties are: for example, it is perfectly possible for global ethicists to be pacifists or advocates of the use of force in instances of humanitarian intervention. Again, we have seen that the issues of global ethics are connected: war and conflict exacerbate poverty, and poverty makes war and conflict more likely. In Chapter 9 we shall consider bioethical issues, which are also connected with poverty. Being poor or lacking infrastructure in a conflict or post-conflict situation affects health as well as increasing one's vulnerability and the likelihood that one will be exploited.

FURTHER READING

- Dower, N. *The Ethics of War and Peace* (Cambridge: Polity Press, 2009).
- Held, V. "Terrorism and War". *Journal of Ethics* **8** (2004): 59–75.
- Honderich, T. *Humanity, Terrorism, Terrorist War: Palestine, 9/11, Iraq, 7/7* (London: Continuum, 2006).
- International Coalition for the Responsibility to Protect website. www.responsibilitytoprotect. org/index.php/component/content/article/383 (accessed June 2011).
- International Commission on Intervention and State Sovereignty (ICISS). *The Responsibility To Protect* (Ottawa: International Development Research Centre, 2001). www.iciss.ca/report2-en. asp (accessed May 2011).
- Kinsella, D. & C. Carr (eds). *The Morality of War: A Reader* (Boulder, CO: Rienner, 2007).
- Pattison, J. *Humanitarian Intervention and the Responsibility to Protect* (Oxford: Oxford University Press, 2010).
- United Nations 2005. "2005 World Summit Outcome" fact sheet. www.un.org/summit2005/ presskit/fact_sheet.pdf (accessed May 2011).
- Wheeler, N. *Saving Strangers: Humanitarian Intervention in International Society* (Oxford: Oxford University Press, 2000).
- Wheeler, N. & F. Egerton. "The Responsibility to Protect: 'Precious Commitment' Or a Promise Unfulfilled?" *Global Responsibility to Protect* **1**(1) (2009): 114–32.

9 GLOBAL BIOETHICS

INTRODUCTION

"Bioethics" is the ethics of biological and medical technology, and deals with moral questions arising from advances in these fields. Examples of topics in bioethics are: reproductive technologies; medical termination or enhancement of life; donation or sale of organs and other "body parts"; cloning; research and experiments using humans and non-human animals; genetic engineering; and stem-cell research. Bioethics is an area of global ethics that is becoming increasingly important as issues of scientific and technological development affect global biological and health injustices. While historically bioethics was concerned with a doctor's duty to patients and the doctor–patient relationship, in the contemporary environment bioethics concerns are key issues of broader public and political controversy. If you think about which ethical issues most excite the media and politicians, you will probably find that bioethics makes up at least half of the top ten. For example, worries about cloning caused national debate in the UK and a parliamentary debate in 2000 and 2001; "Dolly the sheep" – the first successfully cloned mammal – became a household name and a national treasure. Having been highly controversial while alive, in death she is stuffed and can be viewed at the Connect Gallery, National Museum of Scotland.

Dolly is a good example of why bioethical issues are so controversial. They raise new issues that challenge conceptions about what life is and, importantly when we consider interventions in humans, what a *human* life is. So although sometimes dismissed as "high-tech" by ethicists involved in global justice, bioethical issues are in fact fundamental to concerns about the nature of human beings and expectations about how human beings should relate to each other. In addition to addressing what human life is and what opportunities are necessary for humans to flourish and be healthy, bioethics addresses public-health concerns and issues of health injustices.

Arguably, health is a foundational concern for all issues of justice, since good health is a prerequisite for flourishing in any other areas of life. Although this chapter will touch on the high-tech issues that are so important in contemporary bioethics, for the most part it will focus on global issues in order to explore those concerns most relevant to global ethics. In this chapter, then, we shall cover such topics as abortion, euthanasia and the sale of body parts such as kidneys, as well as access to essential drugs and research in developing countries.

BIOETHICAL ARGUMENTS

"High-tech" bioethical issues, such as cloning, genetic enhancement and treatment and stem cells, have been particularly prominent in the public sphere over the past ten years. But as well as these "hot topics", which dominate public debate, more traditional bioethical concerns such as abortion and euthanasia continue to be issues that polarize debate and evoke strong moral responses.

Abortion and euthanasia are useful bioethical issues to consider because they show the strength of feeling that surrounds bioethics. Bioethical issues are areas where people often have particularly strong moral convictions so it can be very hard for compromise to be found. Indeed, in some of these debates it is almost impossible to get the two sides to communicate at all; instead they keep on asserting their views and ignoring the opposing position. Abortion and euthanasia might not, at first glance, be regarded as specifically global ethics issues, but, as we shall come to see, the context of globalization is as important for these as for other more obviously global issues. For instance, there are issues of universal access, such as whether abortion is a basic right for women and how it should be globally resourced and protected, as well as issues of medical tourism (which we shall consider later in this chapter), and, finally, issues about abortion and euthanasia speak to core ethical concerns about how life shall be valued, which underlies global-ethics debates no less than other ethical debates.

Abortion

The kind of intractable opposition that often characterizes debate in bioethics is clearly evident in the abortion debate. Those who think that abortion is wrong (the so-called "pro-life" position) assert that the foetus is a person and that abortion is equivalent to murder. In the US, the pro-life movement is well supported and influential; for example, the biggest pro-life organization, the National Right to Life Committee, has more than 3000 local groups with branches in all fifty states. Pro-life movements represent a wide spectrum of political, medical, ethical and religious opinion, ranging from the Center for Biological Reform and the Pro-Life Alliance of Gays and Lesbians to Operation Save America. Some pro-lifers think that abortion is so terribly wrong that violence and even murder is justified if it stops people from carrying out terminations, so abortion clinics have been bombed and medics and staff killed. In 1994, two receptionists in a Massachusetts clinic were killed by John Salvi, a pro-life activist. More recently, in 2009, George Tiller, a physician and medical director of a clinic in Wichita, Texas, was shot dead outside his practice, following months of being highlighted by the pro-life campaign group Operation Rescue.

Those on the other side of the debate (the so-called "pro-choice" lobby) hold equally strong views. They argue that the foetus is not a person and therefore does not have rights; in standard rights theory, as we saw in Chapter 5, only persons can have rights. For some, the morally significant point is that of "viability" (somewhere between twenty and thirty weeks, depending on definition), and after this point abortion is wrong. For others, it is only at birth that the foetus becomes a person and thus of moral significance and a rights-bearer. Pro-choice activists tend to regard abortion as a fundamental women's-rights issue, and something that should be granted globally and on demand. They see rights to abortion and contraception as the most basic of rights: rights to control one's own body, to choose when to reproduce and to protect bodily integrity. For the pro-choice lobby, these "reproductive rights" to contraception and abortion are necessary precursors to exercising all other civil, political, economic and social rights. They argue that the right to bodily integrity is a basic autonomy right and one that all non-slave men take for granted; it should, therefore, be a basic human right for women too. In this debate, then, both sides use strong moral principles and rights rhetoric to support their arguments (Box 9.1).

In the abortion debate, key issues concern what matters in a good life. For instance, many pro-choice thinkers would insist on the importance of the *quality* of life (of the

---

Box 9.1 Arguments in the abortion debate

Pro-life	Pro-choice
Believe in the sanctity of life	Believe in the importance of the quality of life
Respect the foetus's rights to life	Respect women's rights to bodily integrity and to make choices about their own lives
Respect the moral prohibition on murder	Respect autonomy
Believe that the embryo/foetus has the status of a person	Believe that the foetus is not a person and does not have full rights

mother and the potential child), and not just "life". This is an issue that runs through-out bioethics, most obviously in the euthanasia debate (which we shall consider in a later section), but also in debates about designer babies, genetic therapy, stem-cell therapy and many other contemporary issues.

We do not have time to explore all these issues. However, a brief overview of the issues surrounding designer babies will show the range of ethical issues raised, and how profoundly bioethics is concerned with addressing the limits of life and the quality of life. "Designer babies" is a catch-all term and refers to any child that is selected for certain traits and parts. Babies can be "designed" for a number of reasons. The least controversial reasons are health reasons. For instance, sex selection can be used to avoid X-linked disorders (disorders that only affect male children) and *in vitro* fertilization can be used in conjunction with pre-implantation genetic diag-nosis to select non-genetically impaired children. More problematic is the creation of "saviour siblings", who are created not to avoid any disease that they themselves will suffer but as a "match" for an earlier child. In other words, they are "designed" specifically to be a donor (although it may be the umbilical cord rather than the child itself that is actually used). Most controversial are babies who are designed for completely non-medical reasons, simply to meet parental preferences: for instance in cases where deaf couples have sought to select "deaf embryos" for social and cultural reasons and, most importantly, in sex selection. Some argue that there is nothing wrong with selecting a child of a preferred gender while others argue that this is discrimination and particularly problematic in the global context, where overall the preference is markedly for boys. For others it is not an issue of gender discrimina-tion, but of making children into things, the parts and characteristics of which can be chosen. Parents are currently choosing embryos on health and sex grounds, and selecting donor gametes for intelligence, beauty and even race. For instance, one website where you can purchase eggs suggests that non-white couples should con-sider buying eggs from white couples to give their children the best chance in life, and has testimonies from couples who have done this.

An important element of the bioethics debate, that the abortion debate and our brief overview of designer babies illustrate well, is its hugely political nature. The language of the abortion debate – "pro-life" and "pro-choice" – is highly political and polemical. It implies that if you are in favour of a women's right to abortion then you are "anti-life", or if you think abortion should not be permitted you are "anti-choice". These are not labels that many would wish to adopt, so the language of the debate is very important. In bioethics, perhaps more than any other area of ethics, winning the political argument is a matter of swaying public opinion, and this is often a matter of appealing to public emotion: hence, the prominence of "rights language", which, as we discussed in Chapter 5, is particularly useful for political activism.

The importance of public opinion is recognized in bioethics and the power of the "yuk factor" is an issue that bioethicists pay attention to. The yuk factor is used in bioethics to refer to emotional responses, responses that profoundly influence public opinion. It explains why there are times when one procedure is prohibited but another relevantly similar procedure is not. Essentially, practices are dismissed because they are regarded as "revolting", "repugnant", "repulsive" or "grotesque". Conversely, other practices that raise similar ethical issues are welcomed because they have emotional appeal, sometimes referred to as the "cute factor". Technologies with cute factor are generally welcomed and the ethical concerns and risks are under-reported and underemphasized. The cute factor is one reason that new reproductive technologies have been largely embraced by the public: they result in cute babies and happy families, things that are desired by the public. By contrast, embryo research has received no such positive welcome, despite an overlap in ethical issues, such as the need to discard "spare embryos".

The classic example used to illustrate the influence of the yuk factor is the cloning debate. Clones were uniformly rejected as unethical and even inhuman, despite the fact that clones occur naturally in the form of identical twins. What is permitted in terms of high-tech procedures is largely what the public will accept, rather than what can be reasonably defended. This is worrying, because it means that public debate is influenced not by ethical principles and reasons, but by whether or not public emotions can be swayed; hence the use of graphic photographs by anti-abortion campaigners. It also means that laws can be changed – even if the moral reasons have not changed – simply because public opinion has changed. An example of this is that, until very recently, the sale of organs was regarded as absolutely prohibited, an affront to human rights and human dignity: however in the UK today (although in very few other places) very vocal groups have made the possibility of selling organs one that is being actively considered by academics, policy-makers and, increasingly, the public. Indeed, organ sale may be permitted in UK law in the near future. So, in bioethics a kind of relativism exists that gradually permits and accepts new technologies, even if it takes a little time.

Euthanasia

Euthanasia is a matter of public controversy that raises similar issues to abortion: for example, about sanctity of life and quality of life and about what choices individuals should be permitted to make about their own lives. As with the abortion debate, views are strongly held. On one side are those who believe that life is sacred and that euthanasia should never be permitted; on the other are those who believe that it should be the right of individuals to choose when to end their own lives and that it is the quality of life that is important, rather than simply prolonging life. There are some who take less extreme positions, who think that in principle people should be able to choose euthanasia, but who do not wish to see it made legal because they worry that it would have unintended effects. Rather than being an option for those who really want to end their lives, it would put pressure on some to commit euthanasia even if they did not really wish to; for instance, some may feel that they ought to end their lives to avoid needing time-consuming and expensive care and being a burden to their families, or to ensure that they do not use up their children's inheritance paying for treatment or care homes. Those in this middle category could perhaps be convinced one way or the other: they might be convinced to support euthanasia if enough safeguards were put in place to ensure that the individual's choice was authentic; or, conversely, they might be convinced to reject it if it was shown that in fact people did feel under pressure to "choose" this option. However, those who believe strongly that life is sacred are no more likely to be convinced that euthanasia could ever be a morally permitted option than the pro-lifers in the abortion debate. Conversely, those who believe that individuals have the right to determine their own destinies and not to continue living with a poor quality of life – a "life not worth living" – consider euthanasia necessary if people's autonomy is to be respected. They too will not change their minds. At these ends of the debate there is no dialogue: all are convinced that their position is correct.

When it comes to abortion and euthanasia, the competing sides invoke strong moral principles to support their claims: the sanctity of life and quality of life principles. As with so many ethical questions, there is no obvious "right" answer when you approach the dilemma from an ethical-theory position. Moreover, moral deliberation about such matters becomes even more complex when we think about the global dimensions of such issues and not just about balancing the rights of individuals (e.g. the rights of the woman and the rights or interests of the foetus) but about social justice and structural concerns. For instance, what if you add issues of poverty to the picture? Is a women more justified in aborting what would be her fourth child if she knows that having this child will leave her first three children without enough food and malnourished? Some would argue that these are separate concerns and that the fourth child could be adopted. Yet, in many areas of the world there are already significant numbers of unwanted children who would, on the face of it, enjoy a much better life if adopted. For example, in 2007 the *Telegraph* reported that the Indian government had decided to increase the number of unwanted children it allowed to be adopted by families in the US and Europe because, the report said, "there are more than 11 million abandoned children in India, where a growing number of babies are dumped in cots placed outside orphanages in an initiative to deter infanticide" (Womack 2007).

However, international adoption is ethically problematic in itself. One problem is that it opens up or facilitates the possibility of a lucrative and exploitative black or "grey" market in providing such children for Westerners who are keen to adopt and will pay for the service. Indeed, there are even reports of "baby stealing" and child trafficking for international adoption, and cases have been documented from across

Africa, Asia and Latin America. Another possible consequence that worries some people is that these children are detached from their national or cultural identity. Domestic adoption entails separation from birth parents, but international adoption involves also leaving behind a place, language, sets of practices and customs, and so on. Concerns here are similar to concerns about children born using sperm and egg from anonymous donors. In this parallel debate, some argue that there is a right to know your genetic heritage, and this reasoning led to a change to the law in the UK in 2005, which now mandates that all UK donors be identifiable.

The global-ethics approach does not permit us to consider these issues in isolation, as if these individual cases were unconnected to wider issues. For instance, issues about whether contraception is widely available are issues connected to development and women's rights. For example, the average number of children per family household in the US is 2.5 (and less in Europe), whereas across the African nations the "fertility rate" – how many children a woman will have – is more than five. In addition, such issues connect with concerns about population control and environmental sustainability. However, as we shall see in Chapter 10, population numbers are less important than consumption in terms of using scarce resources and contributing to climate change. For example, a recent study from Oregon State University (2009) concluded that on average a child in the US has a long-term effect on raising carbon emissions that is 160 times higher than a child in Bangladesh. Hence there is not necessarily a direct correlation between higher numbers of people and a greater detrimental effect on the environment: the economic conditions of different societies and their rates of consumption are far more important.

TOWARDS GLOBAL BIOETHICS

If we ignore the wider social issues (something the global ethicist must not do), the abortion and euthanasia debates seem relatively simple to analyse: the positions of both sides and the points of disagreement are clear and the reasons and principles invoked in support of both sides are easy to understand and examine. Therefore, you merely need to decide where you stand on these principles: do you accept the sanctity of life principle or not; and, if so, how does this limit what is morally permissible? The controversies over abortion and euthanasia raise key bioethical and philosophical questions about what is personhood, what constitutes human being and what is a good life. For instance, for some, personhood is connected to capacity and therefore personhood applies only to those who have attained minimum standards of agency; for others, personhood begins at conception and remains until death and should be protected and extended at any cost. These fundamental questions about how we conceive of human beings are the core concerns of bioethics and we can trace them through the current areas of controversy such as cloning and genetic enhancement. What is at issue in these debates when we ask whether a certain type of genetic enhancement is permissible is, in fact, the nature of human being, as the question is really this: if we do this are we changing what it is to be human or what it is acceptable to do to another human?

When we consider these core bioethical concerns about the nature of human beings, and therefore what it is permitted to do medically and scientifically from the global-ethics perspective, the debate becomes even more complex. For example, you may conclude that ethically there is (or should be) access to abortion on women's-rights grounds. However, if abortion is illegal in the jurisdiction of one country, is this ethical reasoning in favour of abortion so strong that it justifies breaking the law in that country or travelling to another country in order to attain the service? Moreover, if there is a strong case for making abortion accessible (e.g. if you agree that it is a necessary precursor for exercising all other rights) then are you claiming a positive reproductive right? If so, who has the duty to provide access to the service? At this point we enter the issues of resource allocation and redistributive justice. Issues such as resource allocation are complex enough when we consider them in local contexts: for example, should abortion be paid for by health-care providers or by individuals? How you answer such questions leads to a whole host of other ethical questions. For example, if you conclude that abortion should not be paid for by health-care providers, because it is not a "health concern" (unless it is threatening the mother's health) and therefore should be paid for by individuals, then are you denying those who cannot afford abortion reproductive rights? Moreover, if abortion is a "service" that can be paid for, is the only criterion for accessing it ability to pay, or should it be limited in other ways? For instance, if you are paying for the abortion, do you have the right to abort a healthy foetus for any reason you choose and up to birth, say because it is of a certain sex, or because it has a "minor" medical condition, such as a cleft lip? Again, these are questions about the nature of human beings and what the limits of acceptability are. But, complex as they already are when considered locally, when considered globally the complexity is exacerbated further.

On a global level, questions of resource allocation and distributive justice become more pronounced and more pressing. From a global-justice perspective the question urgently becomes about whether any high-tech treatments can be justified while most of the world's population is without access to basic health care. For instance, can expensive cancer treatment be justified when most people in the global community do not have access to basic public health care? Or perhaps even more pertinently, what about access to *in vitro* fertilization and reproductive treatments designed to "treat" infertility, even though infertility is not strictly speaking a disease? Not having children might be a sadness but it is not an illness. How you answer these questions will depend to a large extent on the positions you adopted in Chapters 3, 4 and 5. If you adopt a strong cosmopolitan approach you will consider the disparity between different parts of the globe as completely unjustified: there are no ethical grounds that could be used to justify giving expensive treatments to some while others lack basic care. If you adopt a weaker position, perhaps endorsing basic or minimal rights, you will argue that a basic standard of public health and health care should be globally available, but that once this is in place additional treatments for those who can afford them is permissible.

In order to address some of these global bioethical concerns, this chapter will not focus on what Western, privileged individuals are permitted or forbidden to do, but on the issues that affect the global poor. The issues chosen are just a few of the many that could have been selected, but they give a good overview of the types of global-ethics issues concerned and they demonstrate the connection of bioethical concerns with other global-justice concerns. Accordingly, we shall address medical tourism, global research, genetic and population ethics, access to essential drugs and the impact of global intellectual property regimes.

MEDICAL TOURISM

The term "medical tourism" is used to describe the movement of people from one legislative area to another to obtain treatment and procedures not available (or less easily available) within the country or state of their origin. Medical tourism includes "reproductive tourism", which denotes practices such as: Irish women travelling to the UK for abortions; German couples travelling to Belgium for pre-implantation genetic diagnosis; and women travelling from northern Europe and the US to eastern Europe, Spain and Greece for donor eggs for reproductive treatments or to India for "surrogacy services". In addition to reproductive tourism, medical tourism includes any other form of treatment where people go outside their national jurisdictions to take advantage either of cheaper treatment or treatment that is illegal in their home jurisdictions. This includes: travelling from countries where physician-assisted suicide is illegal to countries such as Switzerland, where it is legal; travelling to countries with public-health services in order to access free or cheap treatment; travelling to relatively poor countries to purchase organs from live "donors"; or combining tourism with plastic surgery in so-called "cut-and-beach" holidays. One consumer website notes that "A temperate climate and a consistently strong British pound against the local rand have ensured increasing numbers of Brits have been lured to South Africa with the promise of top-quality surgery and the chance to relax in luxury accommodation at a fraction of the cost of procedures in the UK" (Buy Association UK n.d.).

Medical tourism is an important issue for global ethics, in part because it is overtly "international" and directly about people using their ability to travel globally. Often, although not always, medical tourism is a particularly vivid illustration of the way the privileged in the global system are able to take advantage of the poorer and more vulnerable. If there were no global inequities of wealth and differences in laws and standards in different jurisdictions, medical tourism would be impossible. We have already discussed the sale of body parts; it is the case study set out in Chapter 2 and explored in Chapter 4. Revisit the case study for more details about the market in body parts. In this chapter we shall revisit the debate, focusing on the ethics of kidney sale in order to show the structure of bioethical arguments (see Box 9.2).

Some people, including some bioethicists, argue in favour of kidney sale on the grounds that there is a scarcity of organs. Others reject the sale of kidneys for a number of reasons, particularly because of concerns that the global poor will be exploited. Those who are in favour of kidney sale argue that there is nothing especially or inherently wrong with people selling organs as opposed to selling other assets, such as their labour or possessions. A prime reason that bioethicists who support organ sale, such as Janet Radcliffe-Richards (1998), Julian Savulescu (2003) and Stephen Wilkinson (2000, 2003), give in its favour is that to prevent organ sale is to deny individuals' autonomy and their right to make choices regarding their own bodies. There are also a whole host of other arguments, for instance, about whether it "commodifies" persons if they sell organs: that is, whether buying and selling parts of persons makes persons into commodities, into things that are exchanged and given a "price" just like other products or natural resources in a marketplace (with Wilkinson arguing that it does not and others, such as Alastair Campbell [2009] and Donna Dickenson [2008], arguing that it does). Those who take this line argue that bodies are not "owned" and that, therefore, they are not the kinds of things that should be bought and sold. A more practical argument against organ sale is that inequitable distribution of power and wealth makes it impossible for organ sale to be non-exploitative and non-coercive in current global structures.

In this chapter we shall focus on only one of these arguments, the nature of the choice that kidney sellers make, because the place of autonomy is crucial in bioethical reasoning. Bioethicists tend to place individual autonomy over other values. Voluntary informed consent is the primary ethical practice in bioethics, intended to protect individual autonomy, and it is used in both clinical settings and research settings. Those who endorse the pro-sale view argue that as long as the sellers have consented, in other words chosen, to sell their kidneys then the practice is wholly ethical. In this schema, to challenge an autonomous act is not justifiable, because to do so is to fail to respect autonomy. As a result, all that is needed to justify an action is evidence of choice; so in the case of kidney sale, proof that the "vendor" consented is all that is required for an act to be acceptable. In addition, such thinkers argue that it is better to have more choices than fewer, even though these choices are inherently undesirable, and to remove any options is to reduce limited options still further.

Moreover, it is argued, if some people do choose to sell then it must be the case that the alternatives are even worse.

There are a number of arguments used against these claims: (i) that choice does not respect autonomy; (ii) that choosing something does not, in fact, make it ethical; (iii) that some choices – desperate choices – should never be regarded as meeting the standards of voluntary and informed consent. This last claim also denies that more choices are always better, a debate that we shall return to in Chapter 11.

First, then, many would question the concept of autonomy that is being invoked by bioethicists. For instance, all philosophical theories of autonomy recognize that "choice" alone is not sufficient to ensure autonomy. We need to know more about the context and the background to ensure that it is an "authentic" choice, and not one made under outside influence or undue pressure. In addition, and importantly, theories of autonomy insist that for choices to be autonomous they must be considered over a period of time, even the whole of a life. A momentary choice is not sufficient for autonomous choice. This is an obvious requirement, because there are many examples of people making momentary choices they later regret and, in hindsight, do not identify with their "real self" or recognize as genuine choices. This is particularly important in organ trade because much of the empirical evidence suggests that, in fact, vendors do regret their choices and they and their families do not end up in the improved economic and social circumstances they expected.

Second, other thinkers deny that choosing something is enough to make it ethical. Bioethicists often assume that if you have consented then the act is acceptable: Roger Brownsword (2009) refers to this as "the fallacy of sufficiency". He argues from a legal and rights perspective that simply because you "choose" to do something does not make the choice acceptable or negate the possibility that the act is exploitative. There are some rights that you cannot waive – for instance, human rights – simply because you choose to do so; indeed, as we saw in Chapter 5, part of the nature of human rights is that they are inviolable. If "I choose" to be murdered, for pleasure, or perhaps for money for my family (say if all my organs were harvested), does this make the act ethically required or permitted? Most would surely argue that it does not and certainly it violates human rights. Although I have "chosen" it, murder continues to be morally wrong. According to the fallacy of sufficiency, choice or consent alone – however autonomous or free – is not sufficient to make a wrong act, or an exploitative act, ethically acceptable. This recognition that choice is not sufficient to negate the violation of rights is a standard premise in many contexts. For example, in employment law the worker is not permitted to consent to a contract that would entail waiving his or her rights to various safety standards or to a minimum wage. Employment law recognizes that the worker is vulnerable to exploitation, precisely because they might well view employment, even under exploitative conditions, as a better situation than no employment. Essentially, then, there are some instances where choice is irrelevant; some rights and safeguards cannot be waived and consent does not change the wrongness of the act.

The third point is that even if choice were enough to make an act ethical then there are some choices – usually termed "desperate choices" – that, because of the context or other outside factors, can never be considered to be "freely chosen". "Desperate choices" are choices made in desperation, not because they are desirable. In fact, they are inherently undesirable and chosen only when the range of possible choices is extremely limited. When choice is limited the claim that "choice protects autonomy" is problematic. For although it is true that while there are "any" options then, strictly speaking, "choice" remains, it is questionable whether this is enough to constitute "autonomous" or "free" choice. Can all choices, irrespective of their content, be said to have the same ethical status? Many would argue that severe economic and social pressure is enough for a person to be coerced. You do not need to be physically threatened to feel that you have no real choice or that you were forced to do something because of the circumstances.

In order to find more ethical ways through the problem, many other solutions have been suggested: Erin & Harris (2003), for example, suggest a regulated market within the EU. Other proposals are ongoing, and certainly there are some body parts that are routinely paid for in many parts of the world, such as sperm and often eggs (although sometimes these command not payment but "expenses"). On the other hand, there are those who use the example of successful systems of blood donation to argue that payment should never be made for body parts. How you decide this matter – as discussed in Chapter 4 in detail – will depend on which moral and political theories you favour from Chapters 3 and 4. Or perhaps, like Brownsword, you might adopt a rights-based approach and reject some acts altogether on the grounds

---

Box 9.2 The global organ trade

Arguments for:
- There is a desperate need for organs and there are people willing to supply them.
- Not to permit people to choose to sell their organs denies choice and constrains autonomy.
- The "trade" in organs could be safely regulated to avoid exploitative practices.

Arguments against:
- Choice alone is not sufficient to protect autonomy.
- Human rights can be violated even if an action is consented to or chosen.
- "Desperate choices" cannot be said to be "fully autonomous".
- Legalization does not necessarily remove exploitative and coercive aspects of a practice; in fact it can reinforce and institutionalize them.

that they violate human rights and dignity. How such dilemmas play out on the ground and your experiences of them will also affect which theories you endorse. For instance, you may begin as a utilitarian and be unconvinced by rights, but then experience a successful human-rights campaign that effectively outlaws something you believe is detrimental to human good, and this may make you rethink your theoretical commitments.

Research ethics

For drugs to be deemed safe and released on to the market they are tested for safety and efficacy in a series of research trials. There are usually four phases of trials. The first is to examine the pharmacokinetics (how drugs are absorbed, distributed and metabolized) and toxicity, essentially to ensure the drug is safe; this is done on a small group of healthy subjects. The second tests the efficacy of the drug, essentially checking that the drug works. Phase three compares the efficacy and safety of drugs with other treatments, usually in a randomized control trial that involves a much larger group of people than the initial stages and also usually involves a much longer study. The final phase is a more recent addition to the testing process and monitors long-term effects (often this continues after the drug is licensed).

In 2003, commenting on "the ethical aspects of clinical research in developing countries", the European Group on Ethics in Science and New Technologies documented "a trend to transfer clinical trials to countries where cost and constraints of regulations may be more favourable to their implementation, and where the high number of patients, and especially naïve patients, that is patients who have never received a treatment, facilitates the recruitment of patients to be involved in a clinical trial" (European Commission 2003). This is particularly true in the later stages of research, where large population groups are required. Much of the global ethical concern about pharmaceutical research is connected with this use of people in developing countries for large-scale trials: concern that profit-led Western companies run research trials in the developing world at a much lower cost and arguably less concern for safety than in the West. Some Western research carried out in developing countries can, of course, benefit those countries, and some, for example research into curing tropical diseases, may be carried out specifically for that end. But a key ethical question of international research is, roughly, whether people in poorer countries are effectively the "guinea pigs" of richer ones. This parallels some of the concerns above about kidney sale. Are the rich simply exploiting the poor? To what extent does consent make such research permissible? And is consent in the context of great wealth and power disparities really autonomous?

As we discussed above, informed consent is the primary ethical mechanism of bioethics, and intended to protect individual autonomy. Individual informed consent has been regarded as the "gold standard" of ethics. This is true of all ethics – where informed consent and confidentially are the two primary ethical practices – but it is particularly true of research ethics. When conducting research, gaining consent from research participants is absolutely necessary; indeed, it is often effectively the only ethical safeguard required for the trial to proceed. There are very good reasons for this focus on consent; the primary reason for promoting and supporting informed consent is to protect the individual research participant. The codes governing research and providing the ethical framework for good research were first formulated in the Nuremberg Code in 1947, and were direct responses to the atrocities perpetrated by the Nazis. Their primary aim was thus to prevent individuals ever suffering such horrors again in the name of research or scientific progress. The intention was to ensure that the individual could not be sacrificed for the greater good of the community and to protect individuals from the state, a company or any group performing such research. By enshrining the principle of informed consent as a necessary prerequisite of any and all research, the hope was that it would be impossible for harmful research to be conducted. This focus on informed consent established in the Nuremberg Code has been reiterated in all subsequent codes of practice and guidelines concerned with the ethics of research: most importantly, it is established in the Declaration of Helsinki, first drafted in 1964 (and since amended eight times between 1975 and, most recently, 2008). But, as we saw with the discussion above on organ sale, there are problems with relying on informed consent alone, and particularly in the context of wealth and power inequalities where the dangers of coercion and exploitation are particularly high.

Additional criteria

In addition to informed consent, for research to be deemed ethical a number of additional criteria must also be met (Box 9.3). Benefits must be proportionate to the risk involved and there must be appropriate standards of care in place.

The condition that risk to benefit should be proportionate for the individual should be determined before the study is permitted to go ahead. Usually this judgement is

---

Box 9.3 Ethical standards for research

- Voluntary informed consent.
- A fair proportion of risk to benefit for the research subject.
- Appropriate standards of care.
- Successful ethical review.

made by research ethics committees. There is no global homogeneity governing how such committees are made up, but there is significant overlap in the way they function in practice and, as international pharmaceutical companies and research networks function across jurisdictions, harmonization is increasingly taking place. What is important is that all international research goes through a series of ethics reviews and core ethical issues are at least considered. The emphasis on appropriate standards of care derives in part from ethical concerns to protect the patient and is partly grounded in concerns for proper scientific method. For example, if a company or research team is testing a new drug then in order to know that it is effective they need to know not only that it works, but also how it performs relative to other drugs and procedures already available.

What the appropriate standard of care is has been an issue of some controversy in bioethics. Until relatively recently, it was required that the "new treatment" was always tested against the "best available treatment". Until 2002, the wording of the Declaration of Helsinki was unequivocal on this point, and stated that "the benefits, risk, burdens and effectiveness of a new method should be tested against those of the best current prophylactic diagnostic and therapeutic methods" (World Medical Association 2008). However, this interpretation of "best" has been questioned, and previous versions were less definitive, stating that:

> [T]he benefits, risks, burdens and effectiveness of a new intervention must be tested against those of the best current proven intervention, except in the following circumstances:
> - The use of placebo, or no treatment, is acceptable in studies where no current proven intervention exists; or
> - Where for compelling and scientifically sound methodological reasons the use of placebo is necessary to determine the efficacy or safety of an intervention and the patients who receive placebo or no treatment will not be subject to any risk of serious or irreversible harm. Extreme care must be taken to avoid abuse of this option.

The question for global ethics is whether these ethical safeguards are enough to protect research participants globally. In particular, are they sufficient to protect those in the developing world from exploitation? To explore this issue we shall consider a number of case studies. Arguably, all are examples of unethical practice (although the second example is less clear), and thus useful in showing the nature of the vulnerability of research participants and the breadth of the ethical issues involved in research.

The Tuskegee study

The "Tuskegee Study of Untreated Syphilis in the Negro Male" was a research trial run by the US Public Health Service from 1932 to 1972. It was concerned with mapping the trajectory of the disease and its subject group was made up of relatively poor Afro-American men. The trial compared 399 men with syphilis with 201 who did not have the condition in order to determine the natural history of the disease.

There were a number of ethically questionable features of the trial. First, it seems that the participants were not well enough informed for their consent to be valid: the researchers told them that they were being treated for "bad blood" rather than giving them an exact scientific diagnosis and prognosis. You can attempt to justify this on the grounds that the term "bad blood" was one that the participants could understand: it was a commonly used local term that covered a number of conditions (including syphilis, anaemia and fatigue) and therefore arguably an appropriate description for the participants. It could also be argued that the aim was deliberately to mislead the participants, because the researchers knew the exact diagnosis; namely, syphilis, a serious condition unlike the other conditions designated by "bad blood".

Second, the participants of the trial were given what could be considered inducement to participate: incentives that would encourage and even put pressure on them to participate. This is similar to arguments about payment for organs. The question is whether inducement invalidates informed consent or whether consent is still valid. In the Tuskegee case the research subjects received free medical examinations, free meals and burial insurance, which, given the poverty of these men, would have been a not insignificant inducement.

The third ethical concern raised by this trial relates to the ethical requirement that the "best available standard of care" be given to research participants. When this research programme began in 1932, no effective treatment for syphilis was available. The only treatment available was to treat the patient with "heavy metals" such as mercury and bismuth. Such treatments could hardly be said to be effective: they had a reputed cure rate of less than 30 per cent and, more problematically, had toxic and sometimes fatal side effects. So at the outset of the trial it was justified simply to map the trajectory of the disease because there was no effective treatment. In 1947, however, penicillin emerged as an effective treatment for syphilis and made the continuation of a trial offering no treatment unethical, but the programme did not end and the affected men were not given the appropriate treatment. Rather than treat the men, the researchers continued to track their deterioration and death. It is worth noting that to fail to offer treatment to these men was also unethical using the new 2008 Declaration of Helsinki: clearly these trial participants were at risk of "serious or irreversible harm".

The Tuskegee study ended in 1972 as a result of public outrage, over twenty years after an effective treatment for syphilis was available. It was brought to public attention by the *New York Times,* which ran a front-page story on the study. It exposed the horrors of the trial and caused significant embarrassment to the Nixon government. In response to the public outcry a committee was formed to investigate, instructed by the Assistant Secretary for Health and Scientific Affairs. This committee judged that the study was unethical on a number of grounds. Although the men had freely agreed to be examined and treated, they could not be said to have given their voluntary and informed consent because they did not know the real purpose of the study. Indeed, they had wrongly assumed that the purpose of the trial was to care for them – given the free medical exams – and so the committee judged that they had been misled. More importantly, the research participants had not been given adequate treatment for their illnesses; nor were they informed about effective treatment and given the opportunity to leave the study and take up treatment. Essentially, these participants were used as experimental subjects and not as research participants: they were experimented on and left to suffer from a degenerative and fatal condition for the purposes of furthering scientific knowledge. Perhaps researchers could claim not to have broken any ethical rules at the beginning of the study, because the Nuremberg Code and the Declaration of Helsinki had not then become standards of global research practice. But these codes did come into force during the course of the study and should have been applied when they did. However, even if no such codes existed, it is hard to imagine that the researchers thought it was ethical to continue once effective treatment was available.

Clearly the Tuskegee study was disgraceful. But, even if there had not been such blatant disregard for ethical concerns there would still have been ethical problems. In particular, there are three ethical concerns that arise from this trial, which are concerns for all research ethics, but are exaggerated when considering global and cross-cultural research. For example, the Tuskegee study was criticized for not explaining the nature of the trial, but when doing a trial in a different culture, particularly a culture that does not primarily think of disease using a scientific framework, what counts as "informed consent"? Is it actually more "informed" to give a full scientific explanation or to try to describe the aims in non-scientific and familiar terms? How is the "therapeutic presumption" to be countered? Research reports that even though participants are informed of the experimental nature of trials (and are often told that

---

Box 9.4 Questions for research ethics

- How much information is required for consent to be informed?
- How is the therapeutic presumption to be countered?
- What counts as inducement to participate?
- What does the commitment to provide the best standard of care require?

they might be receiving placebos) they continue to believe that they are receiving treatment and participation is in their personal best interest. If a trial is being carried out in an area of Sub-Saharan Africa where there is virtually no basic health care available, does any form of health check or medical attention count as inducement? And, finally, how rigorous is the requirement to give the "best available standard of care", especially in light of the qualifying clauses introduced in 2008? What about trialling less expensive or less high-tech solutions in areas where the high-tech treatments are unaffordable? Are such trials always unethical?

Inducement in unequal conditions

The problems of whether or not informed consent can ever be given in unequal conditions is one we have already begun to consider in our discussions of the market in organ sale. Inducement to participate is a key issue when considering any procedure or research where the primary beneficiary is not the participant. Decisions about inducement are particularly complicated, because if we refuse to allow the poorest to participate for fear of inducement, then arguably we reduce their choices and make them even more disadvantaged: again, a parallel argument to the organ-sale debate. Arguably, to prohibit trials in particularly poor places in order to prevent the pressures of inducement would be the most unethical approach of all. It would prevent the poorest taking part in all scientific research and deny them a choice that is available to wealthier persons. Such a decision would be paternalistic and even an instance of colonialism: refusing the "poor" options and choices on the grounds that the poor are not capable of making these decisions for themselves. Moreover, even if you are "induced", if you end up benefiting then should that option be precluded? Arguably, it is more important that those who have the potential to be induced are

---

Box 9.5 Comments from participants of trials for HIV drugs

"When the project first ended, the staff told me about a new project I might join and I decided to enrol again. If there were no studies, I would not have the opportunity to take anti-HIV medication."

"The study staff give good advice and when this project is over I hope I can enrol in another study. For that matter I hope there will be new studies for me to participate in all the time. If there would be no more studies I don't know if I would have the strength to go on, as I would not know where to get the drugs outside of clinical trials."

(Nuffield Council on Bioethics 2002)

offered the chance to take part in such trials because they have the greatest need of the benefits on offer. For example, if participating in a research trial or a cluster of research trials is the only access that a person (and their family) has to any kind of health check, health care or disease treatment, then even though such care is "inducement", is it not better for the research subject to get access to it in this way than not at all? This is clearly the view of participants of HIV trials, as reported in the Nuffield briefing paper on research in developing countries (see Box 9.5). In such cases perhaps inducement is a "least worst" option and preferable, despite all the problems, to no access to any potential treatment. However, these statements show not only that worries about inducement are genuine but also clearly demonstrate the therapeutic presumption. The participants show no awareness that they might not be receiving active treatment or that it is experimental.

Others reject the practical argument for the "least worst" option on the grounds that it fails the ethical requirements of equality and impartiality: that we are justifying unethical processes because people are poor and therefore vulnerable, and that the people involved have little real choice. On this point, recall O'Neill's argument (see Chapter 7) about our obligations to the poor, where she claims that the poor are particularly vulnerable when it comes to accepting unjust transactions and relationships with those who are richer. In particular, they are characteristically in no position to exercise entitlements and rights. The "have-nots" cannot make *demands*, but only beg for assistance; accordingly, she states that we have duties to ensure that the poor are not exploited precisely because their poverty makes them especially vulnerable to such exploitation.

The Zidovudine case

The final specifically "research" issue that we shall consider further is that of "best standards of care" and whether "best standard" should be interpreted globally or locally. As mentioned earlier, this has attracted much ethical attention and the current Declaration of Helsinki makes qualifications with regard to what counts as "best standard" that previous versions did not. To illustrate the issue we shall again use a real case: a trial carried out by the pharmaceutical company Burroughs Wellcome (now GlaxoSmithKline) in 1985 to test the effectiveness of Zidovudine, an anti-retroviral drug, in reducing the vertical transmission of HIV.

This was a placebo-controlled randomized trial, so there were two treatment arms. Everyone enrolled in the trial had tested positive for the HIV virus. One group of research participants was given the drug and one group was given a placebo. Those in the placebo arm were given no active treatment. This was ethically controversial because there was indeed some form of treatment available. Prior to this trial in the same year, scientists at the US National Cancer Institute had, in collaboration with Burroughs Wellcome and scientists from Duke University, already determined that the drug was effective against HIV, and that it could be given to patients safely, although trials were still ongoing.

At first glance, then, this trial did not follow the requirements of the Declaration of Helsinki that any new treatment be tested against the "the best current prophylactic diagnostic and therapeutic methods"; even if the later wording had been in place at the time, to give a placebo would have put the research participants at "risk of serious or irreversible harm". The researchers in this trial defended their actions and claimed that they had acted ethically. As there was no locally available and affordable treatment, they believed it justified to give the control group a placebo. They claimed that they had not disadvantaged or harmed anyone in the trial because the participants would not have been able to access the "global alternative treatment" and so were not made worse off by the trial.

The difference between the Zidovudine trial and the Tuskegee study is that, in the Tuskegee case, had the participants been made aware of their condition and that there was a treatment, they would have been able to leave the trial and access the treatment, whereas the "placebo" participants of the Zidovudine study could not access the alternative treatment. Thus the researchers argued that there was no treatment available for these particular women and so they were complying with the guidelines. In other words they interpreted "best available" as *actually available in that locality and context* and to *those particular participants*, rather than best available *globally*.

Interpreting "best available" as "best local" or "affordable" is ethically troubling. Essentially, it makes it possible to test any "new" treatment against a placebo if a locality can be found in which treatment is unaffordable or unavailable. In terms of global justice, this reading opens up the poor places of the world to become testing grounds for treatments for the rich. On the other hand, there are times when we do need to test against treatments and standards that are not the "best global standard". For instance, suppose a cheap drug for a prevalent disease, like malaria, is being tested: even if it is not as effective as the best global standard, but it is better than the current local standard and affordable, then it is important that it is tested against this lesser actual standard, marketed and made available. So how "best available standard of care" should be interpreted is a real ethical question, and other issues should be taken into account when deciding what counts as ethical.

CHALLENGES OF GENETICS

The problems we have considered regarding informed consent – including whether it can be voluntary in circumstances of social and economic inequality, the level of understanding necessary for it to be deemed informed, and the problems of the therapeutic presumption – are compounded in the genetic era. Genetic information, unlike other forms of medical information, is always potentially identifying. Simply put, no matter how anonymized genetic information is, there is always a risk of identification (of the individual, related individuals or the group) when the information is compared with a database. The identifying nature of genetic information has led to the individual-focused model of ethics because, in genetics, human beings are fundamentally related beings connected to consanguineous relations, family groups, ethnic groups and wider communities and, potentially, in some understandings of the genome, to "humankind" as a meta-collective. To suggest that genetics requires that human beings are considered as relational rather than individual is not just rhetorical. It raises very practical questions about the appropriateness of current ethical practices, in particular about the effectiveness and appropriateness of informed consent and confidentiality.

In short, if genetic information about one person gives information about others then should ethical mechanisms be devised that share information rather than maintain privacy? For example, do family members or reproductive partners have rights to such information? In other words, should we reject confidentiality as an ethical standard in the genetic era? As Brock (2001) argues, confidentiality assumes that medical information is of real importance only to the patient and should be controlled by the patient. However, this long-held assumption does not apply when it comes to genetic information. For example, if an individual tests positive for a genetic condition, such as Huntington's disease, or as a carrier of the BRCA1 or BRCA2 mutation (indicators for breast cancer), this information has relevance for family members (consanguineous relations may wish to be tested themselves, and sexual partners may want the information when making reproductive decisions). Therefore, the key question is not just whether confidentiality can be practically guaranteed (and the indentifying nature of genetic material suggests it cannot), but rather whether it should be. If third parties have justifiable reasons for knowing another person's status, for instance to discover their own at-risk status or to make decisions about having children, then is it really ethical for an individual to refuse to share this information?

Some would argue that it is not, and that instead of regarding genetic information as belonging to individuals we should consider it as belonging to families or wider groups. Two suggestions are the "family covenant" proposed by David Doukas and Jessica Berg (2001) and the "joint account" proposed by Michael Parker and Anneke Lucassen (2004). If genetic information pertains not only to the individual from whom it is taken, but also to other connected people, such as family members or ethnic groups, is it really acceptable simply to seek individual consent from the person from whom the sample was taken, rather than from the group more broadly? This is an issue that has become particularly pressing when considering research on indigenous populations with relatively homogenous (and therefore potentially valuable) genotypes. In these cases the shared nature of genetic information means that genetic research on one member of the group potentially affects other members of the group who did not consent. I have addressed this issue elsewhere, as have other thinkers, including Henry Greely, Donna Dickenson, Barbara Tedlock and David Winickoff. To illustrate, let us consider the 1994 case of the Hagahai tribe of Papua New Guinea.

The case of the Hagahai

The Hagahai are an indigenous tribe of Papua New Guinea. In this case samples were taken from a few individuals and a patent granted on a cell line containing unmodified Hagahai DNA and several methods for its use in detecting HTLV-1-related retroviruses. The granting of this patent was met with opposition from indigenous rights groups, who deemed it unethical for unmodified DNA to be owned in any circumstance: "no patents on life". In 1996, following protest, the patent was "disclaimed"; the Hagahai cell line remains in the public domain and is now available to the public at the American Type Culture Collection as Number: CRL-10528 Organism: Homo Sapiens (human) at a cost of $290.

Similar practices have been recorded in the Solomon Islands and Panama, to give two further examples. There has been much debate about whether or not these practices constitute "bio-piracy". For instance, Vandana Shiva (1997, 2001, 2005) has criticized not only the taking of samples from indigenous groups, but also the use and commodification of traditional knowledge to develop drugs or for patents. Other famous examples of bio-piracy are attempts by Western companies to patent plants; for example, turmeric and the Neem tree. These have been objected to on the grounds that there is no "invention" and "every grandmother knows" the therapeutic quality of these plants.

Respecting groups and communal goods

The patenting of unmodified DNA raises ethical issues that are not addressed by individual ethical practices. For instance, even if informed consent was correctly obtained from a member of an indigenous group, this would not recognize the rights and interests that third parties legitimately have in the genetic information. Moreover such individual practices do not protect collective rights and interests, such as those of culture, heritage and ownership. The crucial issue is not just that other group members did not consent, but more importantly that other ethical issues are neglected: group vulnerability, discrimination and exploitation. These group ethical issues are of obvious importance in the case of vulnerable indigenous groups, but they are also important for vulnerable families, for example those who are in danger of being discriminated against on genetic grounds.

As a result of these types of criticism and the clear injustices done to indigenous groups, communal ethical frameworks are being sought; this is described as the "communal turn" in bioethics. The communal turn is most evident in population genetics and research (rather than in clinical genetics, where, despite the suggestions for family models discussed above, individual practices largely continue to dominate). This communal turn has been described particularly clearly by Ruth Chadwick, who has outlined moves to group models as well as discussing the public good in this context. The communal turn is an attempt to recognize that there are ethically significant communal goods as well as individual goods that need to be respected in ethical frameworks.

Group consent

The recognition that there are communal goods that need protecting can be seen in the now standard insistence that there is prior consultation with communities in areas where research is intended to take place. Often some kind of group consent will be sought, particularly when research involves indigenous groups. While group consent does recognize that there are group interests, it has also been criticized. Not least is the argument that group consent, like individual consent, is based on the false premise that if something is chosen it must be ethical. Accordingly, it is argued that group consent does little to address key issues such as exploitation, coercion and commodification, because it does not address underlying structural concerns, such as the power of vested interests (including scientific, commercial and national interests). If consent is the only appropriate tool then it would be acceptable for an indigenous group collectively to consent to destroy a unique biosphere or other important resource simply because they choose to.

Trust model

Other group models have been suggested. Perhaps most prominent in the literature are the "trust model" and benefit sharing. The trust model is usually employed in

---

Box 9.6 Types of group models

- Group consent
- Trust
- Benefit sharing

---

large-scale population studies such as biobanks (e.g. UK Biobank). It is used when informed consent is impractical for two reasons: (i) because samples and consent are taken at the beginning of the project when it cannot be known what specific research will be done, so that it would be false to say that consent was "fully informed"; (ii) because biobanks are a resource for many research projects, so to return to donors and seek consent for every new study would be impossible. Therefore, rather than fully informed consent, "broad consent" is given. However, importantly, this is not "simple broad consent"; rather, what is permitted is limited by the trust framework.

The donor gives broad consent on trust that their material will be used as promised in the original consent, and this is ensured by ongoing ethical and governance mechanisms. Thus key to the effectiveness of trust models are the additional ethics and governance mechanisms that are introduced to supplement consent and to ensure that the samples are used in accord with the expectations of the donor and within the conditions of the original consent. Different types of ongoing ethics and governance models can be adopted. Winickoff has suggested that possible mechanisms might include membership on the trust's board, a donor committee or the board of trustees, or contributing to access mechanisms. In UK Biobank, all research must comply with the "ethics and governance framework" and access and intellectual property policies ensure that this is the case. In addition, there is an ethics and governance council whose remit is to monitor and oversee UK Biobank.

The trust model offers ethical protections that purely individual models do not. Yet its effectiveness depends on the strength of the ethical oversight mechanisms established. Weak trust models may actually increase possibilities of exploitation and coercion if they fail to enforce additional ethical safeguards.

Benefit sharing

Perhaps the most important communal model for global ethics, in that it has been used particularly effectively by some developing communities, is benefit sharing. Benefit sharing does exactly that: it shares the benefits of any profit from research with the community from which the samples, knowledge or other materials or information were derived. Benefits that have been suggested by the Human Gene Organization (HUGO) include health care, public-health-services technology transfer and contribution to the local community infrastructure (e.g. schools, libraries, sports, clean water). The logic of HUGO's reasoning is that the genome is a common good and as such it should be a globally governed resource and the benefits shared globally.

The main problem with benefit sharing is that it does not benefit all equally. Benefit sharing (despite the rhetoric of common good) does not take the globe as its area of concern, but only the community or locality where research or innovation is to occur. Therefore, even when benefit sharing is managed really well, only a particular group benefits. This would not be a problem if all groups could negotiate equally good benefit-sharing agreements, but they cannot. Benefit-sharing agreements come down to what a group has to offer the researchers, and sadly often all a group has to offer is that it will demand fewer "shared benefits" than the next-door village, community or nation. Therefore, despite its aims, benefit sharing may actually reinforce distributive differences and enhance injustice.

This said, benefit sharing has worked well for some groups – for instance, for groups that have something unique to sell – and there are instances where great deals have been negotiated. For example, in 1987 a team of botanists was studying plants in the Kani community in the Thiruvananthapuram forest in the southern part of the Western Ghat region of India, when they inadvertently discovered that locals were able to resist fatigue far more effectively than they were by eating a certain plant later identified as "*arogyapacha*". The scientists went on to develop this synthetically and commercialize the energy-enhancing properties of the plant, and not only gave a proportion of profits to the Kani as the "inventors", but also undertook to implement enhanced cultivation of the plant.

Thus even though benefit sharing is not a perfect group model, it offers at least a partial solution to the problems of bioethical injustice. In addition, together with other group models, it highlights the injustice of current practices and shows clearly that there are ethically significant goods to be protected that individual models of bioethics simply ignore.

PATENTS AND INTELLECTUAL PROPERTY

A final issue we shall consider, and one that is particularly important for global ethics, is the ethics of intellectual property and the ethical problems of the patent system in relation to the development of essential drugs and affordable access to such drugs. This topic relates directly to Chapter 6, where structures of global governance were discussed. Most important in this debate is the international property rights framework, in particular patent rights and the limitations of TRIPS.

90–10 disequilibrium

The 90–10 disequilibrium refers to the fact that only 10 per cent of total health-related research and development is devoted to 90 per cent of the global disease burden. In other words, 90 per cent of the global disease burden is made up of diseases that affect the global poor, such as malaria, but only 10 per cent of the total money spent on researching and developing drugs is dedicated to combating these illnesses.

Reasons for this are many, but chief among them is the high cost of developing and bringing a new drug to market: according to GlaxoSmithKline it costs on average around $1.2 billion to bring a drug to market and typically takes ten to twelve years. Given this, pharmaceutical companies invest in research and development only for medicines that can recoup the large cost of their development, so which medicines are developed is determined not by need but by the potential profits that can be gained. It is not the diseases of the poor in the developing world that have priority, but rather diseases of large numbers of people in industrialized countries. NGOs such as the Gates Foundation and Clinton Foundation have become increasingly important forces for addressing the diseases of the global poor, and their contribution to combating polio, HIV and malaria should not be underestimated.

Health Impact Fund

Options that have been suggested in order to overcome the disequilibrium include compulsory licensing (legally making patents available to others), patent pools (more than one company agreeing to share their patents with each other for mutual benefit rather than compete with each other), incentive schemes and prizes. The greatest focus at the moment is on the "Health Impact Fund" proposed by Aiden Hollis and Thomas Pogge (2008). The Health Impact Fund proposes a supranationally funded prize system, with the size of payment reflecting the reduction in global health burden attributable to the medicine. Initially it would be funded by approximately 0.03 per cent of the GNI of all countries. A prize is then offered for those who produce drugs that will reduce the global health burden. The prize is annual for up to ten years in order to give a company time to bring a drug to market and profit accordingly. After this period the company must provide open licences (a change from an earlier version, which permitted generic competition from the outset, and one that has led to criticism because it reduces the downward pressure on prices from competition). The aim here is to offset the prohibitive cost of the research and development of any drug.

In addition to the cost of developing drugs there are also further problems caused by the patent system, notoriously exacerbated by TRIPS in 1994. Among other things, this agreement made the production of generic drugs (carried out particularly in middle-income countries such as India and Brazil) difficult and the sale of such drugs to the poorest countries (who do not have the necessary infrastructure to produce them) prohibited. Currently, and in no small measure as a result of patents and TRIPS, it is estimated that a third of the world's population has *no access* to essential drugs and more than half of this group of people live in the poorest regions of Africa and Asia.

The current move by GlaxoSmithKline to reduce the cost of certain drugs (excluding AIDS drugs) – in February 2009 CEO Andrew Witty pledged to limit the price of its products in fifty developing countries to 25 per cent of the UK and US price – does little to meet the needs of the poorest. The poor still cannot afford these drugs. Moreover, if we were to be cynical it could be concluded that this reduction is meant to ensure that these "official drugs" are able to compete with generic drugs in middle-income countries and not intended to address lack of access to essential medicines globally.

CONCLUSION

This chapter has shown how integral bioethics is to the global-ethics debate. It addresses core issues about the nature of human beings and what the acceptable boundaries of life are. Moreover, in discussions about access to essential drugs it shows clearly that how global systems of governance are structured affects issues necessary to survival, such as whether essential drugs for life-threatening diseases are affordable for the poor. The bioethics debate is also particularly useful for showing the connectedness of global-ethics issues: poor health reduces opportunities and poverty makes ill health more likely – a vicious circle.

In addition, the debate about the inadequacy of informed consent also speaks to one of the key theoretical debates in contemporary ethics and particularly global ethics, namely the debate about how to balance the rights and interests of individuals and groups. This is a debate we have already considered, particularly in Chapter 5, and Chapter 8 with regard to human rights and security, and we shall return to it in Chapter 11. In developing new communal and group models, bioethics has begun to address the issue in policy and practice as well as in theory, and these "new models" (such as trust and benefit sharing) could be useful in other areas of the global-ethics debate as possible templates. The discussion of how to recognize group and public goods begun in this chapter will continue in the next chapter, when we consider the nature of environmental goods: goods that are always communal and never individual.

FURTHER READING

- Buchanan, A., D. W. Brock, N. Daniels & D. Wikler. *From Chance to Choice: Genetics and Justice* (Cambridge: Cambridge University Press, 2000).
- Dickenson, D. *Body Shopping: The Economy Fuelled by Flesh and Blood* (Oxford: One World, 2008).
- Dickenson, D., R. Huxtable & M. Parker. *The Cambridge Medical Ethics Handbook*, 2nd edn (Cambridge: Cambridge University Press, 2010).

- Greely, H. "Human Genomics Research: New Challenges for Research Ethics". *Perspectives in Biology and Medicine* **44** (2001): 221–9.
- Harris, J. *The Value of Life: An Introduction to Medical Ethics* (London: Routledge, 2005).
- Holland, S. *Bioethics: A Philosophical Introduction* (Cambridge: Polity Press, 2003).
- Human Genome Organization (HUGO) Ethics Committee. "Statement on Benefit Sharing" (2000). www.hugo-international.org/img/benefit_sharing_2000.pdf (accessed May 2011).
- Marquis, D. "An Argument that Abortion is Wrong". In *Ethics in Practice: An Anthology*, H. Lafollette (ed.), 83–93 (Oxford: Blackwell, 1997).
- Nuffield Council on Bioethics. *The Ethics of Research Related to Healthcare in Developing Countries* (2002). www.nuffieldbioethics.org/research-developing-countries (accessed May 2011).
- Thomson, J. J. "A Defense of Abortion". *Philosophy and Public Affairs* **1** (1971): 47–66.
- Wilkinson, S. *Bodies for Sale: Ethics and Exploitation in the Human Body Trade* (London: Routledge, 2003).
- World Medical Association (WMA) 2008. "WMA Declaration of Helsinki: Ethical Principles for Medical Research Involving Human Subjects". www.wma.net/en/30publications/10policies/b3/index.html (accessed May 2011).

10 GLOBAL ENVIRONMENTAL AND CLIMATE ETHICS

INTRODUCTION

Environmental ethics is a key branch of contemporary global ethics and one that is increasingly important. Environmental ethics has expanded dramatically in recent years and, like global ethics, as discussed in Chapter 1, it is a response to emerging problems and crises. For some, the environmental crisis is *the* overarching global-ethics issue that needs to be addressed because human survival itself is threatened. In attempting to respond to the environmental crisis we can see very clearly the logic of global ethics at work. It makes little sense to construct a less-than-global ethical community when considering how to address global threats such as climate change. No nation or region can address climate change alone. Only a shared response, where everyone takes the actions necessary, will be sufficient to deal with this problem. Climate change is no respecter of national borders and the behaviour of one nation or region affects others. Hence responses to climate change are always "global in scope"; even those who endorse regional protections (such as the strengthening of national borders to protect national resources) cannot but think of the global causes and effects. The second two criteria of global ethics are also clearly met: responses to climate change are necessarily multidisciplinary – scientific knowledge is crucial to legal, moral and political responses; and theory and practice are linked as ethicists struggle to propose just and effective practical solutions (something evident in the work of Caney and Moellendorf, discussed towards the end of this chapter).

In addition to being of obvious global-ethics concern, environmental issues are interrelated with the other global-ethics issues we have considered. In particular, climate change compounds other injustices. For instance, those who are already living a subsistence existence have no spare resources with which to cushion themselves from the effects of severe weather events caused by climate change, such as drought or flood. Nor do they have the means to attain scarce natural resources, such as water and productive land. Moreover, as weather patterns change and land that was once fertile becomes uninhabitable, the total resources available diminish. As well as exacerbating economic injustice, other forms of injustice also increase in an environmentally unstable context and accessing basic health and security becomes more difficult. As natural resources – of fertile land, energy, water and food – become increasingly scarce, the likelihood that there will be conflict to secure them increases. Again, those who are most vulnerable will suffer most: they might suffer from insecurity during periods of conflict; be on the losing side and suffer retribution; their land and lives might be threatened; or they might become refugees and suffer loss of status, property and even citizenship.

Environmental issues are clearly fundamental to resolving global-ethics issues; they are not separate but intimately connected. Again, as in Chapter 9, we are reminded that if we wish to address injustice then we must not consider issues in isolation but adopt holistic models that recognize the interconnections of these issues.

ENVIRONMENTAL ETHICS AND CLIMATE ETHICS

Environmental ethics covers a large area and one that has expanded dramatically over the past few decades. It represents developments in ethical thinking that are not just responses to the current environmental crisis, but are responses to increasing ethical concerns and uneasiness about human duties to the non-human world. For instance, environmental ethics includes questions about the scope of duties and asks what duties, if any, humans have to non-human species and to the environment more broadly.

In fact, a primary issue of environmental ethics is whether rights should be extended beyond human agents. The moral theories we discussed in Chapter 3 were human-centric or anthropocentric; moral duties were limited to how human beings should treat other human beings. Likewise, the political theories of Chapter 4 were concerned with human governance, and Chapter 5 was overtly about *human* rights. In Chapter 9 we saw how ethical frameworks are beginning to be developed that respect groups and common goods and that allot some rights to groups as groups, rather than just to individuals. Parallel arguments are made in environmental ethics about the rights of animals; here there is considerable overlap with bioethics, because much of the focus of this debate has been on whether or not research on animals is justified to produce medicine and other products for humans.

Animal rights

The most prominent thinker in this debate is Peter Singer (1975), whose arguments about the duties of justice we discussed in Chapter 7. Singer argues that the principle of equality applies not just to humans, but also to animals. Therefore, according to Singer, if you accept that equality and impartiality are sound moral principles for governing human relations then you should accept that they are also sound when it comes to governing relations between humans and animals. Not to see this is unjustly to discriminate, without reason to do so: a prejudice Singer terms "speciesism". Singer argues that just as being a member of a different race does not justify exploitation, being a member of a different species does not justify exploitation. Likewise, he argues, the fact that animals may be less intelligent than we are does not justify disregarding their interests any more than we would be justified in disregarding interests of less-intelligent human beings.

For Singer, animals have interests that deserve to be protected because they can suffer, and this suffering should be taken into moral consideration. Beings capable of suffering, happiness or enjoyment have interests that entitle them to moral status and enable us to distinguish moral beings from things. Singer does not propose that the interests of all animals are the same and accepts that there are differences in levels of suffering. He also recognizes that there are difficulties in making comparisons between human and animal suffering. However, he argues that precision is not necessary to make judgements and, in cases where human suffering is less than animal suffering, animal interests should be respected over and above human interests. Singer applies this reasoning to all aspects of human relationships with animals, from eating animals to animal experimentation. Ascribing respect for animals' interests has implications for many aspects of contemporary living. For instance, is it acceptable to eat animals at all, and, if so, in what circumstances? How much does human need count compared to animal suffering? Likewise, is experimentation on animals justified when the need is great?

Environmental value

In addition to the rights of animals, there are also questions about how nature itself should be treated in general. Are there duties to preserve and protect our environment that extend beyond the need to preserve what is necessary for human survival? For instance, is the extinction of species intrinsically bad or is it just instrumentally bad in that in losing a species humans might be losing useful resources (such as medical or food sources)? Likewise, should biodiversity be protected, and, if so, why?

The traditional model of ethics excludes the non-human sphere and regards it as having value only as far as it is of use to humans. Thus any duties to nature are *instrumental*: nature should be protected because it is useful to humanity. Over the past few decades other models of the relation between human beings and the planet have emerged and are gaining prominence as "green approaches" become central to public and policy debates.

Stewardship model

One possible model, which has its basis in Judaeo-Christian thinking, is the "stewardship model". This model – which is now promoted as a secular as well as religious model, for instance by Robin Attfield (2006) – suggests that humans are the stewards or trustees of nature. Thus the ways in which human beings can act towards nature is limited; they cannot do whatever they wish and do not have dominion over nature. This model offers a conception of the duties that human beings have not only to animals to prevent suffering, but also to nature more broadly: for instance, to prevent species extinction and to preserve biodiversity. In the current environmental crisis it suggests that there are not just duties to protect humans but additional duties to protect animals, species and habitats as well as biological and ecological systems.

Deep ecology

Another model that moves beyond instrumental models is that of deep ecology. The principles of deep ecology were set out by Arne Naess and George Sessions (Naess & Sessions 1984; Sessions 1995). They assert the *intrinsic* value – value in and of itself – of non-human life. The flourishing of eco-systems and natural objects is regarded as important independently of being *instrumentally* valuable to human beings. The deep ecology model argues that diversity is valuable in itself and that humans, as one form of life among all the others, have no right to reduce the richness and diversity of the natural world except to support vital needs. Hence, deep ecology roundly rejects any anthropocentric perspective: any view that puts humans at the centre of our concerns.

Beyond instrumental value

This brief look into the developing movements in environmental thinking shows that models are emerging that go beyond ascribing instrumental value to the environment. How you view these models and the status you ascribe to animals and the non-human world in general will change your ethical framework, and you will need to revise the frameworks of Chapters 2, 3 and 4 to incorporate such concerns.

This is easier to do when you adopt some theories rather than others: for instance, if you are a utilitarian how can the environment (if you exclude animals) be valued intrinsically in a calculation about happiness? Similarly, can a *human*-rights-based model be extended to animals and the environment more broadly?

In addition to these questions about the scope of rights and duties beyond the human sphere, environmental ethics is increasingly dominated by climate change and how this should be responded to. For the most part this is an anthropocentric debate and one that is concerned only instrumentally with the environment; it is the threat to human survival and flourishing that is driving the concern with climate ethics rather than concerns about whether we should be respecting the environment as valuable in itself. However, these wider debates about environmental ethics are not irrelevant to climate ethics. For instance, more holistic and sustainable approaches to nature, such as those promoted by deep ecology and the stewardship model, offer motivation to make some of the difficult changes that are required if the environmental crisis is to be addressed.

THE ENVIRONMENTAL CRISIS

Given the dominance of climate ethics in current environmental ethics, the rest of the chapter will focus on this issue of ethical response to the environmental crisis and the suggestions that are being put forward to address current challenges of climate change. Climate change is generally agreed to be something brought about by human actions: anthropocentric climate change. It is primarily caused by the emission of greenhouse gases (GHG) through the burning of fossil fuels, deforestation, aerosol gases, CFCs in refrigeration systems and from animals, manure processing and paddy-field farming. Although the science remains disputed by some, by far the majority of the scientific community agree that climate change is happening and that its effect on the environment and human beings' ability to sustain current standards of living – and even to survive – will be catastrophic.

So for example, the latest report from the IPCC (2007a) predicts that "very large sea-level rises that would result from widespread deglaciation of Greenland and West Antarctic ice sheets imply major changes in coastlines and ecosystems, and inundation of low-lying areas, with the greatest effects in river deltas". And the IPCC has produced a statement on the melting of Himalayan glaciers, which notes:

> [W]idespread mass losses from glaciers and reductions in snow cover over recent decades are projected to accelerate throughout the 21st century, reducing water availability, hydropower potential, and changing seasonality of flows in regions supplied by meltwater from major mountain ranges (e.g.

Hindu-Kush, Himalaya, Andes), where more than one-sixth of the world population currently lives. (2010)

These are just two of the predictions of climate change. More information can be found from the IPCC. The task of this chapter is not to lay out the science – which is easily available – but to focus on the ethical responses to the predictions.

These effects of climate change are already being felt; and, importantly, these effects will increase no matter what actions are taken. The effects of the emissions that have already been produced will continue to be felt for a long time into the future. In addition to the already dangerous changes listed in Box 10.1, there are a number of possible events that, if they occurred, would result in even more catastrophic climate changes. For instance, it is also possible that climate change could result in the failure of the Gulf Stream, which would in turn result in the cooling of northern Europe, making another region of the world potentially uninhabitable.

The effects of climate change will fall disproportionately on the poor, as with so many other issues in global ethics. The already vulnerable – through poverty or ill health – will be more vulnerable to environmental catastrophes and less able to mitigate their effects. For instance, sea-level rises will affect low-lying and low-income states – such as Bangladesh, small island states and the Nile Delta – harder and more immediately than other countries. In part this is purely a geographical accident. However, it is also because they are not able to afford the adaptations that richer, similarly low-lying states – such as the Netherlands – employ. (It is worth noting that even in the Netherlands, according to a report from the Netherlands Environmental Assessment Agency (2006), it is unlikely that current approaches will suffice: "The second half of the century may see serious problems arising from climate change, in particular in the low-lying areas of the country. A sea level rise of several to many metres is expected in the very long term [a few hundred years]. It is questionable

---

Box 10.1 Effects of climate change

- Temperature rise.
- Sea-level rise.
- Extreme weather events, e.g. heatwaves.
- Increased floods, hurricanes, droughts.
- Large regions of the world becoming uninhabitable.
- Large-scale displacement of human communities.
- Species extinction.
- Ocean acidification.
- Destruction of land and sea infrastructures.

whether conventional techniques can be used to maintain the current level of safety.")
Likewise, rises in temperature are more easily managed by countries with agriculture
infrastructure that can deal with droughts; earthquakes and tidal waves are more easily
managed by those who live in appropriate housing rather than shanty towns; floods
are more easily managed by rich countries that can bear the cost of immediate aid and
that have health-care systems that can quickly address the threats of emergency diseases; and so the list goes on. Thus one form of injustice compounds other injustices
and the result is further disadvantage and injustice for those already at the bottom of
the heap.

Such compounding of injustices is, without doubt, a serious ethical issue. Yet
because the injustice is so clear and the need to address it so striking, in a strange
way climate change is a less controversial issue – when it comes to ethics – than some
of the other issues we have addressed. For instance, if we think back to Chapter 9,
there are strong disagreements between ethicists; they profoundly disagree on issues
such as whether individuals should be able to sell their organs if they choose or
whether sex selection should be permitted. When it comes to climate change there
is little *ethical* disagreement. In short, climate change is an extreme threat to human
survival and flourishing and therefore it is imperative that it is addressed. This is true
whatever moral theories one adopts from Chapter 3: for utilitarians the greatest good
requires that climate change is addressed because the consequences for not doing so
will be a vast increase in human suffering; for deontologists human dignity and rights
require that climate change be addressed; and for virtue ethicists, if human beings
are to flourish and be able to exercise the virtues, climate change must be addressed.
The political differences of Chapter 4 are also less pronounced; even realists, who
seek only national advantage, have to engage in global negotiation to produce treaties and agreements that will lead to the necessary practical solutions. As discussed
above, this is an issue that no nation can hope to influence alone.

Addressing climate change

However, simply because all agree about the ends does not mean that there is agreement about the means. Thus the ethical debate in climate ethics is primarily about
what measures can be put in place and whether they can be justified. Is the situation
so severe that draconian measures are needed? Would it be permissible to coerce
individuals and communities to reduce their emissions, even if it required a dramatic reduction in standards of living for the wealthy and denied the poor rights of
development? Are enforced population-control measures permissible, for instance
negative measures such as penalties for reproduction or positive measures such as
payment for sterilization? And who should bear the cost of managing the effects of
the climate change already in progress?

A further question that merits some attention is: who is responsible for addressing climate change? Nations clearly have roles in global negotiations, regulation and enforcement of agreed measures. Much current focus is on international responses based on consensus between nations. The most prominent example of nations making international agreements and taking action is the Kyoto Protocol, which, as of November 2009, 187 countries had signed up to; this was followed by the 2009 Copenhagen Accord, which endorses the continuation of the protocol and its targets, but is not itself legally binding.

The Kyoto Protocol is a protocol of the United Nations Framework on Climate Change, and is a global attempt to address the problems of global warming and GHG emissions. The key objective set out in the protocol was for countries to meet targets for emissions in 2012 relative to their 1990 levels. On average this target is a 5.2 per cent reduction, which means that different nations may have different targets: the UK has a target of 8 per cent reduction, whereas Australia is permitted a slight increase. Progress towards this goal has been a partial success (or partial failure), although it is generally agreed that the 2012 target is likely to be met overall. As of 2005, many of the "economies in transition" (EIT), such as Poland and former Soviet Republics, had made significant reductions that exceed their 1990-related targets (up to 35 per cent reductions), possibly owing to the downscaling of the inefficient industries of the communist era. By contrast, during the same period, the other non-EIT developed nations that have ratified the protocol together increased their emissions on average by 5 per cent. Clearly, then, nations have a role in implementing and regulating practical solutions (see Box 10.2) and in managing any kind of carbon quotas or trading policies such as those set out in the Kyoto Protocol.

However, there are problems with relying on nations alone; for instance the Kyoto Protocol is widely criticized for doing too little to address the severity of climate change, and key nations, such as the US and Turkey, have neither signed nor ratified the protocol (although they are named as "parties" to it and their emissions are

---

Box 10.2 Possible practical measures to address climate change

- Carbon quotas.
- Carbon trading policies.
- Carbon taxes.
- Clean development initiatives.
- Adaption programmes.
- Gas extraction from landfill programmes.
- Renewable energy programmes.
- Waste reduction and re-use.

---

included in the targets and calculations). Likewise, there are issues about how such agreements can be enforced and monitored. In 2009, the then UK Prime Minister Gordon Brown looked into the viability of monitoring individual nations with a view to policing their emissions. This proposal received interest and support from French President Nicolas Sarkozy and was followed by a suggestion by US President Barack Obama that spy satellites could be employed to do this. Yet global enforcement mechanisms have yet to be put into place.

So we need to ask what other actors there are who might make a difference. For instance, even though the US has not signed the Kyoto Protocol, some US states have taken measures to address climate change: California is committed to reducing GHG to 1990 levels by 2020 and other states, including most New England states, have pledged to reduce GHG emission to 10 per cent lower than 1990 levels by 2020. Likewise, regions can make a difference: for example, in 2005 the EU introduced a limited emissions and trading scheme that "keeps track of the ownership of allowances in the same way as a banking system keeps track of the ownership of money", in the words of the European Commission (2010).

Institutions and firms can also have roles in influencing both nations and the individuals who work for them. Likewise, individuals have duties; arguably, those in the West, who have largely been the creators and beneficiaries of climate change, have the greatest duties. Some individuals act to compensate for their use of scarce resources by using carbon offsetting schemes, which allow individuals to offset their own carbon footprints by funding "green projects", such as alternative energy sources or tree planting. Suggestions have been made for institutionalizing such duties and ensuring that individuals take responsibility for their own carbon footprints. For instance, the UK government has explored the possibility of implementing a "personal carbon trading system", in which individuals would be given a quota of carbon emissions and, if they wished to use more (e.g. in energy or travel), they would have to purchase additional permits from those who had not used their full quota. This

---

Box 10.3 Responses to climate change

Mitigations:
- Reducing emissions.
- Reducing fossil fuel use.
- Reducing animal emissions.

Adaptions:
- Renewable fuel.
- Sea defences.
- Technological defences, such as genetically modified crops.

---

scheme was not, in fact, taken forward, but the fact that such possibilities are being explored suggests that this is an issue policy-makers are acting on.

Thus the ethical debate is not about whether or not we should address climate change, but rather about how we should do it justly. Given the overwhelming evidence, there is little disagreement about the ethical importance of addressing climate change: the debate is about how to motivate change and how to set about it in practice. For the most part – as we shall see in the final section of the chapter – the ethics debate focuses on mitigation and adaption policies with particular focus on how to reduce GHG emissions in just ways. A primary focus, especially for the global ethicist, is how to ensure that those who are already on the receiving end of much injustice and who lack economic, social and cultural goods are not further damaged by climate change: that those already vulnerable are protected against the effects of climate change and that the right of the poor to develop is not undermined by policies that reduce emissions. However, there are those who propose more radical solutions to climate change; for instance, forced reductions in emissions and forced population control to reduce the scale of the crisis.

Duties to human survival

In a famous paper, "Living on a Lifeboat" (1974), Garrett Hardin argues that if the environmental crisis is to be resolved, then we have duties explicitly to protect the planet so that human beings survive, and that this entails a radical rethinking of what our ethical duties to the poor are. Hardin argues that we should not think of the environmental crisis as a global problem that requires a global solution, in the way set out above: he calls this the "we're all in this together", "spaceship model". He suggests that this model – which assumes that because we all share the planet we should share resources – leads to the destruction of resources and allows "misguided idealists to justify suicidal policies for sharing our resources through uncontrolled immigration and foreign aid". Hardin argues that for resources to be protected – which they must be for human survival and in order to respect the rights of future generations – they must be owned by somebody and access to them must be limited. This is an argument he put forward in an almost equally famous earlier paper, "The Tragedy of the Commons" (1968). The "tragedy" of common property is that because it belongs to all (rather than particular individuals and groups) no one takes responsibility for preserving it into the future. Hardin believes that the tragedy of the commons is evident in the pollution of global commons such as air, water and land and fish stocks.

Rather than a "spaceship" with shared resources to which all have an entitlement, Hardin proposes that it is more realistic to think of the globe as an ocean that is scattered with lifeboats. These lifeboats are the rich countries (which hold about a third of the world's population) and the poor swim in the ocean towards the lifeboats, desperately trying to clamber aboard. The lifeboats are nearly at capacity and at best can take a few more people; but, to do this would be to reduce the "safety factor": the capacity to respond to crisis, such as drought or flood (arguably more important in the current climate situation where emergencies are increasingly likely).

What are the options for those in the lifeboats? Hardin (1974) argues that if we take the usual justice approach, we will attempt to bring all those in the sea into the lifeboats. The result of this is that "the boat swamps, everyone drowns". In Hardin's words *complete justice, complete catastrophe*. He argues that we should refuse to allow any additions to the lifeboats and set guards at their perimeters. If people feel guilt about this for reasons of justice, his reply is "get out and yield your place to others". He regards any other approach as unrealistic, and in fact unethical, because it will result in further environmental degradation and the destruction of all human life.

Hardin's lifeboat ethics has implications not only for immigration and aid policies, but also for health programmes, international law and all forms of global govern-ance. In particular, he worries about population increase – especially of the poor whose populations grow twice as fast as the rich – and advocates coercive popula-tion control as a means of lessening environmental degradation. Hardin points out that every human being uses environmental resources and thus, as population rises, there are fewer resources to be shared. He argues that populations should be naturally checked by drought and famine but that these natural means of population reduction have been artificially reduced by food and development aid. Such aid, he believes, is misguided and irresponsible and should be refused: "however humanitarian our intent, every Indian life saved though medical or nutritional assistance from abroad diminishes the quality of life for those who remain, and for subsequent generations". According to Hardin, our duties to future generations require that we reject the usual claims of justice and recognize the claim of these alternative duties: "prosperity will be satisfied with nothing less".

Not surprisingly, the lifeboat model has received little support from ethicists – especially global ethicists – as it contravenes key principles of moral theories, such as universalism and impartiality, discussed in Chapter 3, and most political theories, from cosmopolitanism to rights theories, discussed in Chapters 4 and 5. Not only is Hardin's theory of justice criticized as failing ethical and moral premises, but his empirical claims about the effect of population growth are questionable. For instance, while all humans do use resources, the quantity of those resources is vastly different; as we saw in Chapter 9, if we were concerned with resource depletion it should be the US population we control and not poor populations. So, to use Hardin's logic, to protect the world's resources for future generations our duty might well be to sink the lifeboats, and insist that all live using sustainable measures. Alternatively, population increase may be addressed as development occurs; however, along with development comes increased resource use and environmental impact. Population reduction alone is not a solution to the environmental crisis.

A rights-based approach

There are strong pragmatic reasons for us to address climate change; it is arguably the biggest threat to human survival and therefore should be at the top of the list if we wish human beings to continue to survive, let alone flourish. This pragmatic and consequentialist approach is most prevalent – particularly in public and policy debates – and most debate is about how to reduce environmental degradation and pollution (few thinkers adopt non-global approaches such as Hardin's). But consequential reasoning is not the only form of moral reasoning that suggests we have collective and individual duties to address climate change. For instance, deontological arguments can be made and a number of prominent global ethicists have adopted rights-based approaches. Foremost among these is Simon Caney. He adopts a human-rights approach to argue that climate change needs addressing with the utmost haste and also to guide thinking about how solutions should be formulated and implemented in practice. Caney's concept of human rights is a standard one, as discussed in Chapter 5. For him, all individuals possess human rights irrespective of their social or cultural circumstances, and these rights take priority over other values. Rights, for Caney, are "moral thresholds"; they delineate an acceptable standard beneath which no one should be allowed to fall. (Think back to the discussion about Shue and "basic rights".) He defends instrumental rather than intrinsic conceptions of human rights but argues that this makes little difference to the ethical arguments or the duties that rights impose when we consider climate change.

In his paper "Climate Change, Human Rights and Moral Thresholds" (2009b), Caney notes the increasing attention to climate change in human-rights documents. To this end he cites the "Male' Declaration on Human Dimension of Global Climate Change" (CIEL 2007) and the 2008 resolution of the Human Rights Council of the United Nations (OHCHR 2008), which recognize the threat climate change poses to human rights. Caney identifies three rights that climate change threatens: rights to life, health and subsistence. Because climate change is brought about by human action, he is able to base his argument on a negative-rights claim that there is a right not to be harmed by the action of others.

Caney presents these three rights as basic, minimal requirements in order to gain as much consensus as possible from across the theoretical and political spectrum. Elsewhere he also argues that "the right to property" and "the right not to be subject to enforced relocation" are also jeopardized; but because these are perhaps more contentious he omits them from "Climate Change, Human Rights and Moral Thresholds" in order to strengthen the force of his argument. Thus he considers the "right to life", for instance, in its negative formulation of the International Covenant on Civil and Political Rights (OHCHR 1976) as the right not to be arbitrarily deprived of life. This is a little different from Shue's basic conception of rights as set out in Chapter 5, which suggested that such basic rights require not only being "left alone",

> **Box 10.4 Basic human rights threatened by climate change**
>
> - The right to life.
> - The right to health.
> - The right to subsistence.

but also some basic protection from threats, something that Shue argued removed the distance between negative and positive rights. However, Caney adopts a minimal, negative account of the right to life and argues that inviolability must entail that no one acts so as to deprive people arbitrarily of their lives. Anthropogenic climate change does just this: by human action people are arbitrarily killed. This happens in the severe weather events that are a result of climate change, such as hurricanes and floods, and in extreme weather conditions such as heatwaves. Caney thus argues that it is unquestionable that a human right to life is violated by climate change and by actions that contribute to climate change.

Caney continues with similar arguments for the right to health and the right to subsistence. Again he frames these as negative rights not to be harmed: the right that others do not act so as to create serious health threats; and the right not to be deprived of the means of subsistence by others' actions. Again he states that it is clear that climate change violates these rights. The severe weather events of climate change bring in their wake epidemic diseases that constitute severe threats to health. The right to subsistence is violated as drought increases and food security is undermined; sea levels rise and agricultural land is lost; floods increase and crops fail; and severe weather events destroy harvests. By way of illustration, in his paper "Human Rights, Climate Change and Discounting" on a similar topic, Caney (2008) notes that "a temperature increase of 2.5°C will [it has been estimated] result in an extra 45–55 million people suffering from hunger by the 2080s; a temperature increase of 3°C will result in an increase of 65–75 million people of those who are threatened by hunger; and a temperature increase of 3–4°C will result in an increase of 80–125 million in that category". Thus, for Caney, one does not even need to think about positive duties; on the basis of negative human rights alone, climate change requires immediate action.

Rights of, and obligations to, future generations

The rights of future generations is becoming an increasingly important global-ethics concern, and perhaps nowhere more so than in issues of environmental justice. As we saw in Chapter 9, increasingly the decisions we are making about the sort of people who can be created and the global infrastructure we put in place to distribute health resources have a fundamental impact on future generations; to an important extent the decisions we make today will curtail and limit the choices of future generations. This is even more the case in climate ethics, where our actions already have – if scientific evidence is to be believed, and the weight of opinion is that it is – curtailed and limited life options for future generations. There is a danger that, if changes are not made very quickly, such limitations will make life for our descendants difficult in unimaginable ways. Indeed, some argue that human survival itself is threatened.

For some, our duties to future generations are less important than our current duties of justice. These arguments are similar in structure to the non-cosmopolitan arguments we discussed in Chapter 4. Just as, as we saw in Chapter 4, non-cosmopolitans argued that our duties to distant others were less than our duties to those in close proximity, so some argue that our duties to temporally (rather than geographically) distant others are fewer or less important than our duties to those who are temporally nearer. This is a view famously championed by Bjørn Lomborg (2001), who argues that money could be better spent on addressing current injustices rather than on climate change. Indeed, he questions the whole "downward trajectory" of the current depressing rhetoric of climate change and cites increasing prosperity in support of his claims. However, given the increasing and overwhelming evidence regarding the dangers of climate change and the impact of climate change on other forms of injustice, this view is not convincing. In addition, the rhetoric of increasing prosperity is problematic given the recent world recession and economic crisis as well as the predicted problems of funding an ageing population. This said, it is important to remember that environmental issues are not the only global-ethics issues to address, and thought needs to go into how to balance the competing claims of justice (to both current and future generations).

Those who defend the rights of future generations do so using the type of reasoning employed by cosmopolitans that we saw in Chapter 4, or by those defending impartiality or universalism that we saw in Chapter 3. They deny that accidents of birth, such as race, gender or class, are morally relevant and therefore they should not feature in moral decision-making. Location in time, no less than geographical location, is arbitrary and irrelevant to moral calculations.

POSSIBLE SOLUTIONS

Given the wide political and ethical agreement that something must be done to address climate change – both in terms of mitigating its effects and funding adaptive technologies and defences – the key ethical question is who should bear the burden of these costs. Who should be required to cut back emissions and on what grounds? How can a fair model be developed that recognizes historical and current beneficiaries and that does not unreasonably prevent the development of those who, as yet, have benefited very little? When it comes to deciding who should be responsible, we should also remember that the costs of adapting to climate change are already significant. Even if GHG emissions ceased wholly and immediately (something that is impossible), the effects of emissions to date will continue to be felt for a significant time to come. For instance, as we have mentioned already in this chapter, temperatures will continue to rise, as will sea levels, and with these there is likely to be an increase in extreme weather events, such as more rain and, with it, flooding, high temperatures and hurricanes.

When considering the possible solutions below it is important to remember that there is no status quo option with regard to climate change. To leave things as they are does not mean that things will stay the same, with the poor and vulnerable continuing to enjoy (or suffer) the same standard of life. To do nothing means that those who are already poor and vulnerable will become more so because the effects of climate change – such as severe weather events – affect them disproportionately because they are unable to adapt as well as the rich.

In the literature, and in public debate, possible principles to govern the development of policies under current discussion are the principles of "equality", "polluter pays", "beneficiary pays" and the "ability to pay". Most of the practical solutions suggested – such as carbon taxes and trading policies – broadly attribute responsibility to those currently polluting. However, a focus on current emissions rather than on past polluters (and beneficiaries) of carbon emissions can lead to injustice. For instance, one might support "clean development initiatives" that are expensive in developed countries, but argue that there is a case for developing countries to be exempt from such requirements (or subsidized by already developed countries) at least until the point where a reasonable standard of living is reached. It would seem unjust if all countries were treated alike, as the developed world has already produced emissions and experienced economic development, whereas the developing world has yet to reap the benefits of development and experiences only the burdens of climate change caused by the developed world.

Box 10.5 Possible principles for addressing climate change

- Equality of burdens.
- Equality of quotas.
- Polluter pays.
- Beneficiary pays.
- Ability to pay.

Equal burdens

It is for these reasons that claims to equality – so central to many global-justice claims – are somewhat problematic in the ethics of climate change, because it may be that to treat actors equally is to treat them unjustly. The problem of treating all global actors equally is discussed by Moellendorf (2009a). He addresses the approach of the Kyoto Protocol and the United Nations Framework Convention on Climate Change, which takes a historical baseline of 1990 and then requires differential reductions in accordance with this. Thus the burdens are intended to be equal for all. Moellendorf argues that this does not sufficiently take into account the background of injustice, but rather requires all to share the burden, including underdeveloped countries. He suggests that this does not respect the right to development because it requires underdeveloped countries to pay costs that may stall development in order to maintain higher standards of living in developed countries. In addition, reduced emissions fall on different parts of the world in different measures. For instance, the reductions of the rich may seem significant, but they may be reductions of luxuries, whereas the reductions of the poor may be losses of essentials: again this threatens development rights. Moellendorf (2009a) argues that "a principle that does not permit emissions increases in many of the poorest countries ... is incompatible with the right to development".

Equal shares

Another equality-based approach is one of "equal shares". Like equal burdens, the idea of equal shares has been discussed with regard to future policy and is the assumption of models that assign per capita quotas. Again, equality has intuitive justice appeal because it allots the same share of emissions to all, and the same reduction.

The advantage of this over the equal-burden model is that it does allow some space for growth for the poorest – who are yet to use their whole quota of emissions – while requiring large reductions for the richest. Moellendorf reports that on one model, using figures from the US Census and IPCC's Fourth Assessment Report (2007b), if years 2000 and 2050 were taken as end points then Bangladesh would be allowed emissions 4.5 times those of 2000. Thus there is some accommodation of the right to development. In addition, it also allows emissions permits and trading for those states that emit less than their target. This allows richer states to buy additional emissions targets, which is arguably more efficient and less difficult than cutting emissions. In addition, it benefits poor states by making their lack of emissions a source of revenue.

Polluter pays

Another model is "polluter pays", which argues that those who created climate change are responsible for addressing its ill effects. It is a backward-looking model that seeks to lay the responsibility on those who caused the calamity. This is an intuitively strong view that meets concerns for justice; it seems fair and puts financial responsibility in the same place as moral responsibility. Again, part of this principle is built into the Kyoto Protocol in that a 1990 baseline is set: however, as Moellendorf has argued, this is not sufficient to respect the rights of the poor.

As well as fitting with assumptions about justice, the polluter pays model seems also to fit our real-world intuitions about who should pay. If we consider countries to be the agents responsible, then it is likely that the wealthier countries would be responsible for the cost of financing mitigations and adaption to climate change. Given that, for the most part, it is wealthy countries that have been the polluters (and also largely the beneficiaries) at the expense of low- and middle-income countries, this model again seems to be broadly fair. Certainly a number of low- and middle-income countries, such as Brazil, have thought so and endorsed such principles.

But, although the polluter pays principle seems to be just and fair, there are a number of difficulties. First (true, to some extent, of all responses to climate change) there is the problem of uncertainty. Estimating the ill effects of climate change is notoriously difficult, as shown by the scientific and political controversies with regard to the extent and danger of climate change. Given the difficulties in estimating ill effects, it is not surprising that it is even harder to estimate who caused which harm with enough accuracy to insist on reparations. Second, are polluters responsible for the ill effects *before* it was known that such actions contributed to climate change, or only for pollution since around the 1990s, when it began to be known that carbon emissions contributed to climate change? To make polluters responsible for effects that they can reasonably be said not to have known about seems unjust, and this reduces the intuitive appeal to fairness that is, at first sight, such a strength of this principle.

Beneficiary pays

Whereas the polluter pays principle places the responsibility for the effects of pollution squarely on those who directly cause or have caused the pollution, the "beneficiary pays" principle holds those who have benefited from the development that has led to climate change responsible for meeting its costs: "responsible", that is, for paying the costs – it does not say that those who benefit from pollution must have had something to do with *causing* pollution. Again, the principle is essentially quite simple. Those who *benefit* from projects that increase global warming and despoil the environment are liable to pay for putting things right, or for reparations to those harmed by those projects. In "Historical Emissions and Free Riding" (2004), Axel Gosseries defends a version of this view, arguing that by virtue of a society's benefiting from, for example, large-scale industrialization, it can incur a moral obligation to compensate those who have been harmed by its effects. This may be the case even if those who benefit could not reasonably have been held responsible – causally or morally – for the event. So, if we in a developed nation now benefit from huge power plants built by our ancestors who knew nothing of global warming and its disastrous consequences, we may *still* owe reparations to people adversely affected by the smoke that bellows out of their chimneys. This is not because we are responsible for it happening or for not stopping it, but simply because we gain the benefits while others do not. Furthermore, such a system could be "progressive", meaning that people pay proportionately according to their means, so that the richer pay more than the poorer because they can afford to do so without hardship. So, for example, to use a proportion of income tax, a percentage of people's earnings, to fund the restoration and maintenance of national parks is consistent with a progressive version of the beneficiary pays principle.

Caney has resisted this view in "Environmental Degradation, Reparations, and the Moral Significance of History" (2006). He raises several problems with both the polluter pays and beneficiary pays principles. Suppose, says Caney, that we combine the two principles and then suppose that one party – a country, government or corporation, *A* – causes an environmental injustice that benefits *A* and also benefits another *B*. On the combined view, both *A* and *B* are liable to pay for the injustice; but *how* liable? How do we apportion blame in this case? We might think that *A* should bear more of the cost, because it caused the event as well as benefiting from it. Yet it could surely be the case that *B* benefited from *A*'s act of injustice far more than *A* did. In fact, we could also imagine a scenario in which *A* causes but does *not* benefit from the act whereas *B* does not *cause* it but does rather nicely out of it. What then? Caney argues that the beneficiary pays principle is less attractive because:

> it is a deeply entrenched view that those who cause a harm have some moral obligation to address that pollution. If I release some toxic waste in a river then surely, *ceteris paribus* [all else being equal], I should pay. To deny the Causal Account [the polluter pays view] any role would be highly counter-intuitive. (2006: 472)

However, despite Caney's criticisms, the beneficiary pays principle continues to have appeal, not least because the polluters and beneficiaries are broadly similar groups. So this principle may be useful as a partial solution.

Ability to pay

The "ability to pay" principle has gained popularity, partly because of the pressing need to address climate change and the awareness that if sufficient action is not taken soon then it may be too late. Accordingly, those who endorse this model argue that there is no point arguing about historical injustices and attributing blame if those identified are either unable or unwilling to pay. So rather than attempt to track difficult networks of causal injustices, we should instead be pragmatic and consider just who can afford to finance the changes that are so necessary. They suggest we adopt an ability to pay model. The model is forward-looking rather than backward-looking, focusing on what can be done now and who has the most resources to do it. It suggests that the burdens of climate change should be carried by the wealthy and in proportion to their wealth.

The main problem with this approach is that it does not seem fair. Why should having the resources to pay for mitigations and adaption of climate change make it your responsibility? This seems unjust, and not a principle that is operated in other areas of justice. The ability to pay principle thus lacks the intuitive appeal to fairness that both the polluter pays and the beneficiary pays principles have. However, if the wealthy do not pay then who will? Furthermore, would such a system be less fair than familiar "progressive" income taxation, where the wealthier give a higher proportion of their income than the less well off? Doing nothing has consequences and it is the poor and vulnerable who will bear the greatest burden if there is no action. If it is a choice between the already disadvantaged suffering (and often to the extent that they fall below a minimally acceptable standard of living) or the advantaged suffering (and in a way that does not affect their survival ability or cause them to fall below a minimal standard), it would be unjust for the already disadvantaged to suffer. In addition, when one considers that, if the actors we are discussing are countries, it is the wealthy countries that are the overall polluters – beneficiaries as well as those with the ability to pay – then this concern is somewhat reduced. However, as Caney has argued, we should beware of equating these groups too quickly. For instance, China and India are current polluters, but they have not been polluters historically, nor are they primary beneficiaries over time and certainly they are not the countries with the greatest ability to pay. Nonetheless, a major advantage of the ability to pay approach is that it avoids much of the uncertainty of establishing causal links between the causes and effects of climate change, which so bedevils the polluter pays principle and, although less so, the beneficiary pays principle.

Hybrid principles

Like so many solutions in global ethics – including all those we have discussed, from development measures to research ethics in bioethics – the option adopted does not have to be *either* one approach *or* another. There are many instances where mixed approaches can be chosen. Often these are practical choices that allow the benefits of the different approaches to be used.

One such hybrid model is proposed by Caney (2010); another similar approach is put forward by Moellendorf (2002), which supplements the polluter pays principle with the ability to pay principle. By so doing they attempt to produce a solution that has the strengths of both principles: a principle with the strong appeal to justice and fairness of the polluter pays principles and with the practicality of the ability to pay principle.

Caney (2010) regards the justice appeal of the polluter pays principle as important and thus adopts this as a first principle by which to fund the mitigations and adaptions necessary to meet the challenges of climate change. However, he does not think this is enough, in part because of the criticisms above regarding uncertainty and the difficulty in addressing pollution caused by previous generations. He argues that these difficulties mean that the polluter pays principle can be used only to address a portion of the effects of climate change. There will always be some causes that cannot be traced or are not appropriate to chase. For instance, he argues, some contemporary polluters, such as India and China, are not able to pay reparations for their emissions. He argues that such countries should be partly exempted from the polluter pays principle because to insist on payment would perpetuate and increase poverty. Therefore, he argues, duties to address climate change should not cause people to fall beneath a certain standard of living. His claim, then, is that the polluter pays principle should be the first principle of climate change, but one that is qualified in order that people are not forced to pay for emissions that are necessary for survival or if such payment will cause people to fall below a minimum standard of living: the "*Poverty-sensitive polluter pays principle*".

To supplement this poverty-sensitive polluter pays principle and address the remainder of the ill effects of climate change he adopts an ability to pay principle. To show why there is a duty for those who have the ability to pay to do so, even when they have not contributed to the harm, Caney (2010) draws on arguments about duty of aid (similar to those of Singer, discussed in Chapter 7) to suggest that there are not only negative duties not to harm, but positive duties on those with the ability to pay. He argues that one should "pay" to the point where the duties are not "too demanding". He also distinguishes between those who attained their wealth unjustly (e.g. by benefiting from slavery) and those who attained it justly. He argues that both groups have duties to pay but that those who attained their wealth unjustly have a greater responsibly: the "*historically-sensitive ability to pay principle*". Including some element of historical considerations introduces a backward-looking element to this essentially forward-looking principle. This allows him to retain some of the sense of justice of the polluter pays principle, even in the ability to pay principle, and so to satisfy concerns about fairness.

CONCLUSION

This chapter has brought together many of the issues of global ethics. What is the scope of justice? As well as being global does it also extend to non-human species? And are there duties to the natural world in itself, for instance to biodiversity and habitats? And what about future generations? How do we factor in to our calculations the rights of those yet to be born and who might never be born as against those who are already living and in need? Moreover, what is justified in limiting the rights of individuals for the greater good of reducing climate change? Can human rights be trumped in order to address the crisis? Some argue that the crisis is so dangerous that it is justified to deny some human rights (e.g. the right to reproduce or to develop) and to curtail civil liberties (e.g. to enforce reduced travel and energy conservation).

How you decide these issues will again depend on the decisions you made with regard to your ethical toolbox. Which of the moral, political and rights theories of Chapters 3, 4 and 5 do you endorse? If, like Caney, you regard human rights as inviolable, this will influence what responses to climate change you favour. If you are an egalitarian cosmopolitan like Moellendorf, you will defend the global poorest's rights to development as justice rights while proposing means that reduce climate change. Perhaps the extreme nature of climate change will change the views you hold and make you rethink your previous moral and political commitments. However, whatever else, the complex way in which environmental injustice affects other areas of injustice has shown the necessity for the interconnected and broad approach advocated in global ethics.

FURTHER READING

- Attfield, R. *Environmental Ethics* (Cambridge: Polity Press, 2003).
- Caney, S. "Climate Change and the Future: Time, Wealth and Risk". *Journal of Social Philosophy* **40** (2009): 163–86.
- Caney, S. "Climate Change, Human Rights and Moral Thresholds". In *Climate Change and Human Rights*, S. Humphreys (ed.), 69–90 (Cambridge: Cambridge University Press, 2009).
- Caney, S. "Equality in the Greenhouse?" *Journal of Global Ethics* **5** (2009): 125–46.
- Caney, S. "Climate Change and the Duties of the Advantaged". *Critical Review of International Social and Political Philosophy* **13** (2010): 203–28.
- De-Shalit, A. *Why Posterity Matters* (London: Routledge, 1994).
- Garvey, J. *The Ethics of Climate Change: Right and Wrong in a Warming World* (London: Continuum, 2008).
- Hardin, G. "Living on a Lifeboat". *Bioscience* **24**(10) (1974): 561–8. www.garretthardinsociety. org/articles/art_living_on_a_lifeboat.html (accessed May 2011).

- Moellendorf, D. "Treaty Norms and Climate Change Mitigation". *Ethics and International Affairs* **23** (2009): 247–65.
- Naess, A. & G. Sessions. "A Deep Ecology Eight Point Platform" (1984). www.haven.net/deep/council/eight.htm (accessed May 2011).

11 GLOBAL GENDER JUSTICE

INTRODUCTION

To add an additional chapter on women in a book of this type is controversial, particularly for those with concerns about gender discrimination. The danger in having a chapter on gender issues is that women's issues might be seen as separate from most issues in global ethics, when clearly this is not the case. All the issues we have addressed in the course of this book affect women at least as much as they do men. Yet the lower status of women relative to men means that, however much men suffer from the injustices of, for example, poverty or climate change, women suffer more. In Chapter 10, for instance, we considered the ways in which environmental injustice compounds other forms of injustice to make those "at the bottom of the heap" likely to be more disadvantaged because these injustices exacerbate each other. Those at the bottom of all heaps will be women. Clearly, rich Western women are rarely in this particular category, but the poorest of the poor are always women and children. Accordingly, despite the dangers of what we can call "exceptionalism" about women, it is important to have a chapter on women to highlight their plight and the particular difficulties women face in addition to sharing with men all the global injustices we have already considered. Moreover, any worries about exceptionalism should be lessened by the discussion of gender issues throughout the volume. For instance, the case studies of Chapter 3 on FGC were concerned with gender justice, as was much of the case study of Chapter 4 on the sale of body parts where the plight of egg vendors was raised, an issue that was returned to in the discussion of reproductive rights in Chapter 9.

Women as a group – despite the difference in different women's situations in different contexts – share some concerns about justice. While there may be different forms of gender discrimination in different places it is a fact recognizable in the experience of all women. In Catharine MacKinnon's (2006) words, "Gender inequality is a global system": "nowhere is sexuality not central to keeping women down". In addition, a chapter on gender justice forcibly demonstrates the connectedness of issues in global ethics and the similarities as well as the dissimilarities of the lives of real individuals. Finally, a feminist approach reminds us that the issues of global ethics are not abstract problems that need theoretical solutions, but are about the experiences of suffering, hardship and injustice that real people suffer and see their families and communities suffer.

FEMINIST APPROACHES TO GENDER JUSTICE

This chapter will not only look at women's issues, but also use arguments that come from feminist theory and activism. Before doing this, a few words about feminists and feminism are necessary. First, there is not one feminist position: indeed, feminist positions vary dramatically and often the hardest fought battles are fought within feminism. Tracking types of feminism is notoriously difficult and complex; schools of feminist thought range from "Marxist" through "radical", "radical libertarian", "cultural", "radical cultural" and "liberal", to "neoliberal". Moreover, it is hard to map exactly who fits into which group, which makes using labels to categorize feminists extremely problematic. These labels are really useful only for mapping broad trends. But, despite the fights between strands of feminism, what all these positions have in common is that they believe there are women's issues that need to be addressed; all wish to improve the situation of women. Second, because thinkers address women's issues, sometimes using distinctively feminist theory, this does not mean that they are not working in the mainstream of global ethics, nor that their arguments are not just as appropriate in any of the previous chapters of the book. This should go without saying, not least because you have already met a number of feminist theorists and their arguments in earlier parts of the book. However, it is important to note that a standard way to dismiss the criticisms of global injustice that we shall meet is to assert that feminist arguments are not part of mainstream ethical argument. This is false: they are very much a part of global-ethics responses, and, as you will see, not only offer insightful critiques of some mainstream positions, but also point the way to resolve certain key problems of global ethics.

GENDER DISCRIMINATION

It has become fashionable to state that there is now little need to attempt to empower women because the "women's liberation" battle has been won. There have indeed been some huge advances in the status of women, in practice in some places and in theory everywhere. However, this is not to say that equality has been achieved. A brief look at some of the facts of the matter demonstrates the extent of current disparities. Despite the fact that there are exceptionally powerful individual women – Condoleezza Rice, Margaret Thatcher and Hillary Clinton are often cited as examples – feminists would argue that gender discrimination and oppression are still evident in all cultures, although they may be manifested differently, and certain women may be able to escape some of the worst features (particularly white, wealthy and educated women). But despite the fact that there are some very powerful individual women, international politics, international corporations and the institutions and associations of global governance are overwhelmingly dominated by men; there has yet to be a female Secretary General of the UN, for example. Moreover, dictators, warlords and juntas are almost all male (although there are also violent women and female soldiers, and if we think back to the case study on torture, this accounts for part of the public interest that surrounded the role of Private Lynndie England in the torture at Abu Ghraib). Women, then, are less powerful than men even if one uses the crudest measures of "who has power", and this is still universally the case even though there are areas in the world where this is changing in some arenas – for instance in the political sphere, particularly in the Scandinavian countries.

When considering data on gender inequality, the starkest figures are always those relating to global inequality and the disparities between north and south (which we discussed in Chapter 7). According to the 2009 Human Development Report (UNDP 2009) the inequities in various measures of gender in development are enormous. For instance, in some of the richest countries in the world the average annual incomes for women in 2007 were in excess of US$25,000, and as high as US$50,000 in some instances (the figures for the UK and the US were US$28,241 and US$34,996 respectively). In comparison, many countries, including almost all of Sub-Saharan Africa, experienced annual female incomes of less than US$1,000 per year, and sometimes substantially less.

However, the overall figures do not tell the full story about the gender disparities that occur within *all* countries without exception. In *no* country do women on average earn the same as men. These disparities can be seen in the section of the Human Development Reports that use the Gender Empowerment Measure, which explicitly shows gender inequality. While for the most part this follows the level of development, with high development correlating with a high gender-empowerment measure, there are a number of anomalies. For instance, Japan is in the group of very high human development, but has a gender empowerment measure of 0.567, which is lower than Uganda, which has a measure of 0.591. As for Europe, Cyprus is also in the group of very high human development, but only 15 per cent of female professional and technical workers are women, which is lower than in Ethiopia, where it is 30 per cent. Singapore is also in the very-high-human-development category, but it has *no* women in ministerial positions, compared to *all* the countries in the low-human-development category (UNDP 2009). Thus it is not the case that gender disparities disappear with development or that progress towards inequality is inevitable. In fact, gender disparities are evident globally and in all places.

The precise calculation of such figures is understandably fraught with the usual difficulties of statistical collation and analysis, but the overall trends are nevertheless obvious. This is true whatever index we look at. If we consider adult literacy rates, for instance, Mali has a female literacy rate of 18.2 per cent and male rate of 34.9 per cent; Niger has a female rate of 15.1 per cent and male rate of 42.9 per cent; the Democratic Republic of the Congo has a female rate of 54.1 per cent and male rate of 80.9 per cent; and Afghanistan has the lowest recorded adult female literacy rate of 12.6 per cent, while the male rate is 43.1 per cent.

In order to make better comparative sense of these figures, the UNDP, as part of its calculation of its Human Development Report, has constructed a Gender-related Development Index. This reasonably complex statistical measure seeks to highlight the national inequalities between men and women using a series of indices relating life expectancy, health, education and standard of living. According to the 2009 report, again using statistics derived from 2007, Australia topped the Gender-related Development Index scale, followed, in order, by Norway, Iceland, Canada, Sweden, France, the Netherlands and Finland. At the very bottom of the scale was Niger, although it ranked very close to other African states such as the Democratic Republic of the Congo, the Central African Republic, Mali, Sierra Leone and, again anomalously (in the sense of not being a Sub-Saharan state) Afghanistan. These inequalities between men and women are not just evident in statistics, but just as starkly in terms of norms and practices with regard to standard ways women are treated globally, such as the seemingly universal attempts to control women's bodies.

CONTROLLING WOMEN'S BODIES

In Chapter 10 we considered environmental ethics and concerns about population control. A key issue discussed was what level of force or coercion is permissible in addressing issues that are so pressing – and so necessary to humanity's survival – such as addressing global climate change. If force or coercion is justified in population control, then clearly these policies will directly affect women and women's freedom. In Chapter 9, on bioethics, we briefly touched on reproductive rights and claims that the ability to choose how and when to reproduce is a fundamental human right for women. If rights to reproduce are partly connected to bodily integrity then population control measures will not fall equally on men and women. While certain of men's rights will be curtailed – for instance the right to form a family (if this is interpreted as extending to the right to choose the size of your family) – population control does not usually affect men's rights of bodily integrity. It is, of course, *possible* that population control *could* impact on men's bodily integrity, for instance if male sterilization were forced on people; but this is actually far less common (it is estimated that less than 5 per cent of the sterilizations that took place in the European eugenics programme at the beginning of the twentieth century were on men). Again, it seems that policies in different areas of global ethics fall more heavily on women than on men and there are long histories across the globe of attempts to control women's reproductive behaviour. Given the extent of these measures it is hard not to see these as part of the domination of women, either within communities or as a way of dominating the community as a whole by dominating the women within it. For extreme examples of this second form, where women are dominated in an attempt to dominate the community as a whole, think of rape as a tactic of war (something we shall consider in a moment). In the words of Alison Jaggar (2005), "because women are typically seen as the symbols or bearers of culture, conflicts among cultural groups are often fought on the terrain of women's bodies, sometimes literally in the form of systematic rape".

Controlling reproduction

One way in which women's bodies have been controlled is in terms of controlling sexual relationships and reproduction. This is done at micro and macro levels. At a micro level, this can be done within the family; a particularly brutal example is the historical use of chastity belts. A common way to control female sexuality is FGC, which, as we saw in Chapters 2 and 3, is a widespread procedure globally. Other ways in which sexual relationships and reproduction are controlled include ensuring there is no possibility of sexual relationship, for instance, by chaperoning women, or by forbidding women to leave the house or rooms in a house. None of these controlling measures are applied to boys and men. In addition, if sexual relationships do occur, blame usually falls disproportionately on the woman rather than the man. This is true in all cultures.

Macro-level controls on women's sexual freedom and reproduction include laws prohibiting contraception and abortion, laws that deny women divorce and laws that limit the free movement of women. Population-control measures are clear examples of such control. For instance, China's one-child policy has, at times, included forced sterilization to enforce it. Population-control policies include education, providing contraception, abortion and sterilization. However, many have pointed out that there are global double standards in population-control measures. In the developing world the emphasis is on encouraging women to have fewer children, something that is often not in their best interest if they live in a society where women's status is determined by motherhood or where children provide the only source of security and support in old age. Conversely, in the developed world there is concern about falling reproductive rates and about how to support a large elderly population. Moreover, when population-control measures are enforced it tends to be female children who are abandoned or female foetuses aborted. Sen's paper "More than 100 Million Women are Missing" (1990) highlights this ghoulish aspect of gender discrimination.

One aspect of population control that has been receiving increasing attention is forced or coerced sterilization. Forced sterilization has a long history of use in Europe and the US. In the early twentieth century it was widely practised as part of public-health measures to improve population health. Women from a variety of groups were forcibly sterilized in order to ensure that they did not pass on their "deviancy" to the next generation; they included those suffering from mental disabilities, the "feeble minded", the "sexually deviant" (which could be interpreted to include promiscuity, lesbianism and adultery) and those from undesirable ethnic groups, particularly "gypsies"(a general term to include many Roma ethnic groups, usually from central and eastern Europe). Forced sterilization continues in many parts of the world today, as does "induced consent", in which women are encouraged to undergo sterilization and even given payment or other forms of inducement as part of population-control measures.

The continuation of forced, or at least coerced, sterilization of Roma in Europe was brought to light in a now famous report: *Body and Soul: Forced Sterilization and Other Assaults on Roma Reproductive Freedom* (Center for Reproductive Rights & Poradňa 2003). This report described continuing practices of forced sterilization in Slovakia, although the practice is not limited to Slovakia and has since been documented in many other countries. The report documents sterilization as a common experience of Roma women. Women in labour in hospital, on the point of being given a Caesarean section, are told to sign a consent form. This form gives consent not only to a Caesarean section, but also to tubal ligation. In April 2010, Amnesty International reported that, according to Chinese media reports, "officials in Puning City, Guangdong Province aim to sterilize 9,559 people, some against their will, by 26 April" in order to comply with the family-planning targets on which the one-child law is also based. Since 2002, forced sterilization has been regarded as a crime against humanity, along with other forms of sexual and reproductive violence against women that we shall now consider.

Rape as a crime against humanity

Rape has always been used as a tactic to dominate women in times of both peace and conflict. It is a cliché to say that rape is about power rather than sex, but one that is clearly as true in conflict situations as in other situations. The rape of men is overtly used (in gangs, prison and armies) to punish, humiliate and dominate, and the situation with women is similar. Yet, although rape has been a recognizable tactic of war for generations – think of the Viking fourfold tactic of killing, raping, pillaging and enslaving – only in the past few decades has this issue begun to be given the attention it deserves. For instance, the Nuremberg trials did not prosecute the crime of rape, even in cases that were commonly attested to.

This has begun to change in the past few decades, and rape has now become a war crime and a crime against humanity, in response to the recent conflicts in Rwanda and former Yugoslavia. Estimates suggest that around 500,000 women were raped in Rwanda and up to 50,000 in Bosnia and Herzegovina. The *Akayesu* judgment defined rape as a crime of genocide in the UN International Criminal Tribunal for Rwanda. The Court judged that "sexual assault formed an integral part of the process of destroying the Tutsi ethnic group and that the rape was systematic and had been perpetrated against Tutsi women only, manifesting the specific intent required for those acts to constitute genocide" (UN General Assembly Security Council 1999). The International Criminal Tribunal for the former Yugoslavia deemed that Muslim women of Bosnia and Herzegovina had been subjected to rape as part of ethnic cleansing and that this constituted a crime against humanity. This was then enshrined in the International Criminal Court in the Rome statute, which includes rape, sexual slavery, enforced prostitution, forced pregnancy and enforced sterilization as crimes against humanity. Currently rape is being used as a weapon in the Democratic Republic of the Congo, where in 2009 there were over 7000 instances of rape registered; the true figures are believed to be much greater (Human Rights Watch 2009).

MALE FRAMEWORKS AND THEORIES

In addition to bearing the brunt of global injustices, both in terms of poverty and climate change, as well as from the human-inflicted injustices of rape and violence in times both of peace and conflict, women are also neglected in the theories and mechanisms we use to address injustice.

Feminist theorists (and indeed other theorists, such as the virtue ethicists we discussed in Chapter 3) have criticized the dominant liberal model for missing out much of what actually constitutes the experience of the moral life. We have seen some of these arguments in Chapters 9 and 10. For instance, in Chapter 9, when we discussed kidney sale, we explored criticisms of a narrow conception of individual choice. Likewise in Chapter 10 we saw that the individual-rights model leaves out ethical duties to future generations and to non-humans; again, this neglects key ethical issues. Narrow ethical models that can identify only some ethical concerns fail in what they leave out. These are core feminist claims. Feminists argue that social, relational and contextual issues must be considered if we are to ensure ethical practice. For instance, some feminists advocate "relational autonomy", which insists that context and relation are essential to any adequate understanding of autonomy. Thus the "autonomy as individual choice" model – which, as we saw in Chapter 9, is key in bioethics – does not respect autonomy considered in this relational sense. On the relational view, for a choice to be autonomous it must take account of the pressures and commitments of real individuals, rather than unrealistically presenting individuals as free and unencumbered. Feminist applications of this view include gender concerns to modify the standard model of autonomy, for example by modifying rights theories and by presenting alternative female models of the self and of ethics quite generally.

In so doing, feminists critique the models of human beings that underpin the moral and political theories we discussed in Chapters 3 and 4, as well as the rights-based models discussed in Chapter 5. A standard feminist concern (Hampton 1997; Held 2006) is that the pictures of human being that these models of justice are based on are male models. By "male" they mean to signal that these models present human beings as essentially isolated and separate agents who make "rational" (and often self-interested) ethical judgements. By contrast, "female" models tend to recognize context and relationship and see these factors as very much influencing the types of ethical and political decisions that can be made. In addition the "male" model tends to present all individuals as essentially the same: by contrast, feminist thinkers such as Iris Marion Young (2009) have championed the recognition of context and difference. Others have taken these insights about rationality and context and sought to reform universal frameworks so that they are better placed to address women's rights and gender justice issues globally: Martha Nussbaum (1999, 2000) is an example.

WOMEN'S RIGHTS AND HUMAN RIGHTS

Rights models have been particularly criticized by feminists as conflicting with feminist responses and with those who value relationships and caring for others. Rights, particularly in their strongest form of rights as trumps (recall Dworkin's account; see Chapter 5), assert the needs of an individual over and above those of others. Rights are therefore confrontational rather than constructive. Indeed, this is one of the reasons that rights are so effective as political and activist tools (an issue we also discussed in Chapter 5). As global ethicists, then, we should recognize the importance and usefulness of the liberal model of rights as well as the problems with it. Indeed, the usefulness of rights is recognized by many non-rights-based theories of ethics, such as the ethics of care, which we come to later in this chapter, particularly in the political and policy arena. There is nothing like the language of rights to focus attention on particular injustices and to galvanize campaigns and support for causes. However, despite the effectiveness of human rights in general, there are many feminist and women's rights criticisms of the theoretical human-rights framework. Many of the criticisms were famously and memorably put by MacKinnon in a paper entitled "Are Women Human?", writing fifty years after the UDHR, and asking: are women human yet? Her response is worth quoting at some length (see Box 11.1).

This essay is now contained in a book of the same title that considers theoretical and practical issues in women's rights. In particular, it tracks the status of rape and violence in conflict in papers from 1981 to 2006, as well as considering pornography and the status of women's rights in various contexts, and providing a commentary on the status of women's rights as opposed to human rights. MacKinnon's forceful statement vividly illustrates the claims made at the beginning of this chapter regarding the suffering of women, sometimes referred to as "double jeopardy": women suffer from whatever injustice their community suffers from, whether poverty, ill health or conflict; but women also suffer from being women and from the additional oppression and exploitation they suffer as women.

Box 11.1 Are women human yet?

"If women were human, would we be a cash crop shipped from Thailand in containers into New York's brothels? Would be we sexual and reproductive slaves? Would we be bred, worked without pay our whole lives, burned when our dowry money wasn't enough or when men tired of us, starved as widows when our husbands died (if we survived his funeral pyre), sold for sex because we are not valued for anything else? ... Would we, when allowed to work for pay, be made to work at the most menial jobs and exploited at barely starvation level? Would we have our genitals sliced out to "cleanse" us (our body parts are dirt?), to control us, to mark us and define our cultures? Would we be trafficked as things for sexual use and entertainment worldwide in whatever form current technology makes possible? Would we be kept from learning to read and write?

"If women were human, would we have so little voice in public deliberations and in government in the countries where we live? Would we be hidden behind veils and imprisoned in houses and stoned and shot for refusing? Would we be beaten nearly to death, and to death, by men with whom we are close? Would we be sexually molested in our families? Would we be raped in genocide to terrorize and eject and destroy our ethnic communities, and raped again in that undeclared war that goes on every day in every country in the world in what is called peacetime? If women were human, would our violation be *enjoyed* by our violators? And, if we were human, when these things happened, would virtually nothing be done about it?" (MacKinnon 2006: 41–2)

Arguably, then, the human-rights system is ordered according to male priorities rather than female priorities. For instance, MacKinnon (2006) suggests that it is likely that women would not prioritize civil and political rights (first-generation rights) but rather social and economic rights. This is because if you lack effective economic and social rights then civil and political rights are "largely inaccessible and superficial". MacKinnon's critique suggests that women's rights initiatives have done little to address this. For instance, she argues that CEDAW says little about the evils of sexism and the inferior treatment of women, whereas others welcome CEDAW as a huge advance in women's rights and some feminists see it as too radical, emphasizing the difference between women and men to too great an extent. The latest initiative is the launch of UN Women (the UN Entity for Gender Equality and the Empowerment of Women) in the summer of 2010, which is intended to mainstream gender issues and to accelerate progress towards meeting the needs of women.

Reforming rights

Most feminists embrace rights and the way that rights rhetoric can be used to advance women's causes. However, they suggest that rights should be supplemented with other ethical frameworks to ensure that the injustices that are difficult to recognize on the rights model are not neglected. Thus rights should be revised and reconstructed to include relational and contextual concerns. For instance, Held (2006) argues that it is not rights themselves that are the problem but the way they have been presented and implemented. She argues that rights need not be, or should not be, individualist in the way they have often been presented but that, in fact, we should reinterpret respecting rights as requiring care of others to the extent that we attribute rights. Rights are then a way of signalling and recognizing that we respect others as fellow members of the group.

In *Globalising Democracy and Human Rights* (2004), Gould also addresses the issue of rights and the need to revise them, with insights from feminist thinking and the ethics of care. Gould is a champion of human rights, but presents human rights in a way that counters at least some of the criticisms of the liberal model of rights. Like other feminist theorists, Gould rejects the extreme individualism that characterizes much liberal theory, especially rights theory. Following many critics of liberal individualism, Gould asserts the relationality and connectedness of human beings, which militates against a conception of human beings as isolated, separate individuals. Thus she supports a view of human beings as social and relational beings, or, in her words, as "individuals-in-relations". In this view, the individualism of liberal theory is tempered, as all activity includes recognition of others, their needs and the individual's relation with them. Accordingly, while the focal agents of her model are "individuals", these individuals are not the autonomous separate moral loci of

---

Box 11.2 Rights for Gould

"Human rights are always rights of individuals, based on their valid claims to conditions for their activity, but individuals bear these rights only in relation to other individuals and to social institutions. Right is in this sense an intrinsically relational concept."

(Gould 2004)

---

liberal individualism but are contextually embedded beings who are relational and connected beings. By basing her philosophy and rights constructs on such under-standings of the self, Gould is able to recognize the related and communal nature of human beings without denying the moral significance of the individual (Box 11.2).

Gould argues that rights cannot be considered properly *without* recognizing the relatedness and connectedness of human beings. On her view, if humans were not related and connected then rights would not be possible. Who would recognize and respect rights in a disconnected world of separate individuals? For rights to work in any context, Gould argues, requires a relational understanding, because if people did not care about others and consider their needs then the claims of rights would be empty. Human rights could be asserted, but there would be no grounds for taking them seriously and fulfilling them. In Gould's scheme then, while individuals remain the key moral loci as rights-bearers, they are not isolated but embedded in caring relationships. This is something we shall return to in the final section of the chapter, on the ethics of care.

PROTECTING WOMEN

There are dangers in arguing that rights should be embedded in social relationships, because some social structures and relationships might actually deny and constrain the exercise of individual rights. To exercise a right is not as simple as much of rights theory suggests, even in instances where clear violation is taking place. It has been said that what much of rights theory *per se*, and the political theories of justice discussed in Chapter 4, fail to take into consideration are the structural injustices within groups that affect minority or vulnerable groups of people *within* recognized structures.

If we return to the discussion of Rawls in Chapter 4, Rawls suggests that one institution taken to be part of the "basic structure" to which justice applies is the family. But he does not speak about possible injustices within the family or power structures in this context. As discussed above, women in their social and political situations tend to see rights not just as statements of individual demands but rather as relational and contextual. So the question of who has power in any instance is core to feminist thinking, and a useful question for global ethicists to ask in any situation. In this instance, feminists ask about the power differentials within such groups and wonder whether gender injustices are in fact nurtured and perpetuated within institutions such as the family. For instance, in *Justice, Gender, and the Family* (1989), Okin argues that Rawls's theory of justice (which, as we saw in Chapter 4, has been highly influential in the theory of global justice) does not, as it stands, address the pervasive injustice of gender inequalities that are rooted and perpetuated in the structures and practices of traditional families. This type of hidden power imbalance and the resulting injustices is illustrated clearly in the discussion of community goods and individual rights of exit.

The right of exit

The usual solution to conflict between group rights and individual rights has been to insist on a "right of exit". The assumption is that if it is always possible for individuals to leave their groups then they will be protected from any undue suppression or oppression within the groups. However, this solution ignores power imbalances within groups and the reality of women's situations. For while it might be *theoretically* possible that women within a group have a "right of exit", *in practice* exercising such a right would be unthinkable. This position is put by Okin (1999, 2002), who argues that if the right of exit is to be a satisfactory protection then it must not be just a formal right to be free to leave a religious or cultural group, but that this must be a realistic right of exit. Okin argues that although professing to protect such rights, liberal theories do not in fact do so, as they fail to recognize the real constraints that render such a right irrelevant to young women. She argues that in many of the cultures where a right of exit might be needed by young women, in particular, these women are in fact less able to effectively exercise such a right than their male counterparts, if at all.

Okin recounts the expectations of women in such cultures and the differences in the ways girls and boys are brought up and treated. She argues that most cultures control the lives of girls far more than they do boys, so that it is naive to imagine that women have the same practical means to attain a right of exit, never mind that for many young women exiting the community is unthinkable and unimaginable.

Thus, although a formal right of exit may exist, actually to make this choice – effectively to leave the cultural or religious group – is not a realistic option for these women. They respond with distress to restrictions but a right of exit is not something they would choose. To leave the religion or perhaps seek legal redress in order to prevent an unwanted marriage would be for the women to reject what is, in fact, most important to their family and community: an impossible suggestion. Thus, the right of exit is no protection from injustices within groups as soon as the reality of the situation is considered. In Okin's (2002) words, "what kind of a choice is one between total submission and total alienation from the person she understands herself to be?" In addition many women would be more damaged if they left the group than if they submitted to the demands of the group; emotionally, psychologically and even at times physically.

Forced marriage

Anne Phillips has considered similar issues in *Multiculturalism Without Culture* (2007) where she critiqued policies of multiculturalism and its blanket deference to "culture". Phillips explores key issues of concern to feminists, from the veil to the shortcomings of the right to exit. She defends multiculturalism, with a focus on protecting individuals and people and the way in which culture matters to them rather than on protecting "culture" as a monolith. She explores the difference between some of the assumptions around arranged and forced marriages and the kinds of claim made about the differences between these, thus addressing much the same issues as Okin does, and discusses what solutions can be put in place to overcome the difficulties Okin raises. Like Okin, she is concerned with questions about coercion such as: "if young people give in to parental blackmail and the threat of ostracism by their community, does this mean they were 'forced' into marriage?" Phillips uses information from studies in the UK and cites the words of young women interviewed about their own experiences. She concludes that many of the women have been pressurized and some might even be said to have been coerced (although they would not think of it in such ways). She explores different levels of parental involvement and decision-making in different cases, and suggests that the distinction between what is voluntary and what is coerced is far from clear. Yet, on the other hand, Phillips is wary of policies that assume that women do not have agency, as there is a danger that this is also discriminatory and disempowering of these women. She cites a number of judgments that, on the face of it, have sought to protect women, but that hide cultural prejudices and fail to respect these women as they would non-minority women. One particular judgment suggested that a women was "less able than a girl from a different background to assert herself against her parents, and more likely to succumb to their pressure". Phillips is concerned about this is because it suggests that certain women's choices should not be respected and effectively "infantilizes ethnic minority women".

Phillips's solution is to change how one approaches the issue, and to focus less on the point of choice. She rejects an extreme liberal view of choice: that anything that is chosen is "freely chosen", an approach we discussed in Chapter 9 around the ethics of kidney sale. For her, "what looks like a free agreement is in reality often coerced, because the person entering it had no real alternatives"; she cites exploitative work and prostitution as examples. Her solution is to suggest that we should not focus on the "choice", on whether something is freely chosen or not, but rather on the nature of the choice. Essentially, the crucial question about an action or state of affairs (e.g. a marriage, a relationship, a job or role) is not Has she chosen it?, but instead, Is what is being chosen ethically acceptable? If not, then whether she freely chooses it or not is irrelevant; there are similarities to Nussbaum here in terms of not equating what is acceptable with what is acceptable to the individual woman. She draws on the work of the feminist thinker Carole Pateman's view of contracts, arguing that a contract – even if agreed by both parties – can still be exploitative if it establishes a relationship of subordination: in other words, if it puts one person under the power of another. Furthermore, she is concerned about the longevity of that power. For instance, a one-off contract (I'll swap you this for that) is less concerning than a long-term commitment. Marriage is exactly that kind of long-term contract: it gives one person power over another and it requires submission over a long period of time. In Phillips's words; "the point about forced marriage is not just that people are forced into it, but that what they are forced into is marriage".

Nussbaum's capability approach

The discussion of women's experience and rights returns us to a discussion at the beginning of this book: that of universalism and relativism introduced in Chapter 3, and the case of FGC. How do we respect both the context and the group, which is essential to respecting the reality of human experience, while ensuring that individuals (often women) are not subjugated and oppressed in those relationships?

Nussbaum – a broadly liberal feminist, but with (as we saw in Chapter 3) strong Aristotelian commitments – offers a strong universalist response, believing that we can protect women only by promoting universal pictures of human being. Nussbaum (1999) argues that simply to defer to culture is to ignore the injustices done to women; and she emphasizes that many injustices are done to women precisely because they are women, and that these injustices are institutionalized and structural. Moreover, she argues, in her work on women and development (Nussbaum 2000), women within patriarchal cultures may have "adaptive preferences". In other words, their preferences and wishes adapt to what is available; they will internalize the role of being second class and say that it is right and proper and that, moreover, it fits their own wishes.

As we saw in Chapter 3, she dismisses cultural-relativist claims; similar arguments to those she used against FGC could be used against any practice. She defends herself against critics, saying:

> [W]e can hardly be charged with imposing a foreign set of values upon individuals or groups if what we are doing is providing support for basic capacities and opportunities that are involved in the selection of any flourishing life and then leaving people to choose for themselves how they will pursue human flourishing. (1999: 9)

On the other hand, she does recognize the dangers in the universal approach, in particular those of colonialism and of imposing one's own values just because they are one's own values. But, as discussed with regard to FGC, not to engage is to "risk erring by withholding critical judgement where real evil and oppression are surely present".

To achieve the balance needed she proposes a variation of the capability approach. Nussbaum's approach is somewhat different from Sen's (discussed in Chapter 7), in that she suggests a list of capabilities that are central for all human living. Nussbaum's full list of capabilities is found in Chapter 3, Case study 3.4, and does not need to be repeated here. She argues that a list is necessary if we are to be able to recognize when people lack necessary functionings so that we can put in place policies to address that lack; and moreover that "without some such notion of the basic worth of human capacities, we have a hard time arguing for women's equality and for basic human rights". Her list is derived from asking what activities are so central that they are necessary for a fully human life.

Thus Nussbaum's response is to apply universal measures, such as her version of the capability approach, in different contexts; she argues that the capability approach recognizes both that humans have common needs, problems and capacities, and that these are manifested in different circumstances. Included in the different circumstances are those of gender. To illustrate this she uses a number of examples of real women's situations in the developing world and shows how the capability approach recognizes their experiences of double jeopardy: the problems they face that men share and the problems they face specifically because they are women. One example she gives is that of a widow, Metha Bai, who was unable to work outside the home because her culture forbade women such work. As a result her survival, and that of her children, was threatened in a way that was a result of gender discrimination rather than simply poverty. Thus, for Nussbaum, Metha Bai faces obstacles and injustices that men in the same position do not face. Nussbaum's conclusion regarding respecting individuals and culture is to insist on ensuring that women have the capabilities in her list. In her words, "the capabilities approach insists that a women's affiliation with a certain group or culture should not be taken as normative for her unless, on due consideration, with all the capabilities at her disposal, she makes the norm her own". Like Okin, she recognizes that formal choice is not the same as real choice and, moreover, that those who have grown up with limited choices may internalize these traditions and come to accept their own second-class status as "right" and "natural". For both Nussbaum and Okin, one has to do more to provide real choice.

Dangers of neocolonisalism

While work such as Okin's and Nussbaum's has been welcomed and hugely influential on theorists' thinking about global gender justice, it is not without its critics. Famously, in a 2005 paper, Alison Jaggar praises the work they have done on mainstream gender justice but argues that their approaches have obscured key injustices. Most importantly, they have focused too much on the local oppression of women by local men and patriarchal culture but neglected the causes of poverty and the fact that the West, including Western women, is implicated in this poverty. She argues that to understand the abuses suffered by poor women, we need to understand practices in the context of broader political and economic systems. She cites Western "inspired" and "imposed" neoliberalism as the source of much poverty: moreover, "since women are represented disproportionately among the world's poor and marginalised, neoliberal globalisation has been harmful especially to women – although not to all or only women". She reminds us that cultures are not separate or monolithic, and that to a large extent cultures are shaped by Western direct and indirect interventions. Thus, she argues, "stark contrasts between Western and non-Western cultures cannot be sustained". Nor are Western cultures necessarily superior. To begin with, there is much violence in Western cultures and practices such as veiling and seclusion are not universally regarded as anti-women: Jaggar cites support for these practices from non-Western women. To miss this context is to promote a misguided picture of poverty and of what is actually discrimination, rather than practices that are unfamiliar to Western women. Moreover, Jaggar argues that to ignore the gendered nature of neoliberal globalization is to fail to see the West's (and Western women's) responsibility: it promotes a "West is best" philosophy that is in contradiction of many women's actual experiences and allows Western women to avoid their own complicity.

CARE ETHICS

So far in this chapter we have focused on feminist criticisms of the current approach and suggestions for reforming current theoretical and rights approaches. In this final section we shall consider care ethics, which is sometimes regarded as an "alternative ethic" to rights-based and deontological approaches. "Care ethics" or "the ethics of care" is presented as a women-friendly theory of ethics that is often contrasted to "the ethics of justice". The ethics of care – with its emphasis on character and the whole person rather than the moral act – is in the tradition of virtue ethics discussed in Chapter 3. Given this, it could be seen, with the other moral theories discussed in Chapter 3, as a Western theory rather than a *global* ethics theory. In one sense that is true (as it is for nearly all the moral theories discussed), although care ethics, like all moral theories, has global application. Moreover, care ethics, with its emphasis on persons in relation to each other and the importance of family and communal ties, can be seen as particularly accessible to communal thinking as associated with the non-Western world (e.g. similarities have been drawn with Asian value claims). Thus care ethics is an appropriate final theory to introduce in an introduction to global ethics.

Although care ethics is often presented as a distinctly female ethics, many of the tenets of care ethics have become mainstream as virtue ethics has itself become established. For instance, Joan Tronto (1993) argues that care ethics is a universal approach, because care is universally necessary: all human beings need to be cared for. However, while having universal applicability, care ethics focuses not on abstract others as a one-model-fits-all picture of the person, but allows focus on real individuals with needs that differ from other real individuals. In Held's words, in the ethics of care others "are not the 'all others', or 'everyone', of traditional moral theory; they are not what a universal point of view or a view from nowhere could provide. They are, characteristically, actual flesh and blood other human beings for whom we have actual feelings and with whom we have real ties" (1990: 338).

The ethics of care begins with a model of the self in which individuals are not isolated, but are relational and interdependent. So moral decisions must be taken in the context of the relational, social and embedded nature of human being. From this perspective, the self, person or agent of most moral and political theories is an abstracted individual: for Held (2006), the "person seen as a holder of individual rights in the tradition of liberal political theory is an artificial and misleading abstraction". Key contemporary proponents of the ethics of care are Held (2006) and Nell Noddings (1984).

This approach began not in moral theory as such, but in moral psychology and with the work of Carol Gilligan, and particularly her famous book *In a Different Voice* (1982). Gilligan, a developmental psychologist, documented the observation that men and women follow different moral approaches. Most particularly, she demonstrated that women were not "irrational" or "morally underdeveloped", as they appeared in standard models of moral development, but in fact used different moral frameworks and had different moral priorities from men. Rather than using a justice framework for moral reasoning, women use a care framework. Gilligan documented a number of key differences in the different moral frameworks: first, in the care framework, priority is given to responsibility and relationships rather than to rights and rules. Second, the focus is contextual and narrative rather than formal and abstract, so rather than

---

Box 11.3 Characteristics of the ethics of care

- Emphasizes responsibility and relationships, not rights and rules.
- Is contextual and narrative, not formal and abstract.
- Focuses on personal processes and activity, not one-off acts or choices.

---

apply universal rules or principles, attention is given to the specific needs of the particular individual. Third, ethics is concerned not with just one-off acts, but with the ongoing process and the activity of care. In all these three criteria the similarities with the virtue-ethics approach discussed in Chapter 3 can be seen.

In the ethics of care the first question is What is the caring response?, rather than What is the "right act"? Here you can see the similarity with virtue ethics, where the focus is on acting virtuously, being motivated by good character traits such as generosity and honesty. Not only does the ethics of care offer an alternative to the ethics of justice, but it also criticizes the ethics of justice for promoting damaging models of ethics. Thus Held (2006) suggests that the liberal model is "not a morally good model for relations between persons". Rather than promoting good relationships, it encourages contractual understandings of how we should relate to each other. It changes our understandings of relationships with other people and with society from

---

Box 11.4 Voices of subjects in Gilligan's work

A male view of morality

"I think it is recognising the right of the individual, the rights of other individuals, not interfering with those rights. Act as fairly as you would have them treat you. I think it is basically to preserve the human being's right to existence … Secondly, the human being's right to do as he please, again without interfering with somebody else's rights."   (Gilligan 1982)

A female view of morality

"We need to depend on each other, and hopefully it is not only a physical need but a need of fulfilment in ourselves, that a person's life is enriched by cooperating with other people and striving to live in harmony with everybody else, and to that end, there are right and wrong, there are things which promote that end and that move away from it, and in that way it is possible to choose in certain cases among different course of action that obviously promote or harm that goal."   (Gilligan 1982)

---

those of connectedness, reciprocity and giving to those of contract and rights. Thus it encourages more self-interested individual approaches, which Held and others argue are not the best model for society.

However, this does not mean that the ethics of care has rejected all aspects of the individual model. For instance, Held argues that autonomy and rights concepts are still important. They are important for understanding how we manage our relationships and accept, manage, maintain or resist the social ties and relationships in which we find ourselves. In her words, "we maintain some relations, revise others, and create new ones, but we do not see these as the choices of independent individuals acting in the world as though social ties did not exist prior to our creating them". Held argues that conceiving of autonomy in this way – as a relational concept – provides a far richer understanding of human being than the isolated liberal model. Likewise, Tronto argues that a model without care is incomplete and thus inferior, so that we need to at least supplement justice ethics with insights from care ethics.

Simply because the ethics of care began in developmental psychology, drawing on specifically female accounts of morality, this does not mean that one needs to endorse this as a *female* issue. Relational thinking and the insights of care ethics apply to all. Held, for instance, uses the paradigm of the caring relationship to stretch to "citizenship". So you do not need to accept, as many virtue ethicists and feminist ethicists do not, that there are "male" and "female" models that are fundamentally different in order to endorse the tenets of care ethics. Indeed, many have argued that the insights of care ethics and virtue ethics are necessary to fix the gaps in utilitarian and deontological theories. For instance, Marcia Baron, a Kantian thinker, argues that many of the virtue ethics insights about what has been left out of standard theories can be used as suggestions of how to modify and develop Kantian theories (Baron *et al.* 1997). Likewise, the implications of separating female ethics as "caring and loving" and male ethics as "rational and principled" are dangerous for ethics and for women and their situations. As Nussbaum (1999) points out, while women can be valued for caring, they are often disvalued for caring and they disvalue themselves: "women's propensity to care for others veers over into an undignified self-abnegation in which a woman subordinates her humanity utterly to the needs of others". Nor would we wish to excuse men who fail to care or who give inadequate attention to their relationships and context. Conversely, we do not wish to deny rationality and principled and abstract thought to women. The danger is that such a model makes men and women different species, but it would in the end *justify* the social structures that so subordinate women. In Nussbaum's words, "it is wrong to observe the way women are under injustice and conclude directly from this that they should and must be that way". Such duality would be the worst situation for women. Thus, the danger is that, rather than showing this dichotomy between men and women to be false, care ethics might end up supporting it. However, the ethics of care properly understood does not do this: both rationality and care are required for whole human beings and for ethics. As Nussbaum continues, "duly scrutinized and assessed, emotions of care and sympathy lie at the heart of the ethical life. No society can afford not to cultivate them."

CONCLUSION

This chapter has brought together many of the issues we have considered, from poverty to exploitation, and explored how women suffer disproportionately from injustices (and sometimes from the solutions to those injustices, for instance in population control). We have seen how women as a group – despite constituting just over half the global population – are systematically and routinely discriminated against. For some women these discriminations are relatively minor, for instance receiving lower pay or suffering sexual stereotyping; for others they are more serious and take the form of abuse and violence; whereas for others still, such as Metha Bai, they are a matter of very survival. Gender injustice is recognizable in the experience of all women – shown clearly by all the data – and the denial of it is part of the oppression.

Considering issues of gender justice raises issues for global ethics more broadly. The discussion of "male" models and human rights reminds us forcibly that ethics is about people and their relationships. This is as true for men as for women, and if we forget this there is a danger that our arguments will become intellectual games, or designed to meet policy targets, rather than tackling the injustice that real women and men actually experience. Considering gender reminds us that we are all human, with our own lives, needs, relationships, joys and sorrows. In so doing it offers insights that we can use to reform and develop global ethics. For instance, on this recognition, feminist models go some way to overcoming a key difficulty of contemporary ethics (perhaps *the* key difficulty) of how to balance the rights of individuals and groups. When considered abstractly, this looks impossible; however, when we recognize that individuals are not separate units, but connected to loved ones, to family and groups, and that groups are collections of real people, the differences begin to look more solvable.

This is not to say that feminist theorizing has all the answers, as even a short chapter has shown that there are huge disagreements between feminists, most obviously between liberal feminists and those critical of the liberal model. However, all the theorists we have looked at agree that the real-world context of women's situations matter and that, when compared to their male counterparts, women are still second class. The key point for our purposes, then, is that if these issues of gender justice were addressed, we would be better placed to tackle many of the broader issues of global ethics. It is hoped that this chapter, and this book, have outlined some of the perspectives from which this can be done.

FURTHER READING

- Center for Reproductive Rights & Poradňa. *Body and Soul: Forced Sterilization and Other Assaults on Roma Reproductive Freedom* (New York: Center for Reproductive Rights, 2003). http://reproductiverights.org/en/document/body-and-soul-forced-sterilization-and-other-assaults-on-roma-reproductive-freedom (accessed May 2011).
- Held, V. (ed.). *Justice and Care: Essential Readings in Feminist Ethics* (Boulder, CO: Westview Press, 1995).
- Held, V. *The Ethics of Care: Personal, Political and Global* (Oxford: Oxford University Press, 2006).
- Jaggar, A. "'Saving Amina': Global Justice for Women and Intercultural Dialogue". In *Real World Justice*, A. Follesdal & T. Pogge (eds), 37–63 (Dordrecht: Springer, 2005).
- Mackenzie, C. & N. Stoljar. *Relational Autonomy: Feminist Perspectives on Autonomy, Agency, and the Social Self* (Oxford: Oxford University Press, 2000).
- MacKinnon, C. *Are Women Human? And Other International Dialogues* (Cambridge, MA: Harvard University Press, 2006).
- Nussbaum, M. *Sex and Social Justice* (Oxford: Oxford University Press, 1999).
- Nussbaum, M. *Women and Human Development: The Capabilities Approach* (Cambridge: Cambridge University Press, 2000).
- Phillips, A. "Free to Decide for Oneself". In *Illusion of Consent*, D. I. O'Neill, M. L. Shanley & I. M. Young (eds), 99–118 (University Park, PA: Penn State University Press, 2008).
- Saul, J. *Feminism: Issues and Arguments* (Oxford: Oxford University Press, 2003).
- United Nations Development Programme (UNDP). *Overcoming Barriers: Human Mobility and Development*. Human Development Report 2009. http://hdr.undp.org/en/reports/global/hdr2009/ (accessed May 2011).
- Young, I. M. *Justice and the Politics of Difference* (Princeton, NJ: Princeton University Press, 2009).

CONCLUSION

There is no simple solution or resolution that can be offered by way of a conclusion to a book about the theory and practice of global ethics. As we have seen, the global challenges that are facing the contemporary world are many and various, and can seem so immense that it can be hard to see a way forwards; for instance, the challenge of "solving" the problems of poverty or climate change can seem overwhelming. However, it is hoped this book has given you some ideas about ways that the problems can be tackled and arguments to support such changes. By this point you should have developed your own approach, know your way around your ethical toolbox and have some confidence in approaching the dilemmas of global ethics. Whatever approach you have adopted, you should now be ready to put it into practice and contribute to making a more just world; or, if you are thoroughly sceptical about change for the better, you should at least be able to support this (controversial) position.

You will, it is also hoped, be aware of just how interconnected global-ethics issues are. For example, ill health makes it more difficult to work or travel, thus making poverty more likely. Poverty then creates opportunities for exploitation and makes the poor vulnerable: willing to be trafficked, say, or to sell their organs. Climate change exacerbates poverty and migration, which in turn put pressure on resources, which then exacerbates climate change. Climate change also makes conflict more likely and in turn conflict makes poverty, violence, rape and torture more likely. In short, those at the bottom of the heap are likely to suffer from more than one form of injustice: the double (and possibly triple and quadruple) jeopardy we discussed in Chapter 11. Given this, perhaps the only conclusion appropriate to draw is to insist that global-ethics issues cannot be addressed in isolation from each other; you cannot, for instance, put in place "fair" systems of migration or delivery of health or quotas for GHG emissions without recognizing the wider structural ethical issues. You must recognize both that "local" issues cannot be separated from "global" issues and that issues in one sphere of ethics and policy connect to others: injustices in one area compound injustices in another. Consequently, any ethical approach that separates different issues – or fails to consider the wider contextual issues – is not ethical, because it is wilfully ignoring important contributors to injustice.

This returns us to the beginning of the book and to the discussion of global ethics. While it is true to say that there is no one global ethic, there is a distinctive approach that has certain characteristics and requirements: the threefold global-ethics approach is global in scope, is multidisciplinary and connects theory and practice. This approach ensures that the needs of all are considered and that global ethics remains concerned with the poor, vulnerable and exploited. Whether or not this will continue, or whether global ethics will be "captured" and come to serve the needs of some interested group or another (as, arguably, professional ethics does) is yet to be seen. This depends largely on how the area of global ethics develops. Will it become a more clearly definable discipline, or will it continue to be practised by people from many different disciplines? Only time will reveal the future of global ethics. But as long as global ethicists remain true to the "global-in-scope criteria", they should continue to be a voice for those who are relatively powerless and who suffer most from global injustices. In addition, if the second and third criteria are respected, global ethics will also continue to seek practical and engaged solutions and not regress into an irrelevant abstract debate.

BIBLIOGRAPHY

Abegunde, D. O., C. D. Mathers, T. Adam, M. Ortegon & K. Strong 2007. "The Burden and Costs of Chronic Diseases in Low-income and Middle-income Countries". *Lancet* **370**: 129–38.

Ackerly, B. A. 2008. *Universal Human Rights in a World of Difference*. Cambridge: Cambridge University Press.

African Commission on Human and People's Rights (ACHPR) 1981. "African Charter on Human and People's Rights". www.achpr.org/english/_info/charter_en.html (accessed May 2011).

Alkire, S. 2002. *Valuing Freedoms: Sen's Capability Approach and Poverty Reduction*. Oxford: Oxford University Press.

Alora, A. T. & J. M. Lumitao 2001. *Beyond a Western Bioethics: Voices from the Developing World*. Washington, DC: Georgetown University Press.

Amnesty International 1997. "What is Female Genital Mutilation?" www.amnesty.org/en/library/info/ACT77/006/1997 (accessed May 2011).

Amnesty International 2004. *Threat and Humiliation: Racial Profiling, Domestic Security and Human Rights in the United States*. New York: Amnesty International USA.

Amnesty International 2010a. "Proposed China Death Penalty Reforms May Have No Great Impact on Executions" (23 August). www.amnesty.org/en/news-and-updates/proposed-china-death-penalty-reforms-may-have-no-great-impact-executions-2010-08-23 (accessed July 2011).

Amnesty International 2010b. "Thousands at Risk of Forced Sterilization in China" (22 April). www.amnesty.org/en/news-and-updates/thousands-risk-forced-sterilization-china-2010-04-22 (accessed May 2011).

Anderson, M. 2009. "NGOs and Fair Trade: The Social Movement Behind the Label". In *NGOs in Contemporary Britain*, N. Crowson, M. Hilton & J. McKay (eds), 222–41. Basingstoke: Palgrave Macmillan.

Anker, C. van den & J. Doomernik (eds) 2006. *Trafficking and Women's Rights*. Basingstoke: Palgrave Macmillan.

Annan, K. A. 1999. "Two Concepts of Sovereignty". *The Economist* (16 September). www.economist.com/node/324795 (accessed May 2011).

Anscombe, G. E. M. 1997. "Modern Moral Philosophy". In *Virtue Ethics*, R. Crisp & M. Slote (eds), 26–44. Oxford: Oxford University Press.

Anstey, K. W. 2002. "Are Attempts to have Impaired Children Justifiable?" *Journal of Medical Ethics* **28**: 286–8.

Archibugi, D. & D. Held (eds) 1995. *Cosmopolitan Democracy: An Agenda for a New World Order*. Cambridge: Polity Press.

Aristotle 2002. *Nicomachean Ethics*, S. Broadie & R. Christopher (ed. & trans.). Oxford: Oxford University Press.

Ashcroft, R. E. 2005. "Access to Essential Medicines: A Hobbesian Social Contract Approach". *Developing World Bioethics* **5**(2): 121–41.

Assaad, M. B. 1980. "Female Circumcision in Egypt: Social Implications, Current Research and Prospects for Change". *Studies in Family Planning* **11**: 3–16.

Attfield, R. 1999. *The Ethics of the Global Environment*. Edinburgh: Edinburgh University Press.

Attfield, R. 2003. *Environmental Ethics*. Cambridge: Polity Press.

Attfield, R. 2006. *Creation, Evolution and Meaning*. Aldershot: Ashgate.

Baer, P., T. Athanasiou & S. Kartha 2007. *The Right to Development in a Climate Constrained World: The Greenhouse Development Rights Framework*. Berlin: Heinrich Böll Foundation.

Bandy, J. & J. Smith (eds) 2005. *Coalitions across Borders: Transnational Protest and the Neoliberal Order*. Lanham, MD: Rowman & Littlefield.

Barnes, P. 2006. *Capitalism 3.0: A Guide to Reclaiming the Commons*. San Francisco: Berrett Koehler Publishers.

Barnes, P. 2008. *Climate Solutions: A Citizen's Guide*. White River Junction, VT: Chelsea Green Publishing.

Barnett, A. & H. Smith 2006. "Cruel Cost of the Human Egg Trade". *The Observer* (30 April). www.guardian.co.uk/uk/2006/apr/30/health.healthandwellbeing (accessed May 2011).

Baron, M. 1995. *Kantian Ethics Almost Without Apology*. Ithaca, NY: Cornell University Press.

Baron, M. W., P. Pettit & M. Slote 1997. *Three Methods of Ethics*. Oxford: Blackwell.

Barr, M. D. 2002. *Cultural Politics and Asian Values: The Tepid War*. London: Routledge.

Barry, B. 2001. *Culture and Equality*. Cambridge: Polity Press.

Barry, C. & T. Pogge 2005. *Global Institutions and Responsibilities*. Oxford: Blackwell.

Bauer, P. 1972. *Dissent on Development*. Cambridge, MA: Harvard University Press.

Bauer, P. 1981. *Equality, The Third World, And Economic Delusion*. Cambridge, MA: Harvard University Press.

Bauer, J. R. & D. A. Bell 1999. *The East Asian Challenge for Human Rights*. Cambridge: Cambridge University Press.

Baxter, B. 2005. *A Theory of Ecological Justice*. London: Routledge.

BBC 2006. "Organ Sales 'Thriving' in China". http://news.bbc.co.uk/1/hi/5386720.stm (accessed May 2011).

Beitz, C. 1999. *Political Theory and International Relations*. Princeton, NJ: Princeton University Press.

Bellamy, A. J. 2005. "Is the War on Terror Just?" *International Relations* **19**: 275–96.

Benhabib, S. 2002. *The Claims of Culture: Equality and Diversity in the Global Era*. Princeton, NJ: Princeton University Press.

Bentham, J. [1823] 1907. *An Introduction to the Principles of Morals and Legislation*. Oxford: Clarendon Press.

Bentham, J. 2011a. *Anarchical Fallacies: An Examination of The Declaration of the Rights of the Man and the Citizen Decreed by the Constituent Assembly in France*. In *The Works of Jeremy Bentham*, vol. 2, J. Bowring (ed.). Edinburgh: William Tait. http://app.libraryofliberty.org/?option=com_staticxt&staticfile=show.php%3Ftitle=1921&chapter=114226&layout=html&Itemid=27 (accessed May 2011).

Bentham, J. [1843] 2011b. "A Critical Examination of the Declaration of Rights". In Bentham (2011a).

Bijoy, C. R. 2007. "Access and Benefit Sharing From The Indigenous Peoples' Perspective: The Tbgri-Kani 'Model'". *Law, Environment and Development Journal* **3**: 1–19.

Booth, K., T. Dunne & M. Cox 2001. *How Might We Live? Global Ethics in the New Century*, Cambridge: Cambridge University Press.

Bowman, K. 2004. "Bridging the Gap in the Hopes of Ending Female Genital Cutting". *Santa Clara Journal of International Law* **3**: 132–63.

Brazier, M. 1999. "Regulating the Reproduction Business?" *Medical Law Review* 7: 166–93.

Brecher, B. 2007. *Torture and the Ticking Bomb*. Oxford: Wiley.

Bresser, A. H. M., M. M. Berk, G. J. van den Born *et al.* 2005. "The Effects of Climate Change in the Netherlands". Bilthoven: Netherlands Environment Assessment Agency. www.rivm.nl/bibliotheek/rapporten/773001037.pdf (accessed May 2011).

Brink, D. O. 1989. *Moral Realism and the Foundation of Ethics*. Cambridge: Cambridge University Press.

Brock, D. W. 2001. "Genetics and Confidentiality". *American Journal of Bioethics* 1: 34–5.

Brock, G. 2005. "The Difference Principle, Equality of Opportunity, and Cosmopolitan Justice". *Journal of Moral Philosophy* 2: 333–51.

Brock, G. 2009. *Global Justice: A Cosmopolitan Account*. Oxford: Oxford University Press.

Brock, G. & H. Brighouse 2005. *The Political Philosophy of Cosmopolitanism*. Cambridge: Cambridge University Press.

Brown, D. 2006. "Richest Tenth Own 85% of World's Assets". *The Times* (6 December). www.timesonline.co.uk/tol/news/world/us_and_americas/article661055.ece (accessed May 2011).

Brownsword, R. 2009. "Rights, Responsibility and Stewardship: Beyond Consent". In *The Governance of Genetic Information: Who Decides?*, H. Widdows & C. Mullen (eds), 99–125. Cambridge: Cambridge University Press.

Buchanan, A. 2007. *Justice, Legitimacy, and Self-Determination: Moral Foundations for International Law*. Oxford: Oxford University Press.

Buchanan, A., D. W. Brock, N. Daniels & D. Wikler 2000. *From Chance to Choice: Genetics and Justice*. Cambridge: Cambridge University Press.

Buy Association UK n.d. "Cosmetic Surgery in South Africa". www.buyassociation.co.uk/lookinggood/cosmetic-surgery-in-south-africa.html (accessed July 2011).

Cabrera, L. 2004. *Political Theory of Global Justice: A Cosmopolitan Case for the World State*. London: Routledge.

Campbell, A. V. 1999. "Presidential Address: Global Bioethics – Dream or Nightmare?" *Bioethics* 3: 183–90.

Campbell, A. V. 2009. *The Body in Bioethics*. Abingdon: Routledge-Cavendish.

Caney, S. 2001. "International Distributive Justice". *Political Studies* 49: 974–97.

Caney, S. 2005a. "Cosmopolitan Justice, Responsibility and Global Climate Change". *Leiden Journal of International Law* 18: 747–75.

Caney, S. 2005b. *Justice Beyond Borders: A Global Political Theory*. Oxford: Oxford University Press.

Caney, S. 2006. "Environmental Degradation, Reparations, and the Moral Significance of History". *Journal of Social Philosophy* 37: 464–82.

Caney, S. 2008. "Human Rights, Climate Change and Discounting". *Environmental Politics* 17: 536–55.

Caney, S. 2009a. "Climate Change and the Future: Time, Wealth and Risk". *Journal of Social Philosophy* 40: 163–86.

Caney, S. 2009b. "Climate Change, Human Rights and Moral Thresholds". In *Climate Change and Human Rights*, S. Humphreys (ed.), 69–90. Cambridge: Cambridge University Press.

Caney, S. 2009c. "Equality in the Greenhouse?" *Journal of Global Ethics* 5: 125–46.

Caney, S. 2009d. "Human Rights, Responsibilities and Climate Change". In *Global Basic Rights*, C. Beitz & R. Goodin (eds), 227–55. Oxford: Oxford University Press.

Caney, S. 2009e. "Justice, Morality and Carbon Trading". *Ragion Pratica* 32: 203–27.

Caney, S. 2010. "Climate Change and the Duties of the Advantaged". *Critical Review of International Social and Political Philosophy* 13: 203–28.

Caney, S. 2011. "Climate Change, Energy Rights and Equality". In *The Ethics of Global Climate Change*, D. Arnold (ed.), 77–105. Cambridge: Cambridge University Press.

Carens, J. 1987. "Aliens And Citizens: The Case For Open Borders". *Review of Politics* 49: 251–73.

Cauquelin, J., P. Lim & B. Mayer-König 1998. *Asian Values: An Encounter with Diversity*. Richmond: Curzon Press.

Center for International Environmental Law (CIEL) 2007. "Male' Declaration on the Human Dimension of Global Climate Change". www.ciel.org/Publications/Male_Declaration_Nov07.pdf (accessed May 2011).

Center for Reproductive Rights & Poradňa 2003. *Body and Soul: Forced Sterilization and Other Assaults on Roma Reproductive Freedom*. New York: Center for Reproductive Rights. http://reproductiverights.org/en/document/body-and-soul-forced-sterilization-and-other-assaults-on-roma-reproductive-freedom (accessed May 2011).

Cheney, A. 2006. *Body Brokers: Inside America's Underground Trade in Human Remains*. New York: Broadway Books.

Coady, C. A. J. 2004. "Terrorism and Innocence". *Journal of Ethics* **8**: 37–58.

Cohen, G. A. 1993. "Equality of What? On Welfare, Goods and Capabilities". In *The Quality of Life*, M. C. Nussbaum & A. Sen (eds), 9–29. Oxford: Clarendon Press.

Cohen, J. 2004. "Minimalism About Human Rights: The Most We Can Hope For?" *Journal of Political Philosophy* **12**: 190–213.

Cohen, J. 2010. *The Practice of Global Citizenship*. Cambridge: Cambridge University Press.

Cohen, J. C., P. Illingworth & U. Schuklenk (eds) 2006. *The Power of Pills: Social, Ethical and Legal Issues in Drug Development, Marketing and Pricing*. London: Pluto Press.

Commers, R., W. Vandekerckhove & A. Verlinden (eds) 2008. *Ethics in an Era of Globalisation*. Aldershot: Ashgate.

Council of Europe 2010. "Convention for the Protection of Human Rights and Fundamental Freedoms" (European Convention on Human Rights). http://conventions.coe.int/treaty/en/Treaties/Html/005.htm (accessed May 2011).

Crocker, D. A. 2008. *Ethics of Global Development*. Cambridge: Cambridge University Press.

Dallmayr, F. 2002. "Asian Values and Global Human Rights". *Philosophy East and West* **52**: 173–89.

Daniels, N. 1985. *Just Health Care*. Cambridge: Cambridge University Press.

Daniels, N. 2008. *Just Health: Meeting Health Needs Fairly*. Cambridge: Cambridge University Press.

Darwall, S. (ed.) 2003. *Consequentialism*. Oxford: Blackwell.

Darwall, S., A. Gibbard & P. Railton 1997. *Moral Discourse and Practice: Some Philosophical Approaches*. New York: Oxford University Press.

de Bary, W. T. 1998. *Asian Values and Human Rights: A Confucian Communitarian Perspective*. Cambridge, MA: Harvard University Press.

Department of Homeland Security 2010. *Yearbook of Immigration Statistics: 2009*. Washington, DC: US Department of Homeland Security, Office of Immigration Statistics. www.dhs.gov/xlibrary/assets/statistics/yearbook/2009/ois_yb_2009.pdf (accessed May 2011).

Dershowitz, A. 2002. *Why Terrorism Works: Understanding the Threat, Responding to the Challenge*. New Haven, CT: Yale University Press.

De-Shalit, A. 1994. *Why Posterity Matters*. London: Routledge.

Dickenson, D. 2002. "Commodification of Human Tissue: Implications for Feminist and Development Ethics". *Developing World Bioethics* **2**: 55–63.

Dickenson, D. 2003. *Risk and Luck in Medical Ethics*. Cambridge: Polity Press.

Dickenson, D. 2008. *Body Shopping: The Economy Fuelled by Flesh and Blood*. Oxford: One World.

Dickenson, D., R. Huxtable & M. Parker 2010. *The Cambridge Medical Ethics Handbook*, 2nd edn. Cambridge: Cambridge University Press.

Dobson, A. 1998. *Justice and the Environment: Conceptions of Environmental Sustainability and Dimensions of Social Justice*. Oxford: Oxford University Press.

Donchin, A. & L. Purdy 1999. *Embodying Bioethics: Recent Feminist Advances*. Lanham, MD: Rowman & Littlefield.

Doukas, D. J. & J. W. Berg 2001. "The Family Covenant and Genetic Testing". *American Journal of Bioethics* **3**: 2–16.

Dower, N. 2002. "Global Citizenship: Yes or No?" In *Global Citizenship: A Critical Reader*, N. Dower & J. Williams (eds), 30–40. Edinburgh: Edinburgh University Press.

Dower, N. 2007. *World Ethics: The New Agenda*, 2nd edn. Edinburgh: Edinburgh University Press.

Dower, N. 2009. *The Ethics of War and Peace*. Cambridge: Polity Press.

Dower, N. & J. Williams (eds) 2002. *Global Citizenship: A Critical Reader*. Edinburgh: Edinburgh University Press.

Doyal, L. & I. McGough 1991. *A Theory of Human Need*. Basingstoke: Palgrave Macmillan.

Dworkin, R. 1977. *Taking Rights Seriously*. London: Duckworth.

Dworkin, R. 1984. "Rights as Trumps". In *Theories of Rights*, J. Waldron (ed.). Oxford: Oxford University Press.

Eade, J. & D. O'Byrne (eds) 2005. *Global Ethics and Civil Society*. Aldershot: Ashgate.

The Economist, Banyan correspondent 2010. "People, the Philippines' Best Export". Blog post (9 February). www.economist.com/blogs/banyan/2010/02/philippines_and_its_remittance_economy (accessed May 2011).

Emsley, S. 2005. *Jane Austen's Philosophy of the Virtues*. Basingstoke: Palgrave Macmillan.

Erin, C. A. & J. Harris 2003. "An Ethical Market in Human Organs". *Journal of Medical Ethics* **29**: 137–8.

European Commission 2003. *Opinion on the Ethical Aspects of Clinical Research in Developing Countries: Opinion no. 17*. Luxembourg: Office of Official Publications of the European Communities. http://ec.europa.eu/archives/european_group_ethics/docs/avis17_en.pdf (accessed May 2011).

European Commission 2010. "Registries: Transitional Measure to End on 20 April with the Reinstatement of the National Registry of Lithuania". http://ec.europa.eu/clima/news/articles/news_2011041901_en.htm (accessed July 2011).

Evangelista, M. 2008. *Law, Ethics and the War on Terror*. Cambridge: Polity Press.

Faini, R. 2006. "Remittances and the Brain Drain". IZA Discussion Paper No. 2155. Bonn: Forschungsinstitut zur Zukunft der Arbeit (IZA). ftp://repec.iza.org/RePEc/Discussionpaper/dp2155.pdf (accessed May 2011).

Foot, P. 2001. *Natural Goodness*. Oxford: Oxford University Press.

Fortress Europe 2010. "Death at the Border: Press Review, 1988–2009". http://fortresseurope.blogspot.com/2006/01/press-review.html (accessed May 2011).

Frankfurt, H. 1989. "Freedom of the Will and the Concept of a Person". In *The Inner Citadel: Essays on Individual Autonomy*, J. Christman (ed.). New York: Oxford University Press.

Fukuyama, F. 1998. "Asian Values and the Asian Crisis". *Commentary* **105**: 23–7.

Garvey, J. 2008. *The Ethics of Climate Change: Right and Wrong in a Warming World*. London: Continuum.

Gentleman, A. 2008. "Poor Donors Duped by Organ-Transplant Racket in India". *New York Times* (29 January). www.iht.com/articles/2008/01/29/asia/kidney.php (accessed May 2011).

Gilligan, C. 1982. *In a Different Voice: Psychological Theory and Women's Development*. Cambridge, MA: Harvard University Press.

Global Humanitarian Assistance (GHA) 2010. *Global Humanitarian Assistance Report*. Wells: GHA. www.globalhumanitarianassistance.org/report/gha-report-2010 (accessed May 2011).

Goodin, R. 1995. *Utilitarianism as a Public Philosophy*. Cambridge: Cambridge University Press.

Goodin, R. 2003. *Reflective Democracy*. Oxford: Oxford University Press.

Goodin, R. 2008. "What is So Special about Our Fellow Countrymen?" In *Global Justice: Seminal Essays*, T. Pogge & D. Moellendorf (eds), 255–84. Saint Paul, MN: Paragon House.

Goodwin, M. 2006. *Black Markets: The Supply and Demand of Body Parts*. Cambridge: Cambridge University Press.

Gosseries, A. 2004. "Historical Emissions and Free Riding". *Ethical Perspectives* **11**: 36–60.

Gould, C. 1988. *Rethinking Democracy: Freedom and Social Cooperation in Politics, Economy, and State*. Cambridge: Cambridge University Press.

Gould, C. 2004. *Globalising Democracy and Human Rights*. Cambridge: Cambridge University Press.

Goyal, M., R. L. Mehta, L. J. Schneiderman & R. A. Sehgal 2002. "Economic and Health Consequences of Selling a Kidney in India". *Journal of the American Medical Association* 2: 1589–93.

Greely, H. 2001. "Human Genomics Research: New Challenges for Research Ethics". *Perspectives in Biology and Medicine* 44: 221–9.

Hampton, J. 1997. *Political Philosophy*. Boulder, CO: Westview Press.

Hardin, G. 1968. "The Tragedy of the Commons". *Science* 162: 1243–8.

Hardin, G. 1974. "Living on a Lifeboat". *Bioscience* 24(10): 561–8. www.garretthardinsociety.org/articles/art_living_on_a_lifeboat.html (accessed May 2011).

Hare, B. 2006. "Relationship Between Increases in Global Mean Temperature and Impacts on Ecosystems, Food Production, Water and Socio-economic Systems". In *Avoiding Dangerous Climate Change*, H. J. Schellnhuber, W. Cramer, N. Nakicenovic, T. Wigley & G. Yohe (eds), 117–94. Cambridge: Cambridge University Press.

Harris, J. 2005. *The Value of Life: An Introduction to Medical Ethics*. London: Routledge.

Harris, J. & C. A. Erin 2003. "An Ethical Market in Human Organs". *Journal of Medical Ethics* 29: 137–8.

Harsanyi, J. 1980. "Rule Utilitarianism, Rights, Obligations and the Theory of Rational Behavior". *Theory and Decision* 12: 115–33.

Hathaway, O. 2004. "The Promise and Limits of the International Law of Torture". In *Torture: A Collection*, S. Levinson (ed.), 199–213. New York: Oxford University Press.

Häyry, M. 2004. "There is a Difference Between Selecting a Deaf Embryo and Deafening a Hearing Child". *Journal of Medical Ethics* 30: 510–12.

Hayward, T. 2007. "Human Rights Versus Emissions Rights: Climate Justice and the Equitable Distribution of Ecological Space". *Ethics and International Affairs* 21: 431–50.

Heimir, G. & M. Holmgren (eds) 2001. *Ethical Theory: A Concise Anthology*. Peterborough, Ontario: Broadview.

Held, D. 1995. *Democracy and the Global Order: From the Modern State to Global Governance*. Cambridge: Polity Press.

Held, V. 1990. "Feminist Transformations of Moral Theory". *Philosophy and Phenomenological Research* 50 (supplement, Autumn): 321–44.

Held, V. (ed.) 1995. *Justice and Care: Essential Readings in Feminist Ethics*. Boulder, CO: Westview Press.

Held, V. 2004. "Terrorism and War". *Journal of Ethics* 8: 59–75.

Held, V. 2006. *The Ethics of Care: Personal, Political and Global*. Oxford: Oxford University Press.

Held, D. & A. McGrew (eds) 2000. *The Global Transformation Reader: An Introduction to the Globalisation Debate*. Cambridge: Polity Press.

Heller, J. 1972. "Syphilis Victims in US Study Went Untreated for 40 Years". *New York Times* (26 July), 1, 8.

Helm, P. (ed.) 1981. *Divine Commands and Morality*. Oxford: Oxford University Press.

Herodotus 1996. *Histories*, J. Marincola & A. DeSelincourt (eds & trans). Harmondsworth: Penguin.

Hersh, S. M. 2004. "Torture at Abu Ghraib: American Soldiers Brutalized Iraqis. How Far Up does the Responsibility Go?" *New Yorker* (10 May). www.newyorker.com/archive/2004/05/10/040510fa_fact? (accessed May 2011).

Hobbes, T. 1994. *Leviathan*, E. Curley (ed.). Indianapolis, IN: Hackett.

Hohfeld, W. N. 1919. *Fundamental Legal Conceptions*. New Haven, CT: Yale University Press.

Holland, S. 2003. *Bioethics: A Philosophical Introduction*. Cambridge: Polity Press.

Hollis, A. & T. Pogge 2008. *The Health Impact Fund: Making New Medicines Accessible to All*. New Haven, CT: Incentives for Global Health, Yale. www.yale.edu/macmillan/igh/hif.html (accessed May 2011).

Honderich, T. 2006. *Humanity, Terrorism, Terrorist War: Palestine, 9/11, Iraq, 7/7*. London: Continuum.

Hoy, P. 1998. *Players and Issues in International Aid*. West Hartford, CT: Kumarian Press.

Human Genome Organization (HUGO) Ethics Committee 2000. "Statement on Benefit Sharing". www. hugo-international.org/img/benefit_sharing_2000.pdf (accessed May 2011).

Human Rights Watch 2009. "Democratic Republic of Congo (DRC): Events of 2009". www.hrw.org/en/node/87600 (accessed July 2011).

Hursthouse, R. 1997. "Virtue Theory and Abortion". In *Virtue Ethics*, R. Crisp & M. Slote (eds), 217–38. Oxford: Oxford University Press.

Hursthouse, R. 1999. *On Virtue Ethics*. Oxford: Oxford University Press.

Ikonya, P. 2009. "There Are No Cameras Here". www.irct.org/what-is-torture/voices-of-torture-victims/there-are-no-cameras-here.aspx (accessed May 2011).

Inter-American Commission on Human Rights 1979. "American Convention on Human Rights". www. cidh.org/Basicos/English/Basic3.American%20Convention.htm (accessed May 2011).

Intergovernmental Panel on Climate Change (IPCC) 2007a. *Climate Change 2007: Impacts, Adaptation and Vulnerability*, M. L. Parry, O. F. Canziani, J. P. Palutikof *et al.* (eds). Cambridge: Cambridge University Press.

Intergovernmental Panel on Climate Change (IPCC) 2007b. *IPCC Fourth Assessment Report: Climate Change 2007*. www.ipcc.ch/publications_and_data/publications_and_data_reports.shtml (accessed July 2011).

Intergovernmental Panel on Climate Change (IPCC) 2010. "IPCC Statement on the Melting of Himalayan Glaciers". www.ipcc.ch/pdf/presentations/himalaya-statement-20january2010.pdf (accessed May 2011).

International Commission on Intervention and State Sovereignty (ICISS) 2001. *The Responsibility To Protect*. Ottawa: International Development Research Centre. www.iciss.ca/report2-en.asp (accessed May 2011).

Jackson, R. 2005. *Writing the War on Terrorism: Language, Politics and Counter-Terrorism*. Manchester: Manchester University Press.

Jaggar, A. 2005. "'Saving Amina': Global Justice for Women and Intercultural Dialogue". In *Real World Justice*, A. Follesdal & T. Pogge (eds), 37–63. Dordrecht: Springer.

Jenkins, R. 2005. "Globalization, Corporate Social Responsibility and Poverty". *International Affairs* **81**: 525–40.

Jha, V. 2004. "Paid Transplants in India: The Grim Reality". *Nephrology Dialysis Transplantation* **19**: 541–3.

Jones, P. 1994. *Rights*. New York: St Martin's Press.

Kant, I. 1797. *On a Supposed Right to Tell Lies from Benevolent Motives*, T. K. Abbott (trans.). http://oll. libertyfund.org/?option=com_staticxt&staticfile=show.php%3Ftitle=360&chapter=61937&layout= html&Itemid=27 (accessed May 2011).

Kant, I. [1788] 1993. *Critique of Practical Reason*. New York: Macmillan.

Kant, I. [1785] 1997. *Groundwork of the Metaphysics of Morals*, M. Gregor (ed.). Cambridge: Cambridge University Press.

Katumba, R. 1990. "Kenyan Elders Defend Circumcision". *Development Forum* (September): 17.

Kenyatta, J. 1938. *Facing Mount Kenya: The Tribal Life of the Kikuyu*. London: Secker & Warburg.

Khan, A. A. 2004. "Pakistan's Kidney Donor Crisis". http://news.bbc.co.uk/1/hi/world/south_asia/4092325.stm (accessed May 2011).

Kinsella, D. & C. Carr (eds) 2007. *The Morality of War: A Reader*. Boulder, CO: Rienner.

Klein, N. 2009. *No Logo: No Space, No Choice, No Jobs*. London: Picador.

Knoppers, B. & R. Chadwick 2005. "Human Genetic Research: Emerging Trends in Ethics". *Nature* **6**: 75–9.

Küng, H. 1993a. *A Global Ethic: The Declaration of the Parliament of the World's Religions*. London: SCM Press.

Küng, H. 1993b. "Declaration Toward a Global Ethic". www.parliamentofreligions.org/_includes/FCKcontent/File/TowardsAGlobalEthic.pdf (accessed May 2011).

Locke, J. [1689] 1980. *Second Treatise of Government*, C. B. MacPherson (ed.). Indianapolis, IN: Hackett.

Lomborg, B. 2001. *The Skeptical Environmentalist: Measuring the Real State of the World*. Cambridge: Cambridge University Press.

MacIntyre, A. 1982. *After Virtue: A Study in Moral Theory*. London: Duckworth.

Mackenzie, C. & N. Stoljar 2000. *Relational Autonomy: Feminist Perspectives on Autonomy, Agency, and the Social Self*. Oxford: Oxford University Press.

Mackie, J. L. 1977. *Ethics: Inventing Right and Wrong*. Oxford: Oxford University Press.

MacKinnon, C. 2006. *Are Women Human? And Other International Dialogues*. Cambridge, MA: Harvard University Press.

Macklin, R. 1999. *Against Relativism: Cultural Diversity and the Search for Ethical Universals in Medicine*. Oxford: Oxford University Press.

Mandelbaum, M. 1994. "The Reluctance to Intervene". *Foreign Policy* **95**: 3–18.

Mandle, J. 2006. *Global Justice: An Introduction*. Oxford: Blackwell.

Marchetti, R. 2008. *Global Democracy: For and Against*. London: Routledge.

Marquis, D. 1997. "An Argument that Abortion is Wrong". In *Ethics in Practice: An Anthology*, H. Lafollette (ed.), 83–93. Oxford: Blackwell.

Marx, K. [1844] 1977. "On the Jewish Question". In *Selected Writings*, D. McLellan (ed.), 49–62. Oxford: Oxford University Press.

Marx, K. & F. Engels [1845–46] 1999. *The German Ideology*, C. J. Arthur (ed.). London: Lawrence & Wishart.

McNaughton, D. 1988. *Moral Vision: An Introduction to Ethics*. Oxford: Blackwell.

McNeill, D. & A. L. St Clair 2009. *Global Poverty, Ethics and Human Rights: The Role of Multilateral Organisations*. London: Routledge.

Mendus, S. 2009. *Politics and Morality*. Cambridge: Polity Press.

Meyer, A. 2000. *Contraction and Convergence: The Global Solution to Climate Change*. Foxhole: Green Books.

Midgley, M. 2000. "Biotechnology and Monstrosity: Why We Should Pay Attention to the 'Yuk Factor'". *The Hastings Center Report* **30**: 7–15.

Mill, J. S. [1863] 1987. *Utilitarianism*. Harmondsworth: Penguin. www.efm.bris.ac.uk/het/mill/utilitarianism.pdf (accessed May 2011).

Miller, D. 1995. *On Nationality*. Oxford: Oxford University Press.

Miller, D. 2007. *National Responsibility and Global Justice*. Oxford: Oxford University Press.

Miller, S. 2005. "Is Torture Ever Morally Justified?" *International Journal of Applied Philosophy* **19**: 179–92.

Moellendorf, D. 2002. *Cosmopolitan Justice*. Cambridge, MA: Westview Press.

Moellendorf, D. 2005. "The World Trade Organization and Egalitarian Justice". *Metaphilosophy* **36**: 145–62.

Moellendorf, D. 2009a. *Global Inequality Matters*. Basingstoke: Palgrave Macmillan.

Moellendorf, D. 2009b. "Treaty Norms and Climate Change Mitigation". *Ethics and International Affairs* **23**: 247–65.

Morgenthau, H. & K. Thompson 1985. *Politics Among Nations*. New York: McGraw-Hill.

Mulhall, S. & A. Swift 1996. *Liberals and Communitarians*, 2nd edn. Oxford: Blackwell.

Murdoch, I. 1970. *The Sovereignty of Good*. London: Routledge & Kegan Paul.

Næss, A. 1973. "The Shallow and the Deep, Long-Range Ecology Movement: A Summary". *Inquiry* **16**: 95–100.

Næss, A. 1989. *Ecology, Community and Lifestyle: Outline of an Ecosophy*, D. Rothenberg (trans.). Cambridge: Cambridge University Press.

Naess, A. & G. Sessions 1984. "A Deep Ecology Eight Point Platform". www.haven.net/deep/council/eight.htm (accessed May 2011).

Nagel, T. 1991. *Equality and Partiality*. Oxford: Oxford University Press.

Narayan, U. & S. Harding (eds) 2000. *Decentering the Center: Philosophy for a Multicultural, Postcolonial and Feminist World*. Bloomington, IN: Indiana University Press.

Nardin, T. 1983. *Law, Morality and the Relations of States*. Princeton, NJ: Princeton University Press.

National Archives n.d. "Declaration of Independence". www.archives.gov/exhibits/charters/declaration. html (accessed May 2011).

National Constituent Assembly 1789. "Declaration of the Rights of Man and of the Citizen". www.hrcr. org/docs/frenchdec.html (accessed May 2011).

Netherlands Environmental Assessment Agency 2006. "The Effects of Climate Change in the Netherlands". http://www.pbl.nl/en/publications/2006/TheeffectsofclimatechangeintheNetherlands (accessed July 2011).

Neumayer, E. 2000. "In Defence of Historical Accountability for Greenhouse Gas Emissions". *Ecological Economics* **33**: 185–92.

Noddings, N. 1984. *Caring: A Feminine Approach to Ethics*. Berkeley, CA: University of California Press.

Nozick, R. 1974. *Anarchy, State, and Utopia*. New York: Basic Books.

Nuffield Council on Bioethics 2002. *The Ethics of Research Related to Healthcare in Developing Countries*. www.nuffieldbioethics.org/research-developing-countries (accessed May 2011).

Nullis-Kapp, C. 2004. "Organ Trafficking and Transplantation Pose New Challenges". *Bulletin of the World Health Organization* **82**(9): 639–718. www.who.int/bulletin/volumes/82/9/feature0904/en/ index.html (accessed May 2011).

Nussbaum, M. 1988. "Nature, Function, and Capability: Aristotle on Political Distribution". *Oxford Studies in Ancient Philosophy* **6** (supp. vol.): 113–37.

Nussbaum, M. 1996. "Double Moral Standards? A Response to Yael Tamir's 'Hands off Clitoridectomy'". *Boston Review* (October/November). http://bostonreview.net/BR21.5/nussbaum.html (accessed May 2011).

Nussbaum, M. 1999. *Sex and Social Justice*. Oxford: Oxford University Press.

Nussbaum, M. 2000. *Women and Human Development: The Capabilities Approach*. Cambridge: Cambridge University Press.

Nussbaum, M. & A. Sen (eds) 1993. *The Quality of Life*. Oxford: Clarendon Press.

Office of the United Nations High Commissioner for Human Rights (OHCHR) 1975. "Declaration on the Protection of All Persons from Being Subjected to Torture and Other Cruel, Inhuman or Degrading Treatment on Punishment". www2.ohchr.org/english/law/declarationcat.htm (accessed May 2011).

Office of the United Nations High Commissioner for Human Rights (OHCHR) 1976. "International Covenant on Civil and Political Rights". www2.ohchr.org/english/law/ccpr.htm (accessed May 2011).

Office of the United Nations High Commissioner for Human Rights (OHCHR) 1984. "Convention against Torture and Other Cruel, Inhuman or Degrading Treatment or Punishment". www2.ohchr. org/english/law/cat.htm (accessed May 2011).

Office of the United Nations High Commissioner for Human Rights (OHCHR) 2008. "Resolution 7/23: Human Rights and Climate Change". www2.ohchr.org/english/issues/climatechange/docs/ Resolution_7_23.pdf (accessed July 2010).

Okin, S. M. 1989. *Justice, Gender, and the Family*. New York: Basic Books.

Okin, S. M. 1998. "Feminism, Women's Human Rights and Cultural Differences". *Hypatia* **13**: 35–52.

Okin, S. M. 1999. *Is Multiculturalism Bad for Women?* Princeton, NJ: Princeton University Press.

Okin, S. M. 2002. "Mistresses of Their Own Destiny: Group Rights, Gender and Realistic Rights of Exit". *Ethics* **112**: 205–30.

O'Neill, O. 1996. *Towards Justice and Virtue: A Constructive Account of Practical Reasoning*. Cambridge: Cambridge University Press.

O'Neill, O. 2000. *Bounds of Justice*. Cambridge: Cambridge University Press.

O'Neill, O. 2001. "Agents of Justice". In *Global Justice*, T. Pogge & D. Moellendorf (eds), 188–204. Oxford: Blackwell.

O'Neill, O. [1987] 2008. "Rights, Obligations and World Hunger". In *Global Ethics: Seminal Essays*, T. Pogge & K. Horton (eds), 139–55. Saint Paul, MN: Paragon House.

Oregon State University 2009. "Family Planning: A Major Environmental Emphasis". http://oregonstate.edu/ua/ncs/archives/2009/jul/family-planning-major-environmental-emphasis (accessed May 2011).

Organisation for Economic Co-operation and Development (OECD) 2003. *Fighting Corruption: What Role for Civil Society? The Experience of the OECD*. Paris: OECD. www.oecd.org/dataoecd/8/2/19567549.pdf (accessed May 2011).

Organisation for Economic Co-operation and Development (OECD) 2010. *Development Co-operation Report 2010*. Paris: OECD.

Page, E. A. 2006. *Climate Change, Justice and Future Generations*. Cheltenham: Edward Elgar.

Parker, M. & A. Lucassen 2004. "Genetic Information: A Joint Account?" *British Medical Journal* **329**: 165–7.

Parry, B. 2004. *Trading the Genome: Investigating the Commodification of Bio-Information*. New York: Columbia University Press.

Paskins, B. 1976. "What's Wrong with Torture?" *British Journal of International Studies* **2**: 138–48.

Pateman, C. 1988. *The Sexual Contract*. Cambridge: Polity Press.

Pattison J. 2010. *Humanitarian Intervention and the Responsibility to Protect*. Oxford: Oxford University Press.

Phillips, A. 2007. *Multiculturalism Without Culture*. Princeton, NJ: Princeton University Press.

Phillips, A. 2008. "Free to Decide for Oneself". In *Illusion of Consent*, D. I. O'Neill, M. L. Shanley & I. M. Young (eds), 99–118. University Park, PA: Penn State University Press.

Pogge, T. 1992. "Cosmopolitanism and Sovereignty". *Ethics* **103**: 48–75.

Pogge, T. 1994a. "Cosmopolitanism and Sovereignty". In *Political Restructuring in Europe: Ethical Perspectives*, C. Brown (ed.), 89–122. London: Routledge.

Pogge, T. 1994b. "An Egalitarian Law of Peoples". *Philosophy and Public Affairs* **3**: 195–224.

Pogge, T. 1998. "A Global Resources Dividend". In *Ethics of Consumption: The Good Life, Justice, and Global Stewardship*, D. Crocker & T. Linden (eds), 501–36. Lanham, MD: Rowman & Littlefield.

Pogge, T. 2001. "Eradicating Systemic Poverty: Brief for a Global Resources Dividend". *Journal of Human Development* **2**: 59–77.

Pogge, T. 2002. *World Poverty and Human Rights: Cosmopolitan Responsibilities and Reforms*. Cambridge: Polity Press.

Pogge, T. 2005. "World Poverty and Human Rights". *Ethics and International Affairs* **19**: 1–7.

Pogge, T. 2008. *World Poverty and Human Rights*, 2nd edn. Cambridge: Polity Press.

Pogge, T. & K. Horton 2008. *Global Ethics: Seminal Essays*. Saint Paul, MN: Paragon House.

Pogge, T. & D. Moellendorf 2008. *Global Justice: Seminal Essays*, Saint Paul, MN: Paragon House.

Polman, L. 2010. *War Games: The Story of Aid and War in Modern Times*. London: Viking Press.

Posner, E. A. & D. Weisbach 2010. *Climate Change Justice*. Princeton, NJ: Princeton University Press.

Rachels, J. 2007. *The Elements of Moral Philosophy*, 5th edn. London: McGraw-Hill.

Radcliffe-Richards, J., A. S. Daar, R. D. Guttmann *et al.* 1998. "The Case for Allowing Kidney Sales". *Lancet* **351**: 1950–52.

Rawls, J. 1999a. *A Theory of Justice* (rev. edn). Cambridge, MA: Harvard University Press.

Rawls, J. 1999b. *The Law of Peoples*. Cambridge, MA: Harvard University Press.

Resnik, D. B. 1998. "The Ethics of HIV Research in Developing Countries". *Bioethics* **12**: 286–306.

Robertson, J. 2001. "Preconception Gender Selection". *American Journal of Bioethics* **1**: 1–9.

Robinson, F. 1999. *Globalizing Care: Ethics, Feminist Theory and International Relations*. Boulder, CO: Westview Press.

Rohda, H. 1993. "Cultural Relativism as Cultural Absolutism". *Human Rights Quarterly* **15**: 315–38.

Ruddick, S. 1989. *Maternal Thinking: Towards a Politics of Peace.* London: Women's Press.

Ruddick, S. 1997. "Maternal Thinking". In *Feminist Social Thought: A Reader*, D. T. Meyers (ed.), 583–603. New York: Routledge.

Saul, J. 2003. *Feminism: Issues and Arguments.* Oxford: Oxford University Press.

Save the Children 2007. "Crisis in Darfur and Chad". www.savethechildren.org.uk/en/41_crisis-in-darfur-and-chad.htm (accessed July 2011).

Savulescu, J. 1999. "Sex Selection: The Case For". *Medical Journal of Australia* **171**: 373–5.

Savulescu, J. 2003. "Is the Sale of Body Parts Wrong?" *Journal of Medical Ethics* **29**: 138–9.

Scanlon, T. M. 1998. *What We Owe to Each Other.* Cambridge, MA: Harvard University Press.

Scheper-Hughes, N. 2003a. "Commentary: A Beastly Trade in 'Parts'. The Organ Market is Dehumanizing the World's Poor". *Los Angeles Times* (29 July). http://pqasb.pqarchiver.com/latimes/access/377365761.html?FMT=ABS&FMTS=ABS:FT&type=current&date=Jul+29%2C+2003&author=Nancy+Scheper-Hughes&pub=Los+Angeles+Times&edition=&startpage=B.15&desc=Commentary%3B+A+Beastly+Trade+in+%27Parts%27%3B+The+organ+market+is+dehumanizing+the+world%27s+poor (accessed May 2011).

Scheper-Hughes, N. 2003b. "Keeping an Eye on the Global Traffic in Human Organs". *Lancet* **361**: 1645–8.

Schukelenk, U. & R. Ashcroft 2000. "The Ethics of Clinical Research". *Bioethics* **14**: 158–72.

Sen, A. 1979. "Equality of What?" The Tanner Lecture on Human Values. www.tannerlectures.utah.edu/lectures/documents/sen80.pdf (accessed May 2011).

Sen, A. 1982. *Choice, Welfare and Measurement.* Oxford: Blackwell.

Sen, A. 1985. *Commodities and Capabilities.* Oxford: Oxford University Press.

Sen, A. 1990. "More than 100 Million Women are Missing". *New York Review of Books* (20 December).

Sen, A. 1997. "Human Rights and Asian Values". Sixteenth Morgenthau Memorial Lecture on Ethics & Foreign Policy. New York: Carnegie Council on Ethics and International Affairs. http://www.cceia.org/resources/publications/morgenthau/254.html/_res/id=sa_File1/254_sen.pdf (accessed May 2011).

Sen, A. 1999. *Development As Freedom.* New York: Knopf.

Sen, A. 2009. *The Idea of Justice.* Cambridge, MA: Harvard University Press.

Sen, A. & B. Williams (eds) 1982. *Utilitarianism and Beyond.* Cambridge: Cambridge University Press.

Sessions, G. (ed.) 1995. *Deep Ecology for the Twenty-first Century.* Boston, MA: Shambhala.

Shachar, A. 1998. "Group Identity and Women's Rights in Family Law: The Perils of Multicultural Accommodation". *Journal of Political Philosophy* **6**: 285–305.

Sheldon, S. & S. Wilkinson 2004. "Should Selecting Saviour Siblings be Banned?" *Journal of Medical Ethics* **30**: 533–7.

Shimazono, Y. 2007. "The State of the International Organ Trade: A Provisional Picture Based on Integration of Available Information". *Bulletin of the World Health Organisation* **85**: 901–80. www.who.int/bulletin/volumes/85/12/06-039370/en/ (accessed May 2011).

Shiva, V. 1997. *Biopiracy: The Plunder of Nature and Knowledge.* Cambridge, MA: South End Press.

Shiva, V. 2001. *Protect or Plunder? Understanding Intellectual Property.* London: Zed Books.

Shiva, V. 2005. *Earth Democracy: Justice, Sustainability and Peace.* London: Zed Books.

Shlomo, A. & D. Avner (eds) 1992. *Communtarianism and Individualism.* Oxford: Oxford University Press.

Shue, H. 1980. *Basic Rights: Subsistence, Affluence, and US Foreign Policy.* Princeton, NJ: Princeton University Press.

Singer, P. 1972. "Famine, Affluence, and Morality". *Philosophy and Public Affairs* **1**: 229–43.

Singer, P. 1975. *Animal Liberation: A New Ethics for our Treatment of Animals.* New York: Random House.

Singer, P. 1993. *Practical Ethics.* Cambridge: Cambridge University Press.

Singer, P. 2002. *One World: The Ethics of Globalization.* New Haven, CT: Yale University Press.

Singer, P. 2009. *The Life You Can Save: Acting Now to End World Poverty*. New York: Random House.

Sinnott-Armstrong, W. 2006. "Moral Skepticism". *The Stanford Encyclopedia of Philosophy* (Summer 2009 Edition), E. N. Zalta (ed.). http://plato.stanford.edu/entries/skepticism-moral/ (accessed May 2011).

Sklair, L. 2001. *The Transnational Capitalist Class*. Oxford: Blackwell.

Sklair, L. 2002. *Globalization: Capitalism and its Alternatives*. Oxford: Oxford University Press.

Steinhoff, U. 2007. *On the Ethics of War and Terrorism*. Cambridge, MA: Harvard University Press.

Tamir, Y. 1996. "Hands off Clitoridectomy". *Boston Review* (Summer). http://bostonreview.net/BR21.3/Tamir.html (accessed May 2011).

Taylor, C. 1994. *Multiculturalism*, A. Gutmann (ed.). Princeton, NJ: Princeton University Press.

Tedlock, B. 2006. "Indigenous Heritage and Biopiracy in the Age of Intellectual Property Rights". *Explore* 2: 256–9.

Thomson, J. J. 1971. "A Defense of Abortion". *Philosophy and Public Affairs* 1: 47–66.

Thomson, J. J. 1985. "The Trolley Problem". *Yale Law Journal* 94: 1395–415.

Tong, R. 2001a. "Towards a Feminist Global Bioethics: Addressing Women's Health Concerns Worldwide". *Health Care Analysis* 9: 229–46.

Tong, R. 2001b. *Globalizing Feminist Bioethics: Crosscultural Perspectives*. Boulder, CO: Westview Press.

Tronto, J. C. 1987. "Beyond Gender Difference to a Theory of Care". *Signs: Journal of Women in Culture and Society* 12: 644–63.

Tronto, J. C. 1993. *Moral Boundaries: A Political Argument for an Ethic of Care*. London: Routledge.

Tronto, J. C. 1995. "Woman and Caring: What can Feminists Learn about Morality and Caring?" In *Justice and Care: Essential Readings in Feminist Ethics,* V. Held (ed.), 101–17. Boulder, CO: Westview Press.

Tronto, J. C. 1996. "Care as a Political Concept". In *Revisioning the Political: Feminist Reconstructions of Traditional Concepts in Western Political Theory*, N. J. Hirschmann & C. Di Stefano (eds), 139–56. Boulder, CO: Westview Press.

UK Biobank 2007. *Ethics and Governance Framework*. www.ukbiobank.ac.uk/docs/20071011_EGF_Version_3_1_0October_2007withTOR.pdf (accessed May 2011).

United Nations 1948. "The Universal Declaration of Human Rights". www.un.org/en/documents/udhr (accessed May 2011).

United Nations 2005. "2005 World Summit Outcome". www.un.org/summit2005/presskit/fact_sheet.pdf (accessed May 2011).

United Nations Children's Fund (UNICEF) 1999. "Iraq Surveys Show 'Humanitarian Emergency'". www.unicef.org/newsline/99pr29.htm (accessed May 2011).

United Nations Department of Economic and Social Affairs (DESA) 2009. *Rethinking Poverty: Report on the World Situation 2010*. New York: United Nations. www.un.org/esa/socdev/rwss/docs/2010/fullreport.pdf (accessed June 2011).

United Nations Development Programme (UNDP) 1994. "A New Design for Development Cooperation". In *Human Development Report 1994: New Dimensions of Human Security*. http://hdr.undp.org/en/media/hdr_1994_en_chap4.pdf (accessed May 2011).

United Nations Development Programme (UNDP) 1998. "Glossary of Terms". http://hdr.undp.org/en/humandev/glossary/ (accessed May 2011).

United Nations Development Programme (UNDP) 2009. *Overcoming Barriers: Human Mobility and Development*. Human Development Report 2009. http://hdr.undp.org/en/reports/global/hdr2009/ (accessed May 2011).

United Nations Framework Convention on Climate Change 1997. "Paper No. 1, Brazil: Proposed Elements of a Protocol to the United Nations Framework Convention on Climate Change, presented by Brazil in Response to the Berlin Mandate". Item 3 of the Provisional Agenda of the Seventh Session of the Ad Hoc Group on the Berlin Mandate, FCCC/AGBM/1997/MISC.1/

Add.3 (30 May). http://unfccc.int/cop4/resource/docs/1997/agbm/misc01a3.htm (accessed May 2011).

United Nations Framework Convention on Climate Change 1998. "Kyoto Protocol to the United Nations Framework Convention on Climate Change". http://unfccc.int/resource/docs/convkp/kpeng.pdf (accessed May 2011).

United Nations General Assembly 2005. "Resolution Adopted by the General Assembly: 60/1, 2005 World Summit Outcome". http://unpan1.un.org/intradoc/groups/public/documents/un/unpan021752.pdf (accessed May 2011).

United Nations General Assembly Security Council 1999. "Report of the International Criminal Tribunal for the Prosecution of Persons Responsible for Genocide and Other Serious Violations of International Humanitarian Law Committed in the Territory of Rwanda and Rwandan Citizens Responsible for Genocide and Other Such Violations Committed in the Territory of Neighbouring States Between 1 January and 31 December 1994". http://www.un.org/ga/54/doc/tcir.pdf (accessed July 2011).

United Nations Security Council 1999. "Report of the Second Panel Established Pursuant to the Note by the President of the Security Council of 30 January 1999 (S/1999/100), Concerning the Humanitarian Situation in Iraq". S/1999/356. www.casi.org.uk/info/panelrep.html (accessed June 2011).

United Nations Women 2008. "Eliminating Female Genital Mutilation: An Interagency Statement". www.unifem.org/materials/item_detail.php?ProductID=110 (accessed May 2011).

US Citizenship and Immigration Services 2010. "Implementation of the Convention Against Torture". Code of Federal Regulations §208.18. www.uscis.gov/ilink/docView/SLB/HTML/SLB/0-0-0-1/0-0-0-11261/0-0-0-14927/0-0-0-15320.html (accessed July 2011).

US Department of State 2005. *Victims of Trafficking and Violence Protection Act of 2000: Trafficking in Persons Report*. www.state.gov/g/tip/rls/tiprpt/2005/index.htm (accessed May 2011).

US Department of State 2006. "Legislative Requirements and Key Terms". In *Country Reports on Terrorism 2006*, ch. 7. www.state.gov/s/ct/rls/crt/2006/82726.htm (accessed July 2011).

US Senate 1976. *US Senate Executive Report 102-23: US Senate Report on Ratification of The International Covenant on Civil and Political Rights (102d Cong., 2d Sess.)*. http://sitemaker.umich.edu/drwcasebook/files/senate_committee_on_foreign_relations_report_on_the_iccpr.pdf (accessed July 2011).

Van Hooft, S. 2009. *Cosmopolitanism: A Philosophy for Global Ethics*. Stocksfield: Acumen.

Varmus, H. & D. Satcher 1997. "Ethical Complexities of Conducting Research in Developing Countries. *New England Journal of Medicine* **337**: 1003–5.

Verkaik, R. 2003. "Heathrow's Neighbours Lose Fight for a Quiet Night". *Independent* (9 July). www.independent.co.uk/news/uk/crime/heathrow-neighbours-lose-fight-for-a-quiet-night-586216.html (accessed July 2011).

Walzer, M. 1973. "Political Action and the Problem of Dirty Hands". *Philosophy and Public Affairs* **2**: 160–80.

Walzer, M. 1997. *Just and Unjust Wars*. New York: Basic Books.

Walzer, M. 2002. "Five Questions about Terrorism". *Dissent* (Winter). www.dissentmagazine.org/article/?article=622%3Cbr%20/%3E (accessed May 2011).

Walzer, M. 2004. *Arguing About War*. New Haven, CT: Yale University Press.

Waters, M. 1995. *Globalization*. London: Routledge.

Weiss, T. 2007. *Humanitarian Intervention*. Cambridge: Polity Press.

Wenar, L. 2008. "Property Rights and the Resource Curse". *Philosophy and Public Affairs* **36**: 2–32.

Wheeler, N. 2000. *Saving Strangers: Humanitarian Intervention in International Society*. Oxford: Oxford University Press.

Wheeler, N. & F. Egerton 2009. "The Responsibility to Protect: 'Precious Commitment' Or a Promise Unfulfilled?" *Global Responsibility to Protect* **1**(1): 114–32.

White House 2003. "President Discusses Beginning of Operation Iraqi Freedom". http://georgewbush-whitehouse.archives.gov/news/releases/2003/03/20030322.html (accessed June 2011).

Widdows, H. 2004. "Religion as a Source of Moral Authority". *Heythrop Journal* **45**: 197–208.

Widdows, H. 2005. "Global Ethics: Foundations and Methodologies". In *Global Ethics and Civil Society*, D. O'Byrne (ed.), 74–88. Aldershot: Ashgate.

Widdows, H. 2007a. "Is Global Ethics Moral Neo-Colonialism? An Investigation of the Issue in the Context of Bioethics". *Bioethics* **21**: 305–15.

Widdows, H. 2007b. "The Self in the Genetic Era". *Health Care Analysis* **15**: 5–12.

Widdows, H. 2008. "Why and What Global Ethics?" In *An Ethics in an Era of Globalisation*, M. Commers, W. Vandekerckhove & A. Verlinden (eds), 95–133. Aldershot: Ashgate.

Widdows, H. 2009a. "Between the Individual and the Community: the Impact of Genetics on Ethical Models". *New Genetics and Society* **28**(2): 173–88.

Widdows, H. 2009b. "Persons and Their Parts: New Reproductive Technologies and Risks of Commodification". *Health Care Analysis* **17**: 36–46.

Widdows, H. & C. Mullen 2009. *The Governance of Genetic Information: Who Decides?* Cambridge: Cambridge University Press.

Wilkinson, S. 2000. "Commodification Arguments for the Legal Prohibition of Organ Sale". *Health Care Analysis* **8**: 189–201.

Wilkinson, S. 2003. *Bodies for Sale: Ethics and Exploitation in the Human Body Trade*. London: Routledge.

Winickoff, D. E. 2003. "Governing Population Genomics". *Jurimetrics* **43**: 187–228.

Winickoff, D. E. & R. N. Winickoff 2003b. "The Charitable Trust as a Model for Genomic Biobanks". *New England Journal of Medicine* **349**: 1180–84.

Wolff, J. & A. De-Shalit 2007. *Disadvantage*. Oxford: Oxford University Press.

Womack, S. 2007. "India Opens Way to More British Adoptions". *Telegraph* (9 April). www.telegraph.co.uk/news/worldnews/1548082/India-opens-way-to-more-British-adoptions.html (accessed July 2011).

World Health Organization (WHO) 1999. *The World Health Report 1999: Making a Difference*. www.who.int/whr/1999/en/whr99_en.pdf (accessed May 2011).

World Medical Association (WMA) 2008. "WMA Declaration of Helsinki: Ethical Principles for Medical Research Involving Human Subjects". www.wma.net/en/30publications/10policies/b3/index.html (accessed May 2011).

World Trade Organization 1994. "Trade-Related Aspects of Intellectual Property Rights". www.wto.org/english/docs_e/legal_e/27-trips_01_e.htm (accessed May 2011).

Young, I. M. 2009. *Justice and the Politics of Difference*. Princeton, NJ: Princeton University Press.

WEBSITES

ATTAC: www.attac.org/

Bill and Melinda Gates Foundation: www.gatesfoundation.org/Pages/home.aspx

CEDAW: www.un.org/womenwatch/daw/cedaw/

Co-operative Bank, "Tackling Global Poverty": www.co-operative.coop/corporate/ethicsinaction/poverty/

International Coalition for the Responsibility to Protect: www.responsibilitytoprotect.org/index.php/component/content/article/383

International Criminal Court (ICC): www.icc-cpi.int/menus/icc

International Criminal Tribunal for Rwanda (ICTR): www.unictr.org/

International Labour Organization (ILO): www.ilo.org/global/lang--en/index.htm

International Monetary Fund (IMF): www.imf.org/external/index.htm

International Rehabilitation Council for Torture Victims: www.irct.org/what-is-torture/voices-of-torture-victims.aspx

OECD, Bribery and Corruption: www.oecd.org/topic/0,3373,en_2649_37447_1_1_1_1_37447,00.html

Public Interest Lawyers: www.publicinterestlawyers.co.uk

Tobin Tax Initiative: www.ceedweb.org/iirp/

UK Biobank: www.ukbiobank.ac.uk/

United Nations Children's Fund (Unicef): www.unicef.org/

United Nations Conference on Trade And Development (UNCTAD): www.unctad.org/Templates/StartPage.asp?intItemID=2068

United Nations Development Programme (UNDP): www.undp.org/

United Nations Educational, Scientific and Cultural Organization (UNESCO): www.unesco.org/new/en/unesco/

United Nations Environment Programme (UNEP): www.unep.org/

United Nations High Commissioner for Refugees (UNHCR): www.unhcr.org.uk/

United Nations International Criminal Tribunal for Rwanda: www.unictr.org/

United Nations Millennium Development Goals: www.un.org/millenniumgoals/bkgd.shtml

United Nations Populations Fund (UNPFA): www.unfpa.org/public/

UN Women (the UN Entity for Gender Equality and the Empowerment of Women): www.unwomen.org/

William J. Clinton Foundation: www.clintonfoundation.org/

World Bank: www.worldbank.org/

World Food Programme (WFP): www.wfp.org/

World Health Organization (WHO): www.who.int/en/

World Trade Organization (WTO): www.wto.org/

INDEX